THE SUPER-AMERICANS

Books by John Bainbridge

The Super-Americans

Garbo

The Wonderful World of Toots Shor

Little Wonder,
or The Reader's Digest and How It Grew

Another Way of Living

Like a Homesick Angel

John Bainbridge

❧ THE ❧
SUPER-AMERICANS

A Picture of Life in the United States,
As Brought into Focus, Bigger than Life,
In the Land of the Millionaires—Texas

With an Introduction by Lon Tinkle

This account of life among the Super-Americans
originated in *The New Yorker* as a series of articles,
which have been somewhat altered and considerably extended.

ISBN (Paperback): 0-03-085488-1
ISBN (Hardbound): 0-03-085697-3
Library of Congress Catalog Card Number: 75-155502

First issued 1961
New edition published 1972
Printed in the United States of America

Second Printing, July, 1972

FOR WILLIAM SHAWN

INTRODUCTION

When John Bainbridge's *The Super-Americans* was first published in the autumn of 1961, Stanley Walker, reviewing it in the *New York Times Book Review,* called it "the best book about contemporary Texas ever written." If anybody knew whereof he spoke, it was Walker. He had come back "home to Texas" a few years before, after a brilliant career as writer and as city editor of the old New York *Herald Tribune.* A few other Texan critics held down the whistle for *The Super-Americans,* but in general it was, for the natives, an anger-breeding survey. Texans, as Bainbridge proved conclusively in his study, have never placed much value on criticism. To say that they resent it would be the understatement of the year. And so, for many Texans, the amused affection (not amused contempt, as some thought) with which this talented and clear-sighted outlander viewed Texas seemed just another Eastern put-down, another in a steady flow of outsiders' books designed to deflate the vaingloriousness of a state lucky enough to be sitting on some of the richest mineral resources in the world, a kind of good luck that had intensified the congenital Texas habit of boasting and bragging, of revelling in being "uncouth." Some Texans who were atypical were locally known as "couth Texans." The phrase was meant to collapse its audience into paroxysms of laughter and ridicule. How could the "couth" Bainbridge understand "uncouth" Texas?

In fact he understood it so well—and, as in the case of nearly all real understanding, with so much sympathy—that he was able to see that Texas, however unique the claims its citizens might make for it, was essentially a mirror for the nation of its own youth, its own adolescent struggle between ungainliness and a desire for shape, its own problem of the resolution of buoyant energy with wisdom and maturity.

After only a year among "the natives," Bainbridge was able to observe that the reality, the experience, of Texas was a kind of rerun for the rest of the nation of its growing pains. More specifically, in the most brilliant insight in a book full of brilliant insights, Bainbridge realized that Texas (Whitman's "barbaric yawp" might have served to characterize its genial and frisky and breezy vitality) stood in relation to the rest of the nation as the United States itself stands in relation to a Europe hypercritical of the New World lifestyle, with its emphasis on youth and ardor.

For this reason, and for others perhaps less striking, *The Super-Americans* is still "the best book about contemporary Texas ever written." There have been many similar surveys in the decade since it first appeared, but none has supplanted *The Super-Americans'* evocation of Texas mores, the Texas life-style, or its judgment on the values Texans accept, both consciously and unconsciously.

It is rather amazing that this should be so, for the Sixties have been a landmark decade in Texas, a decade of profound chastening and of profound change. When Texans contemplate the major historical "moments" of this decade in the Lone Star State, they are stunned by the sense of the existential contingency of life, that is to say, by the incredible role played in communal as well as in individual life by the unforeseeable. No hurricane, not Carla in Galveston nor two later ones in Brownsville and Corpus Christi, no physical disaster equalled the traumatic experience for Texans of the assassination in Dallas of President John F. Kennedy. The blithe innocence of Texans, so little aware of the true nature of evil floating and coalescing in the world, was shattered by this tragedy that produced in the collective soul of the state a tormenting sense of guilt—and of shame. Strangely, perhaps, no such soul-searching, and certainly no such national condemnation, attended the assassination of Robert Kennedy in California or of Martin Luther King in Tennessee. But neither of those states is a paradigm, a microcosm, of the nation, as Bainbridge so astutely shows Texas to be. Nobody demanded of Californians or Tennesseans that they wear sackcloth and ashes, but the whole nation demanded that Texans suffer in order to be redeemed. Bainbridge's awareness of this kind of psychological "transfer" is one of the enduring perceptions in his book, a reinforcement of his thesis that the country finds in Texas a repetition of its own not always easy growth into maturity.

Other things of tragic import, as well as some that are sanguine, have profoundly changed Texas in the Sixties. For the first time, and as a result of the Kennedy assassination, the Lone Star State provided the nation with a native-born Texan as president. The glory of this fact was pulverized, however, by the division in the country that followed President Johnson's decisions in regard to the war in Vietnam. As Johnson's popularity diminished, so did the national interest in Texas. Norman Mailer's novel about two Texas youths who love to hunt and kill, *Why Are We in Vietnam?*, persuaded many readers all over the country to accept the thesis that Texans were fundamentally predatory. Again, in the harsh light of American involvement in Vietnam, Texas was chastened, its brio punctured.

One might suppose that the extrovert brio and bravura with which so many Texans like to season their public images —as Bainbridge steadily shows—would have been sliced at least in half by the assassination of John F. Kennedy and the toppling of Lyndon B. Johnson.

There were, however, one or two ego-nourishing bonanzas to offset the disasters.

Most significant of these was the federal government's limelighting for global audiences the Apollo flights and the control boards located in the NASA installation south of Houston. All of a sudden Houston emerged as one of the great science centers of the twentieth century. And in the television broadcasts of the history-making flights—before the largest simultaneous watching public in history—the "image" of Texas took on a new and needed element of serious intellectual achievement, and not merely serious but awesome. Thanks to NASA's location in South Texas, the state reaped a golden harvest of good will, and Houston almost overnight became "the place where everyone's going."

But all this was in the Sixties, after *The Super-Americans* was published. If Bainbridge were freshly writing it today, no doubt there would be more topical items about Houston and fewer about Dallas; no doubt some of the names would be different. Nonetheless, the spirit of his book—and the perceptions—would be the same.

In early 1971, *Fortune* magazine devoted an issue to Houston. In stating that Houston is the place where everyone is going, *Fortune* was not speaking alone of astronauts and men of science, nor of international "celebrities" (such as the Duke of Windsor) seeking out the services of such famous men of medicine as Dr. Michael DeBakey and Dr. Denton Cooley. *Fortune* was speaking of the massive business relocations in the warm Gulf Coast climate, the transfer of populations of industries and corporations to a city that claimed only a million inhabitants in the Fifties but which by the beginning of the Seventies had become the nation's fifth largest city, its second port in volume of freighter business, and its first in petroleum and petrochemical industries. Houston had become the number one symbol of the customary Texan worship of size, of bigness.

But Houston was, of course, or rather is, something else, as Bainbridge would have quickly noted. It is the first really grand metropolis in the Southwest. With its broad and extensive downtown streets, its spaciousness allowed by the fortunate dispersal over wide areas of its towering skyscrapers, its structure of one self-sufficient village contiguous to another as in New York and London, with its flair for contrasts (a city of the Old South but also of the Southwest—a city called by one expert "a whiskey and trombone city," but also a city extremely cosmopolitan, a port city with international riffraff, a city with two estimable universities, and yet a city where the school board is often governed by hicktown limitations), Houston is now a metropolis of considerable culture, with perhaps the finest symphony orchestra in the whole Southwest (whose resident conductors have included Stokowski and André Previn), the finest theater installation in the region—Nina Vance's Alley Theatre—and no doubt the finest art museum, bracketing both the modern and traditional, the Houston Museum of Fine Arts. And its many lively and attractive bookstores are now unrivalled in the state for volume of business, a distinction held by Dallas only a decade ago.

So, since publication of *The Super-Americans,* Houston has emerged as a center of international renown and importance. Yet strangely, for all its global aura, it remains a very "Texan" symbol.

Meantime, in Austin, and again while almost no one was looking, the Texas "image" was being spectacularly improved as the University of Texas, the second richest university in the world (second only to Harvard, thanks to its possession of rich oil lands), set about becoming, under the guidance of an inspired Texas-born chancellor, Harry Huntt Ransom, a truly great institution. With an imaginative audacity that soon caused Texans to acknowledge that he was a man of exceptional talents—even if he had begun his career as a mere "professor"—Harry Huntt Ransom brought to the Austin campus a prize panoply of brilliant professors wooed away from grander institutions, gave them the salaries they deserved and found fellowships for the kind of students they deserved, brought in for special sojourns creative men in every field, and above all—with his skill as a book man—

bought and sought for the university the choicest library acquisitions up for grabs by the richest institutions in the world. He turned what had been a big and baffled state university into one of the acknowledged great universities of this country, distinguished for its "big name" faculty, its revivified university press, its periodical publications, its innovative programs, its openness to ideas, and its amazing collections.

The anti-intellectualism that prevails in the power groups in Texas seemed at last successfully challenged by a state institution, a university great as well as big. As it turned out, for a time in the Sixties Texas appeared to be on its way to a maturity whose absence is present, so to say, on every page of *The Super-Americans*.

One other significant change in traditional Texas also helped to make the Sixties a memorable decade. This was the lessening, however slight, of the dominant role of oil in the state's economy. It is now fairly conventional to assert that just as cotton and cattle have had their day in Texas—their primacy defeated by worldwide competition—so has oil. Light industry is now the rage, capitalizing as it does on modern inventiveness and on technology. For example, the brains who directed the tremendous seismological research for oil—the men who put together Geophysical Research Corporation and Geophysical Service, Inc.—have converted their oil-exploration business into Texas Instruments, Inc., manufacturers of transistors and of all sorts of delicate detection devices for the government. Oil has been in trouble ever since the end of World War II and international access to the incredibly immense oil reserves of the Middle East. Competition from foreign oil has especially plagued the "independents" of Texas, who don't have the international holdings and combines of the great oil corporations. And the ever-present attack upon the validity of the depletion allowance, making more headway than ever before, at least in regard to the percentage granted, has plunged the oil fraternity into gloom. Whereas oil conventions used to be signals for celebration and conviviality, they are often now defensive and depressing. When Bainbridge wrote his study, oil was still flying high and cavorting like a *remuda* of wild mustangs, obvious kings of the Texas domain. Oil power is still the number one power in the state, but its elite has lost some of its buoyancy and confidence. Other kinds of wealth and power are challenging it. But as yet this is not reflected in the life-style of Texans, and Bainbridge's close attention to the values of the oil "kings" makes as good reading and is still as true as ever. But a decade from now one might not be able to find his observations as valid.

So, a reader coming to this book for the first time, ten years after its publication, need not fear that he is encountering a museum piece, no matter how witty and flashing. *The Super-Americans* is not in any serious sense "dated," as it now becomes the melancholy duty of this "native" to show.

Just as the frank admission that the Sixties had indeed shaken Texas with unexpected disasters or achievements or changes was necessary, so must one now rehearse certain disquieting events that in the opening year or so of the Seventies clearly testify to the prophetic accuracy of *The Super-Americans.*

Despite stunning progress, the University of Texas, for reasons not yet entirely clear, began to backslide at the end of the Sixties. In the academic year of 1970-71, many thoughtful Texans were agreed that the great university, of such recent éclat, had been set back by twenty years. Chancellor Ransom, the distinguished primary architect of its growth, resigned his post, although still a number of years from mandatory retirement age. His next-in-line, the president of the university, Norman Hackerman, resigned. The immensely respected Dean of the College of Arts and Sciences, Dr. John Silber, resigned. Three of the university's most envied professors—all "imports"—resigned. Fulminations in the press between the Chairman of the University's Board of Regents, who regards his mandate as the fulfillment of the wishes of the taxpayers of the state in regard to the kind of university they want, and dissident students yielded for a time almost daily confrontations. The reader who follows Bainbridge carefully will not be surprised by any of this. His pages subtly evoke the ever-present power in the state of "bossism," of might making right, without query or debate or discussion.

When Bainbridge's book first came out, many thought he was being hypercritical when he was only providing statistics. His dim view of Texans' enthusiasm for education is supported all the more in 1971 by a survey supplied by the National Education Association and printed in the state's perhaps most typical newspaper, *The Dallas Morning News*. The editorial page of *The News*, which normally is cheerleader for Texas fans, admits gloomily that Texas, fifth in population among the nation's states, ranks thirty-seventh in "average elementary schoolteachers' salary," and fortieth "in average salary paid secondary schoolteachers." In regard to per capita support of higher education, Texas ranked thirty-first. Money priorities are, of course, one reason for the troubles at the University of Texas at Austin. One other dismal statistic: thirty per cent of Texas' students drop out of school after the ninth grade; but in Hawaii, for example (and Minnesota, for another example), fewer than ten per cent of high school students drop out before graduation.

Bainbridge's caustic comments about the level of political life in Texas also stirred up the animals, as Mencken used to say. On the very evening in January of 1971 when Texas' newly elected governor (returned for a second term) was to be heralded with five separate inaugural balls, the biggest potential scandal in Texas politics in many a moon was made public. On that day the federal Securities Exchange Commission alleged that four or five of the highest political officers in the state, plus a number of subordinates, had conspired to manipulate stock prices of a Texas insurance company for a private gain—among them all—of more than half a million dollars, realized in one month, and related, according to ugly rumor, to special legislation. The national newspapers have been filled with the rumors, or allegations; formal trial is still, at this writing, several months off. What delight Bainbridge would take in the comment of one of the implicated: "I haven't done anything wrong; I've just done what everybody else has been doing all the time."

Not only in politics, education, and crime rate (Texas is still the national champion), and in the acceptance of federal aid while condemning it in principle (an art which has now reached perfection, as a look at the recent scandal over making a state park, with federal funds, of Mustang Island will show), but in many other matters Bainbridge remains a peerless recorder of inconsistencies and foibles.

Two quick samples: he indicates the hopeless confusion of political labels in the state. The natives said: "He'd understand, if he just knew us better." Well, they are now smitten with non-understanding themselves. In 1971, former Governor John Connally, an intimate friend of LBJ and the most potent politician currently active in Texas, was appointed— to the astonishment of the entire nation—Secretary of the Treasury. Just what exactly this means nobody knows. Many believe Connally will "cross over" in 1972 and join the Republican party, maybe as running-mate for Richard Nixon. As Bainbridge said, you can't tell the players without a program. A lot of people, Texan and otherwise, couldn't tell in this case even with opera glasses and a score card. What team is a player on when he runs both ways?

Finally, Bainbridge enjoys the details of exhibitionistic spending, of moneyed high jinks, in what passes for "society" in Texas. These details caused real anguish in his Texas readers. But not enough to occasion reform. The social game goes on as a vast competition. Still, it would be hard to beat the coming-out party this past season in Dallas of a wealthy young girl whose father admitted that his daughter's debutante career found him in white tie and full dress for the first time in his life. For his daughter's "presentation," he had imported four chefs from Vienna, and he didn't stop there. He had the grand ballroom of the local Sheraton Hotel temporarily redesigned to resemble the Viennese State Opera House, a place where the host had never been. So what? If the décor were good enough for the Old World, it would do in Texas, right? The cost of the ball was, appropriately, in excess of $100,000. But it was worth it to him: a local paper devoted the entire issue of its Sunday magazine to the occasion. Memories, memories! *Alt Wien!*

The Super-Americans indeed! In naming them, Bainbridge proved that he had captured the essence of them. His piercing but affectionate portrait is still true, painted as it was with great skill, the mind back of it enlightened and civilized and above all undeceived.

LON TINKLE

Dallas
June 1971

I am as little disposed to flatter my contemporaries as to malign them.

—ALEXIS DE TOCQUEVILLE
Democracy in America

Chapter One

It is currently fashionable among the more advanced spirits in this country to look upon Texas with an air of amused condescension. This attitude, though not heartily relished by Texans, is historically appropriate, for Texas is a new boy, standing in relation to the rest of the United States as the United States stands to Europe, or, for that matter, as Rome stood to Athens, and since time began new boys have been subject to the elaborate patronization of old boys. The practice of low-rating Texas does not, of course, spring solely from the superiority that age naturally feels toward youth. Twenty-two states are younger than Texas, Utah among them. Who bothers to denigrate Utah? To be sure, the widespread mockery of Texas, like the old European custom of patronizing America, originally stemmed from the newcomer's relative immaturity, but something much more provocative has since come into play: envy. "As long as the region was church-rat poor, there was nothing for the other sections to be jealous of," the eminent historian and native Texan Walter Prescott Webb recently observed. "But today . . . we in Texas have become a sort of whipping boy for the other regions. Wherever we go, people tell us stories, most of them unfavorable to Texas. . . . Texans may have done things that foster this attitude of not too delicate criticism and invective. But there is no doubt that a good part of the hostility stems from the fact that Texas is booming." Beyond the mere envy of prosperity is the envy, more far-reaching in its implications and less easy to evaluate, of a certain cast of mind. The life-style in Texas is marked by bravado,

1

zest, optimism, ebullience, and swaggering self-confidence. "In the East, the young men fight for jobs with the telephone company, so they'll be safe and secure," Joseph O. (listed in the Dallas telephone directory as Joe O.) Lambert, Jr., a Louisiana boy who has made good in Texas in landscaping—"the bush business," as he offhandedly calls it—real estate, and allied lines, once said. "Down here, young fellows have to be drafted for that sort of work. This whole world is new, wide-open. Anybody, any person of ability, can set out here and make it go."

This exuberant, razzle-dazzle approach to life is sometimes referred to in Texas as the "wheeler-dealer" spirit. Nobody seems to know, or care, where the term originated (in gambling halls, no doubt), but everybody knows what a wheeler-dealer is: a canny, adventurous millionaire whose approach to business is strictly free-style. In what appears to be an unquenchably lighthearted and casual mood, he is constantly in the process of extending his enterprises by buying, selling, borrowing, merging, and trading. His transactions, always called deals, usually involve sums of at least seven digits; to save time in calculating, he customarily drops the last five. He keeps no regular hours. He may spend the morning at his office and by late afternoon be fishing in the Gulf or watching the races at Aqueduct or Santa Anita. He shuns conferences, paperwork, consultations with lawyers, and other time-consuming activities that pass for accomplishment in the life of the ordinary businessman. A few months ago, a pair of old-line Texas wheeler-dealers named Leo Corrigan and Toddie Lee Wynne flew to Hong Kong, where they entered into competitive bidding against not only local moneyed groups but also Japanese, British, and Wall Street interests for a forty-thousand-square-foot parcel of Hong Kong's choicest real estate. After a spirited session lasting two and a half hours and ending with the one-hundred-and-tenth bid (for $2,480,000), the Texans walked off with the prize—a typical triumph of wheeler-dealer-manship. "The others had to spend so much time in conference that they lost out," Corrigan later explained. "We had complete authorization with us."

A wheeler-dealer makes most of his deals over the telephone, and prides himself that his word is as good as his signature on a contract. For him, business is a game. He operates on the sporting principle that he wants to make a profit but wants the other fellow to come out all right, too. His cardinal rule is to trade in such a way that whoever does business with him today will want to do business with him again tomorrow. In Texas, the sharp but free-and-easy wheeler-dealer spirit extends even into banking circles, which nearly everywhere else are havens of decorum. "A bank in Florida called us up the other day," DeWitt Ray, a vice-president of the Republic National Bank, in Dallas, recently recalled. "'We've got a couple of customers down here in the citrus business,' they said. 'These fellows need a couple of million to carry them over the harvest. We understand you know how to loan money. If you think you'd like to loan some here, we'll send a couple of men up with all the facts and see if you're interested.' 'Tell you what we'll do,' we said. 'You just sit tight. We'll have a man down there by morning to look into the proposition.' Which we did. And within twenty-four hours after the phone call we closed the deal." This bright-eyed, bushy-tailed attitude toward lending money has made Republic the largest bank in the Southwest, and, six years ago, enabled it to monumentalize itself in the form of a shiny, forty-story, twenty-five-million-dollar skyscraper surmounted by what appears to be a gigantic trained seal holding an electric beacon, which casts a beam for a hundred miles over the surrounding prairie. The new building, which, when completed, was the tallest in the Southwest, has a main banking floor nearly as long as a football field; this is a vast, unobstructed expanse of wood and marble, and looped around it is an eye-catching balcony faced with a hundred thousand dollars' worth of glistening gold leaf. The bank opened its new quarters with a housewarming party, which got under way with a cocktail buffet for forty-five hundred guests. They were diverted by mountains of food, oceans of whiskey, and continuous entertainment, which included comedians, jugglers, can-can dancers, and a symphony orchestra. The party lasted two days and cost about a quarter of a million dollars. Among the guests was an Eastern banker named Raymond N. Ball. "We gave him a tour of the bank," DeWitt Ray said. "One of the things that impressed him was the big, handsome chairs in our board room. On the back of each of them are the bank's initials, RNB, in raised gold letters. Mr. Ball said something about how those happened to be his initials also. Some time after that, I was talking to Fred Florence—he was our president then—and I mentioned what our Eastern friend had said about the chairs in the board room. 'Let's send him one of those goddam chairs,' I said. 'It'll give him a kick.' 'Hell, yes,' Fred said. 'Let's do it.' So we did, and ordered a replacement for the board room. Now, I don't know, but I'll bet if you admired the chairs in the board room of a bank back East, somebody would tell you how old they were and that would be the end of that."

The inhibited practices of Eastern businessmen are regarded by wheeler-dealers more with sorrow than with anger. "It's not their fault. They just don't know how to work streamlined," B. Hick Majors, a millionaire Dallas real-estate broker who has handled a number of big deals for the protean wheeler-dealer Clinton W. (Clint) Murchison, said recently. A few years ago, when Murchison acquired control of an insurance company, he induced Majors to take over as its president. "I tried it for a year," Majors says, "but it was too tame. I missed the wheeling and dealing. Why, if I'd stayed much longer, I'd have got slowed way down, like those Eastern fellows. You know, they don't understand the way we do business down here. They want to fool around exchanging a lot of papers. They can't believe it when they sit around here and see how we frame a deal over the phone in fifteen minutes that it would take their lawyers months to handle. After those Eastern fellows been around for a while, though, they begin to go along in the small denominations. But when they get into the big denominations, then they start going slow again. They never

4

really seem to catch on to the basic idea, which is that it's the *ratios* that count. Just the *ratios*. Them noughts at the end don't mean nothin'."

Clint Murchison has earned the admiration of his fellow wheeler-dealers for his audacious disregard of the noughts at the end. "Figures don't scare Clint," one of Murchison's operatives says. "He figures if it's a good deal it will walk. Like the Lamar Life Insurance Company deal, over in Jackson, Mississippi. I told Clint about that one—how he could buy a hundred thousand shares of the company at a hundred and five. It sounded good to Clint. 'Take my plane and go over there to Jackson and buy it for me,' he said. Well, I went over, but when I got there, it looked like the thing was a little bigger and more complicated than Clint had figured, so I called him up. He was just taking off for Mexico on a hunting trip. 'There's nothing complicated about it,' he said. 'A hundred thousand shares at a hundred and five. That's ten point five. Just a simple business deal. Go ahead, and don't worry about it.'"

The wheeler-dealer spirit, of course, is not unique to Texans. Though not always referred to by the same term, the quality is a basic component of the adult American personality. Cecil Beaton, discovering it to be an admirable attribute shared by all Americans, has described it as their "exhilarating insouciance." Whatever name it is given, the trait is one that Americans have always been proud of. These days, however, they are aware that it is gradually being toned down, dulled, and eroded, and will soon enough be replaced by a creeping punctilious conformity. The attrition is under way everywhere, but in Texas it has made scarcely a dent. Texans have kept their original store of exhilarating insouciance just about intact. Americans who haven't begrudge them this. Such outsiders also begrudge Texans their possession of the frontier. To most Americans, Texas is the last real frontier (when Harvard College was two hundred years old, it has been noted, they were still shooting Indians around Dallas), and in this country the frontier still holds a mystical fascination. According to the idealized concept, life on the frontier has always been simpler and happier, and a man could be luckier there. As things fall out nowadays, the so-called American Dream, which has as its point getting very rich, preferably overnight, seems to come true most often in Texas. So it appears that the popular attitude toward Texas is compounded not only of hostility born of envy but of resentment born of nostalgia. There is more to it than that. Non-Texas Americans find much in Texas to praise, but, adopting the traditional Old World attitude toward the New, they usually find much more to criticize. The faults of Texas, as they are recorded by most visitors, are scarcely unfamiliar, for they are the same ones that Europeans have been taxing us with for some three hundred years: boastfulness, cultural underdevelopment, materialism, and all the rest. In enough ways to make it interesting, Texas is a mirror in which Americans see themselves reflected, not life-sized but, as in a distorting mirror, bigger than life. They are not pleased by the image. Being unable to deny the likeness, they attempt to diminish it by making fun of it. As a consequence, Texas has become the butt of jokes too numerous—not to mention tedious —to count. Still, the image remains. In the end, perhaps, it may not be possible to escape the fact that the epitome of America is Texas and the epitome of Texas is its most picturesque product, its millionaires. They are the Super-Americans, making up a little civilization—the United States in microcosm.

Above all else, Americans are noted around the world for what de Tocqueville, the most perceptive of observers, termed their "irritable patriotism." This trait is, as one might expect, found in exaggerated form in the land of the Super-Americans. With the natives, bragging has become almost a natural function, like breathing. At a recent cocktail party in Dallas, a visiting journalist was introduced to a handsome, impeccably groomed young matron with golden hair, velvety eyes the color of wood violets, and a becomingly superbious air. She seemed a sublime specimen of the Super-American until, as so often happens, she elected to open her mouth. "Mistah,"

6

she said, "Ah'm sick and tahed of readin' those trashy stories
you-all keep writin' ahbowt Texas. They ah just so unfaih they
make mah blood boil. Ah know this state real well. Ah'm a
native Texan. Ah grew up on a ranch in the Panhandle, up
neah Amarillo. Mah granddaddy [nobody in Texas has a
grandfather, or a father] owned fouh hundred thousand acres
and when he passed on, he divahded it up among his fouh
sons. So mah daddy's ranch has a hundred thousand acres.
Theah's a great big beautiful house on it. The livin' room is
thihty by fohty. Daddy lives a very cultured life. You should
see his books! Hundreds of them! And his paintin's! Two
Renoirs, a Chagall, a Manet—scads and scads of them. Daddy
weahs Peal shoes. Always has. He sends to England foh them.
Just won't weah any othah kind. Fouh years ago, Daddy sold
all his cattle, foh one million dollahs. Now he leases his land
foh pasture, foh a dollah an acre, and he doesn't have all
those worries. If you could get to know Daddy, Ah just know
you wouldn't repeat all those trashy lies they ah always tellin'
about us."

Daddy not being immediately available, the visitor was introduced to an older woman of stately bearing. Her grandfather, it soon developed, though the possessor of neither a
ranch nor a pair of Peal shoes, did own the first house in Dallas
to have wallpapered rooms. A casual boast, on the surface, but
pregnant with old-family implications. Some Texas millionaires
—especially those who have had money for a generation or
two—seem to suppress their natural desire to brag out loud and
assume, instead, a tight-lipped smugness, which is apt to turn
into a truculent uneasiness. Apparently unsure of recognition
as a member of the peer group, they seem constantly on the
verge of throwing aside their affected complacency, grabbing
by the shoulder whoever they feel has not been properly
impressed, and demanding, "Look here, don't you know who
I am?" Many sojourners in Super-America have remarked the
prevalence of a kind of implied boasting, and some, like the
wife of a Northern corporation executive who served a three-
year tour of duty there, have found that it takes the form

7

of airily dismissing all things non-Texan. "Every time I went to a party," she recalls, "they'd notice that I didn't have a mushy accent, and they'd ask where I came from. 'Chicago,' I'd say. Then they always gave me a pitying look and said, 'Well, then you *are* glad to be here.' At first it made me laugh. Then it made me mad. I'm no Chicagophile, but I figured, Who do they think they are, running down Chicago? I used to try to think of something to say back to them, you know, like how pretty the lake front is in Chicago, or what a nice art museum we have there, or something, but they never seemed to listen. They would just look the other way, or through me or past me, and pretty soon I'd be standing there sort of muttering to myself. Well, I fought 'em for nine months. Then I found I couldn't lick 'em, so I joined 'em."

Many Super-Americans, like Dillon Anderson, the Houston lawyer and former special assistant to President Eisenhower for national security affairs, scrupulously avoid boasting and sometimes privately express the wistful hope that others might follow suit. "All Texans ought to be silent for the next ten years," Anderson remarked a while ago, but he gave no sign that he expected his admonition to be heeded. This is understandable, in view of the fact that bragging in Super-America, far from being generally frowned upon, is often openly encouraged. "'Texans have ample reasons to be proud of their heritage, even to brag,' Dallas *News* Book Editor Lon Tinkle said Tuesday at a meeting of the Dallas Federation of Women's Clubs," one reads in a newspaper. The question arises: If Tinkle, a graduate of the Sorbonne, a professor of French and Comparative Literature at Southern Methodist University, and one of the state's cosmopolitan and cultivated citizens, comes out for bragging, who can be expected to come out against it? Certainly not the newspapers, which relentlessly urge Texans to hold firm to the belief that they and their state are special and superior. "Texas is a country in itself," the Dallas *News* proclaimed recently, in a typical editorial. "It started out that way, and, in resources, tastes, spirit, and aspiration, it is a land apart, like none other in the world."

This popular thought was echoed by the Houston *Post* in its editorial commendation of Sam Rayburn for having replied, when asked if he planned to return to Texas upon the adjournment of Congress, "There isn't any other place in the world I want to go." "Some commentators may accuse him of being narrow-minded in taking such a Texanic view of the world," the editorial said, "but millions of Texans . . . know exactly what he means. Washington is all right, and other spots in the world are all right, but Texas is THE place."

Texanic ("Texanic" is often used as a heightened form of "Texan," and so is "Texian") journalists like to emphasize the separateness of Texas by only half-humorously referring to the United States as a "Sister Republic" and by describing Texas as "a State which may rule the world some day, if it can only shrug off the hampering arm of the rest of the U.S.A." For the same reason, they have a taste for feature stories such as the one concerning a Mexican laborer named Pedro Hernandez, who was tried on a charge of false claim to citizenship. Asked by the judge if he had previously been in the United States, he answered that he hadn't. "But this report says you worked in the United States as a contract laborer last year," the judge said. "Is this right?" "No, Your Honor," Hernandez replied. "I was working in Texas." According to the Dallas *Times Herald,* William Blakley, a former cowboy and present millionaire who was appointed to fill Lyndon Johnson's seat in the Senate, was asked on a television program if Texas is a Southern or Western state. "Texas is Texas," Blakley replied. The Fort Worth *Star-Telegram,* editorially endorsing this stand, added, "As far as Texans are concerned, that is enough." Even the advertisements have a Texanic quality. "Texas Is Still the Land of Milk and Honey," the Suniland Furniture Company recently assured readers of the Houston *Post.* "Texans, one and all," the Suniland folk adjured, "be thankful for your heritage." When the Royal Dutch Airlines inaugurated service to Texas, their newspaper ads announced, "KLM Now Serves Texas and 74 Other Countries." Texans appreciate clever touches like that, just as they do the pixie habit of radio announcers who follow the time signal with the phrase "Texas Standard Time."

Satisfaction is also derived from reading the annual Associated Press dispatch from London about the dinner of the Anglo-Texas Society, a group of "two hundred distinguished Britons who love the Lone Star State," and who gather once a year to pay it tribute on the anniversary of the Texas Declaration of Independence from Mexico. "One of the proudest moments of my life was when I was taken for a Texan," Lord Jellicoe, a Society member, said in his speech at the 1960 dinner, held in the House of Commons. Texans were pleased to learn that that dinner concluded with the reading by Lord Bossom, the eminent architect, of a message from Prime Minister Harold Macmillan, who declared, after appropriate remarks about the splendid characteristics of Texans, "Friendship between Texas and Great Britain is a most important thing."

When Super-Americans put aside their newspapers and pick up a book by one of their native authors, like Mary Lasswell's 1958 work "I'll Take Texas," they are almost certain to find a literary *smörgåsbord* groaning with rich, patriotic tidbits. "After exploring Texas over a period of three years," Mrs. Lasswell, who returned to Texas after a long time spent in other parts of the country, writes in one of her less rhapsodic passages, "I am forced to conclude that God made Texas on His day off, for pure entertainment, just to prove what diversity could be crammed into one section of earth by a really Top Hand." At an autographing party, Mrs. Lasswell suggested that "all Texans should be required by law to leave the state so they can fully realize how great it is," adding, "Why, if Texans really knew all the state has, they would be insufferable. Texas brags are in many cases genuine understatement." Her book, not unexpectedly, was very well received in Texas, one gallant critic likening it to Proust.

A somewhat more reserved reception was given a recent work in the same genre—"Home to Texas," by Stanley Walker, another native who returned, but one whose judgment, in the opinion of his sympathetic friends, may have been slightly impaired by many years in New York. At least, that is the way they account for the book's occasional blasphemies (carefully attributed by the author to his Uncle Ernest), such as "There have been some wonderful Texans, but in general Texans have little to brag about. The state was settled mostly by second-rate folks on the lam from Tennessee. What can you expect from such people?" For every subversive thought like that, Texans are exposed to a thousand like the lyric flight contained in Mrs. Perry Wampler Nichols' recent work, "Deep in the Hearts of Texans," which makes the faithful choke up with pride. "Visitors stepping into this land of bluebonnets and endless skies find weaving about their hearts, like webs spun by giant spiders, the love of something friendly and great," Mrs. Nichols writes. "To them is given a serenity and peace. Longer-lingering guests feel the tentacles of their hearts reaching out in desire to take root here where the soul may climb its upward path unhindered by the rush—the dirt—the cynicism—of more thickly populated and commercial places. With regret—some leave, and in the departing, find a wistful part of themselves remaining. Others come from far lands—discover Texas—and join the family, soon to find that they have been adopted by the oneness of Texas love."

Adopted sons and daughters who are not totally blinded by the oneness of Texas love are apt to discover that the land of bluebonnets has itself become rather commercial. At least, Texas now leads the nation in the production of oil, cotton, beef cattle, natural gas, sheep, petrochemicals, goats, carbon black, rice, mules, bees, wool, pecans, helium, mohair, roses, spinach, and quite a few other items. In industrial production, Texas has moved up during the past twenty years from nowhere to tenth place, and in aircraft production to second. Within a generation, the population of the state has doubled. No city in Texas had more than sixty thousand people at the beginning of the century. Today, eleven cities have more than a hundred thousand. Houston has nearly a million. And all this, according to the signs, is just the beginning.

The accomplishment so far, especially in view of the natural handicaps, would no doubt be acclaimed a Great American Success Story if it had been made by any people but Texans. Or if Texans would let the record speak for itself. As a race, they seem constitutionally incapable of this. They try to make everything bigger by talk. Everybody knows, for instance, that Texas enjoys a high degree of self-sufficiency, but Texans have a way of taking off from there to talk and act as if they believed Sam Houston's pronouncement, reprinted from time to time in their newspapers, that "Texas could exist without the United States, but the United States cannot, except at very great hazard, exist without Texas." Texans are generally, if sneakily, admired for their streak of independence, but other Americans are not uniformly charmed when Texans act not only as if they had a patent on this trait but as if it had been invented by one of their own; namely, a certain Brit Bailey, whose last request was that he be interred standing up, since he had never looked up to any man and didn't aim to in the hereafter. Bailey, a whiskey-drinking curmudgeon, is referred to in Texas in terms that in other sections of the country would be applied to a figure like Paul Revere. If Revere's name is mentioned in Texas, the natives are apt to ask, "Isn't he the fellow who ran for help?"

The teaching of history is another example of the Texas penchant for the extra-hard sell. Texas history is treated in the schools as if it were as important as United States history. Much is made of the colorful but scarcely significant circumstance that Texas has been under six flags (Spain, France, Mexico, the Texas Republic, the Confederacy, and the Stars and Stripes) and of what Texans consider their state's uniqueness in having been a republic before it joined the Union. Students are also reminded that upon entering the Union the Texas Republic reserved the right to split into five separate states and thus be represented by ten United States senators instead of two. In Texas schools, Thermopylae, if it is mentioned at all, comes out as a bush-league skirmish compared with the Alamo. And so it goes. Why? "All our big talk is the result of an inverted mass inferiority complex, and if anybody around here heard me say that, I'd be run out of town," a psychologically oriented member of an old Texas family has said. This explanation, bringing to mind Vernon Parrington's observation that "an inferiority complex is a common mark of the frontier mind," contains more high-toned terminology than the one offered by Dr. Perry Talkington, a Dallas psychiatrist who is a native and widely travelled Texan. "It's natural that people here should take pride in their achievements," Dr. Talkington remarked a while ago. "They have been made in the face of real hardships. It's like raising children. They give you a lot of trouble, and that's one reason you love them."

Perhaps the Texan who has produced the most thoughtful analysis of what outsiders consider his countrymen's excessive pride is Walter Prescott Webb. "Westerners have developed a talent for taking something small and blowing it up to giant size, as a photographer blows up a photograph," Dr. Webb wrote in a *Harper's* article on the American West, a region in which he includes Texas. "They are like a musician performing on a giant stringed instrument with many of the strings missing," he went on to observe. "The missing strings put extravagant demands on the performer. He must make the best of what he has; he must compensate by ingenuity, agility, and improvisations for the missing strings. His range is limited, his repertoire reduced. He cannot follow the musical conventions, will try anything, and we should not be surprised that the effects are sometimes odd." Showing no interest in winning a popularity contest, he also noted, "Historically, the West has no depth, no long background of slow development. Its story is told in current events. It came on the scene too late to participate in the founding of the nation or to prevent its dissolution in the Civil War. The result is that it has not yet produced a great statesman. Only two Presidents, Herbert Hoover and Dwight Eisenhower, have come from the region; only one was born there. . . . Aside from the Battle of San Jacinto, there has never been a military conflict on Western soil that had the slightest influence on national affairs. . . .

What is the biographer going to do for a region that has so few men of distinction? What is the historian going to do with a country almost without chronology or important battles or great victories or places where armies have surrendered or dead soldiers were buried? How can he make a thick history out of such thin material?" Without answering the harder questions, the Dallas *News* dismissed Dr. Webb in a chiding editorial that was gentle in tone compared to other entries in the furor his article inspired. "Dr. Webb should look up that old song, 'Home on the Range,'" the editorial concluded. "He should note the lines 'For seldom is heard a discouraging word, and the skies are not cloudy all day.' Then he should learn to sing them. He would not be so depressed over the picture of the Great West."

The incessant repetition of the tribal chant singing out their uniqueness and superiority produces in the natives the expected result: they begin to believe their own publicity, or at least they give the impression of doing so. This often leads them to actions that have a limited appeal to others. For example, when gasoline rationing was decreed during the Second World War, Texans took the position that since they had plenty of gas in their own back yard, they should be excused from submitting to this inconvenience. The Governor at the time, Coke Stevenson, refused to set up rationing machinery until Leon Henderson, head of the Office of Price Administration, made a special trip to Texas and persuaded him to enforce the law. Another wartime conservation measure required that the length of coffins be reduced from six feet six inches to six feet three inches. This order was attacked by Texas undertakers, who were apparently influenced by the tribal myth that Texans are taller than other Americans. Recently, in connection with the legal skirmishing between Texas and the federal government over ownership of the oil-rich Texas tidelands, Governor Price Daniel solemnly announced that as one measure for combatting the United States he had "reactivated the Texas Navy as a patriotic organization to preserve the rights and boundaries of this state." Though all Texans were

14

aware that the Texas Navy, a force in being a century earlier, had become a mythical body whose best-known Admiral was Miss Ginger Rogers, they gave Daniel's pronouncement a second thought when he went on to request the owners of the two hundred and eighty-six thousand pleasure boats in Texas to "register their craft as ready for emergency service at any time." This development led the Dallas *News* to remark that "Daniel was quite serious about the whole thing," despite "just a touch of humor." Even as a jest, the proposal is in the tradition, for it implies that Texans will fight to prove that they are not subject to the same laws as other Americans, and it conjures up the agreeably fanciful picture of two hundred and eighty-six thousand craft filled with Texans sailing out, Dunkirk-style, to strike a blow for self-interest.

The Texans' "unintelligible passion of race pride," to use a term that the British historian D. W. Brogan applies to Americans generally, is demonstrated with equal vigor in their loftier pursuits, such as literature. In the spring of 1958, a group of Texas literary men got together in Austin to discuss their native belles-lettres, which they agreed, to the surprise of nobody, are in a glowing state of "renaissance." The conclave ascended to a peak when one participant compared the development of Texas literature with that of Greek literature, to the straight-faced enjoyment of his confreres. Other home-grown arts, like opera, are treated with equal respect. In the fall of 1957, when the Dallas Civic Opera made its début with a production of Rossini's seldom performed "L'Italiana in Algeri," the amusements critic of the Dallas *News*, John Rosenfield, began his endorsement of the performance by describing it as "sensational and horizon-lifting," and went on from there. By the end of his notice, he was declaring, "For Dallas has, above all, the Neiman-Marcus complex or what has been called the Dallas *News* complex. This is that Dallas' best must be the most unique in the world. Good enough is not at all good enough."

That mixture proved a trifle rich even for a few Texans,

among them Rosenfield's counterpart on the Houston *Post*, Hubert Roussel. "Whom are such absurdities meant to impress?" he asked in his column. "Certainly not the sophisticated citizens of Dallas, for that would make them 'the most unique' sophisticates in the world not alone in the grammatical sense of the double superlative." Later, Rosenfield responded by quoting a few excerpts from Roussel's review of a performance by the three-year-old Houston Grand Opera Association —"most astonishing prodigy on the nation's musical scene . . . triumphant declaration of maturity . . . completely glorious victory . . . most brilliant and original achievement"—which seemed to indicate that the Houston critic was capable of handling at least the single superlative.

The Dallas newspapers' treatment of their Civic Opera's first season, though not lacking warmth, was about as lively as an obituary notice compared to the attention they accorded the second, which was given a fillip by the fact that Maria Callas was appearing with the company when she received word from Rudolf Bing that the Metropolitan had decided it could manage without her. This event, announced by the Dallas *News* in a page-one, five-column headline and reams of copy, was wildly welcomed, because, as the *News* put it, "no amount of money could have brought us the worldwide publicity." For days afterward, the story grew, giving the increasingly strong impression that Bing had become so jealous of the Dallas Civic Opera, whose season consisted of three performances, that he fired Miss Callas in order to vent his spleen. "We extend our deep sympathy to the City of New York," an advertisement of Neiman-Marcus remarked, "whose Metropolitan Opera Company apparently finds itself incapable of coping with a power and genius of this dimension." So noble and protective was the attitude displayed on all sides toward Miss Callas that one might have been led to believe that the Manhattan-born diva was a native Texan. Indeed, one excited journalist did refer to her as "Dallas' singing tigress." Long after the tigress had departed, the newspapers continued to boast about the splendid publicity that her misfortune had brought their fledgling musical organization. As one of the more colorful accounts put it, "Dallas Civic Opera's red-hot blast off the pad of civic culture and into orbit all can see is now history."

The boasting that Texans do on their home ground, though not unimpressive, is inferior in both quantity and quality to what they are capable of when on foreign soil. This is to be expected. "If the Americans are more sensitive at home than they are abroad, they are more boastful abroad than they are at home," the Scottish journalist Alexander Mackay remarked a long time ago. The observation still applies, and especially to Texans. One reason for their notably expansive behavior abroad has been suggested by James Mathis, a prizewinning reporter for the Houston *Post*. "We carry the seeds of exaggeration wherever we go," he wrote, "because a great many Texans simply can't resist acting out the expected role." Mathis made this reflection in a series of newspaper articles he prepared in 1957 with the aim of searching out the reasons for the generally hostile attitude toward Texas. The Texas reputation for boasting, he found, was one important factor. "No Texan anywhere can escape the general tendency to tag all Texans upstart liars and boring braggarts," he said, and added that, as a result, whereas "once the greeting abroad was one of warmth, friendliness, and curiosity, we are quite likely now to be confronted with suspicion, amusement, scorn, and ridicule." While acknowledging that "many Texans have been big braggarts almost from the time Texas was colonized," Mathis expressed the opinion that the professional boasters, those responsible for the cross that all Texans must bear, are but "a tiny speck—estimates go as low as one-tenth of one per cent." This statement was printed on page 1 of the *Post*. An inside page of the same edition carried a photograph of the state's Governor, at a conference in Virginia, standing next to an unusually tall soldier. "'I've got a bigger one down in Texas,' Governor Price Daniel seems to be telling Third Infantry soldier," the caption said. The missionary work that Mathis undertook has not yet borne bountiful fruit—even in his own paper. A few weeks after his series concluded, the *Post* publicly backslid when, in a full-page institutional advertisement, it discreetly boasted, among other things, "Texans do things a little bigger, perhaps a little better than most."

Like most Texas boasts, this one is not without some basis in fact. Texans are dedicated to the bigger things in life. Indeed, the zeal with which they worship bigness is impressive even to other Americans, whose "singular preoccupation with quantity," in Santayana's phrase, has for long been a source of wonderment to travellers from abroad. "To say that something is large, massive, gigantic," a nineteenth-century German visitor reported, "is in America not a mere statement of fact but the highest commendation." Tyrone Guthrie recently noted our easy assumption "that a big country, a big building, or a big potato is not just bigger than a small one; that there is inherent virtue in jumbo size." And Edward Weeks, of the *Atlantic*, has recalled how his friend Raoul de Roussy de Sales, the French writer who lived for many years in this country, used to be amused by the American infatuation with bigness. "When I listen to Americans talking on shipboard," he told Weeks, "or in a Paris restaurant, or here in New York, it is only a question of time before someone will come out with that favorite boast of yours—'the biggest in the world!' The New York skyline, or the Washington Monument, or the Chicago Merchandise Mart—the biggest in the world. You say it without thinking what it means."

The passion for bigness—the confusion of size with greatness —is, like nearly everything else, carried to extremes in Texas. Visitors encounter it the moment they set foot in any Texas airline, railroad, or bus terminal and glance at the souvenirs on display—an oversized teacup on which is printed "Texas Demitasse"; a map of the United States showing what purports to be Texas occupying nine-tenths of the area; a silver serving spoon bearing the words "Texas Teaspoon"; and other native artifacts indicating the preoccupation with magnitude. In everything, size is the measure of excellence. Nothing is thought worth much attention unless it is the biggest, the highest, the most. It really means something to Texans that their San Jacinto Monument, just outside Houston, is a little higher than the Washington Monument and that their Capitol, in Austin, has a similar edge on the Capitol in Washington. They also take satisfaction in knowing that of all the states Texas has the most farms, the most churches per capita, the biggest state fair, the most airports, the most insurance companies, the most species of birds, the most banks, the most football teams, and the most holidays, among other things. The board chairman of a Texas bank, consulting with an architect who had been engaged to plan a new building, summed up his ideas by saying that he wanted the new structure to be the tallest in town, so he could "spit on the First National." Another architect, who had designed a residence in the city of Midland for a millionaire named Fred Turner, was soon afterward hired by a fellow millionaire Midlander, who was not without the competitive instinct. "I don't give a damn what kind of a house you build," the competitor said. "Just be sure it's a hell of a lot bigger than Fred Turner's." Perhaps the purest, most succinct statement of the philosophy that superiority is inherent in size has been made by an amiable Dallas millionaire named D. H. (Dry Hole) Byrd, whose nickname is derived jointly from his initials and from the fact that after he had brought in his first producing oil well he drilled fifty-six dry holes in succession. Byrd has made many gifts to his alma mater, the University of Texas, not the least important of which, he feels, is the biggest drum in the world. Known as Big Bertha, the instrument measures eight feet in diameter and three feet eight inches in width; on its head is the printed intelligence "The World's Biggest Drum." As a spectator in the Cotton Bowl not long ago, Byrd watched with apparent pride and satisfaction as Big Bertha, mounted on a hand-drawn truck, was hauled onto the field. "You know," he said reflectively, as a few booms from the drum reverberated richly around the stadium, "to have the biggest of anything—that's something."

Chapter Two

The fact that for over a hundred years Texas was the biggest state in the Union has no doubt been the single most important influence in fostering in its citizens the cult of size. Though Texas is now outranked by Alaska, which is roughly two and a half times as big, the century-long conditioning will not be quickly undone. Governor Daniel, who as a United States Senator had naturally opposed statehood for Alaska, greeted the accomplished fact with a show of good sportsmanship tinged with indigenous pride. "Texas will extend the hand of welcome to a state large enough for us to talk with on equal terms," he said. Many other Texans took a middle-ground attitude, of the sort reflected in a Houston *Post* headline that read, "Texans to Submit Meekly on Size but Not Quality." Those who adopted this semi-defeatist point of view were scored by the Dallas *News* columnist Lynn Landrum for "being afflicted with the limber-tail." He exhorted all his countrymen to hold fast "to the proposition that in the matter of size, Texas has the greatest amount of real estate above water in the Union," and went on to explain, "Nobody can prove how much there is to Alaska because seven-eighths of it is covered by water—frozen water, that is. . . . Alaska is nothing but an Arctic hypothesis in deep freeze. That's all." Even though Texas is no longer the biggest state, it covers an area so vast that it offers to Americans something of the same challenge in spatial comprehension that the United States offers Europeans. To cross Texas by automobile from north to south or east to west—a trip of approximately eight hundred miles—takes about an hour longer than to drive from New York to Chicago or from Paris to Rome. People who traverse Texas by car are quite ready to believe that Texas is more than five times the size of New York State and that it is bigger than any country in Europe except Russia.

After vastness, diversity is the most striking component of the geographical personality of Texas. Newcomers usually expect to find nothing much except an enormous, dusty, treeless plain, like the main setting of the movie "Giant," and in most of the state that is what they do find, as anyone who has made the sensationally dull six-hundred-mile trip from Dallas to El Paso is wearily aware. Taken as a whole, however, Texas is surprisingly varied. In East Texas, one travels through piney woods and over rich, waxy black soil; on the Gulf Coast, over picturesque, bayou-dotted flatlands; in the irrigated Lower Rio Grande Valley, through a subtropical land bursting with green plants and fruit blossoms; and, in the Big Bend country beyond, through a jagged, virtually uncharted wasteland forbidding to some and enticing to others. Practically anything geographical that exists anywhere in the United States, mountains included, can be found in Texas. Its eight-thousand-foot Guadalupe Peak is the highest mountain east of the Rockies. Along with lakes and rivers, Texas has three hundred and seventy miles of coastline and twelve deep-water ports; the largest, Houston, ranks second to New York in tonnage handled.

Despite its mixture of geographical characteristics, Texas produces in few travellers the *coup de foudre,* or love at first sight, that Jacques Maritain says strikes so many Americans upon first looking into France. In Texas, the response is more likely to be love at long last. A major reason for the lack of immediate appeal is the fact that Texas, on balance, may be the least scenically rewarding state in the nation, with the possible exception of North Dakota or Nebraska. The niggardliness of Nature in her scenic endowment of most of Texas was pointed up by recent findings of the Texas Highway Department, whose operatives asked eight and a half million visitors

21

what aspect of the state most impressed them; six per cent said the scenery. The fact that during the past three years the tourist trade has fallen off one-fifth in Texas while increasing one-fifth in the rest of the country has no connection, as Texans see it, with their state's natural attractions.

"The truth of the matter is that one could spend a lifetime of vacations in Texas and not completely exhaust what it has to offer," the Houston *Post* said last year. More tourists would spend at least one vacation in Texas, the residents have taken to telling one another, if word about its offerings got around. "Tourist states are not born—they are made," Tom H. Taylor, director of the Travel and Information Division of the Texas Highway Department, told the Houston Advertising Club a few weeks ago. And the way to begin making a tourist state of Texas, he went on, is to spend three hundred thousand dollars advertising it. Such spending, some non-advertising men feel, may stimulate tourism but never appreciation, an emotion that is reserved largely for native Texans, a few of whom— the writers John Graves, Stanley Walker, and Lon Tinkle, among them—are able to communicate a sense of what it is about Texas that can produce affection deep enough to bring tears to the eyes of otherwise undemonstrative people. For them, the landscape of Texas is not only endlessly fascinating but as important as the sun. In many visitors, however, prolonged exposure to the high degree of uniformity of Texas town and country induces a consuming boredom. However varied the landscape they have seen, their prevailing impression of the state is apt to be that of a smooth, limitless expanse of unrelieved beige. The natural difficulties that Texas puts in the way of a newcomer's quick attachment have been evident for some time, according to a group of early settlers' letters presented a couple of years ago to the University of St. Thomas, in Houston. "I am not charmed by this country and I don't meet anybody that is," one new resident reported in 1835 to a friend in his native Georgia. "If I had a family, I would not bring them here to live for ten of the best leagues of land in Texas." Even then, however, there were differences of opinion. David Crockett, for example, at about the same time described Texas to his kin as "the garden spot of the world."

Writing of the British climate in his "Notes on England," Taine said, "I always come back to this, for there is no more powerful influence." The observation applies with equal felicity to the Texas climate. "One Texas claim is that it does not have a climate, just weather," J. Frank Dobie, the eminent Texan, writer, and savant, remarked in a recent issue of *America Illustrated,* the United States Information Agency magazine circulated in Russia. "The weather was here before Columbus sailed, and it has had a more powerful effect on the lives of the inhabitants than all the Spanish expeditions, flag flying, and gubernatorial administrations recorded in history books. Also, it has done more than any other one factor to make braggarts out of Texans. You can tell a Texan who is out of the old rock from the other kind by how and what he brags on. . . . He brags on the weather, and for his purpose the worst is the best. He brags in reverse." Texans are seldom without adequate material for reverse bragging. Regardless of the season, Texas weather easily lives up to its reputation for being changeable (if you don't like the weather, according to the old saying, wait a minute), disagreeable, and bizarre.

The climate of Texas varies from humid, on the Louisiana border, to arid, on the far western plains, and from subtropical in the Lower Rio Grande Valley, to temperate, in the Panhandle. Because of the climatic range, a vacationer can be sunbathing in Corpus Christi while a rancher is shivering in Amarillo. However, there is in the Texas climate one constant —wind. It may be a waft or it may be a gale, but it never lets up. Texans seldon use the word "wind" in referring to the ever-present phenomenon. "We always have a nice breeze," they are likely to say, frequently holding on to their hats. The unceasing wind makes it hard to play a decent game of badminton out-of-doors, but it does make Texas a kite-flier's paradise; a kite can be put into the air almost any time and soon be carried nearly out of sight with no more effort on the flier's part than paying out the string. Because gas is the primary source of heat and power in Texas, the air, as a rule, is noticeably clean and clear. "Life in a gas-burning city has many virtues," Stanley Marcus has said. "Your shirt cuffs aren't soiled within an hour after you've reached town. Your nasal tissues aren't seared with soot, and your eyes aren't attacked by flying missiles, as in New York. Women can wear white gloves for a week, stone buildings stay white, and there is never smog to blot out the sun." Or almost never. In November, 1959, Dallas had a whole day of smog, which the *News* celebrated by printing a photograph taken at noon of the city's hazy skyline along with a story headlined: "Dallas Smog Different: It's Healthy."

Outside the Panhandle plains, Texas as a rule has very little snow, although in the past five years there have been heavy, highway-clogging snowfalls in the northern and western sections of the state—twice since 1955 El Paso has had the unusual experience of being covered with eight inches or more—and in other sections snow has ceased to be a breathtaking novelty. Dallas has had enough of it to measure in three of the past five winters, and in February, 1960, when a snow blanket spreading seven hundred miles from east to west and four hundred and fifty from north to south settled over the state, even Houston received three inches of "the strange, white stuff," as the *Post* referred to the element that had been seen locally only a half-dozen times before. Still, the average snowfall in Dallas amounts to only one and seven-tenths inches a year and in Houston to only three-tenths of an inch. In winter, the normal pattern consists of a succession of generally moderate, frequently sunny days temporarily terminated by the sudden arrival of a norther—a cold front that sweeps down from the Arctic and often reduces the temperature forty degrees or more while one is attending a movie. An especially bitter storm of this kind is called a blue norther, because it makes its entrance amid a dark-blue haze created by the clash of the Arctic blasts with the prevailing southerly winds. On the afternoon of January 9, 1957, the temperature in Dallas was a balmy eighty-three degrees. Shortly after dark, a typical blue norther arrived, on a thirty-seven-mile-an hour wind that for the first thirty minutes forced the temperature down a degree a minute. By morning, the thermometer registered twenty-five degrees. A norther that blew into Weatherford on November 16, 1959, dropped the temperature from sixty-three to thirty-eight in an hour and a quarter. On November 28, 1960, the thermometer in Houston read eighty-one; the next day, forty-three. Texans take an admirably relaxed attitude toward northers and the inconveniences they cause, such as the need to organize an impromptu expedition on a freezing afternoon to rescue children and husbands who had started out in the morning dressed for summer. Northers usually last for only a few days; with the return of the southerly winds another spell of mild weather begins. The season for northers, extending from late autumn into early spring, is also the season for sand and dust storms, which generally whistle in from the west at speeds up to eighty miles an hour, tingeing the atmosphere with a reddish glow, irritating the eyes, and on occasion cutting visibility within an hour from fifteen miles to practically zero.

Spring in Texas is distinguished not only by the magnificent blanketing of the countryside with vast seas of bluebonnets but also by the onset of the tornado season. Texas has more tornadoes than any other state except Kansas. If tornado statistics took into account area as well as frequency, Texas would be outranked by two or three more states. Even so, it would have no reason to take a back seat, for in the past fifty years roughly one of every eight tornadoes recorded in the United States occurred in Texas. Twisters have become an accepted fact of Texas life; storm cellars are in the nature of standard household equipment in the rural areas, and during the tornado season, which continues into early summer, prudent motorists travelling through areas alerted by severe weather warnings keep their car radios turned on in order to learn of the formation and expected movement of tornadoes.

Generally, however, tornado warnings are regarded about as

casually in Texas as forecasts of heavy rains are elsewhere. Late one afternoon in April, 1957, a woman who had recently taken up residence in Dallas was called to the phone by a neighbor, who said, in a voice as excited as if she were asking to borrow a cup of sugar, "If you've never seen a tornado, take a look out the window." A funnel-shaped cloud approaching the city was by then clearly visible to thousands of Dallas residents, many with cameras in hand, who had taken to the streets and rooftops to get a good look at the twister; it killed nine persons, injured a hundred and seventy others, and destroyed or damaged eight hundred homes and other buildings. Two years later, almost to the day, ten tornadoes ripped through the center of the state and killed six persons. Texas now averages about six dozen twisters a year. Since 1957, spring in Texas has also been marked by violent hailstorms, torrential rains, overflowing streams, and rampaging rivers. The devastating floods have time and again turned streets in Fort Worth, Dallas, San Antonio, and other cities and towns into rivers, drowned scores of persons (ten during one weekend in 1960), and made hundreds homeless, and, all told, have caused well over two hundred million dollars' worth of damage.

Before 1957, Texas had gone through seven years of uninterrupted drought, which parched the plains and dried up the rivers and streams. The drinking water in many parts of the state became so brackish that outsiders were unable to get it down; the natives, uncomplaining, simply stepped up their intake of Coca-Cola and Dr. Pepper, and either had spring water delivered to their homes at fifty cents a gallon or bought a cheaper but potable variety in five-gallon jugs at supermarkets. Dry weather also makes the chiggers, an indigenous pest, seem a worse nuisance than ever. Chiggers—the larval form of parasitic mites that are found on grass and bushes, attach themselves to the skin, and cause intense itching—turn up in the spring and early summer in such force that drugstores in Texas feature entire counters of various kinds of powders, sprays, ointments, and other medications to use against them.

No nostrum has yet been developed to combat the chigger successfully, so the Texans take the annoyance in stride, their light-hearted view being reflected in the newspaper articles always printed at the beginning of the chigger season, like a recent one in the Houston *Post* that chummily referred to the pest as a "much-misunderstood imp."

While dry weather promotes imps, wet weather promotes snakes. "The snakes have been stirred up by the floods, and certainly we can assume there are a number of copperheads and water moccasins loose," an official of the Harris County Flood Control District said in Houston last year. "Families should probably warn their children about them." Apparently not all did, for ten days later, a six-year-old Houston girl told her parents she had cut her finger on a piece of glass while playing on the lawn of her house; the injury, it was discovered barely in time to save her life, had been inflicted by a poisonous snake. In some sections of Texas, rattlesnakes, which account for approximately half of the state's poisonous snake population (water moccasins, coral snakes, and copperheads comprise the most common other varieties), are so abundant that local organizations like the West Texas Peace Officers and the Junior Chamber of Commerce of Sweetwater stage annual rattlesnake roundups. More than two hundred and fifty hunters, including a number of women, took part in the 1960 Sweetwater roundup, which lasted three days and resulted in the capture, alive, of nearly seven thousand snakes, mostly diamondback rattlers. The snake situation is not, however, all fun and games, as a Dallas housewife recently discovered, when, cleaning a storage closet, she saw on the floor what looked like the electrical cord of the vacuum cleaner. "I picked it up to hang it back where it belonged," she said later. "Then it wiggled."

So many people get bitten by snakes, especially in the ranching country, that such incidents are hardly considered news, though the papers do print stories, usually two or three paragraphs long and on an inside page, about people who get bitten by snakes in towns and cities. In the past few months, there have been newspaper articles about a yard worker bitten by a rattlesnake while cutting grass at a home in Dallas; a Houston mother, on the way through a public park to pick up her children, bitten by a copperhead; a woman vacationing near Burnet bitten by a water moccasin that also bit her two dogs; an eleven-year-old and a four-year-old Fort Worth child, each playing in his own yard, bitten by copperheads; and a two-year-old Smithfield girl, "bitten," as the one-paragraph story rather vaguely put it, "by a snake Friday at her home." (Actually, the incidence of snake bites in Texas is less than the incidence of rat bites in New York City. During an average month, Health Commissioner Leona Baumgartner recently stated, twenty-seven rat bites are reported in New York. Nobody has estimated the number that go unreported.) By and large, Texans take a casual attitude toward snakes, though perhaps not to the same degree as the wife of a Nolan County rancher, Mrs. William Howe, who nonchalantly acknowledged in an interview with Frank X. Tolbert in June, 1960, that during the past thirty years she had been "rattlesnake bit" twelve times. "I haven't since June 10, 1959, so things are kind of quiet around here," she said.

When spring floods and their attendant inconveniences can be forgotten for another year, summer comes in with heat that is, typically, immoderate. The so-called normal July temperature ranges from eighty in the northern part of the state to eighty-four in the southern. Many summer days are very abnormal. On June 15, 1960, the temperature reached a hundred and two in Dallas, a hundred and four in Waco, a hundred and five in Abilene, a hundred and six in Midland, and a hundred and nine in San Angelo. These readings, being Weather Bureau figures, were, of course, taken in the shade. Just for the fun of it, a native of Boston who lived for a few years in Houston kept a record one August, during his vacation, of the temperature in the sun at noon in his yard. The average for the thirty-one days, according to his findings, was a hundred and thirty-one degrees. Some parents consider such warmth to be of limited benefit to young children, and make a practice of keeping them indoors from about ten in the morning until around four in the afternoon. This precaution tends to prevent accidents like the one that happened in Waco a few summers ago to a thirteen-month-old infant named Clara Elizabeth Cook, who toddled out of her house onto the sidewalk on a hundred-degree day and, when found by her mother a few minutes later, had to be taken to the hospital for second-degree burns of both feet. Once a heat wave begins, it tends to be prolonged; it is not unusual for nearly any Texas city to have a dozen consecutive days when the temperature is in the nineties or half a dozen when it is above a hundred.

The chief weapon for contending with the heat, which in some sections—notably Houston—is combined with memorable humidity, is air-conditioning. "Hell, since we've had air-conditioning, I've gotten over being apologetic about Texas weather," Angus Wynne, Jr., a Dallas real-estate operator and civic leader, said recently. "You go to Chicago or New York in the summertime and it's intolerable. You can't breathe. You can't find one comfortable spot. They're just not prepared for the heat. Down here we are. Everything is air-conditioned, so it's no trick to be comfortable." Along with air-conditioning (deplored by a few of the extra patriotic, because, they say, it enables Yankees to exist in Texas), the natives use a number of old-fashioned stratagems in the annual summer battle. For one thing, they dress for comfort. In summer, men's jackets are obligatory during the daytime only for some such occasion as a city wedding or funeral. Slacks and a sports shirt make an accepted costume for office workers and many professional men. On the street, shirtsleeves are the rule. Any summer day, a stranger can be spotted instantly among a group waiting at a corner for a traffic light to change. The stranger stands at the curb; the natives step back into the entryway or shadow of the nearest building—bracing themselves against it, if necessary—to enjoy a few seconds of shade. When nothing else is at hand, the experienced stand in the pencil-thin shadow cast by a telephone pole.

Along toward the end of September, the heat begins to subside, and in October and November Texans can reasonably expect good weather. However, they are kept on the *qui vive* by the knowledge that the hurricane season in Texas extends from the end of July through November. Though hurricanes have not bothered Texas much in recent years, they have figured so redoubtably in the state's meteorological history that during the hurricane period priests of the Galveston-Houston Catholic diocese are under instructions to include in masses a prayer "for the driving away of storms." By the time the hurricane season has passed, winter has arrived, with its northers, and a new round of climatic excitement has got under way.

The great distances and the wayward climate of Texas combine to discourage the habit of walking. Texas children, to judge by the morning and afternoon traffic jams around the schools, are taught early to shun the habit. Anybody strolling in a residential section of a Texas city is an object of considerable interest to passing motorists and police prowl cars. During the Civil War, a British military observer noted that "no Texan walks a yard if he can help it. Many mounted regiments were therefore organized, and afterwards dismounted." Nowadays, about the longest distance a Texan regularly covers on foot is from his house to his garage. "Most Texans walk slowly, as if it went against the grain," Stanley Walker has remarked, "and they regard the automobile as the only way to get from here to there." Folklore has it that all Texas millionaires get around in one of their several Cadillacs, which they trade in for new ones as soon as the ashtrays need emptying. "The deal isn't quite that good," W. D. De Sanders, president of the Lone Star Cadillac Company, of Dallas, which sells a couple of thousand new Cadillacs a year, said a while ago. "Only about twenty per cent of your millionaires trade after one year. Most of them keep a car for two. And I'm here to tell you, these people that got money, they're pretty smart. They try to buy them as good as they can." A conspicuous minority of Texas millionaires have never bought even one Cadillac. For example, H. L. Hunt, one of the wealthiest men in the state, drives medium-priced cars, which he usually keeps longer than two years. Some other Texas millionaires buy Chrysler Imperials, the choice of Jake Hamon, or Lincolns, the choice of R. E. (Bob) Smith, who has four.

In spite of a sizable promotion campaign, the Rolls-Royce has not become a fad among Texas millionaires. "Texans don't like to be unique," William McGhee, who handles the Rolls-Royce distributorship in Fort Worth, has explained. Last year, however, one Rolls-Royce was sold in Dallas and seven in Houston. Being diffident in respect to cars, D. D. (Tex) Feldman drives a Bentley. Foreign sports cars are becoming increasingly popular in Texas. One of the first Texas millionaires to become interested in them was Clint Murchison's son John, who was urged by a friend who owns an agency to buy a Mercedes-Benz 300 SL. "Why, that was going to run to something like ten, twelve thousand dollars," Murchison recalls, looking almost as dismayed as if his friend had tried to sell him the Brooklyn Bridge. Murchison decided to start out with a Porsche, which he bought wholesale. A few months ago, John Mecom, a Houston oilman who likes to start at the top, began tooling around town in a new Ferrari. Many Texas millionaires who eschew the genuine article have invested in what they consider the American equivalent, the Thunderbird, which offers them all the comfort and excitement of an easy chair. Notwithstanding all such vagaries, the Cadillac, of course, is no stranger in Texas. Though five other states—California, New York, Illinois, Michigan, and Ohio, in that order—buy more new Cadillacs per capita than Texas, appearances indicate that, in the words of Art Buchwald, "Texas is the most Cadillac-conscious state in the Union." So much so, he added, that he had no trouble understanding this laconic conversation overheard in Houston:

"Did you hear Zeke got a new car?"

"What kind?"

"Dark blue."

A number of Texas millionaires, like Leo Corrigan and Michel Halbouty, have a Cadillac for themselves and one for their wives; Halbouty also has a Chevrolet, used primarily by his domestic help. Though servants often drive when taking the children to school and performing other chores, nearly all Texas millionaires and their wives prefer to take the wheel themselves. Only about two per cent of the Cadillacs sold in Texas are models designed to be chauffeur-driven. Almost without exception, Texas millionaires buy air-conditioned automobiles. (In Texas, even hearses are air-conditioned.) "Once in a great while, we sell a car that isn't air-conditioned," De Sanders says. "We consider those special orders. I remember one we sold to a man that hated any kind of air-conditioning, but his wife made him trade it in for a regular model. She had a French poodle that was used to living in an air-conditioned house. The dog refused to get into an un-air-conditioned car." Because nearly all Texas millionaires own two or more cars, it is not unusual to hear one of them say, upon offering to drive somebody somewhere, "Excuse me, I'll go get a car." The use of the indefinite instead of the definite article is common enough to go unnoticed.

Fast, heavy cars, like the Cadillac and the Chrysler, are well suited to Texas driving. Speed is desirable because of the absence of much to attract the eye en route, and weight because of the possible added protection it provides. The second factor is of considerable importance, because more people are killed every year in traffic accidents in Texas than in any other state except California—and Texas has a population about three-fifths that of California. In traffic deaths during the 1960 Christmas holidays, Texas even beat California, twenty-seven to twenty-five. Since 1939, when Texans started keeping accident records, more than forty-three thousand persons have been killed and one and three-quarters million injured on the state's streets and highways. A Texan born today has but one chance in ten of escaping injury in a traffic accident before he reaches sixty.

On the average, traffic accidents in Texas kill twenty-four hundred persons and injure a hundred and ten thousand every year. This is a substantial contribution to the position that the United States holds in the rate of deaths from motor-vehicle accidents—first in the world. In Texas, as everywhere, a great many accidents are caused by speeding and by drunken driving, but an even more important cause, some experts believe, is the fact that Texans behind the wheel tend to excel by far all other Americans in aggressiveness, perhaps in this respect outclassing even the Germans. As Assistant Chief of Police Charles Batchelor, of Dallas, has put it, "The worst fault of drivers is their violation of the rights of others." The frontier spirit dominates the driving habits of Texans, each of whom seems to take the position that every other motorist is a poacher. In the circumstances, courtesy can be expected on the splendid Texas highway system only from the lily-livered. It follows that the auto-rebuilding industry in Texas long ago achieved a plateau of prosperity.

To rank next to the top in traffic deaths is nothing to brag about, the Dallas *News* once remarked in an editorial, but at the same time it is an indication of real Americanism, for the killings result from "the same human qualities that made America great—willingness to risk, driving energy, rugged individualism." Dallas, which works hard to promote traffic safety and on whose streets only eighty-four people were killed in auto accidents in 1960 (more than in any other American city in its population class), has an enviable record compared to other Texas cities, and frequently wins prizes. Even in a bad year, when traffic accidents soar, the Dallas police department will proudly announce that it has won an award for "outstanding achievement in the maintenance of accident records." Houston perennially holds the distinction of leading the state in traffic deaths. Its record for one year, set in 1959, stands at a hundred and five. The total dipped to eighty-six in 1960; however, traffic injuries that year exceeded those in 1959 by about a thousand. As it happened, none of them was caused by a blind resident, who was arrested in June for driving an automobile while intoxicated. That made the seventh time he had been charged with the same offense.

If driving in Texas when the weather is fair can be a memorable experience, driving when there has been any precipitation can be as exciting as Russian roulette. Rain, snow, sleet, or ice makes it extremely difficult for Texas motorists to complete their appointed rounds without mishap. The minute any moisture appears on the streets, Texans begin driving as if they had all been taken suddenly drunk. Cars skitter around the streets, banging and scraping and smashing into each other and into telephone poles and people. For instance, on February 19, 1959, Dallas had three-tenths of an inch of snow; it also had seventy-five automobile collisions. One day the following September, half an inch of rain fell on the city; police recorded sixty-six minor and thirteen major traffic accidents. "Everybody out there seems to be running into everybody else," a radio newscaster said in announcing the early-evening returns on one such day. "Fender-bending episodes and bumper-to-bumper pile-ups were the favorite forms of wreck-creation," one of the newspapers noted next morning, in a passage that reflects the bonhomie with which Texans treat the subject. When the precipitation is heavier, as it was on February 24, 1960, the "slam-bang crescendo of crashes," in a newspaper phrase, naturally grows louder: between three in the afternoon and ten that night Dallas was the scene of two hundred and twenty-six collisions. Houston motorists have done better. They made February 12, 1960, the day the city had three inches of snow, a banner day by chalking up two hundred and seventy-five accidents—the record so far.

In recent years, some measures have been taken to make Texas highways less stimulating. For one thing, the Governor set up a Highway Safety Commission, consisting of two hundred and fifty members, who were summoned to Austin for their first conference in the Fall of 1958. On their way into the city, quite a few members were caught in a radar check on its outskirts and given tickets for speeding. Governor Daniel has also supported the Texas Traffic Safety Council, which is carrying on a crusade aimed at persuading Texans to do things a little smaller on the highways. "On a cold cash basis," the Council has announced, "safety experts say a traffic death costs the state's economy $40,000. In other words, an average

Texan killed by an auto would contribute about $40,000 to the economy of the state." Many people feel that this approach, appealing to what might be called patriotic materialism, will get results.

For long-distance travel, Texas millionaires prefer airplanes. Railroad passenger service in Texas tends to be sketchy—for example, none is available between Houston and Austin—but the state is served by seven major domestic and two foreign airlines, as well as by a number of small ones operating within the region. In addition, Texans own some six thousand private airplanes. Only Californians own more, and per capita Texas has the most. One fine October weekend in 1959, the Houston oilman Pat Rutherford and his wife gave a party at their ranch, southwest of Austin, for the Lyndon Johnsons; fifty-three private planes brought some of the eight hundred guests. The 1960 Christmas catalogue of Neiman-Marcus offered "His" and "Her" airplanes for "a husband or wife who's utterly impossible to buy for." "Hers" was priced at twenty-seven thousand, "His" at a hundred and forty-nine thousand. The private-aircraft business in Texas is sufficiently big and brisk to cause the large dailies to include in their classified advertising a section headed "Airplanes, Accessories." The cities that have the largest number of private planes are Dallas, Houston, Fort Worth, and San Antonio, in that order, and their airports (Dallas has eight) start humming every decent weekday morning at around seven, when dozens of private planes carrying oil operators and other businessmen begin taking off at three-minute intervals. This activity moves into high gear again in the late afternoon, when the flying executives start coming home for dinner. On fall weekends, the airports in cities with major football games scheduled are taxed to the limit. Novels and movies about Texas sometimes give the impression that the native millionaires travel in nothing but four-engine airplanes, complete with bar, galley, and a uniformed crew that includes a ravishing hostess. As a matter of fact, some years ago Glenn McCarthy did own a Boeing Stratocruiser, which cost him two million dollars. He also owned a few other planes at the time, and on occasion filled his air armada with family and friends and took off for a few days of fun in some such place as Mexico or Canada. Now only one Texas millionaire seems to be in the four-engine class—John Mecom, who recently bought a Lockheed JetStar for a million three hundred thousand dollars. In the manner of most Texas millionaires, Mecom uses the JetStar, as well as nine smaller planes that he also owns, mainly for business purposes. Though not a jet owner, D. D. Feldman has a Lockheed Learstar, which can fly non-stop from coast to coast and costs in the neighborhood of four hundred and fifty thousand dollars.

As for the Texas millionaires who shy away from being thought unique, many of them choose either a DC-3, which seats fifteen, or a Lockheed Lodestar, which seats eleven; these range in price from a hundred and eighty-five thousand dollars to two hundred and twenty-five thousand, depending on their equipment. Smaller two-engine planes popular among Texas millionaires include the Cessna 310, the Beechcraft Twin Bonanza, and the Aero Commander, which range in list price from sixty thousand dollars to eighty-nine thousand and are normally outfitted with radio, radar, and other equipment costing from twenty-five thousand to fifty thousand more. Quite a few Texas millionaires who are licensed pilots own one or more single-engine planes seating two or four persons and selling for upward of ten thousand dollars. In addition to the purchase price, which can as a rule be depreciated over a five-year period, the fixed expenses normally include hangar rental, hull and liability insurance, taxes, gas, oil, maintenance, and the salary of the crew, which on larger planes usually consists of a pilot and a co-pilot. Altogether, the annual cost of owning a substantial but not gaudy plane in the class of the Aero Commander (the kind President Eisenhower used on trips to Gettysburg) and flying it two hundred and fifty hours a year—par for Texas millionaires—is approximately forty-five thousand dollars. To maintain a larger plane, like a Beechcraft D-18, calls for an annual expenditure of about sixty-five thousand dollars, and a plane in the Lockheed Lodestar class uses up about ninety-two thousand dollars. The actual outlay is considerably less, since Texas millionaires generally charge off as a business expense something like sixty or seventy per cent of the total cost of operating a private plane.

Along with many advantages, the possession of a private plane offers an occasional, peculiar difficulty, such as the establishment of just the right relationship between the owner and the pilot, a man who is at once an employee and sometimes master of his employer's life. Experience is often required to achieve the proper balance between formality and familiarity. "When we got our first plane, we had this perfectly divine pilot," the wife of a Texas millionaire told an acquaintance not long ago. "Duncan was his name. He'd been in the R.A.F. He was real cute. A very superior-type person. Cultured. We enjoyed having him around—he was fun, you know—and we just got in the habit of taking him along with us wherever we went. When we'd go down to Austin for a football game, we always got a seat for Duncan, too. We'd go to parties afterward, and he'd go along with us. He had this cute British accent, and lots of people just thought he was an English friend of ours. Which he was. It was fun. We had a ball. We were down in San Antonio during Fiesta, and Duncan went with us to a lot of parties—he always took his dinner jacket on trips. We were having a divine time. Then, at one of these parties, this stuffy old hostess—her granddaddy built the Alamo, or got killed there, or did something very historical—she came over to me and said, 'Well, my dear, I didn't know I was going to have the pleasure of entertaining your chauffeur, too.' Well, I mean. How cotton-pickin' snooty can you get? We'd never thought of Duncan that way, of course, but, I don't know, after that it wasn't quite the same. We got to feeling funny about taking him places. It got so we were really between a rock and a hard place trying to think up excuses for not inviting him along. He looked so hurt when we'd leave him at the airport. You know, like a pet dog that's been whupped. Finally, we couldn't stand it any longer. We decided the only thing was to get rid of him altogether. Just fire him. So we told him we were going to sell the plane. Now we have an older pilot. He's good, but he's not cute. He just stays with the plane."

Another problem faced by the owners of most private planes is the occasional delays in taking off and landing and the other inconveniences that are inevitable around busy public airports. A. S. Crutcher, president of a pipeline-equipment company in Houston, and the owner of four planes, became so piqued a few years ago at what he considered the inadequate facilities of the municipal airport that he bought eighty-eight acres of land on the outskirts of the city and turned it into a private airport, complete with a thirty-four-hundred-foot runway and a hangar, at a cost of about sixty thousand dollars. So many Texas millionaires own private planes that their novelty has long since worn off. A few months ago, during a dinner party in Tyler that was attended mainly by millionaires, a guest mentioned that she and her husband were taking off later in the evening for New York so they could see one of their horses run at Belmont the following day. They had plenty of room in their DC-3, she said, and would be delighted to take along anyone who cared to spend a day at the races. The invitation stirred up about as much enthusiasm as the offer of a lift home would in other circles. When Texas millionaires are discussing plans for an out-of-town trip, one is likely to ask another, "Are you going commercial?" It is not considered declassé to travel on commercial airlines; it is just the difference between taking a taxi and being driven in one's own limousine.

With swift transportation readily at hand day and night, Texas millionaires are able to indulge a frequent whim to get away from Texas. "Ah, the Texans," Leo Rosten remarked in a recent article on Hollywood. "They flock into Beverly Hills and Bel Air with increasing gusto and alarming bankrolls. As one philosophical producer put it, 'Deep in their hearts, Texans must *hate* Texas. They certainly don't waste any time, once they strike oil, in moving to Beverly Hills.'" Though California is a favorite migrating ground for Texas millionaires, very few have taken up permanent residence there. They may hate Texas, but they hate the California income tax more. Texas millionaires commonly maintain one or more out-of-state residences, which they visit periodically to escape the vagaries of the weather at home. Scarcely any, however, have become expatriates. To sojourn long and often in more congenial climes is socially acceptable; to give in and move away for good is regarded as desertion. Nevertheless, a disinclination to violate that taboo is almost incidental in keeping Texas millionaires from fleeing permanently. The important reason they are quite willing to stay in Texas and put up with things as they are is that Texas is the place where they can most easily realize their basic aspiration, which is, of course, to make money.

Chapter Three

The movement is not of millionaires away from Texas. On the contrary, the movement is of people into Texas in the hope of becoming millionaires. A dramatic and almost ultra-typical illustration of this phenomenon is Midland: in 1930, a sleepy village of some five thousand persons, including a handful of millionaires; today, a bustling city of more than sixty-seven thousand, including scores of millionaires. However it is approached, Midland, which looms up improbably on the desolate prairie halfway between Fort Worth and El Paso, looks like a mirage. Suddenly on the horizon one catches sight of what seems to be a collection of skyscrapers surrounded by hundreds of miles of wasteland. The sight, no more convincing from a distance than a theatrical backdrop, turns on a closer look into real stone and steel office buildings (one of them rising to twenty-two stories), newly paved streets, new residential subdivisions, new schools, new churches, and new people. Seventy per cent of the population are under thirty-five. The sprouting of Midland resulted from the discovery, in the nineteen-thirties, of the Permian Basin, a vast reservoir of oil, underlying much of West Texas, which at present accounts for more than half of the state's petroleum production. Because more than six hundred oil and oil-service companies have offices in Midland's skyscrapers, the city is known as The Brains of the Permian Basin. (Odessa, which is twenty miles to the southwest and furnishes supplies and labor for the twelve hundred-odd oil fields, is naturally called The Brawn.) The builder of many of the new skyscrapers is a local millionaire, a banker's son and rather colorful dresser named Jack B. Wilkinson, who has memorialized himself in the Wilkinson Building, the Wilkinson-Foster Building, the Wilco Building, and the V & J Tower, "V" standing for his wife, Virginia, and "J" for everybody in Midland knows whom.

Another builder, however, had a larger hand in shaping Midland's history. This was a visionary speculator named William Hogan, who, on the strength of the discovery of oil in West Texas, put up a twelve-story structure called the Petroleum Building in 1929. He was ahead of his time. The real oil boom came several years later, and meanwhile his building, which was practically without tenants, inevitably became known as Hogan's Folly. When oil operators did start streaming into the region, Midland offered ample, ready-made office space, and this was one major reason they made it their headquarters. Another reason is that Midland was also able to provide adequate hotel accommodations. In the mid-twenties, the late Clarence Scharbauer, a pioneer cattleman and one of the town's wealthiest and most public-spirited citizens, had come to the conclusion that what Midland needed was a good hotel. He accordingly had one built, and when it was completed, in 1927, he paid for it by writing a check for a million dollars. As the city grew, he enlarged the hotel—it is now a six-story, block-long, air-conditioned structure containing three hundred and fifty rooms—and financed the expansion in the same uncomplicated manner.

Ever since the Hotel Scharbauer was opened, its lobby has served as Midland's informal stock exchange. There ranchers and oilmen gather every weekday to trade and deal, their transactions amounting to some fifty million dollars a year. "It used to be if you got to the hotel at seven in the morning and stayed until nine, you'd see anybody you wanted to see, whether it was about oil or cattle," a long-time resident of Midland recalls. "In those days it was decorated in what you might call Western Victorian. Big, heavy furniture. Mounted steer heads on the walls. Plenty of brass spittoons. The Coffee Shop had a tile floor, and men waiters in aprons. It's all been what they call modernized. No more steer heads. No more spittoons. Waitresses in the Coffee Shop. Even TV in the lobby. That's what's happening to Midland and everything else out this way." Since the establishment of the Petroleum Club and the Country Club, the lobby of the Scharbauer has ceased to monopolize Midland's financial life, but it is still the favorite headquarters of the old-timers. For the most part, these are elderly ranchers who, through no particular fault of their own, became immensely rich after oil had been discovered on their land. "They were standing there blowing the bass tuba the day it rained gold," an irreverent Texan has said of innocent bystanders such as these. The millionaires who spend their days in the Scharbauer lobby, sitting on chairs and couches reserved for them by custom, could not justly be accused of putting their money on their backs. In winter, they customarily wear a nondescript, wrinkled suit or a pair of trousers and a scuffed leather jacket; in summer, trousers and a wildly figured sports shirt; in all seasons, pointed Western boots and a light-colored Western hat, which a native apparently never removes except when sleeping. The men around the Scharbauer share a lean, hard, acquisitive look, and they are not garrulous. They seem to take as much pride in their taciturnity as in their shabby appearance. What talking they do is generally about business, and even when it isn't, it is chiefly related to money.

One evening a while ago, a wizened, tight-lipped habitué in his sixties walked out of the Coffee Shop, made his way across the lobby, and sat down in a chair next to another weather-beaten codger, who was looking straight ahead at a blank wall. After the new arrival had sat down, pulled up his trousers, crossed his legs, taken out his watch, looked at it, wound it, and put it back in his pocket, he opened the conversation.

"Evenin', Cap," he said.

Cap went on staring. He pulled his hat down a trifle lower to shade his eyes. After several seconds had passed, he said, "Evenin', Sam."

Several minutes passed before either spoke again. "How yuh doin'?" Sam said.

Cap took a kitchen match from one pocket and a jackknife from another. He sharpened the end of the match. "Nothin' to brag on," he said.

After another long silence, Sam said, "How was the trip to San Antone?"

Cap picked his teeth with the matchstick for a few minutes. "Easy," he said.

Both Sam and Cap scrutinized the blank wall. "See they got another floor on the new bank building," Sam, the talkative one, said at last.

Cap continued to pick his teeth. "I seen it," he said.

Sam took a pack of cigarettes from the pocket of his shirt, opened the package with deliberation, took out a cigarette, and lighted it. "Hope I live to see it finished," he said.

After apparently giving the matter considerable thought, Cap said, "You will."

Sam took a few more puffs of his cigarette, pinched off the burning end with his thumb and forefinger, and carefully put the butt in the cigarette pack. "I doubt it," he said.

Nothing was said for several minutes. Cap completed his dental ritual and put the match behind his ear. Sam removed his hat, scratched the back of his head, and put his hat back on again, spending a good deal of time adjusting the tilt of the brim. After a while, Cap, who had turned his head slightly, said, "Here comes your partner."

A man perhaps ten years younger than Cap and Sam had walked into the lobby. He was wearing a crumpled, dust-covered brown suit, orange-colored boots, and an electric-blue tie. He walked over and stood in front of Sam and Cap. They looked up.

"They finish your well today?" Cap asked.

"Nope," the partner said. "Down to fourteen thousand feet. Couple more days."

"Then what'll you have—forty-eight million?" Cap said.

"You kiddin'?" the partner said. "Anyway, I ain't goin' back out there for a spell. They told me there's some man out there around the well lookin' for me. One of Uncle Sam's men, they think."

"Revenue man, eh?" Sam said. "Fifty-eight tax?"

"I reckon," the partner said. "I already give 'em twelve thousand and some dollars. I don't mean to be givin' 'em any more. And I'm not about to go lookin' up Uncle Sam's man. He can try and find me."

Sam and Cap nodded approvingly.

"That a new tie you got on there?" Sam asked.

"Yessir," the partner said. "Cost me two and a half dollars. I didn't mean to pay all that. I was goin' to get another one, cheaper, but the clerk, she talked me into this here one for two and a half dollars."

The older man gave the tie a long, critical look. "Ain't that a little rip there down at the bottom?" Sam said.

"I seen that," the partner said, examining an end of the tie. "I can sew it up with a needle and thread. That shouldn't oughta happen with a tie that costs two and a half dollars."

"Specially shouldn't happen to a feller with forty-eight million dollars," Cap said.

"You kiddin'?" the partner said. "I'm goin' to find me some thread and a needle." He left.

"If he ain't got forty-eight million now, he will before he dies," Cap said.

Sam said nothing.

They resumed their scrutiny of the wall.

In considerable contrast to the natives who frequent the Scharbauer lobby are the scores of eager, hard-driving young men, many of them graduates of Yale, Princeton, or other Eastern universities, who have flocked to Midland since the end of the Second World War. Because of this immigration, Midland claims to have more college graduates per capita than any other city. Regardless of where they come from, the young men are known generically in Midland as the Ivy Leaguers or the Yalees. Some have arrived with a stake, others

44

THE SUPER-AMERICANS [III]

with nothing but the desire to get rich. Quite a number have done so. After migrating to Midland, George Bush, son of a Connecticut senator, co-organized an oil company that now has among its assets four offshore drilling rigs worth around nine million dollars. Murphy Baxter, son of a successful Dallas insurance executive, not long ago drilled a discovery well in a rich field, which he is developing in partnership with the Phillips Petroleum Company, and from which, his friends figure, he should make around five million. One of the new men is a former Notre Dame football player named Joseph O'Neill, whose preparation for a career in the oil business consisted of a stint as an F.B.I. man. He arrived in Texas in 1948, borrowed some money to get started, and has learned enough about his new career to have accumulated about twenty million. Robert E. Stripling, who served as chief investigator of the House committee that investigated Alger Hiss, later moved to Midland to practice law and is now doing nicely in the oil business.

These and some fifty thousand other immigrants have discovered that Midland is a mixed blessing. The financial prospects it offers are bedazzling, but they must be pursued in a place that few people without an ardent financial attachment to it would look upon as Eden. A Midland civic group once invited O'Neil Ford, an articulate San Antonio architect who is not noted for his mild opinions, to address them on the subject "Midland and the Future." Ford's prognosis was not sanguine. At the conclusion of his remarks, which contained a number of unflattering references to Midland's climate, a member of the audience rose and said, "Well, if Midland is all as bad as you say it is, what do you suggest we do about it?" "Abandon it," Ford replied. Like Ford, most visitors are inclined to take notice of the Midland weather, especially if they arrive during the first three months of the year, when sandstorms in the city can become so intense that for two days and nights in succession it is impossible to see across the street. At times in other months, the sand-bearing wind sweeping in from the surrounding desertlike prairie makes it necessary to use headlights when driving through the city in midday. "Cli-

45

matic conditions are almost ideal," a publication of the Midland Chamber of Commerce says, "being uniform, temperate, and healthful"—a statement that is likely to be recalled with vividness by visitors getting used to the novelty of grinding sand between their teeth as they talk on the street.

The attitude of Midlanders toward their weather ranges from stoic to laudatory; they deal with it as best they can. Without noticeable exception, every householder encloses his property within a brick or cement-block wall six or eight feet high. Lacking this protection, he could not, for example, barbecue a steak in his back yard unless he was willing to have it garnished with a fine coating of sand. Without walls around them, Midlanders' houses would be permanently banked on all sides with drifting sand, and their children's outdoor recreation would tend to lack variety, being limited to playing in a sand pile. On Country Club Drive and on streets like Bedford, Harvard, and Princeton, where Midland's millionaires live, the houses are clustered together like a colony of ant hills, and, owing to their general bleakness, the neighborhood has the aspect of an improbable, high-cost housing project. However, some have a distinctive touch, such as the mansion of R. B. (Bum) Cowden, who belongs to one of Midland's old ranching families and is an enthusiastic big-game hunter. Mounted in concrete on either side of the entrance to his house are the tusks of an elephant he once shot. Midlanders also contend with their weather by using ingenuity to stay out of it. At five in the afternoon, when the business offices close, Wall Street and the other main downtown thoroughfares are full of people; by five-thirty they are practically empty. The object in Midland is to spend the least possible time getting from one air-conditioned place to another. On weekends, Midlanders in droves climb into their cars and planes and take off for Dallas, Santa Fe, La Jolla, or some more distant spot that offers another nearly ideal climate. "I think I've got the travel-lingest congregation in the world," a Midland minister has said. "When a weekend comes along, they just seem to break up and scatter in every direction. The weather here isn't too good for my business."

Once the visitor gets over his preoccupation with the weather, he gradually becomes aware of the spirit that pervades Midland—a kind of bristling, chip-on-the-shoulder vigor. "It's the same thing you find in the French Foreign Legion," O'Neil Ford has said, bestowing another compliment. Stanley Weiner, who has been in the oil business in Midland most of his life, says, "People here aren't any prouder. It's just that they take larger satisfactions from what they can accomplish because everything out here is so goddam hard to do. Making a garden, for example, is a major accomplishment. After you've lived here a couple of years, though, you're sold on it. Sure, we all like to get away once in a while. I like to go to Vegas and other places, but I like getting back even better. When I come driving across the prairie and I see those skyscrapers, I get a great charge. Of course, Midland is a good place to make money, too."

Quite a few Midland millionaires have, like Weiner, a natural inclination to talk about Midland's financial attractiveness as if it were of secondary importance. "A lot of things bring a man out here," H. E. Chiles, an early migrant to Midland, told a visitor a while ago. "The West is something that gets into your blood. It's an intangible, but once you feel it it's as real as daybreak. There's a spaciousness out here. This is a place that's good for the masculine ego. It's a place where a man can come and carve a niche for himself if he's willing to put out the effort." Chiles, a lean, alert, carefully groomed man in his early fifties, is among those who did carve a niche. A graduate of the University of Oklahoma, he moved to West Texas with his wife in 1939 and set up an oil-well-servicing company. He started with two trucks and three employees; his wife constituted the office force. His company now has some six hundred employees, and if he were to sell it, he could put from six to ten million or so in the bank. "I wouldn't want to do it again," he once remarked at the Petroleum Club, sipping a Coke in deference to an ulcer, "but I love this business, and

I love this place. There aren't more than thirty days in a year when we can't play golf here. Of course, that means we're sometimes playing in a twenty-mile-an-hour wind, but we're out there. Golf is the big sport. You can't go anywhere. So we live a semi-outdoor life in our back yards. When the sun goes down, it's very pleasant. Of course, you have your hot winds in the daytime, as everywhere on the desert. We're on the desert. We might as well face it, and we do. All our windows are weather-stripped. We build walls to keep the sand out. And when the sand is blowing, we stay indoors, just like the goddam Arabs. But in spite of the sandstorms, we have a very desirable climate here. It won't let a man get soft."

Being self-made, Chiles is typical of the great majority of Midland millionaires. "The only people here with second-generation money are the ranching families," a Midland historian has remarked. "Just about all of them hit oil, and practically all their descendants have stayed here. Like Junior Scharbauer. He's probably the leading one. Junior is a hell of a good citizen and a damned good businessman. He's worth a hundred million, but he works real hard. The last thing he wants is for anybody to call him one of the idle rich."

Though old ranching families like the Scharbauers are in the minority, Clarence Scharbauer, Jr., believes they are more representative of Midland than the newcomers are. "I know these new people," he said a while ago. "They're real nice men. I've played golf with a lot of them. But you can't know Midland if you don't know the people who've been here a real long time. These people are the real, honest-to-goodness people. With these people their word is as good as their bond. They're the real people. We're different out here. We never wanted any publicity. Absolutely not. We just want to go along livin' like everybody else."

In his dress and speech, at least, Scharbauer succeeds in resembling nearly everybody in the lobby of his hotel, off which he has his offices. When he received a visitor there one afternoon, he was attired in worn, pale-blue cowboy trousers, a wide leather belt with a large silver buckle, Western boots, and a shirt with no tie. At thirty-five, he is tall, husky, blue-eyed, and rosy-cheeked, and he talks so slowly and sparingly that he gives the impression of taking off Gary Cooper. With his mother, he owns, among other things, nine ranches, scattered from the Panhandle to New Mexico and totalling half a million acres. Though his cattle business ranks as one of the largest in the country, it accounts for a relatively small part of his holdings. "Hell, we're in the oil business ten to one what we are in the cattle business," he says. "We never got in on the drilling part. Just the royalties. I'm a cowman, like my father. I'm happier at the ranch talkin' to thirty-dollar-a-month cowboys than over at the Petroleum Club talkin' to somebody that's tryin' to promote somethin'. Spring and fall—six, eight, ten weeks—you won't find me here more than one day a week. That's roundup time. I'm out there workin'. I'm up at three in the mornin', just like everybody else, and I put in the whole day workin', just like everybody else. That's how I learned to run this business. In the school of knocks, like my father. He wasn't anything but a cowman, but if Midland needed something, like a hotel or a radio station, he saw they got it. And everything he did just turned to money. Hell, I've been wealthy all my life. I grew up with this thing. I was born with it. There's nothin' new about it to me. It never made any difference. I just grew up in the country, and I just like that regular, plain life. I'm not crazy enough to start drinkin' or be a playboy. I'm just a little country boy. That's the way I like it."

While the Scharbauers, the Cowdens, and members of the other old ranching families entertain each other a great deal at home, the social life of most of the Midland millionaires centers on the Midland Country Club, which has eight hundred and twenty-five members. One of them invited a couple visiting the city to dinner at the club on a recent evening following a day that had been marked by a moderate sandstorm. The wind had subsided, and there was only a fine powder in the air as the visitors walked out of the hotel and stepped into a Cadillac driven by their host. "Beautiful night, isn't it?" he said, heading toward the club. "This is the kind we have from May until late in the winter—temperature between sixty and sixty-five. And very dry. That's because the elevation here is about twenty-seven hundred feet. That's also the reason we don't have any mosquitoes. There's always a nice breeze at night, and that has a cooling effect. All in all, we're pretty lucky. We're especially lucky to have a nice country club, since there's very little out here in the way of bright lights. About the only entertainment we have is what we create. And we really have only two nice places to go—the Country Club and the Petroleum Club. That may seem strange when you consider that Midland is supposed to be the richest city per capita in the country. Of course, we're very young. We haven't had much time to spend on frivolous things. The oil business is pretty demanding. Ninety per cent of the people you will meet at the Country Club are in the oil business. So ninety per cent of the talk you'll hear will be about oil."

The prognostication turned out to be quite accurate. Over cocktails, the visitors were introduced to O. C. Harper, C. V. Lyman, J. P. (Bum) Gibbins, and a number of other prominent old hands in the oil business, and during dinner they made the acquaintance of one of the younger hands, a so-called Yalee, and his wife, who have been in Midland for eight years. It came out one way and another at dinner that the Yalee, a native of Boston, had graduated from medical school and, fulfilling a plan he made in his youth, started a career in medical research. He was on the staff of a New York foundation and was married and the father of two children when he was visited by a college classmate who had made a sizable fortune in Midland. The Yalee was bitten by the bug, and determined to cut himself in on the bonanza. Practically overnight, he resigned from his foundation post and set out for Midland with his family. The move was temporary, he told his wife; as soon as he had made a pile, they would return to New York and he would resume his career. As things have fallen out, he has done well enough in the oil business to be able to live very well—far better than on the usual research-foundation salary. Compared to his lucky contemporaries, how-

50

ever, he is scarcely even a run-of-the-mill success. He has put up with the same things they have—the sandstorms, the frustrations implicit in the search for oil, the generally meagre existence—but reaped next to none of the rewards. It became evident at dinner, when he was seated next to the visitor's wife, that as a result he has developed into a rather bitter, angry young man. By the end of the meal, he had drunk as much as was good for him and had become taunting and argumentative, taking issue loudly with whatever his dinner companion said. His gift for friendly conversation did not improve over brandy. At length, driven by what demons it is impossible to guess, he uttered what in his world is apparently the ultimate insult. Point-blank, he accused the visitor's wife of not being rich. "How much have you got in the bank?" he snarled. "I'll bet you haven't got enough to bait a mousetrap!" And so the party ended.

Chapter Four

With not very many exceptions, the thing that has put Texas millionaires on Easy Street is oil. To be thus enriched is the epitome of Super-Americanism, since oil is by far the most important source of modern wealth in the United States. Regardless of vintage, more than a third of this country's large fortunes were gathered in the fruitful and beguiling vineyards of oil. In our time, oil has become not only America's biggest industry—the shares of publicly owned oil companies alone have a value exceeding fifty billion dollars, or more than those of the steel, automobile, and chemical industries together—but also, perhaps, its most characteristic. Indeed, one of its knowledgeable admirers, James A. (Jim) Clark, who writes passionately about petroleum in the Houston *Post*, ascribes to his corporate inamorata the distinction of being "the only native American industry the world has ever known." Certainly the oil industry comes as close as any to approaching the "ideal essence," in Santayana's phrase, of American business. Besides meeting the basic requirement of bigness—of the country's ten largest industrial corporations, five are oil companies—the industry is notably young, inventive, brash, enterprising, powerful, well intentioned within the limits of enlightened self-interest, and, because it regards itself as sorely misunderstood, perpetually uneasy.

Beyond all that, the oil business possesses to a unique degree one other quality that is peculiarly American—adventurousness, that national trait which has been inspiring wonderment in European visitors ever since de Tocqueville observed that "the whole life of an American is passed like a game of chance." It may be this built-in spirit of adventure, or a longing for it, that lies behind the widespread American custom of referring to labor of practically every kind as if it were merely a risky but enjoyable diversion—the advertising game, the retailing game, the building game, the frozen-food game, and so on. In most forms of commercial enterprise, this practice reflects the American gift for self-delusion; in the oil business, however, it is quite legitimate. For the oil business is not only a game but—what is even better suited to the American taste—a game of chance. "It's just like running a dice table—one that's honest, open, and all aboveboard," Ted Weiner, a Fort Worth oilman, has remarked. A confrere, Thomas W. Blake, Jr., who makes his headquarters in Houston, has said, "What it comes down to is big-time gambling with all the latest scientific helps." Neither Blake nor Weiner nor any other professional oilman would be so stuffy as to say he was in the petroleum industry. If he felt like putting on a few airs, he might describe himself as being in the oil business, but as a rule the professionals refer to their work simply as "the oil game"—or, as a Russian-born Super-American named Paul Raigorodsky puts it, with even more economy, "oil game." "Oil game is not like monastery or old ladies' home," Raigorodsky has said. "It can be rough. In oil game, you keep your eyes open. You play for keeps."

Considering the nature of the oil game, it is not surprising that those who engage in it are inclined to express themselves in language more appropriate to a casino than to a monastery. "I ran a fifty-dollar bankroll, beginning in 1921, up to—well, what I'm supposed to have today," the Dallas oilman H. L. Hunt said in 1954, when he supposedly had about two billion. The word "play" turns up with conspicuous frequency in the oilman's vocabulary. "That was a big play," he says of an oil field in which there has been great activity, and he speaks of production in the tidelands as "the offshore play." To him, every transaction, including marriage, is a "deal," and he generally identifies himself on his business cards and stationery as an "Oil Operator," and in the telephone directory as "oil oprtr"—a term of such marvellous aptness that one might expect, upon visiting his office, to find him wearing a green eyeshade and conducting his business at a baize-covered table. As the operators see it, the oil game is the most exciting gamble of the century and possesses the prime requisite for a national pastime in a democracy: any number can play.

Though the oil game has produced many millionaires, it has produced many more paupers. This is the favorite adage of oilmen, especially millionaire oilmen. An equally cheerful truism is that many who have made the most noteworthy contributions to the game have received the meagrest rewards. The precedent was set by a former New York & New Haven Railroad conductor named Edwin L. Drake, the man who is usually given credit for inventing the game. Naturally, the Russians claim that they did. It is true, as the Houston operator and part-time historian Michel Halbouty points out in his frequent public speeches, that Marco Polo sniffed oil at Baku in the thirteenth century, but that, Halbouty goes on, does not prove the Russian claim, because eighteen hundred years earlier Herodotus, the celebrated Greek foreign correspondent, returned from the island of Zante, in the Adriatic Sea, with an eyewitness account of oil springs there. The Greeks took this scoop in stride, that being their way. The rest of ancient oil history is no less fascinating.

By the time Edwin Drake got into the act, a process had been devised for extracting from coal a product called coal oil, or kerosene, which had taken the place of whale oil for lighting. Around 1854, it occurred to a New York lawyer and promoter named George H. Bissell that the petroleum that for two hundred years had been seen oozing out of the earth around Titusville, Pennsylvania, might be as efficient as kerosene and considerably cheaper. His belief confirmed by tests made at Yale University, Bissell took the lead in organizing a company, with headquarters in New Haven, to put the product on the market. The company's first employee was Drake, an acquaintance of one of the stockholders, who was hired in

1858, at a salary of a thousand dollars a year, to go to Titus-ville and, in the unconfining terms of his directive, "raise & dispose of Oil." Neither an engineer nor a businessman, Drake was a bearded thirty-eight-year-old Yankee with a common-school education who had prepared for this novel assignment by working in a textile factory, as a hotel clerk, and, most recently, as a railroad conductor. He had two positive, visible qualifications: he was available, having temporarily left the railroad because of a back ailment, and he carried a railroad pass—a not inconsiderable recommendation in view of his em-ployer's wispy resources. As it turned out, Drake's real talent was stubbornness. After a year and a half of experiment, humiliation, and defeat, he completed, in August, 1859, what is generally considered the world's first oil well; it was sixty-nine feet deep. The boom that followed cast up several mem-orable figures. Among the more entertaining were John D. Rockefeller, who went on to become the oil game's first all-time All-American, and John (Coal Oil Johnny) Steele, who created the popular archetype of the oil millionaire by falling heir to an income of some seven thousand dollars a day and assiduously getting rid of it all in highly conspicuous consump-tion.

The bonanza eluded Drake, though he remained at the scene of the boom for five years. Bissell's company collapsed in 1864, and Drake found work with another firm, at about the same salary. He did have one piece of good luck; for a couple of terms he served as justice of the peace in Titusville, a post that brought him twenty-five hundred dollars a year. Then he moved to New York, where he set himself up as an oil-stock and oil-property broker, lost everything, and dropped out of sight. Shortly before the tenth anniversary of the com-pletion of the first oil well, it was discovered that Drake, suffer-ing from spinal neuralgia, had been without work for three years and was living with his wife and four children in a sum-mer cottage, lent by a friend, on the New Jersey shore. Their income consisted of what Mrs. Drake earned from sewing. When the oilmen in Titusville learned of Drake's predicament, they managed to get together a fund of nearly five thousand dollars to help him out. Four years later, in 1873, the Pennsylvania legislature voted Drake, then a hopeless invalid, an annual pension of fifteen hundred dollars for having made a discovery that, the legislators said, "has greatly stimulated various industries and has also added directly to the revenues of the commonwealth more than one million dollars." Drake died in 1880, leaving behind him a fortune of good will. "Honest and upright," a former business associate eulogized, "he risked his all to develop the oil interest in Pennsylvania, but, like many another enterprising man, he shook the boughs for others to gather the fruit."

During the rest of the nineteenth century, the petroleum industry came increasingly under the domination of John D. Rockefeller, who was so dedicated to gathering its fruits that he was willing to do the job all by himself. In fact, he was so anxious to handle the project alone that anybody who tried to help him was put out of business or otherwise discouraged. This naturally took a lot of fun out of the oil game. However, changes came about as time passed. In its modern form, the game dates from January 10, 1901, when a remarkable gusher of oil erupted from a hole, eleven hundred and sixty feet deep, dug into a marshy hillock called Spindletop, one mile south of Beaumont, Texas. That event, a turning point in our history, marked the end of the oil monopoly and the beginning of the liquid-fuel age. Before Spindletop, Rockefeller's Standard Oil Company directly controlled eighty-three per cent of all oil production in the United States; within a year Standard was competing with Texaco, Gulf, and a few other incipient giants. Before Spindletop, too, the uses of petroleum had been limited mainly to lighting and lubrication; insufficient supply had made it too costly for fuel. In its first year, the initial Spindletop well alone produced as much oil as all the thirty-seven thousand Eastern wells together. By 1902, a hundred and thirty-eight wells were producing at Spindletop; their combined production was more than that of the rest of the world. Suddenly, oil had become a source of cheap power, an abundant fuel that was to break the coal monopoly, propel automobiles and airplanes, and alter the face of the nation.

Behind all this was the man who originally shook the boughs at Spindletop—a one-armed, self-educated, prideful native of Beaumont named Pattillo Higgins, son of the local gunsmith. Owing to some unusually sportive behavior, Higgins had left town as a youth; in his early twenties, after working for several years as a lumberman, he returned to Beaumont to go into the real-estate business and teach in the Baptist Sunday school. Soon afterward, from observation and a do-it-yourself course in geology, he came to the conclusion that oil could be found under Spindletop. Despite the unanimous contrary opinion of experts (it was their comic way to offer to drink all the oil that Higgins could find in the vicinity), he spent ten years and as much money as he could make and borrow—some thirty thousand dollars—trying to demonstrate his eccentric theory. When, at last, he was unable to raise another dollar, he enlisted the interest, through an advertisement in a trade paper, of a trained mining engineer, Anthony F. Lucas, who took up the pursuit with equal fervor. Lucas carried it on until he had invested about as much as Higgins and had been obliged to begin selling his household furniture to buy groceries. Still he persisted. At length, he secured from a pair of Pittsburgh oil operators named James Guffey and John Galey, who were backed by the Mellon brothers, enough financing to complete the first well at Spindletop. All that Guffey and Galey required in return was that Lucas turn over to them practically all the interest he had acquired in Spindletop property. Lucas thus handily escaped becoming a millionaire. After drilling the gusher (which bore his name), Lucas continued exploring for petroleum for four years, and then moved to Washington, D.C., where he resumed his original business as a mining engineer and kept it up until his death, in 1921. Though the material returns from his historic feat were negligible, he received some rewards of a more enduring nature. Not only did the citizens of Beaumont name a street after him and erect a monument in his honor, both after his death, but, during his lifetime, a hundred of the more generous among them presented him with a large solid-gold watch charm cleverly decorated on one face with a gusher and on the reverse with a Texas star containing a large diamond and surrounded by five small ones.

No such honors were heaped on Pattillo Higgins. A year after Spindletop, when his theory was rather fully proved and a number of his friends were enjoying their new status as millionaires, he tried to organize a company that would permit him to get in on the big play. The people of Beaumont accorded this proposal their unqualified indifference, and Higgins left town again, this time for good. During the rest of his long life, he roamed the state, at first in a horse and buggy and later in an old Ford, making a living by prospecting for oil and dealing in oil lands. He died in San Antonio in 1955, at the age of ninety-two, and there was found among his effects a document that said, in part, "Mr. Higgins deserves the whole honor of discovering and developing the Beaumont oil field. He located the exact spot where all the big gushers are now found." The paper was signed by thirty-two Beaumont citizens and attested by the county clerk. Public recognition, such as it was, had come at last.

Of all the developments of the oil game that Higgins saw in his lifetime, no doubt the most important was a drastic change that occurred in the nineteen-thirties. This step was taken as the result of a discovery by a pioneer named Columbus M. Joiner, a genial and likable man who was known to almost everybody as Dad. Like most of his precursors, Dad, who came from Alabama, had scant formal education. His entire schooling, he once said, added up to seven weeks. He early acquired a fondness for reading—the Bible and Shakespeare were apparently his favorite reading matter, considering the frequency with which he quoted them—and late in life estimated that he had read at least ten thousand books. After starting work at twelve, he migrated to Tennessee, qualified as a lawyer, served two years in the legislature, and moved on to Oklahoma, where he turned his attention to oil. In his first venture, he made a four-hundred-per-cent profit; he bought an oil lease for five dollars and sold it for twenty-five. If he had kept the lease, which was on property that proved to be very productive, he would have made more than six million dollars. At any rate, the transaction served to launch Dad on a career that later brought him the title King of the Wildcatters. (The term has since been vitiated by indiscriminate use; wildcat kings are now about as common as gypsy kings.) Dad drilled his first well in Oklahoma in 1913, made and lost two fortunes, and took out for Texas.

In 1925, when he showed up in Dallas, he was sixty-five and broke; for the next five years, he said later, he didn't have enough money to buy a new suit of clothes. He was able to keep on operating because his pleasant, homely manner inspired confidence in small investors and because he had chosen to prospect in East Texas, a region where leases could be obtained cheaply, for the understandable reason that no oil had been found there or, in the publicly expressed judgment of the geologists of all the large oil companies, ever would be. With a small amount of borrowed money, Dad secured a lease on some thousand acres in Rusk County, on a farm owned by a widow named Daisy Bradford. Then he scraped together enough additional money to, in the oilman's phrase, "po'-boy" a well. As the term suggests, to po'-boy a well is to drill one as cheaply as possible, using a makeshift rig, second-hand pipe, old tools, much sweat, and great ingenuity. To nobody's astonishment, the first Daisy Bradford well turned out to be a duster, or dry hole. After selling a few fractions of his lease to raise a little more money, Dad moved his ramshackle rig to a new location and sank another well. This was as dry as the first. The men on his crew, who had been working in return for an interest in the lease, got discouraged and left. To replenish his capital funds, Dad issued and sold scrip backed by his lease, rounded up another crew, and started drilling a third well. Mrs. Bradford contributed to the project by serving free meals to the men working on the well, and a local banker who had a small interest in the lease put on overalls and donated his spare time to helping out on the rig. On October 3, 1930, the Daisy Bradford No. 3 came in, a gusher. Dad Joiner had tapped the largest single pool of oil ever discovered in the United States. It was a fabulous reservoir, spreading over an area of some two hundred and forty square miles.

For a while, Dad's discovery threatened to ruin the industry. With oil available in such abundance, the market skidded toward collapse; eighteen months after the Daisy Bradford strike, oil had dropped from a dollar and thirty cents a barrel to as low as five cents. Efforts were made to boost the price by voluntary restriction of production, but Texas was not ready for that. The more eager and rugged among the small producers ignored the quota plan and took to running "hot oil." There were fights and bloodshed in the fields. The oil game got very rough. Texas called out its National Guard (the general in command, as it happened, was also chief counsel of the Texas Company) to patrol the East Texas fields. Finally, to straighten things out, a major rules change was agreed upon. Whereas it had previously been the right of a producer to pump as much oil as he wished, state and federal laws were now enacted giving Texas and other oil-producing states the authority to set the amount each operator would be allowed to produce. As a result of the new rule, the oil game soon became orderly and prosperous.

Dad Joiner's discovery erased the effects of the depression in East Texas and populated the landscape with a sizable body of new millionaires. Dad himself, being in the bough-shaking tradition, was not among them, or at least not for long. Paying a visit to Dallas to buy a new suit and celebrate, Dad, then seventy, found himself exceedingly popular. Before he had had a chance to do much shopping, he negotiated a deal with one of the foxiest traders in the business. Dad wound up with what amounted to a token sum, and this became the object of his creditors' lively interest. Within hours after the successful Bradford well came in, a lawsuit had been filed against Dad, and in the ensuing four years, he once recalled, he was the defendant in more than a hundred and fifty others. By the time he had freed himself from the lawyers, he was worn to the bone; he gave up the oil game and lived the rest of his years in a modest house on Mockingbird Lane, in Dallas. He died there in 1947, at the age of eighty-seven. If he had left an estate, he might well have made a bequest to the Dallas Public Library. In retirement, he was known as its best customer.

Ever since Spindletop, the headquarters of the oil game has been Texas, which now produces some thirty-eight per cent of the nation's oil and has approximately half of its reserves. (Texas is also well supplied with a companion product, natural gas, of which it also has about half of the country's reserves— a hundred and twenty trillion cubic feet, to be exact.) Of the two hundred and fifty-four counties in the state, a hundred and ninety-five produce oil. Scattered across Texas are nearly two hundred thousand oil wells, which have now replaced cattle as the state's unofficial insignia. "During the twentieth century," the Texas folklorist J. Frank Dobie has remarked, "oil has brought so much money to the Southwest that the proceeds from cattle have come to look like tips." Probably the most familiar sight on the Texas landscape is the device used to lift oil to the surface—the so-called pumping jack, whose long steel beam bows to the ground in a regular, obeisant motion matching the tempo of the slowly repeated phrase "Thank you very much, thank you very much, thank you very much." Since oil has been discovered in nearly every conceivable location in Texas, pumping jacks can be seen not only on farms and ranches and in swamps, forests, and churchyards but in less likely places; for example, an enterprising operator named Cliff W. Trice recently drilled a number of producing wells in Houston's municipal dump. Driving through the countryside, a traveller is constantly confronted with other reminders of oil—pipelines, refineries, drilling rigs, clusters of storage tanks, exploration crews at work. On the highways, he frequently finds himself caught up in an impromptu parade whose most conspicuous entries represent oil: trucks (seemingly the length of barges) to which are chained tons of dully glowing steel drilling pipe; barrel-shaped trucks carrying sand, acid, and cement for the servicing of wells; station wagons bearing crews of surveyors and geologists; and dusty, serviceable sedans driven by engineers, scouts, and other oilmen, whose connection with the game is often revealed by the presence on the shelf inside the car's rear window of a bright-yellow helmet for wear in the field.

With all this evidence around him, a visitor is soon willing to believe that one out of every eleven Texas workers is employed in the oil business—two hundred and twenty-five thousand people, at latest count—and that petroleum is the state's largest taxpayer, accounting for more than a quarter of the total take. In the cities, the visitor encounters other signs indicating that oil is the keystone of the Super-American economy—particularly the large number of buildings named after oil companies and operators, many of which are surmounted by a striking adornment, such as a gigantic red neon flying horse that revolves incessantly. Furthermore, in all cities of reasonable size those who play the oil game have clubs of their own; their clubhouses range in size from the Midland Petroleum Club's converted (genuine) ranch house to the Houston Petroleum Club's million-dollar spread atop the Rice Hotel.

Perhaps the most meaningful reflection of the place that the oil game holds in the hearts of Super-Americans is the way it is treated in the newspapers. On a year-round basis, they probably devote more space to the oil game than to any other game, with the possible exception of football. Every one of the metropolitan newspapers employs an oil editor; some have, in addition, oil columnists, the most notable being the Houston *Post*'s Jim Clark; the game is often the subject of editorials; and it frequently makes page-one news.

For aficionados, the most interesting part of the paper is the oil section, where the players' day-to-day activities are reported. A glance at this section reveals that the oil game has its own language, even more recondite than that used by *Variety* to cover the amusement game. For example, a typical story in the Houston *Post* begins, "John W. Mecom's Lacy I Armour B well made 4 million cubic feet of gas per day with approximately 60 barrels of 52.4-gravity distillate to the million cubic feet through a 3/16-inch choke on a drill-stem test." An account in the Dallas *News* of another well, this one belonging to an operator named Paul C. Teas, is no less cryptic: "The Dallas independent's No. 1 Skeeter-Slaughter, section 24, block 1, Jasper Hays survey, eight miles southwest of Post townsite, showed its better flow from the Ellenburger at 369 barrels daily." Some stories invest the game with an element of hunting on a Paul Bunyan-like scale ("English L. Jackson, Jr., Tyler, spotted a 5800-foot wildcat three miles east of Elkhart . . ."), and sometimes, to judge from the headlines, the chase ends tragically ("Loving Wildcat Plugged"). The headlines on some other stories make the game sound as violent as a television drama: "Strawn to Be Fractured and Caddo Acidized at Prospect in Stephens." Besides giving the game at least adequate coverage, Texas newspapers, apparently operating on the principle that what's good for the oil business is good for Texas, seldom reveal signs of an excessive straining for objectivity in matters involving petroleum. As a working policy, they tend to criticize the oil game and its players about as often as they knock motherhood and Texas.

Owing to its uniquely favored situation, Texas attracts more players of the oil game than all the other states together. Of approximately twelve thousand oil-producing firms in the United States, some sixty-five hundred are domiciled in Texas. These full-time professional players are divided into two main groups, known familiarly as the majors and the independents. The majors consist of a small number of very large corporations, while the independents consist of a large number of relatively small operators. Altogether, only twenty-one oil companies in Texas are classed as majors; their dominant position is indicated by the fact that the six largest—Humble, Pan American, Gulf, Magnolia, Texaco, and Shell—produce or purchase more than eighty per cent of the oil that comes out of the state. Though the top executives of the major companies enjoy the status of Texas millionaires, the vast majority of that happy breed come from the ranks of the independents—mostly men who started from scratch, or behind it, and created their fortunes singlehanded. "The independents like to be known as 'the little fellows,'" a vice president of one of the larger major companies said recently. "Of course, most of them could buy and sell the president of any of the majors. That's why those of us who work for the majors refer to one another as 'pigeons.'"

In some respects, the interests of the majors and the independents diverge—for example, the majors, with heavy overseas investments, favor the importation of foreign oil, while the independents, whose holdings are mainly domestic, are generally against it—but in most matters they see eye to eye. They are at once competitors and partners—competitors because both are engaged in the search for oil, partners because they frequently share the cost of the search. Beyond that, the independents are allied with the majors by necessity; the majors own practically all the pipelines and refineries, and it is consequently to them that the independents must sell their product if they want to sell it at all. B. G. (Billy) Byars, a prominent independent and the leading citizen of Tyler, Texas, has described the relationship succinctly: "Without the big companies, we couldn't exist. They buy our oil and gas." As it works out in practice, the independents are scouts for the majors. In allotting money for exploration, the big companies are bound by group decisions, accountability to stockholders, and other corporate impedimenta, whereas the independents are bound by nothing but their own judgment and their own bank balance or credit. Partly as a result of their flexible position, the independents make the great majority of new oil discoveries. "The independents find eighty-five per cent of the oil and own fifteen per cent of it," Michel Halbouty, himself an independent, has said. "The majors find fifteen per cent and own eighty-five per cent. That gives you some idea of how important the independents are in this industry."

Though alike in sharing sovereign status, the independents

differ from one another in several ways, such as their backgrounds. The late Everette Lee (Mr. De) DeGolyer, perhaps the most esteemed figure in the history of the oil game, used to divide players into two groups: the "silver-spoon boys" and the "rabbit's-foot boys." The great majority of oilmen—from James Abercrombie, a dairy farmer's son, who sold part of his oil properties a few years ago for fifty millon dollars, to Joseph Zeppa, an Italian immigrant who arrived in this country in steerage at twelve and is now, at sixty-seven, reported to be worth more than fifty million—belong to the rabbit's-foot group, the one in which DeGolyer also had good reason to claim membership. Born in a sod hut in Kansas, he did various jobs to help pay his way through school and took time off between his junior and senior years in college to work for a British oil company in Mexico, where he located a well that produced a hundred and thirty million barrels of oil, a record that has not been equalled. "Sheer luck," DeGolyer remarked when recalling this discovery a few months before his death, in 1956, at the age of seventy. "I was just a kid at the time and it seemed to me there was nothing left in the world to accomplish." As things turned out, he went on to accomplish a good deal, such as becoming the petroleum industry's foremost geologist; the most gifted pioneer in the field of geophysics; the recipient of a couple of dozen honorary degrees and awards, including the John Fritz Medal, which had previously been conferred on other successful scientists like Thomas Edison and Orville Wright; the financial savior and board chairman of the *Saturday Review;* the possessor of one of the greatest libraries in the Southwest; and, by no means incidentally, the accumulator of some forty million dollars.

Only a small handful of men in the oil game have reached the top, as DeGolyer did, by way of the scientific route; most took the road that starts by performing unskilled labor—"roughnecking," as it is called—in the oil fields. Among this group is Billy Byars. Like most players of his generation, Byars, who is fifty-nine, rotund, cheerful, unassuming, and astute, started earning a living early. "I went to the oil fields when I was fifteen, in December, 1917," he says. "I remember it was cold and muddy. Sleeping in tents. I was a roughneck, working on a rig." After drifting from one oil-boom area to another, he managed to secure a half interest in a drilling rig, had luck in wildcatting operations, formed his own company, and went on to pile up thirty million or so.

As in Byars' case, the turning point in the career of most independents can be traced to the acquisition of a drilling rig, and that event is apt to have resulted as much from good luck as good management. The experience in this respect of R. E. (Bob) Smith, one of Houston's most prominent citizens, is in the tradition. On finishing high school, Smith—then a sturdy, six-foot redhead with a quick temper and today, at sixty-six, unchanged except that his hair has turned snow white—worked for several of the large oil companies in Texas, and was fired by the best of them. "I figure I was fired from at least five jobs besides the ones I quit," he has recalled. "The trouble was I couldn't take orders from a man unless they were properly given." Looking for a place where orders were given in a manner to suit his taste, Smith travelled to Tonkawa, Oklahoma, then the center of an oil boom, and was hired as a salesman for an oil-field supply company. In a restaurant one bitter winter night, he overheard a drilling contractor damning the weather and complaining about being stuck in Tonkawa; he said he would leave town on the first train if he could get rid of his two rigs for twenty-five thousand dollars. Smith knew they were worth much more than that, and though he doubted whether the driller was in earnest, he found, upon looking him up in the sober light of morning, that the offer was good. He repaired to the local bank and managed to talk the president—a nephew, as it happened, of the Starr brothers, who had built a considerable local reputation as bank robbers before going to their reward—into lending him twenty-five thousand dollars without collateral. He had no trouble repaying the loan and has not been greatly agitated by financial worries since; his present income has been estimated at about five hundred thousand dollars a month.

Another outstandingly successful Houston-based independent, John W. Mecom, a quiet, unruffled, six-foot-three, two-hundred-and-twenty-pound native Texan, departed from tradition by going to college. He got back on the track, however, by dropping out before getting his degree and going to work as a roughneck. Then, borrowing seven hundred dollars from his mother and an old wooden drilling rig from his father, who had dabbled in oil, he tried his luck, which turned out to be good enough to enable him to pocket a hundred thousand dollars within two years. With this he bought some new equipment and went on expanding until today, at fifty, he could sell his holdings, pay his debts and taxes, and put at least a hundred and ten million in the bank.

After the roughnecks, the second most numerous group of players got into the oil game as lease brokers. These, as Ray E. Hubbard, of Dallas, who used to be one of them, has explained, are more commonly referred to in the trade as "lease hounds" or "lease grafters"—terms which may possibly provide a clue to their professional standing. "Whatever you want to call 'em, their job is to buy up a lease on a piece of property where there oughta be oil and sell it at a profit to somebody else," says Hubbard, a forthright, determinedly roughhewn man. "Bein' a lease grafter don't take much schoolin', and it don't take much capital. What it takes is knowin' how to trade." Hubbard began learning how to trade upon quitting high school in his sophomore year to go into business with his father, a tombstone cutter turned real-estate operator. After trying their luck in Florida and a few other places, they showed up at the right time in Tulsa, Oklahoma, where they accumulated cash and experience as oil-lease brokers. Moving on to Texas, they piled up a comfortable fortune serving as brokers in many big deals, and then, following the usual pattern, became drillers and producers. By the time young Hubbard was thirty-five, he was worth numerous millions, and the number has multiplied so many times since then that, as a friend remarked recently, "Ray now has what you might call aggravated social security." Once, in a philosophical mood,

Hubbard made an observation, perhaps produced by reflection on his own early career, on the importance of intelligence in getting rich. "Anybody that's got money can hire somebody who's smart to make them money," he said. "It's a son of a bitch that hasn't got any money that has to be smart."

That condition has generally been shared by another group of independents, who started out as suppliers, selling drilling pipe, engines, valves, and other equipment needed to play the oil game. One of the more unusual members of this group is a slight, soft-spoken resident of Fort Worth named Sol Brachman, who was born in Russia, raised in Ohio, and graduated from Marietta College, where he was elected to Phi Beta Kappa. His son Malcolm, who also wears the key, graduated *summa cum laude* from Yale, received his M.A. and Ph.D from Harvard, and at twenty-three put in a year at Southern Methodist University teaching nuclear physics. He has since become associated with many of his father's enterprises, which now include insurance and oil production. "We're both Phi Beta Kappas," the elder Brachman is likely to inform new acquaintances within a decent interval after shaking hands. "Some people think on account of that we shouldn't be in the oil business." Despite the handicap, they have done well enough, but their business is, as Brachman puts it, "peanuts" compared to that of another Fort Worth resident, K. W. Davis, who heads the largest independent supply company in the country.

The final, and smallest, group that makes up the independents entered the game by the white-collar route. Of these, probably none has gone farther than a smooth-faced, soft-spoken Dallas resident named Algur H. (Al) Meadows. The son of a Georgia physician, Meadows started his business career selling Ford cars, drifted down to Louisiana, got a job as a clerk in Shreveport with the Standard Oil Company, studied law at night, and after passing the bar organized, in partnership with another young lawyer, a small-loan company. The time was 1928. Within five years the company had opened eight branch offices, including one in Tyler, Texas. Into that office one day in 1933, when Meadows was paying a visit there, walked a drilling contractor named G. E. (Blondy) Hall. He told Meadows he had a contract to drill three wells, and out of the sale of oil from the wells he was to be paid a hundred and five thousand dollars for his work. To complete the wells, Hall explained, would cost about twenty-four thousand dollars; he needed a loan for that amount. Before committing himself, Meadows engaged a firm of geologists to size up the drill sites, and received a highly favorable report. He then made Hall a proposition: instead of lending him money he would give him thirty-five thousand dollars in cash, and in return Hall would turn over to the company his prospective hundred and five thousand. Money being tight, Hall accepted the deal, giving him a profit of eleven thousand and the loan company one of seventy thousand. In the following months, Meadows concluded deals with other drillers on the same terms: for every dollar paid out in cash he received three dollars in oil payments. It dawned soon enough on Meadows and his partner that this line of work beat even the small-loan companies, so they gradually liquidated that enterprise and concentrated on oil. The kind of imaginative thinking that Meadows displayed in his first oil deal has, in the ensuing quarter of a century, shown itself in many ways and has not only earned him the widespread respect of his colleagues but propelled him to the post of executive committee chairman of the General American Oil Company of Texas. This is a far-flung operation of which Meadows was a founder and in which he and his wife, whose jewels brighten up the night, own stock having a market value of about fifty-five million. And that, according to one of their friends, is "the iceberg stuff that shows—what you don't see is many times as much."

Besides variations in origin, the independents differ in the size of their organizations, which range from that of a small independent, whose personnel consists of himself and a part-time secretary working in a one-room office, to that of, say, John Mecom, who employs some five hundred and fifty people, in nine states. An independent may follow a carefully planned long-term program, like Jake Hamon's (he normally drills a hundred wells a year), or a rather short-range schedule, like Paul Raigorodsky's ("My program," Raigorodsky says, "is whatever turns up"). Another, and quite important, distinction can be made between the independents who do business mainly with the majors, fellow-independents, and others inside the industry (a group that might be called the inside operators), and those (the outside operators) who operate primarily with funds solicited from investors outside the industry.

A fairly representative inside operator is Byars, who, like most of his colleagues, particularly inside operators, is open for business by phone twenty-four hours a day. His operations usually begin when he receives an early-morning phone call at home from his secretary, who reports on the mail and other matters. Around nine o'clock, Byars gets into his station wagon and drives himself downtown to his office. On the wall behind his desk is an oil painting, of overwhelming dimensions, of an Aberdeen Angus bull, the late Prince 105 of TT, for which Byars and three other bull fanciers jointly paid the record sum of two hundred and thirty thousand dollars; on another wall is a reproduction of a painting of George Washington, simply framed, and inscribed, "For Billy Byars, Merry Christmas, 1954, Dwight D. Eisenhower." As a rule, Byars stays in his office until noon, handling correspondence, discussing deals with employees, and transacting business on the telephone. "At least fifty per cent of our deals are made by phone," he says. His afternoons are generally spent reconnoitering Royal Oaks, a twelve-hundred-acre ranch he owns, a few miles outside of Tyler, where he raises prize-winning cattle. While there, he keeps on doing business by means of a dozen or so telephone calls. Almost all his contacts are with other old hands at the oil game. "Oilmen like to deal with other oilmen," he said one afternoon at the ranch. "That's because it's easier to deal with somebody who knows the ropes the way you do. People who aren't in this game don't know how deals work, so if they do get into it, right away they start asking for detailed reports and all kinds of figures. The oilman usually carries all that around in his head. He doesn't want to waste his time writing it all out and trying to teach somebody. In this business, you work mostly through friendships. It's a cinch you can't make money off your enemies. You get a stranger in on a deal, and the first thing you know, he wants you to be an accountant and a geology teacher and a petroleum-engineering professor and a few other things. Hell, in the time you spend answering all his questions you could make enough to put him through college. Probably a lot more."

As for outside operators, though reputable ones will not do business with just anybody who has cash to spare (the few who will are apt to be experts in the so-called New York deal; that is, a shady or crooked operation), all are aggressively interested in locating qualified strangers and, for a fee, teaching them how to play the oil game. A few, like D. D. (Tex) Feldman, maintain offices in New York mainly for the purpose of recruiting promising students. The majority, however, are put in touch with investors through brokers specializing in oil, and through financial and investment concerns like the Empire Trust Company, Lehman Brothers, and Ingalls & Snyder, whose staffs have a wide knowledge of the game. Another fruitful source that a successful outside operator can count on consists of friends of satisfied students and alumni. Since outside operators find their best prospects among the very wealthy on the east and west coasts, they apparently feel obliged, in the interests of business, to cultivate the social graces more earnestly than inside operators do. In addition to displaying a higher, or perhaps flashier, degree of sophistication—for instance, an insider's taste in art is apt to lean toward Remington and Russell, an outsider's toward Monet and Mondrian—outside operators are likely to be some ten or fifteen years younger than their counterparts in the other fraternity. And because of the nature of their business, they are found almost exclusively in the larger cities.

Ted Weiner, a quite typical outside operator, is a trim, fashionably tailored, articulate forty-eight-year-old man with confidence and worldliness enough to make his way around the

Racquet Club in New York about as comfortably as around the Petroleum Club in Fort Worth. He lives in a handsome, award-winning modern house designed by Edward Barnes, serves as a director of the Fort Worth Art Center, and has a collection of modern art that includes works by Chagall, Rouault, and Picasso, as well as by a number of Texans, like Charles Umlauf and Cynthia Brants. To travel the short distance from his house to his office, Weiner customarily uses a new white Cadillac sedan, though occasionally he drives a blue Thunderbird. Three mornings a week, on his way to work, he stops off at a dance studio for a private one-hour lesson in ballroom dancing—a pastime that Weiner, who is not given to smoking or drinking, much enjoys. On his terpsichorean mornings, Weiner arrives at his office around eleven, or about an hour later than on the other days. Like Byars and other independents, Weiner does a large share of his business by telephone, and he feels no obligation to set his employees a good example by remaining in his office—which is furnished like a living room and decorated with modern paintings—any longer than necessary.

Whether at home or travelling, Weiner plays golf every afternoon when the weather permits. Because his dedication to golf is exceeded by few other Americans, he scores in the high seventies and low eighties, and so is able to turn in a respectable card when he shoots a round with other good players, like his friend Bob Hope, who has also shown a keen interest in the oil game. It was not Weiner but another Fort Worth operator, W. A. Moncrief, who introduced both Hope and Bing Crosby to the oil game. This occurred several years ago, when Moncrief allowed each a sixteen-per-cent participation in the development of a Scurry County field, in which, after one dry hole, twenty-eight producing wells were drilled in succession. The venture, which returned a profit of a few million apiece to Crosby and Hope, naturally gave ideas to other actors, including James Stewart, who enjoy a reputation for being levelheaded about money. Stewart's investments in oil, which have also turned out very pleasantly, have been made in association with still another Fort Worth operator, F. Kirk (Fran) Johnson, at whose house Stewart and his wife are occasional guests. The petroleum adventures of some other actors have not had such happy endings. "After Bing and I struck oil," Hope told a reporter recently, "a lot of Hollywood people lost millions. Everybody went into oil to try and match our luck, but they lost their shirts. I've got just a few little oil investments in Texas now—about five oil wells."

A veteran player, Weiner took up the oil game at nineteen, in a West Texas town named Wink, where his father, a Lithuanian immigrant who had worked in the Pennsylvania coal mines until he was fourteen and had later made and lost a fair sum prospecting for oil in Arkansas, was running a machine shop that made drilling equipment. "Before going out to Wink," Weiner recalled a while ago, "I attended the New Mexico Military Institute for two years. I dropped out when my dad went broke. For a couple of years, I just drifted around, did a little amateur prizefighting—I had pretty good luck in the Golden Gloves—and then started working for my dad. He had a lot of old parts around the shop, and in my spare time I put together a rig and started wildcatting. That was in the late twenties." Using the classic po'-boy technique, he drilled a number of wells, some good but more bad. "When I got married," he went on, "I owed forty-seven thousand dollars, and had no assets except the credit I'd established. Right after my marriage, I got involved with a real sorry well and went even further into hock. I'd been broke many times, of course, but that was the big one. Then I got lucky and made a good discovery. It was 1938, and the discovery was what turned out to be the Weiner Pool, in Winkler County. That paid off all my debts and made it possible for me to acquire fourteen thousand acres on the Floyd Ranch, in Midland County. There we got in on the Spraberry Pool—a terrific field, though the recoveries have been disappointing. But I drilled three hundred wells, and it has been profitable to me. There was a time when I could have sold out for thirty million. We still have the wells, and they're still producing, and we're still drilling in that area.

"Since then, we've branched out a lot, but the real turning point in my company's career was the Spraberry. I realized then how much it was going to take to develop the areas we'd acquired, so I talked to investment bankers in New York, and they advanced money for development wells. That step led to others. As we developed more properties, we met more people who were interested in investing, and so it has gone. It's not as easy as you might think to find the right kind of investors. We turn down a lot of people with rather small sums, because we don't want to do business with anybody who's going to be hurt if a deal doesn't turn out. We prefer to deal with people who are sophisticated in money matters. For instance, the large investment bankers. They're hardened to the pitfalls in this business. And we look for people who are in it for the long ride—in other words, people whose tax position is such that they can put up a minimum of fifty thousand dollars a year in our various ventures and not bat an eye if they lose it."

Chapter Five

Though identifying the players poses no particular problem, it is not easy to follow the oil game unless one has some familiarity with the special tax rules governing it. These rules, three in number, are central to the game, and together constitute its most fascinating feature to all concerned—majors, independents, investors, and spectators. Rule No. 1 permits a player to deduct twenty-seven and a half per cent of his gross income as "a depletion allowance," provided that this sum is not more than half of his net income. Thus, a player with an annual gross income of a million dollars may keep two hundred and seventy-five thousand dollars tax-free, as long as this does not exceed fifty per cent of his net. Rule No. 2 permits a player who drills a well that turns out to be a dry hole to deduct all the expenses of drilling it from his gross income. Rule No. 3 permits a player who drills a producing well to deduct from his gross income all the "intangible expenses" incurred in drilling the well. The intangibles, comprising items such as geological studies, equipment, labor, fuel, and testing, generally add up to at least sixty per cent of the total drilling costs. The tax advantages granted by this set of rules are, of course, available to everybody—in theory, any number can play the oil game. However, because of the high stakes and big risks, new players now come mainly from the ranks of disquieted taxpayers in the higher brackets.

A person whose income is subject to taxation at ninety per cent has nearly ideal qualifications for getting into the oil game, because nine of every ten dollars he puts into it are what are known in financially enlightened circles as tax dollars. As Ted Weiner has explained, "A tax dollar, to put it bluntly, is the name given to money that would normally be paid to the Internal Revenue Service." Owing to the nature of the income-tax structure, therefore, a taxpayer in the ninety-per-cent bracket has strong inducements to play the oil game. If he wins, he may, under Rule No. 1, keep from each dollar of oil income 27½ cents free of tax; to this he may add ten per cent of the remaining 72½ cents, or 7¼ cents—since his normal tax situation allows him to retain ten per cent of his income, regardless of its source—making a total of 34¾ cents. Instead of reaping ten-cent dollars, he reaps thirty-five-cent dollars. If a player decides to leave the game by selling his holdings, he can cash in his chips and take a capital gain, on which he will be taxed twenty-five per cent; his reward comes not in ten-cent dollars but in seventy-five-cent dollars.

Of course, players lose much more often than they win; Rule No. 2 provides for losing situations, such as the following: A player in the ninety-per-cent bracket puts a hundred thousand dollars into drilling a well, and it is a dry hole; he may therefore deduct the entire sum from his gross income. With his income thus reduced, he pays the federal government ninety thousand dollars less than he would have otherwise; the venture costs him ten thousand dollars. He has lost, but he has had the fun of taking a hundred-thousand-dollar gamble at a sensationally low price. If he has enough chips, he can continue to play, and eventually might beat the odds.

The combination of Rules No. 1 and No. 2 (Rule No. 3, which some operators consider as important as Rule No. 1, is self-explanatory) accounts for the gambit known as "drilling it up"; that is, the widespread practice among oilmen of spending their tax dollars on further exploration and drilling. "What do they do with their money?" Byars once said in discussing oilmen's income. "I'll tell you what they do—they put it back in the ground. Let's say eighty per cent of it is lost. But you have to remember that money used like that is far from a total loss. Dry holes give us a lot of valuable geological information.

Also, all the drilling and prospecting provide jobs, directly and indirectly, for thousands of people, and those people pay taxes. And, of course, the money we put back in the ground results in finding a great deal more oil, and that way we keep on increasing the country's reserves." Naturally, players who have success in drilling it up add to their personal oil reserves, which are just about as good as money in the bank.

Except for a few poor sports who consider their tax position oppressive, the players of the oil game are pretty well satisfied with the rules as they stand. The same near unanimity prevailed for many years in Congress, which acts as the game's rule-making body. Recently, however, Congress has shown an increasing interest in changing Rule No. 1 to reduce the depletion allowance. As a consequence, a lively and often entertaining debate has developed between those who believe that the present depletion allowance is fair and those who believe that, as President Truman put it in a message to Congress in 1950, "no loophole in the tax law [is] so inequitable." The controversy has so far turned up some fairly wonderful nonsense, such as Leon Henderson's classic observation "It is an impoverished science that permits an industry to continue to drill dry holes. The wells that are going to be dry should not be drilled." The same spirit of informed reasonableness exists among partisans on the other side, such as Congressman Frank Ikard, of Texas, who has described advocates of changing the allowance as "bomb-throwing liberals" —a company presumably including many well-known Leftist bomb-throwers like the late Senator Robert A. Taft, who took the view that "percentage depletion is to a large extent a gift . . . a special privilege beyond what anyone else can get." As usually happens in disagreements involving money, the heat obscures the light—a condition that is likely to continue. Just about every oilman regards any reference to the depletion allowance that is not in unqualified support of it as something in the nature of an insult, like aspersing his wife's virtue. "The way these goddam Communists and Socialists talk," a Houston operator said a while ago, with about average passion, "you'd think we were all a bunch of crooks, or something. The hell with those bastards! We don't get a single penny we're not entitled to by law—and by plain goddam common sense besides."

As far as the law is concerned, Congress established the present depletion allowance for oil in 1926. The principle was not new then, and it has since been so widely extended that practically all the extractive industries now receive a depletion allowance. The petroleum percentage is the highest, but the law provides a twenty-three-per-cent allowance to producers of sulphur, uranium, lead, platinum, zinc, and thirty-two additional strategic metals and minerals, and an allowance of five to fifteen per cent to producers of many other substances, including coal, lignite, slate, peat, ornamental stone, and clam and oyster shells. Back in 1942, when Congress was considering an extension of percentage depletion allowances, Senator Robert M. La Follette, Jr., expressed doubt about "vesting interests which will come back to plague us," adding, "If we are to include all these things, why do we not put in sand and gravel?" Sand and gravel are now in, at five per cent.

The petroleum industry's percentage has remained unchanged through both Republican and Democratic administrations and in spite of the fact that efforts to reduce it were made by every Secretary of the Treasury in the twenty years before George Humphrey took office in 1953. The failure of those efforts is evidence of Congressional approval of the depletion principle as well as a tribute both to the oilmen's generosity in financing an effective public-relations program and to the skill of Speaker Sam Rayburn, a renowned Texan, who has managed to keep all measures affecting the allowance confined within the House Ways and Means Committee, where tax bills originate. "Let it out of committee," he once remarked, "and they'd cut it to fifteen, ten, five per cent—maybe take it away altogether. Do you think you could convince a Detroit factory worker that the depletion allowance is a good thing? Once it got on the floor, it would be cut to ribbons."

In 1957, Senator John J. Williams, a Republican of Delaware, using the simple stratagem of proposing an amendment to a tax bill that had already passed the House, brought the depletion measure to the floor of the Senate; the Williams amendment called for a reduction of the allowance to fifteen per cent. In the same session, Senator Paul Douglas, a Democrat of Illinois, introduced an amendment to put the allowance on a graduated scale—twenty-seven and a half per cent for producers with an annual income of less than a million dollars, twenty-one per cent for those with an annual income of one to five million dollars, and fifteen per cent for those with an annual income of more than five million. Both amendments stirred up tremendous apathy. Only five senators besides the sponsors were willing to go even as far as to commit themselves in favor of a roll-call vote; that is, to have their vote for or against even recorded. In 1958, Williams again proposed his amendment; this time it was turned down by a vote of sixty-three to twenty-six. By a slightly smaller margin, the Senate also defeated an amendment introduced by Senator William Proxmire, a Democrat of Wisconsin, that contained the graduated plan offered the year before by Senator Douglas. Since then, Senator Douglas has twice reintroduced his favorite amendment, and it has twice been rejected, most recently in June, 1960, by a vote of fifty-six to thirty.

Among those voting for the Douglas amendment at that session was Senator John F. Kennedy, a fact that was not lost sight of in Texas during the ensuing Presidential campaign. Kennedy's appeal to Texas oilmen was not enhanced by the Democratic platform, which pledged to "close the loopholes in the tax laws by which certain privileged groups legally escape their fair share of taxation," and went on to say, "Among the more conspicuous loopholes are depletion allowances, which are inequitable." Vice-President Nixon declared firmly that he was for depletion all the way. Nevertheless, as Jim Clark pointed out early in the campaign, "Politically, the oil industry finds itself between a rock and a hard place." While the Republican candidate and platform favored depletion, Clark said, "The Democrats have Lyndon Johnson. Furthermore, there is

Speaker Sam Rayburn. These two men have stood like Horatio at the bridge for years defending depletion against all comers. Almost any oilman knows that without 'Lyndon and Mr. Sam' there might be no depletion provision today." Subsequently, the two Horatios gave oilmen public assurances that they would continue at their old stand on the bridge. ("I've never heard of the twenty-seven-and-a-half-per-cent oil-depletion allowance being considered a loophole. I trust that the oil people do not consider it to be. I do not and never have."—Rayburn. "The platform pertains only to loopholes, and I see none in oil."—Johnson.) The oilmen listened, but most liked the Republican talk better, and as a result, Clark said after the election, it was depletion "more than religion that almost cost" the Democrats the Texas vote. Though the consensus among oilmen seems to be that their depletion allowance is not seriously threatened at present, they continue to take frequent, full-page advertisements in Texas newspapers to convince one another that "The Depletion Allowance Is Not a Special Tax Privilege" and that "For Adequate Oil Reserves the Depletion Allowance Must Be Maintained!" Albert B. Fay, Republican National Committeeman from Houston, put the oilmen's position with notable accuracy and brevity when he said recently, "The oil depletion allowance is just like motherhood and country."

To counter Senator Williams and other advocates of changing Rule No. 1, the oil industry has fashioned an elaborate and highly sophisticated defense of the twenty-seven-and-a-half-per-cent allowance. It is essential, first, as an incentive to stimulate the continued exploration for oil, oilmen say, and, second, because of what Scott C. Lambert, general tax counsel of the Standard Oil Company of California, has called "the peculiar nature of the wasting-asset character" of the oil industry. "In reality," Lambert has said, "the miner or oil-and-gas producer is in the inexorable process of liquidating his capital." Every oilman has his own way of stating the proposition that the producer of oil depletes his capital asset. Paul

Raigorodsky puts it this way: "Investing in oil is different from investing in office building. If you invest in building, you have it paid for in twenty years, and building is still there. In oil game, it is different. After twenty years, no oil. In building, you have capital structure. In oil, you have to replace capital structure. That means you have to find more reserves. To do that, you must have incentives and means. Those are supplied by twenty-seven-and-a-half-per-cent depletion allowance."

Advocates of changing the allowance, while they may be inclined to agree with this much of the case, are less impressed with the rest of the industry's defense, which is a veritable labyrinth of arguments and rationalizations of varying degrees of ingenuity. If Senator Williams has his way, so one of the arguments runs, the independents will be driven to the wall, and the majors will become a monopoly. "If it weren't for depletion, we'd all be out of business," Michel Halbouty has said. "Take away depletion and you absolutely wipe out the independents." The industry's champions also make much of the fact that oil is essential to national defense. "Oil, gentlemen, is ammunition," General Ernest O. Thompson, Commanding General of the Texas National Guard and the senior member of the Texas Railroad Commission, which, its name notwithstanding, is charged chiefly with regulating the oil industry in Texas, told a Congressional committee. "In defense," he added, "oil is a prime mover. Why tamper with a system that has twice in a generation brought forth a drilling, which is the only way to find oil, and has made oil available in such quantities that we have been able to win two wars?" And so it goes. A host of shuddersome consequences are, in the eyes of the industry's champions, certain to follow any change in the present depletion allowance. "In a relatively short time," as the comptroller of the Magnolia Petroleum Company once summed it up, with noticeable constraint, "our entire economy and the well-being of every individual in the United States would be adversely affected."

All these arguments overlook the fact that no legislation has been introduced by Senator Williams or anyone else to abolish the depletion allowance. "Eliminating the depletion allowance would be taxing capital," Erwin N. Griswold, Dean of the Harvard Law School, has observed. "There would be no more sense in it than in eliminating the depreciation allowance." The Senate proposals have been to reduce the depletion allowance from twenty-seven and a half per cent—a figure that oilmen are fond of investing with a sacred quality, like ten in connection with commandments, although it was, in the first place, the result of a compromise between twenty-five per cent, favored by the House, and thirty per cent, favored by the Senate. Furthermore, those favoring a change have never minimized the petroleum industry's contribution to national defense; they just wonder whether its rewards for doing its duty have not been disproportionate. Dean Griswold, no foe of the depletion principle, has expressed this view. "I admire its great achievements, and its great contributions to the country, its economy, and its defense," he has remarked. "But there are also many other forms of activity that contribute greatly to the country, its economy, and its defense. Why should they not all be treated the same? Why should the oil industry be the recipient of a tax deduction, enormous in the aggregate, which bears no relation to its costs, or to the capital invested in oil production?"

The main trouble with Rule No. 1, according to those who think it should be changed—a group including many economists and lawyers specializing in taxation—is that the twenty-seven-and-a-half-per-cent rate permits an oil producer to receive tax-free a return exceeding his actual capital investment. In no other industry can a taxpayer enjoy this benefit. Therefore, vis-à-vis players of the oil game, every other individual in the United States is at present adversely affected by the operation of Rule No. 1, which John P. Barnes, a Chicago lawyer who served from 1955 to 1957 as chief counsel of the Internal Revenue Service, has described as "the inequality in our tax law that, in my opinion, is the most indefensible of all." Another lawyer—Harry J. Rudick, of the New York firm of Lord, Day & Lord—has pointed out that because maximum corporate and personal income taxes have increased approximately three-fold since 1926, the allowance is worth much more today than when it was adopted, and that for this and other reasons it has become an "unjustified subsidy." Horace M. Gray, a professor of economics at the University of Illinois, has called the allowance a "private tax-escape device" and remarked that "the Treasury is poorer by exactly the amount by which the beneficiaries of this special privilege are richer," adding, "Other taxpayers who must make good the resulting deficiency in the federal revenue ultimately sustain this loss in the form of tax rates higher than otherwise would be necessary." Estimates of how much federal revenue would be increased as a result of changing Rule No. 1 vary from about two hundred million dollars, in the opinion of its champions, to around a billion, in the opinion of its critics. According to the Treasury Department, a reduction in the allowance to fifteen per cent, as proposed by Senator Williams, would create a net revenue increase of three hundred and ninety million dollars; adoption of the graduated scale favored by Senators Douglas and Proxmire would produce an increase of three hundred and ten million dollars.

However much the champions and the critics of Rule No. 1 may differ on other matters, they are united in the conviction that no change should be made that would work a hardship on the small independent operator, who is customarily referred to as "the little fellow." The solicitude that the champions of Rule No. 1 show for the little fellow is remarkable. In fact, he seems uppermost in their thoughts whenever they argue publicly for retention of the twenty-seven-and-a-half-per-cent allowance. Perhaps nobody has been more consistently eloquent in pleading the cause of the little fellow than General Thompson. In testifying before the committee considering a reduction in the allowance, he said, "It works against the little independent, who is the fellow who finds the oil. They said yesterday that a little fellow can discover it and sell it to somebody. Why should he sell it? Why, in a free nation, could he not produce? All these companies were little at one time. The Texas Company started in Texas, the Gulf Company started in Texas, and the Humble Company started in Texas. Many big companies started there, and why can we not keep an opportunity open for the little man today? Why should he sell out to somebody else? Let him grow and prosper under the wise and beneficent law you passed here. It is a wise law, and gives a little man a chance to live."

The chance given the little man under the law was illustrated in a Senate speech in 1957 by Senator Douglas, who presented figures showing the net incomes of twenty-seven oil and gas companies and the federal income taxes they paid over a ten-year period. The companies, which included none of the big ones, like Standard, Gulf, or Texaco, were identified only by letters of the alphabet, because, Douglas said, he was "striking at the evil but not at any person." In 1954, Company A had a net income of $21,029,648 and paid federal income taxes of $1,252,000, or 5.9 per cent. The same year, Company E had a net income of $5,320,750 and paid no federal income tax. Senator Douglas called attention to Company I, which in 1951 had a net income of $4,477,673 and paid income taxes of $404, or .01 per cent. That sum, Douglas observed, is "a tax bill which is lower than the taxes paid by a married couple with three dependents with an adjusted gross income of $5,600 before deductions and exemptions." Company N also had no reason to doubt the wisdom of the law; its net income for the three years from 1952 through 1954 totalled $7,796,359 and its federal taxes $128,491, or 1.8 per cent. As for Company W, Douglas said, "This is a truly interesting situation. Here is a company, which in 1954 and 1953 had net incomes in excess of $10 million and $12.5 million respectively, but which not only did not pay any taxes in those years but which had net tax credits of $100,000 and $500,000 respectively. . . . What other kind of company in America can have a net income of $10 to $12 million per year and receive a tax credit from the Federal Government? Is their incentive being ruined?" Company Z was even more interesting, Douglas said. "Here is a company which in seven years has paid absolutely no taxes

84

of any kind," he pointed out. "Yet, in those seven years its income varied between $134,000 and $3.2 million a year. What further incentive is needed here? What more could a benevolent Government do for an individual or a company than to forgive all of its taxes?"

Over the ten-year period, Douglas noted, the twenty-seven companies paid an average of 17 per cent of their net income in federal income taxes, compared with the general corporate rate of 52 per cent. According to the government publication *Statistics of Income*, in 1951 depletion allowances amounting to $2,100,000,000 were claimed by corporations. Of the total, 63 per cent was claimed by corporations with assets of $100,000,000 or more, 84 per cent by corporations with assets over $10,000,000 and 96 per cent by corporations with assets of at least $1,000,000. So it would seem that none of the fellows, either big or little, who play the oil game have much reason for wanting to change the rules.

While proclaiming their passionate devotion to independence from the federal government, oilmen are perfectly willing to let their state government take a big hand in telling them how to run their business. On the surface, this may seem to reflect a stunning paradox in the oilman's character, but in the oil game, as in the matter of which the poet spoke, things are not what they seem. The agency to which oilmen most uncomplainingly surrender many of their prerogatives is the Texas Railroad Commission; it consists of three elected members, who receive an annual salary of seventeen thousand five hundred dollars for regulating an industry that does a yearly business in Texas of two and a half billion. The Commission's most important function is to decide how much oil can be produced in Texas each month. This amount, known as "the allowable," is divided among the various fields and then subdivided among the operators in each. The allowable is determined a month in advance, after representatives of the large companies—the ones that own the pipelines and refineries—appear before the Commission and make so-called nominations of their requirements; that is, each company says how much oil it is willing to buy during the following month. Presumably, in setting the allowable, the Commission considers other factors, such as the monthly estimate of future demand prepared by the United States Bureau of Mines. However, students have found that there is almost never any significant difference between the amount of oil the refining companies say they will buy and the allowable authorized by the Commission. That is to say, what the refineries want, the refineries get. The beauty of this arrangement, from the oilmen's viewpoint, is that with supply not allowed to exceed demand there can be no surplus, and with no surplus there can be no conventional pressure to reduce the price. The creation of a surplus is, in fact, illegal; an operator who exceeds his production limit is penalized by Texas law, and if he tries to sell "hot oil" in interstate commerce, he is penalized by federal law. Thus, in the opinion of some economists, the oil industry operates under government-sanctioned monopoly conditions.

Oilmen, however, emphasize that the limiting of production —or, in their inventive language, "prorationing," or the operation of "market-demand law"—is a conservation measure, aimed solely at the elimination of wasteful practices, and that it saved the industry from chaos in the nineteen-thirties. One thing on which oilmen and skeptical economists can agree is that the market-demand law works in a far more wondrous way than Adam Smith's "invisible hand." During the past decade, the oil industry has developed what Morgan Davis, president of the Humble Oil & Refining Co. (Standard Oil of New Jersey's largest subsidiary), has described as "a burdensome surplus-producing capacity." Put another way, the Texas oil industry, while maintaining the most efficient standards of conservation, could produce double or more what it does. Anybody not acquainted with the industry's peculiar economics might think that such an immense potential supply would lead to a reduction in price. Instead, in January, 1957, when the excess productive capacity had become so great that production had been cut to thirteen days a month—the lowest ever reached up to that time—Humble raised the price of crude oil thirty-five cents a barrel. One result was that the country's oil bill was increased, according to J. H. Carmical, a financial writer for the New York *Times*, five hundred million dollars a year. Another was that, in May, 1958, a federal grand jury handed down an indictment charging Humble and twenty-eight other major companies with conspiring to fix the price of crude oil and automobile gasoline. All twenty-nine firms were acquitted in a ten-day, non-jury trial, which came to a close in February, 1960, when District Judge Royce H. Savage declared in an oral decision that in his judgment "the evidence in the case does not rise above the level of suspicion," and added, "I have an absolute conviction personally that the defendants are not guilty." The independent oilmen were as pleased as the majors with the blanket acquittal, which, in effect, gave further official blessing to prorationing. As it works out, the oilmen's willingness to surrender prerogatives has not diminished their independence but enhanced it, for the result has been to give them privileges not legally enjoyed by the business community at large.

In the opinion of Texas oilmen, who have a constitutional prejudice against rejoicing in public, the outcome of the conspiracy trial was one of two pieces of good news in recent years. The other, also received in 1960, was the ruling of the United States Supreme Court that Texas (and Florida), unlike other states, owns the oil and other underwater resources within ten and a half miles of its coast. (On learning of the tidelands victory, worth untold millions to the state in revenue, Governor Daniel made the seven lawyers who had handled the state's case admirals in the Texas Navy.) Except on these occasions, Texas oilmen have been wearing long faces most of the time since 1957, when the oil industry began to be affected seriously by the worldwide glut of oil (if no more were found, experts predict that present reserves would last, at the rate they are now being used, for forty years); to cope with the problem in Texas, the Railroad Commission reduced the number of producing days from a hundred and seventy-one in 1957 to a hundred and four in 1960. Throughout most of the latter half of 1960, production was down to nine days a month. During that period, Texas wells were being operated at about a third of capacity, and the producers were thus foregoing, according to J. H. Carmical, some six million dollars every day in sales.

The reduced output was felt quickly and keenly by the independent oilmen, whose "business is so bad," Jim Clark wrote in July, 1960, "that most of them are just a shade off relief." If their plight did not strike all observers as quite that desperate, nobody has denied that conditions in the past four years have made it harder than before to win at the oil game. "You don't make money on nine days," a Houston player said not long ago. "That hurts everybody, but especially the small operators, the contractors, and the drillers. In 1960, drilling was ten per cent below 1959. The major companies have had to lay off a lot of people. Good geologists come to my office every day looking for work." The same kind of men have also been calling on Jake Hamon. "There's not much you can do," Hamon said recently. "The independents have had to cut down on their staffs, too, besides taking a lot of other economy measures. They're going in for more unitization—a joint operation that saves money but means putting people out of work—and they've even tried economizing by using smaller drilling pipe. Of course, many smaller operators haven't been able to keep going, no matter how hard they economized. They've had to sell out their production to large, integrated companies. You know, things have reached the place where oilmen don't want their sons to grow up and go into the business. Some people are saying this is a finished business—a non-growth industry. I don't say that. But let's say the drama has gone out of it."

Paul Raigorodsky, for one, won't say that. "Let me tell you how dull oil game is," he explained to a friend a couple of months ago. "A big oil company came to me last year with a new kind of deal. All I do is sign some papers, and my income goes up extra hundred and ten thousand dollars a year. Just fell in my lap. I know some of these people selling production

—they're getting mighty fine guaranteed income in return. I'd like to buy all Standard Oil stock right now. Whatever it's selling, it's bargain. Oil game hit bottom last year. Now it's on way up."

Among those who agree that the 1961 outlook is upward are the members of the Railroad Commission, who set the March allowable at ten days—the highest in a year—the *Oil and Gas Journal,* and a growing number of independents, including Ted Weiner, who even in the bad years shunned the gloomy view that was popular among his confreres. "A lot of them go by that old Chinese philosophy—that negative philosophy," he has said. "Our approach is different. We've been optimistic, and just worked along. Last year, we drilled thirty wildcats, and found oil in twelve. If the market is bad, you have to hold on a bit. The important thing is that you've got value in the ground. We've just tiptoed around and dodged around and kept things going. When they started stringent prorationing in Texas, we started looking for gas and oil in South Louisiana, where the allowables are higher. If it gets tough there, we'll try something else. We've got a lot of acreage in Australia —six million acres in one concession, and we've opened an office in Sydney. Union Oil has made a discovery, a good one, in acreage adjoining ours, and that may set the whole area on fire. We've had no trouble raising money for our ventures. There are still a lot of tax dollars coming into the oil business in Texas." Not long ago, a Dallas *News* editorial, discussing current conditions in that business, concluded, "Texas is still the great oil state, and it will be for many years into the future." Even oilmen whose judgment may be hampered by Chinese philosophy are not apt to take issue with that.

Chapter Six

Once the rules of the oil game are understood, play can begin, the initial move depending on which form of the game has been selected. The oil game, like poker—our other great indigenous gambling game, and one that is held in high favor by oilmen—can be played in a variety of interesting ways, ranging in complexity from the equivalent of five-card draw to that of high-low Cincinnati. To provide an exhaustive description of all the possible variations, together with accurate definitions of the terms involved—one-eighth royalty, overriding royalty, turnkey deal, rank wildcat, proven acreage, dry-hole money, and bottom-hole money, to mention a few— would require a work roughly the size of Hoyle, and just about as fascinating. One variation worth noting, because it is by far the most popular with people outside the business, is called the One-Shot. In this, the player, who is usually a novice with only a few thousand dollars to bet, is persuaded by a friend or acquaintance to invest in the drilling of a well by a wildcatter about whom the player knows almost nothing. His chances of winning are so slight that this play has come to be known as the Deadly One-Shot. Even so, it draws from confirmed dreamers an annual outlay estimated at two hundred and fifty million dollars.

"The majority of people who put money in oil spend it in the wrong places," Ted Weiner has remarked. "They throw their money away on flyers when they should turn it over to an organization with the experience and ability to find good deals and develop them. Our organization, for instance, spends three-quarters of a million dollars a year just looking for deals. Each one of our offices has a man who does nothing else. We may screen forty deals before finding one we want. Besides finding the deal, we have lawyers who do all the legal work, and we also drill the wells and operate them for the life of the property. An organization like this can furnish a complete service to the man with tax dollars to invest. When he has recovered his investment, we come in for twenty-five per cent. That's fairly standard procedure with reliable organizations.

"To see how it works, take a simple deal, like a farm-out from a major. One of the big companies decides to farm out some drilling on one of its properties to an independent. We like the deal, and agree to drill a well in return for a percentage of the production if we find oil. Say that we need a hundred thousand dollars to drill the well. We get together three people who put in thirty thousand each, and our organization puts in ten thousand. This deal, like every other one, is based on a principle that is well established in the oil business— spreading the risk. Everything is joint operations. Nowadays, the tendency is to spread the risk even further, because drilling costs have tripled in the last ten years, and also you have to drill deeper. The deepest well ever drilled in this country was the one out in Pecos County that Phillips Petroleum started in 1956. It went down close to five miles, and cost about three million. Incidentally, it was a dry hole. The cost of drilling a well depends on a number of factors. The way it works out, the average well runs to about a hundred thousand, like the one we have on the farm-out. Now, say that we're lucky and we hit. The investors each get back their thirty thousand, in pocketable dollars, out of production of the well. After that, we come in for a fourth of their interest. In other words, after recovering their investment, instead of each getting thirty per cent from the remaining production, each gets three-fourths of thirty per cent, and we take the balance as payment for our service.

"Anybody who's going to put money in an oil deal ought to

find out two things. First, is he going to get a complete return on his investment before the operator starts taking a percentage? Second, is the operator putting in some money of his own? If both answers are in the affirmative, he's probably got the basis for a pretty fair deal."

Regardless of the variation or the deal, the object of the oil game is, in the end, always the same—to drill a hole in the ground and find oil at the bottom. What are the chances of succeeding? The mathematical probabilities fluctuate in accordance with, for one thing, the location of the well. As might be expected, the odds are longest on discovery wells (those drilled where oil has not previously been found) and shortest on development wells (those put down on acreage where oil is already being produced). According to averages compiled by the industry, the chances of drilling a successful discovery well are one in eight, and of drilling a successful development well, three in four. The probabilities also vary from one operator to another; in contrast to the industry's rather doleful record for discovery wells, a number of experienced operators, including Mecom, Weiner, and Halbouty, have a fairly consistent average of about one in five.

More important than how often a player strikes oil is how much he finds. Many a player has been cleaned out because he struck a succession of wells that produced oil but not enough to pay the cost of developing them. Because such wells encourage the throwing of good money after bad, they are more dreaded by oilmen than dry holes. To be within the margin of profitability, according to the industry's estimate, a discovery well must bring in a field that will produce a million barrels of oil. The chances of finding such a field are one in forty-three. The chances of finding a ten-million-barrel field are one in two hundred and forty-three, and of finding a fifty-million-barrel field, one in nine hundred and sixty-seven. The odds soar from there. Of the thousands of wells that have been drilled in this country since the beginning of the century, less than fifty have brought in hundred-million-barrel fields. One of these, the Keystone Field, was discovered in West Texas in 1935 by the late Sid W. Richardson, and proved to contain reserves worth over a billion dollars. Altogether, three hundred and eighty-five wells were drilled in the Keystone, and only seventeen were dry. Rather than talk about this sensational performance, however, Richardson always preferred to call attention to a three-year period when, he said, he invested fifteen million dollars in drilling and "can drink every drop of oil I've got to show for it."

To dwell thus on the gloomy side—at least when anybody is listening—is characteristic of oilmen, who are convinced that nobody knows the trouble they've seen. "The only oilmen the public hears about are the few rich ones," Halbouty, who happens to be among them, has remarked, voicing the typical lament. "They never hear a whisper about the thousands and thousands who have gone broke. How many people know that most independents have to drill eight or nine dry holes to find one producing well? Take Spindletop. Eighty million dollars were invested there, but only thirty million came out. Why, a whole book could be written about oilmen who once were rich and are now hanging around hotel lobbies trying to make some little deal that will pay the rent and buy the groceries. This business is full of heartbreak."

Oilmen can get themselves so worked up about the pity of it all that a recital of their failures is apt to carry an undertone of perverse pride, like the confessions of a redeemed sinner. "Last year," Humble Oil announced in 1958 in a report to the public, "dry holes cost Humble almost $62 million, roughly $13 million more than in 1956. But oil can't be found without drilling for it. And when you drill, the odds are strong you will find nothing. In forty years, Humble has poured half a billion dollars down long, dry holes. That's nearly half as much as the Company's total assets today. Just since 1933, Humble has drilled 3540 dusters, averaging a mile and one-third in depth. End on end, they would probe two-thirds through the earth, or stretch from New York to San Francisco —via the Panama Canal. . . . Dry holes cost the industry about a billion dollars a year—almost 40 cents for every barrel of oil produced. Still more millions are lost on surrendered leases and unsuccessful exploratory work. Only about five per cent of all acreage leased proves even mildly productive. In all, about half of all the money spent on exploration and drilling results in no production." Of course, all the money that oilmen lose on exploration and drilling is completely deductible, and when this fact is included, their story can have a happy ending. For example, though dry holes cost Humble almost $62,000,000 in 1957, the company managed to wind up the year with a net profit of $175,910,400.

When a player beats the odds and finds oil, he enters the final, and most interesting, part of the game. He is now in a position to make money through one of two moves. Either he can sell the oil-producing property and pay the capital-gains tax on his profit or he can develop it and take advantage of the depletion allowance and other tax benefits. Though the second move contains a greater element of risk, it offers opportunity for a larger reward, and is preferred by most players.

A development program requires the drilling of additional wells to provide efficient drainage of the field, the number depending on, among other factors, the size of the property. Since wells cost about a hundred thousand dollars apiece, an operator working even a small field must put his hands on considerable capital. To get development money, approximately nine oilmen out of ten borrow from banks. The exceptions consist of players like Jake Hamon ("I worked for Mr. Interest long enough"), who have accumulated enough funds to finance their operations without going to the bank, and who tend to play a comparatively tight game. Operating on borrowed capital is such a common practice among oilmen that in their circles to be heavily in debt is no cause for chagrin; on the contrary, a talent for relieving financial institutions of large sums is considered a reliable measure of a player's skill. "Murchison, I'm a bigger success than you are," Sid Richardson once told his friend Clint Murchison after negotiating a rather spectacular loan. "Some of my paper is now in London."

Though banks do not advance money to drill discovery

wells as such (oil-producing property can be mortgaged to secure wildcatting funds, however), Texas banks compete in the lending of money to drill development wells. The pattern is generally the same. As collateral for a loan to drill his second well, a player assigns to a bank the lease on his first well. If the second well comes in, he pledges the lease on that for money to put down the third. The lease on the third is then assigned as security for funds to drill the fourth. And so on. The borrow-drill-borrow procedure can be continued as long as a player guesses right more often than wrong, for as he acquires more successful wells than dry holes or marginal wells, he can move steadily ahead. If, however, he guesses wrong more often than right, he reaches what is known in the oil game (the term having been appropriated from the flying game) as the point of no return. He has extended his operations beyond the point where they provide sufficient income to maintain payment on his bank loans, which in principal and interest customarily take from seventy to eighty per cent of his production, and to pay his taxes and living expenses. He cannot add to his income by arbitrarily increasing the amount of his production, because that is set by law. To stay in the game, he is obliged to sell enough property to raise the cash he needs to pay off his debts. Since selling property obviously has the result of reducing income, a player who repeatedly gets beyond the point of no return is at last penalized by losing all his chips and being retired from the game; if he can secure another stake, he may begin again from the starting point. A player who completes the course, avoiding the point of no return, repaying his loans, and finally securing ownership of a hundred per cent of his production, wins the game.

So far, no how-to-win-at-the-oil-game books have appeared, although it is probably inevitable that they will. Anyone undertaking a work of that kind would no doubt get, through attempting to analyze the makeup of the successful players, a few inklings of what it takes to win. Such an inquiry might usefully concentrate on the independent oilmen, since they are the most numerous and the most typical. The collective term by which they are known, the inquirer would early discover, is the basic clue to their character, which is marked, above all, by implacable independence. "The independents," Jim Clark, who has spent his life among them, once remarked, "are earthy-type fellows who don't want anybody else to try to tell them what to do. It goes against their grain to take orders. That's why they don't like to incorporate, because then they can't rely exclusively on their own judgment. Take Glenn McCarthy. He could have saved just about everything if he'd been willing to incorporate. Or he could have made a deal with Sinclair. They offered him a hundred million for his holdings and another fifty million to pay off all his debts. He could have paid his taxes and put seventy-five million cash in the bank. But that's not the way independents operate. No matter what the risk, they prefer to go it alone." Their preference is based, in large part, on the conviction that they are individually at least as capable as the next man, and quite possibly a little more so. In view of this conviction, it is not surprising that their society has no élite—though members who have some connection with Spindletop enjoy a slightly special status. An oilman whose father was a teamster at Spindletop takes as much pride in the fact as a Bostonian does in having a forebear who fought at Bunker Hill. As a group, however, oilmen are not much attracted to ancestor worship. They are, perhaps, about as inner-directed to begin with as anybody in the lonely crowd can be, and success serves to intensify the tendency.

This aspect of their character has been remarked on by Thomas A. Knight, a Dallas lawyer with a mordant wit who has been servicing, to use his term, independent oilmen ever since his graduation from the Harvard Law School, in 1915. "Finding oil," Knight has said, "has a tendency to accentuate the self-confidence and self-reliance of the discoverer, as well as the effect of making him at least temporarily rich. Being rich even for a moment is a happy condition, and the bright boys who discovered oil resolved, if it was at all possible, to perpetuate this condition and constantly to ameliorate it. With a view to never being without material resources, some of them acquired multi-carat diamonds, and the more trustful put chunks of money in the bank accounts of their wives, as a hedge alike against a rainy day and against creditors, and those who optimistically looked forward to a tranquil old age even let smart life-insurance salesmen talk them into buying annuities. Such measures afforded social security of a sort, but they did not gratify the yen of rugged individualists for ever-increasing power and wealth. A man suddenly coming into a million dollars is pretty well satisfied until he begins hob-nobbing with lots of people, each of whom has considerably more than a million dollars. Keeping up with the Joneses is it-self right smart of a stimulant."

The competition among oilmen, as Knight has observed, follows the national pattern, being confined to the material realm. While oilmen do not look down on intellectual pursuits, neither do they look up to them. The fact that the majority of oilmen made their way to the top with but a small amount of conventional book-learning plays its part in anchoring them securely to the native tradition, for, as Robert Hutchins has noted, "education has nothing to do with success in the United States." What oilmen lack in schooling they make up in stamina. One of the first conditions of the happiness, and even the existence, of nations, it has been said, is physical strength —a statement applying with equal force to oilmen. Their folk-lore is filled with tales of physical prowess, like those told of J. P. (Bum) Gibbins, of Midland, a mountain of a man who in his younger days performed feats requiring the strength of a team of horses. "Even now, I bet Bum can whip anybody in town," a Midlander said a while ago. To be handy with the fists is an ability not scorned by oilmen. Most of the successful ones started out in the oil fields, where differences of opinion are seldom resolved according to the etiquette prevailing at Boy Scout encampments. When Glenn McCarthy was po'-boy-ing his first wildcats and found himself unable to pay his men, he had a habit of announcing, "Anybody wants to walk off the job, I'll whip the hell out of him." He was able to maintain a remarkably steady level of employment. The oil fields have since become quite civilized. There has even been talk recently that the roughnecks will unionize. Nevertheless, the oil game is still not for pantywaists.

Nor is it a game for anybody who does not possess the quality defined by Alva Johnston as legitimate nonchalance. The eager beaver and the counting-house man are equally distasteful to oilmen not because oilmen have a low regard for drive or money but because they consider it bad form to press, in the golfing sense, or to be pernickety. The oilman's approach to business is genuinely casual, as is indicated by, for instance, the opinion that Byars once rendered on the value of the legal contract. "A contract in the oil business," he declared, "isn't worth the paper it's printed on. All it's for is to remind you of the terms you agreed on." Much the same view of the basic instrument of commerce is held by Paul Raigorodsky. "You don't need lawyers to make deals," he has explained. "In oil game, you do things differently. Maybe like this: I meet somebody at Petroleum Club who says he has to drill well before first of next month. He asks me if I want piece of deal. That means I'm going in on ground floor. I ask how much it will cost, and he says sixty thousand. I ask him how much he has, and he says quarter of eighth. If it sounds all right, I say, 'O.K. Count me in.' Or I may take eighth, form syndicate, and offer it to five or ten other people, and they all go in because I say it's O.K. All you need is person's word. Legal business comes along later."

This order of doing business, while second nature to oilmen, is apt to bewilder tradition-bound outlanders. "I remember a deal I made in New York with five investors, all new to the business," Weiner has recalled. "They agreed to put up a million and a half to drill five wells. I came back, and we'd drilled four of the wells and were just getting around to drawing up the papers on the deal when a lawyer who'd been hired by the New York investors called at my office. This fellow got to the point right away. 'You know,' he said, 'we don't have so much as a scratch of a pen to bind that deal. We haven't turned over any money to you, and you haven't signed any papers, and yet you've gone ahead with the drilling. Now I'm here to find out just what you intend to do.' Well, I told him we were going to do just what we said we'd do. We had a deal, and we'd all share in it just as we'd planned. As it turned out, before all the papers were drawn up and signed we had oil in the pipeline and three million dollars in the bank."

A typical New York investor might require a short indoctrination course in order to get used to the offhand manner in which Clint Murchison conducts the annual stockholders' meeting of the Delhi-Taylor Oil Corporation, his favorite commercial enterprise. "If you'll all come to order," he said in opening one meeting in Dallas, "I'll run through my annual reading lesson. First, let's have a motion to waive the reading of the minutes of the last meeting. Does anybody so waive?" Somebody waived, and Murchison proceeded to deliver an easygoing review of the year past ("Canadian Delhi is so conservative we kicked it out of Delhi"), a casual forecast of the year ahead ("Gas can't go anywhere but up"), and an announcement of a forthcoming stockholders' meeting of the Canadian subsidiary. "Clint," a stockholder asked from the floor, "how can you make the stockholders' meeting in Calgary and the Kentucky Derby, too?" "Afraid I can't, Roy," Murchison replied. "I'll have to pass up the stockholders' meeting." All present liked that, and after a few more informal questions and answers Murchison said, "I make a motion you make a motion we adjourn." The stockholders obliged, and then retired to Murchison's house for a garden party.

While partaking of bourbon and choice Kansas City strip sirloins broiled on a battery of charcoal braziers, the guests got Murchison to talking about some of his jauntier deals, including one he had made not long before with another prominent oilman, Toddie Lee Wynne. As partners over a period of years, Murchison and Wynne had expanded their joint holdings into a rather elaborate structure, which Wynne wanted to simplify. He accordingly proposed that he buy out Murchison's interest in the American Liberty Oil Company while Murchison, for his part, would buy out Wynne's interest in two life-insurance companies. Murchison agreed, and as they discussed the terms of the transaction, it developed that Murchison thought he should wind up with four hundred and ninety-eight thousand dollars more than Wynne figured. "We flipped a coin for the difference," Murchison said. "Toddie Lee won." Although Murchison lost nearly half a million on the toss, he turned a profit amounting to several times that sum on the sale of the oil company. "After all," he said, "the original investment in American Liberty was exactly one hundred and seventy-five dollars, cash."

The nonchalance that distinguishes the oilmen's character is a luxury they can afford because of their scrupulous regard for fair dealing. A representative oilman would as soon rob his mother as cheat a partner. "I never made a trade where I couldn't go back and make a second trade easier than the first," Sid Richardson once said with pride. "All oilmen aren't roses," Sol Brachman, the equipment supplier, who has been trading with scores of big and little oilmen for many years, has observed. "Some of them don't realize there was a world here before they arrived. But one thing you can say about oilmen is that, generally speaking, they are very honest. And, with very few exceptions, they are good-hearted. As for honesty, I have many, many times charged off accounts, figuring there wasn't a chance in the world of collecting them, and five or six years later these fellows have come in and paid up."

Oilmen do not necessarily adopt the foursquare approach to commerce out of an abiding belief in the chilly principle that virtue is its own reward; rather, they are in the position of not having a great deal of choice. "In this business, you've got to be honest with everybody or you don't get anywhere," Jim Clark has remarked. "That's why deals can be made over the phone, and wells drilled, before any papers are signed. The plain fact is that a crook doesn't last long in this business." In the oil game, a handshake is considered as dependable as a contract. The principle is based on the old-fashioned notion, still in circulation on the frontier, that people can be trusted. "You put faith in a person," Byars has said, "and if he's half-way honest, he'll come through."

In the oilman's world, a respect for the cardinal precept of the square deal is handed down from father to son. "I was tradin' out with one of my partners," Ray Hubbard has said in recalling how the word was transmitted to him. "This partner had got in some tax trouble, and he had to sell out. He'd rooked me once in times past, and I got an elephant's memory, so I was goin' to see he got a rookin' in return. Yes, sir, I decided to give him a rookin' he'd remember. So I told Tom Knight, the lawyer, what the deal was, so he could make out the papers. Tom said, 'What's the matter, Ray? I guess you and Arch had a fallin' out, but you know what time it is, and you know you're stealin' it.' I said, 'Sure I know I'm stealin' it. That's what I got in mind. So go ahead and draw up the papers.' Next mornin', I got to the office and there was my father. He was in his eighties. Not really active in the business but still keepin' an eye on things. 'What you doin'?' he said. 'What do you mean, what am I doin'?' I said. 'I mean that deal with Arch,' my father said. 'That's no good. I know you got the axe on him, but you can't do what you're aimin' to. You gotta pay him what it's worth. I've told you time and again you're the boss, but you're the boss only as long as you run this business to suit me. And it ain't gonna suit me unless you play fair with Arch.' Well, to make a long story short, we played fair with Arch."

Once they have made their own fortunes, many oilmen go out of their way to help business associates and friends by cutting them in on promising deals. This practice, like the dedication to fair play, stems not only from altruism but also from enlightened self-interest, for, in the oilman's typically informal way, it provides the advantages of a profit-sharing plan. As Murchison once advised a friend, "If you've got a good man working for you, make certain he dies rich."

To enjoy the privilege of being independent without becoming arrogant is no easy task, as Europeans are in the habit of reminding us, and it is a particularly heavy burden for oilmen. Their special difficulty originates in the fact that they are, taken together, even more rootless than most Americans (thirty-three million of whom—about one in five—move to a new neighborhood every year), and consequently less affected by the give-and-take influences that spring from group participation. "There's not an oilman alive who has any sense of belonging," Thomas Knight has remarked. "Not a man in Dallas in the oil business wouldn't move someplace else if he could get a better break on taxes. Oilmen have no sense of permanence. They're in an industry rather than in a locality. That's why oil people carry less than their proportionate load in civic affairs." A survey conducted last year by the Texas Mid-Continent Oil & Gas Association among more than five hundred oilmen in five Texas cities showed that less than one out of three even belonged to a local civic or service club. Though oilmen like Michel Halbouty, Ray Hubbard, R. E. (Bob) Smith, Jake Hamon—in fact, a majority of those one is aware of when living in the state—work conscientiously at community enterprises, they constitute the exceptions proving the rule that non-involvement is the oilman's preferred way of life. "I don't make my money in this town," a Fort Worth operator told an acquaintance. "I make it in West Texas and in New Mexico and Canada. Why should I worry what happens here?"

The oilmen's tenuous relationship with the community influences their larger relationship with the country. Of those included in the Mid-Continent survey, one out of five didn't know the name of his Congressman, and less than half said they take any part in political affairs. Oilmen care very little about the public, because, unlike most people in business, they don't need to care very much. The fact that they sell their wares not to consumers but to the big oil companies means that, in a commercial sense, they exist in a world of their own. The public knows about them only vaguely, and this is to their liking, for they prefer to live in privacy. Their infrequent forays into the outside world are seldom felicitous. From time to time in recent years, they have come into view in connection with their efforts to secure passage of legislation removing the price of natural gas from federal control. While opponents of the measure say that the oilmen are out to increase their collective income by about a billion dollars a year, the oilmen say that their primary interest is to save, as Jim Clark has put it, "the industry from the socialist planners in Washington and elsewhere." Whatever their motive, the oilmen have twice succeeded in getting a bill to their liking passed by Congress, but both have been vetoed—by President Truman in 1950 and by President Eisenhower in 1956. Though Eisenhower favored the bill, he felt obliged to veto it because its passage had been accompanied by what he called "arrogant" lobbying. Around this time, Senator Francis Case, Republican of South Dakota, turned down a campaign contribution of twenty-five hundred dollars from an oilman whose interest in the natural gas bill, the Senator sensed, was not altogether impartial.

It is not what the oilmen do but the way they do it that sometimes leads people to believe that the oilmen's philosophy is influenced less by Big Tim Sullivan's view ("God and the People hate a chesty man") than by John Jay's ("Those who own the country ought to govern it"). In any event, the actions of both the independents and the majors do not always contribute significantly to improving the industry's public relations, a matter in which oilmen profess great interest. In the hope of fashioning a reputation as good as the next industry's, they support national trade associations, like the American Petroleum Institute, and numerous regional groups, like the Texas Mid-Continent Oil & Gas Association, which, in turn, manage an imposing array of educational projects, ranging from bread-and-butter institutional advertising to more sophisticated ventures, such as providing subsidies that enable professors to produce deep, or at least dense, books about petroleum. Besides helping to finance these joint operations, major companies like Standard, Gulf, and Texaco, which sell to the ultimate consumer, are far from niggardly in their outlays aimed at creating a favorable public image. "Today, the oil industry is doing everything in its power to make people like it," Jim Clark recently remarked. "And there is little reason why all people in this country should not."

It appears from public-opinion polls, however, that the majority of people are able to keep a fairly close check on their enthusiasm for the oil industry. The reason that its massive effort to build good will has not produced better results, some observers feel, is that, basically, oilmen do not have their heart in it. Otherwise, this reasoning goes, they would not lapse into careless displays of highhandedness. For example, the industry, led by the largest subsidiary of Standard Oil of New Jersey—the largest of the majors and supposedly among the most enlightened in public relations—chose the period of the Suez Canal crisis to raise the price of oil. Whatever the justification for the increase—it was the first in three years—the timing, when Western Europe was forced to depend on oil supplies from this hemisphere, revealed an almost majestic indifference to the public.

If anybody calls attention to their unsociable attitude, the oilmen, who are not notably sporting when it comes to criticism, have a habit of crying foul. They are being persecuted, they say; a sinister, if somewhat vague, force is out to get them. "It is hard to pin down just what that force is," the *National Petroleum News* has remarked. "Obviously, messing up the industry in this country and in the rest of the world would be pleasing to the Communists. Yet repeatedly in these past years it has been evident that there are others than Communists who have designs on the oil industry." These "others," the *News* went so far as to imply, might include "some allegedly 'good' Republicans." To make the point even clearer, eleven independent oilmen, including John Mecom, Michel Halbouty, and H. J. (Jack) Porter, took a full-page advertisement in the Houston *Post* a while ago to deliver what they called "A Declaration of Independents," the essence of which was to equate enthusiasm for the oil industry with patriotism. The declaration said that "without a sound and vigorous American oil industry, our nation could fall easy prey to those who would eliminate the competitive system and the American way of life" and that it was therefore necessary "to stand united against the common and undivided forces which seek to destroy us and the system of competitive free enterprise our industry so clearly typifies." The advertisement had the additional value of clearly typifying the oilmen's standard operating procedure of regarding anybody who does not unstintingly praise their industry as a saboteur, deliberate or unthinking, bent on destroying the country. There is little doubt that they really believe it.

Whatever else it takes to win in the oil game, the *sine qua non* is luck. Recently, H. L. Hunt was asked his formula for making money. "You have to be lucky," he began. Ted Weiner agrees. "Finding oil is ninety-five per cent luck," he has said. "In a way, it's like golf. All the pros make the green in par; it's the lucky players who putt out in one. In the oil game, the pros—the fellows who have a background of experience—are about evenly matched in the number of wells they find. It's the lucky ones who find the big wells. I suppose I've drilled about as many wells as Sid Richardson did in his lifetime, but where he had maybe a thousand million, I have—well, somewhat less." Richardson held the same opinion. "Luck has helped me every day of my life," he once said. "And I'd rather be lucky than smart, 'cause a lot of smart people ain't eatin' regular. I may not be the smartest fellow in the world, but I sure am one of the luckiest. Some people get luck and brains mixed up, and that's when they get in trouble."

A favorite story that oilmen tell, to show what they regard as the relative importance of intelligence and luck in the oil game, has to do with the exploits of the son of a very successful operator. "The boy," an oilman who was acquainted with him has recalled, "was a nice boy, but he wasn't quite right in the head. The trouble came on him gradually, after he'd got out of school and his daddy had set him up in the oil business. Folks began to notice something wrong when he started doing funny things, like when he went into a clothing store to buy a new suit of clothes. He looked at himself in one of those three-sided mirrors, and then he said, 'I like them. I'll take all three.' It got so bad they finally had to put him away in an institution, but by then he'd already had quite a time of it. He started out in the East Texas fields, and he really cleaned up. He didn't pay much attention to geologists' reports or anything else like that. He'd just look around and say, 'This looks like a good place.' And it didn't make any difference where he drilled —he couldn't miss. Then he moved on to Louisiana and began doing business in even more peculiar ways. Finally, he threw away the book completely. He went around giving those farmers fifty per cent override, instead of the usual one-eighth, and the wells just kept coming in, one after another. The boy and the farmers were both making out real good. Then he took to whipstocking some of his wells—that means, after you've dug a well to a certain distance vertically and haven't hit oil, you drill at an angle and hope to strike it, an expensive process— and, to everybody's surprise, practically every one of those wells made money, too. Why, the boy must have made twenty million while he was going crazy."

Unlike most businessmen, who are inclined to credit their unwavering dedication to diligence, thrift, and honesty with boosting them to the top, oilmen, displaying a refreshing candor, take a positive pride in attributing their success to luck. "My West Texas oil field was solely luck," R. E. (Bob) Smith has said. "It has thirty-eight million barrels in reserve and cost me five dollars an acre. The lesson you learn as you get older is that it's luck." The lives of oilmen offer abundant proof of this. Early in his career, John Mecom had a choice between drilling in an area called South Mercy and an area called High Island. Partly on a hunch, he chose the latter, and brought in a well that gave him enough funds to start building his empire. He would have lost everything if he had chosen South Mercy, for when he got around to it later, he found nothing. With minor variations, that is the story of every man who succeeds in the oil game.

It is a truism among the players that the indispensable quality for winning cannot be cultivated. "I have a friend who is an excellent geologist, an absolutely first-class man," Jake Hamon said a while ago. "I helped him get into several deals. There's every reason they should have paid off, and paid off well, but not one of them did. He never hit. There's no logical explanation, except that the man is simply not lucky. Every once in a while, young fellows come in to see me and ask my advice about going into the oil business. I never know just what to tell them, but I always get around to one thing: I ask them if they're lucky. Do they like to gamble? Are they good poker players? And how's their luck generally? If they like to gamble and if they're lucky, they'll probably do all right in the oil business." In the end, all hands happily agree, it is not the smartest or the strongest or the meekest or the poorest in spirit or the purest in heart but just the luckiest who wind up in the oil game's Hall of Fame. That is Super-America all over again.

Chapter Seven

Few documents since the Emancipation Proclamation have stirred as much commotion in Texas as Edna Ferber's novel "Giant," whose protagonists are a pair of Texas millionaires. Ever since the work was published, in 1952, Texans have been denouncing it like sin. The book, they think, slanders not only their millionaires but their state. For an outsider to find a fault in either is, according to the Texas code of conduct, bad form; to knock both is practically an extraditable offense. So it is that, even today, a sojourner in Texas can expect to hear philippics on the evils of ednaferberism. The most heinous, to judge by the frequency with which it is voiced, is that, by way of becoming acquainted with her subject, Miss Ferber spent six weeks in Texas. In the natives' view, her visit was so brief that it amounted to a breach of etiquette, like not removing one's hat in the Alamo, and they keep the memory of the alleged discourtesy green. "Frank Wardlaw, of the University of Texas Press, has just heard how Edna Ferber managed to get material for her novel 'Giant,'" George Fuermann wrote in his Houston *Post* column a while ago. "As Mr. W. heard it, Miss Ferber, while flying across the Southwest in an airliner, sent a note to the pilot: 'Please fly a little lower. I want to write a book about Texas.'" People in the state she wrote about still take pleasure in repeating to visitors, sometimes before they've had a chance to unpack their bags, the observation that William Kittrell, a Dallas philosopher and student of Texas millionaires, made upon discovering that the characters in "Giant" were flying about in their own DC-6s, which, as far as the manufacturer or anybody in Texas is aware, have never been used as private planes. "If Miss Ferber had favored us with her company for a more extended period of time," Kittrell remarked, "she would have learned that while some of our more successful millionaires do indeed own DC-3s, it is not true that two DC-3s make one DC-6." Putting jokes aside, a member of the Houston Board of Education recently made an effort to ban an economics textbook from the city's public schools because it contained a reference to Edna Ferber. In such ways the anti-Ferber campaign goes on and on, having now reached the point where it might begin to seem somewhat absurd, if it were not being waged by Texans. They are impelled to overdo this, like everything else. For if Americans are sensitive ("They are more than this; they are oversensitive," wrote the Scotsman Alexander Mackay. "They are touchy in the highest degree," wrote the Hungarians Francis and Therese Pulszky. "No nation is equally sensitive and impatient of criticism," wrote the Pole Count Gurowski), it is in the nature of things that Super-Americans should be super-sensitive. It can therefore be expected that the communal irritation over "Giant" will be perpetuated, possibly unto the third and fourth generation.

Meanwhile, injured feelings have not kept Texans from doing far more than their share to make "Giant" one of the greatest successes of all Miss Ferber's novels. In addition to buying approximately eight per cent of the copies sold in the United States, they have also done yeoman service in making the movie version a smashing financial triumph. "Again, Texans flocked out for their beating in the guise of entertainment," Jim Mathis, of the Houston *Post,* noted in 1957. "They even laughed as the knife operated. Exhibitors made it all but impossible to see another show, booking the movie into all second-run theatres and drive-ins at the same time. Last week, exhibitors said, a million seven hundred and fifty thousand Texans had paid their way inside to see the movie." The flocking has continued. In the spring of 1961, "Giant" was simultaneously booked into, among others, five theatres in Dallas, six in Fort Worth, and nine in Houston, again setting box-office records. Mathis, who thought the picture "openly dishonest," though "not as incredibly malicious as the book," attributed his fellow-citizens' all-out support of both to "a facet of character peculiar to Texas: an almost masochistic interest in that which slashes deep."

Actually, the explanation is less complicated; it is simply that Texans delight in looking in the mirror, regardless of whether they are pleased by what they see there. Furthermore, their addiction to the looking glass is hardly peculiar to them. Mirror-gazing is second nature to all Americans, and has been for so long that we take it for granted, like happy endings. Foreigners have never ceased to be impressed, or amused, by how perfectly fascinated we are with ourselves. "One thing in him is noteworthy—he is always willing to discuss America," the English novelist W. L. George remarked. "He will state her, explain her, defend her, and the subject never wearies him." Nor does it seem to weary others, considering the multitude of non-Americans who have also been willing to discuss the subject. "No other people, it is safe to say, was ever so besieged by interpreters," Henry Steele Commager has pointed out. "None has had its portrait painted, its habits described, its character analyzed, its soul probed so incessantly. The practice started before Independence and has continued unabated to the present day."

Since 1947, when that observation was made, efforts to feel the nation's head have sharply increased. Not only has the output of foreign commentaries, like that of foreign cars, been stepped up to satisfy the burgeoning American market but the native industry has boomed to the point where many economists believe that full employment has now been reached in the production of books by Americans about Americans. Among the recent works aimed at anatomizing the species are "The Affluent Society," "The Lonely Crowd," "The Organization Man," "The Man Who Feels Left Behind," "The Status Seekers," "The Exurbanites," "The Waist-High Culture," "As Others See Us," "America as a Civilization," "America the Vincible," and "Only in America," to name but a few. Finishing these, Americans can turn to the magazines and go right on reading about themselves. In this vast and expanding literature, there is something for everyone; for example, the ladies will find, in *Look,* the noted literary critic Diana Trilling discussing "The Case for the American Woman," while at the same time the gentlemen will discover, in *Esquire,* the distinguished historian Arthur Schlesinger, Jr., pondering "The Crisis of American Masculinity." As for American children, their dissection in print (not to mention in private conversation) has become a national mania, like dieting, and as interesting.

Americans are infatuated not only with America Past and America Present but even with America Future. Recently, the *Times Magazine* published an article in which three eminent American historians told us what we will be like in 1970. "There will be less need for the 'rugged individualist' and more for the social-minded civil servant," said the first. "Intellectuals will still take an unrealistic view of non-intellectuals," said the second. "The intellectual level will be higher, but we will lack a superculture," said the third. It all really matters to Americans. (Imagine the French caring about how their national character may change in the next decade—or, for that matter, the next century—or the Italians paying respectful attention to what tourists say about them.) "One of the few features of American civilization about which all observers are agreed is its intense self-consciousness," William A. Orton has observed. "There was probably never a great people so eager to hear itself talked about. The Greeks, according to the Apostle Paul, had a similar fondness for visiting lecturers, but they do not seem to have been equally avid for comments on the value of Greek civilization." The Americans heed everybody's comments, for the obvious reason that they are not sure they *are* a great people. Indeed, they do not yet know what they are. Compared, say, to the British, who have had a few centuries to get up in their part, the Americans were handed a script only yesterday.

Behind the Americans' big talk, of course, is a youthful uncertainty stemming from an anxious search for identity. As

John Wain put it recently in the London *Observer*, "Self-discovery, if necessary by means of violence and sacrifice: that is the American preoccupation. Having discovered their land, they now face the discovery of themselves." The Super-Americans, similarly confronted, have reacted according to form by developing what Sawnie Aldredge, a Dallas bibliophile and the proprietor of the bookstore bearing his name, has termed "an insatiable lust to read about Texas and Texans." The potency of the urge is indicated by the imposing array of books aimed at slaking it on display in Texas bookstores. Cokesbury's, the largest in the state, devotes a separate room to indigenous belles-lettres, a genre that has never been in short supply.

Since the days of the Republic, Texans have been apt and diligent recorders, if not interpreters, of themselves. As a result, they have already produced what amounts to a domestic five-foot (or, perhaps more precisely, five-hundred-foot) shelf, and it is substantially extended every year with works like "I'll Take Texas," "13 Days to Glory," "Reluctant Empire," "Home from the Hill," "Spindletop," "The Staked Plain," "Home to Texas," and "The Lusty Texans of Dallas," to name a recent few that Texans have bought by the thousand. Their passion finds another outlet in the devouring of old and esoteric books about Texas. The Aldredge Book Store, for example, does a brisk business in lively volumes like "The History and Geography of Texas As Told in County Names" ($20) and "The History of Dallas County, 1837 to 1887" ($50), as well as in hundreds of less expensive items with a somewhat limited appeal, such as "Orators and Oratory of Texas," "A History of the Texas Baptists," and "My Texas 'Tis of Thee."

Indicative though these signs may be, the most telling evidence of the Texans' voracious appetite for reading about themselves is the fact that for more than a quarter of a century they have, in effect, subsidized their own publishing house. This is the Naylor Company, of San Antonio, which annually publishes some forty new titles, mainly by and about Texans. While the company has begun publishing Southwestern authors who are not Texans in the last few years, it is "still Texasminded to the core," as an officer of the firm said recently, and there is not much in the Naylor list to contradict him; to wit, "When God Made Texas," "Early Days in Texas," "Texas in 1848," "Texas in the Confederacy," "Texas and the Fair Deal," "A Hundred Years of Comfort in Texas," "Those Texans," "Towering Texans," "Texans with Guns," "You Can Always Tell a Texan," "I Give You Texas," "My State: Texas," "Texas Laughs," "Texas Wildcatter," "Texas Wild Flowers," "Texas-broke," "Texas—Proud and Loud," "Texas Treasure Chest," "Texas Rhythm and Other Poems," "Poet Laureates of Texas," "The New Texas Reader," "The Texas Democrat," "The Texas Indians," "Night Fishing in Texas," "Deer Hunting in Texas," "Texas Lion Hunter," "Cavalier in Texas," "Turkeys in Texas," and enough others in this vein to satisfy everybody except, apparently, Texans. Unsated, they spur their writers on to ever-higher peaks of production, not only with legal tender—Hugh Roy Cullen once bought to give to friends fifty thousand copies of a book that, even though it was not written by a Texan, had struck his fancy—but also with laurel. Excellence in the literary line is honored by Super-Americans with their version of the Pulitzer Prize; in other words, they offer three Pulitzer-type prizes. Each is worth a thousand dollars—fittingly, double the Pulitzer.

Taken as a whole, the native writings, though high in volume, are low in revelation of the nature of the people. This is inevitable. Like other Americans, Texans have small talent for self-portraiture, and it may be partly for this reason that they pay uncommon attention to pictures of them done by outsiders. These have not been uniformly fortunate, having tended either toward flattery or—much more often—toward superciliousness. With some reason, therefore, Texans believe that they are currently suffering the lot common a century ago to all Americans, whose feelings, Alexander Mackay wrote in 1849 upon returning to England, "have been wantonly and unnecessarily wounded by successive travellers who have undertaken to depict them, nationally and individually, and who, to pander to a prevailing taste in this country, have generally viewed them on the ludicrous side."

One explanation for the fanciful air that distinguishes the bulk of the commentaries on Texas is the fact that successive travellers who have undertaken to depict Texans have, more often than not, been the kind described by Henry James as sentimental tourists. "The sentimental tourist," James said, "makes images in advance; they grow up in his mind by a logic of their own. He finds himself thinking of an unknown, unseen place as having such and such a shape and figure than such another. It assumes in his mind a certain complexion, a certain color, which infrequently turns out to be singularly at variance with reality."

Thanks to the observations of sentimental tourists, anybody setting out for Texas knows beforehand, among many other things, what the people there will look like. He has been advised by Paul Gallico in the *Reader's Digest* that "the men *are* taller, tougher, handsomer, fightin'er than most. The girls *are* prettier, slimmer, more sparkling." He has been further benefited by the undigested remarks on the Texas male offered by Cecil Beaton in his book "I Take Great Pleasure," written after a recent lecture tour. "Many of the men, lithe and lanky, with their long slender waists, looked like thoroughbred horses," Beaton noted. "Their hips so narrow, their legs so innocuously elegant and lean in cowboy disguise, would make a paunchy Northern businessman green with envy." The female in Texas, the traveller has been assured, will appear no less remarkable than the male. "Texas women," Robert Ruark declared in *Coronet*, "grow taller and stand straighter and their lips are redder and their eyes are brighter than any other women's in the world. Their hair piles higher and their legs sprout slimmer and their sweaters stick out farther." Ruark was teasing when he wrote that (Texans by the score nevertheless congratulated him on his perspicacity), but Bettina Ballard was not when she wrote in *Town & Country* of "the pretty, blond, long-legged women for which Texas is so famous."

Thus briefed, the traveller attends his first big party given by a Texas millionaire and, to his delight, has no trouble at all finding what he is unconsciously looking for. There they are—any number, it seems, of pretty, blond, long-legged women and tall, lean, handsome men. "It's true what they say," the visitor is apt to murmur to himself. Such is the effect of his conditioning and of the shock of recognition that it may be some little while before he begins to notice among the guests a considerable—perhaps even equal—number of short-legged brunettes and squat businessmen as paunchy as any up North. His vision cleared, the unsentimental tourist is at length forced to conclude that for every Texas millionaire as tall, dark, and handsome as Angus Wynne, Jr., there are quite a number as short, round, and balding as Stanley Marcus, and, further, that in spite of an abundance of lovely women, not all Texas millionaires walk with beauties. No matter how long his stay, however, the visitor will probably never be able to decide whether the prettiest women in America can be found in Texas, as Oleg Cassini says, or at the corner of Fifth Avenue and Fifty-Seventh Street in New York, as Cary Grant says. About tastes, of course, there is no disputing.

While the sentimental tourists are demonstrably wrong about the way Texans are constructed, there is no use disputing the proposition that Super-Americans collectively present a more colorful aspect than people of other states. This is because of the way some of them dress. A foreigner set down in, say, Buffalo or St. Louis or Portland or San Diego would have a hard time telling, from the appearance of people on the street, one region from another. Not so in Texas. A stranger set down in any Texas city—even Dallas, sometimes called "the best Northern city in the South"—would see enough men wearing broad-brimmed, light-colored hats, sharp-pointed, high-heeled boots, wide belts, tight-fitting pants, and other distinctive accoutrements to let him know he had arrived in Texas. The number of people in the cities who are turned out in the traditional Texas garb is small, and growing smaller, but it is this minority that gives a painterly quality to the scene and provides what is usually thought of as the Texas style. As for the majority of

Texas millionaires, their dress varies, in part according to where they live. The city dwellers, as a rule, are indistinguishable from other well-tailored American men of means. There is nothing, for example, about the appearance of William or Andrew Fuller or Tom Slick or John Blaffer or H. H. Dewar or Jay Simmons or Jake Hamon (who was once listed among the country's ten best-dressed men) or scores of others that would mark them as Texas millionaires when seen in the lobby of the Pierre, the Mark Hopkins, the George V, the Excelsior, the Nile Hilton, or anywhere else they are likely to turn up.

Since the end of the Second World War, graduates of Eastern universities have flocked to Texas, bringing their alien costume, which has found increasing favor with the natives. Aiding this trend away from regional attire, Neiman-Marcus a few years ago established a men's-clothing section called the Ivy Shop, where, according to the advertisements, "authentic Ivy wares" are sold by "authentic Ivy men." Texans in authentic Ivy wares become increasingly scarce as one travels west from Dallas, and are quite a rarity even in Fort Worth. An oil millionaire in Odessa or San Angelo, for instance, customarily dresses for work in slacks and a sports shirt, while a cattle millionaire puts on a pair of worn trousers, a faded shirt, a Western hat, and dusty boots. For church or a social occasion, the cattleman dresses up in a ranch suit, which is generally made of gray or tan whipcord or gabardine and consists of narrow trousers and a coat with a pleated back. This outfit is almost always made to order, as are his boots. So plain, however, are the everyday clothes of West Texas millionaires that they serve as a kind of protective coloration. Strangers have been known to offer tips to West Texas millionaires for performing small courtesies, such as helping push a car out of a ditch, and West Texas millionaires have been known to accept them.

Though it is far from easy, in the normal course of events, to run across a Texas millionaire got up the way a sentimental tourist expects, it can, with luck, still be done. A recent sojourner in Texas had been in residence half a year before encountering such a specimen, and then only by chance while he was lunching with an investment broker at the Blackamoor Room (so named, the guest was told, because of two ebony statues at the entrance, not because the waiters are colored) of the Fort Worth Club.

"There's our only surviving indigenous boot-and-jewelry man —my friend Sam Lard," the broker said, nodding in the direction of a gray-haired man seated at a nearby table. "Came down here from Kansas without a dime, made a fortune in the creamery business, sold out to Borden's in 1929—Sam had one of the biggest creamery businesses in the country by then— went into ranching, found oil, and Sam had it made, but good. A few years back, he sold one of his ranches in New Mexico— the Ladder Ranch, a famous name—for an even million. Been taking it sort of easy since then. His son Bobby—a boy who won a lot of decorations in the war—lives out in California, and Sam spends a good deal of time out there now himself."

On his way out of the Blackamoor Room, Lard stopped to shake hands with the broker.

"How you doin', Sam?" the broker said.

"Not a goddam thing," Lard said, chewing on an unlighted cigar. "Hardest goddam job in the world, doin' nothin'."

Tall, slim, and ramrod straight, his silvery hair parted in the middle and plastered down at the sides, Lard was wearing a light-tan gabardine ranch suit, boots made of pink-and-blue leather stitched with gold thread, and acres of diamonds. His tiepin was adorned with a diamond at each end, and his tie clip with two diamonds and a ruby. He was also wearing a diamond ring of noble proportions, as well as a Masonic emblem encrusted with diamonds on his left lapel, and, on his right lapel, a rather massive cluster of sparklers.

"That something new, Sam?" the broker asked.

"Yes, sir, just got it last week," Lard said, putting his thumb under the lapel to display the new acquisition. "That's what I call my crest. Designed it myself. See, it's a shield. Got my initials on it. All diamonds. It sorta matches the belt." Lard opened his coat to reveal a glistening belt buckle, about three inches long and two inches wide. "All diamonds," he said.

"Sixty-four big and little ones. Designed that, too. Had it custom-made in California."

"Right smart-looking boots you got on there, Sam," the broker said.

"God-damned if they ain't," Lard said, hitching up a trouser leg. "Designed 'em myself. Had 'em made in San Antone. Little lady that was with me when I went in to order these boots, why, she thought I was plumb crazy because I said I wanted a pair of pink-and-blue boots. Said they'd be too loud. What the hell. They ain't too loud. All that gold thread and all that pink-and-blue inlaid leather—hell, they're *quiet*. Cost two hundred and fifty a pair, and worth every penny of it. Got eight or ten more pairs like it. Gonna have a pair made for Bobby."

"How's he doin' in California?" the broker asked.

"Bobby, he's ranchin' in a Cadillac," Lard replied. "He's levellin' that land, pushin' it around till it'll be flat as a pancake, and he's goin' to charge the whole goddam thing off. I'm goin' to get me some land out there and do the same thing. Got a deal for three hundred and twenty acres. I'm goin' to level it all and charge the whole goddam thing off. Then I'm goin' to take a hundred acres and soil-bank it, and I'm goin' to make a hundred dollars an acre for raisin' nothin'. If ya can't lick 'em, goddam it, join 'em. That's what I say. Well, be seein' ya." Lard exited, glittering.

The wives of Texas millionaires, taken together, are not only very well dressed but noticeably very well dressed. Their clothes are expensive, and they show it. Even their casual outfits look costly, as indeed they generally are. The rich costuming of the wives is the rule whether they live in Dallas or Nacogdoches, San Antonio or Muleshoe. It is probably safe to say, for example, that Mrs. Dudley Dougherty, of Beeville (pop. 15,000), has a wardrobe as fashionable as that of any millionaire's wife in Houston (pop. 925,000). This is due in part to Mrs. Dougherty's habit of flying to Paris every once in a while for a clothes-shopping visit of three or four days. Because of their penchant for elegant clothes, the millionaires' wives, according to some observers, appear to their best advantage at formal parties, where the guests can dress about as elaborately as they wish without any risk of seeming to be overdressed. "There's no middle to anything," a French visitor once said of the fashions she saw in Texas. No matter what the time of day, the millionaires' wives usually look as if they were headed for a party of some sort. As often as not, they are, but even when just going out to lunch at, say, the S & S Tea Room, in a suburb of Dallas, they are inclined to don a splendid costume, consisting of an expensive dress or suit, a full-fledged hat, high-heeled shoes, and a mink stole. "When the temperature drops below ninety, out come the minks," the founder of the S & S Tea Room once remarked. "You've never seen so much mink under one roof. Why, this place looks like a fur salon."

The popularity of mink (which, according to the *Times Literary Supplement,* "today symbolizes prosperity as effective as any sheaf of corn, or fruity cornucopia, in the arms of a seventeenth-century goddess") and the custom of wearing hats are but two contributions of Neiman-Marcus, which exercises the most important single influence on women's clothes in Texas. "Neiman-Marcus sells probably more fine mink than any other store in the country, but there is no way of proving it," a vice-president of the store once advised an acquaintance, with a mixture of pride and rue. The store also does a nice year-round business in headgear, a subject on which the store has strong convictions. "Nine times out of ten when a woman is not wearing a hat, she ought to be," a recent Neiman-Marcus advertisement sharply declared. "She needs a wardrobe of hats as she does a wardrobe of apparel," the admonition continued, "and, wisely selected, the hats can be interchanged to make her look like four different women wearing the same suit." Though partial to Neiman-Marcus, the wives of Texas millionaires also shop for clothes at stores like Sakowitz, in Houston; Stripling's, in Fort Worth; and Frost Brothers, in San Antonio, as well as at shops in San Francisco, New York, and Paris. The gowns they choose for significant social events are likely to be originals. At a recent Assembly Ball in Fort Worth, for example, the guests were clad in creations designed by, among many others, Balmain, Marc Bohan, Ben Reig, Scaasi, Estevez, Sophie, Irene, Galanos, Simonetta, Martini, Fontana of Rome, and Alicia of Fort Worth.

Perhaps nobody appears more often in original gowns at Texas social affairs than Mrs. Roy Woods, the wife of an Oklahoma City millionaire who has trucking, oil, aviation, and other business interests in Texas and frequently visits there. It is quite possible that Mrs. Woods' enthusiasm for clothes is even keener than that of any millionaire's wife to be found in Texas. On trips of any consequence, Mrs. Woods, known to her Texas friends as Alta, likes to travel with her French maid and a different ensemble for each morning, afternoon, and evening. To make sure that her costumes arrive unwrinkled, she has them placed on rolling racks, like those seen on the streets in the New York garment district, and transported to her destination in one of her husband's trucks. At the hotel, a sample room or similar extensive space is taken for the racks. A while ago, she and her husband travelled through Europe in a two-vehicle motorcade, consisting of a limousine carrying Mr. and Mrs. Woods, followed by a truck carrying her things. Later, attending a formal ball in Tyler, Texas, Mrs. Woods, who enjoys talking, reminisced about the trip. As she talked, she occasionally adjusted her gown, a Traina-Norell original made of black feathers, and her white ermine stole, which appeared to be a yard wide and three yards long.

"And then Harry introduced us to this French countess, the rich one with the castle and all," Mrs. Woods said. "That one you should have seen. She was loaded, and I mean in *every* department."

"Not more than you, though, was she, Alta?" one of her friends asked playfully.

"Run that past me again, will you, please, honey?" Mrs. Woods replied, fondling a diamond necklace too enormous not to be real.

The Houston millionaire Hugh Roy Cullen used to say,

"Jewelry is something people use in order to make out that they're better than other people. It's just plain common. I've taught my children that if they feel like buying some jewelry, they should find out how much it costs and then go out and give that amount to a school or hospital. They'll get more satisfaction out of it." Cullen's philosophy has not won notably wide acceptance among Texas millionaires, many of whom sport an impressive star-sapphire or diamond ring, or among their wives, who apparently get some satisfaction out of helping to support Harry Winston, Julius Cohen, Van Cleef & Arpels, Neiman-Marcus, and Cartier, the five firms that divide the bulk of the fine-jewel business in Texas. Van Cleef & Arpels and Harry Winston maintain shops in Dallas, while representatives of Julius Cohen and Cartier make frequent trips through the territory, peddling the ice. All the firms find Texas an excellent market not only for the important stuff but also for tasteful novelties. The current favorite in the latter category is an American twenty-dollar gold piece processed in Switzerland so that, upon release of a concealed clasp, it opens into two halves, the bottom of which contains an almost incredibly small, thin watch that can be lifted to stand on its side, like a tiny travelling clock. This amusing trinket, sold by Harry Winston and costing nine hundred and fifty dollars, is carried by many Texas millionaires and their wives as a good-luck piece, the way people with less originality sometimes carry a silver dollar. That the wife of a Texas millionaire has a decent supply of jewels is so taken for granted that no great stir is caused when, for example, Mrs. Jake Hamon, following a theatre opening, reports that she has lost a thirty-thousand-dollar clip (later found on the street after having evidently been stepped on several times). The pleasantly relaxed attitude with which mishaps of this kind are treated is no doubt born of the knowledge that there is more where that came from.

Numerous though the notable collections are, it seems generally agreed that Mrs. Robert Windfohr, descendant of an old, wealthy ranching family and wife of a successful oilman, has the best jewels in Texas. Not infrequently they figure in the conversational post-mortems of social affairs that she has attended. "Anne was wearing the emeralds," a guest may recall, or "Anne wore the big diamond." The latter, set in a ring, is the so-called Vargas diamond, which was purchased from Harry Winston and is of such dimensions that Mrs. Windfohr is unable to bend the finger she is wearing it on. She has an emerald ring almost as large and, complementing it, a necklace of five large emeralds separated by four slightly smaller pear-shaped diamonds. Her sapphire necklace is of similar design but contains a few more stones. While Julius Cohen was changing planes in Fort Worth on his way to the West Coast a few months ago, he phoned Mrs. Windfohr from the airport to say hello, and was invited, as he has recalled, "to come by for a quick look and some coffee. The quick look brought a quick sale of my Primavera necklace [intertwined platinum and gold branches bearing a few dozen diamonds], and I was on my way West again a few hours later."

A practical woman, Mrs. Windfohr likes to get the good out of her jewels, and customarily has some on display both day and night. At lunch, for instance, she may wear earrings of lapis lazuli and jade and a matching string of beads, as well as a number of rings, all of the pieces being generously proportioned. "Anne usually wears a good deal more than other women could manage," a friend has remarked, "but on her it all looks perfectly right. She was made to wear jewels. All of them are in faultless taste, of course, like everything else she wears." At a recent costume ball given by the Jake Hamons, Mrs. Windfohr's jewels attracted more than usual attention. "Anne was dazzling as an Oriental goddess," one of the guests said afterward. "She was wearing her latest, biggest diamond, that you'd think even a goddess couldn't afford. 'Harry says it's the third-greatest rock in the world today' is the way she described it. It was a little less blinding than a locomotive headlight."

Once a year, a number of Texas millionaires and their wives, when attending social affairs held in connection with such popular annual events as the Southwestern Exposition and Fat

Stock Show, in Fort Worth, and the Houston Fat Stock Show and Livestock Exposition, deck themselves out in elaborate Western getups. Some of the less inhibited—mostly the gay ones lately arrived at the millionary estate—use these occasions to engage in a lively competition to see who can devise the most sensational, eye-catching costume. Much careful thought goes into the planning of these so-called cowboy and cowgirl outfits (actually, of course, they come close to being parodies of the real thing), which are almost always custom-made, and are designed and put into production months before they are to be worn. The cowgirl outfits, consisting, as a rule, of a blouse and either trousers or skirt, together with matching hat and boots, frequently cost as much as one of the higher-priced gowns in a Paris collection. The men's outfits, equally expensive, are often conceived to complement—or, in a common local phrase, "go cute with"—their wives'.

Though every livestock exposition and fair in the state is brightened by a certain number of memorable costumes, opening night at the Fat Stock Show in Houston is as hard to beat for sheer glitter as first night at the Met. At a recent opening, according to the Houston newspapers and other periodicals that give the event wide coverage, Mrs. Bernard Sakowitz, the blond wife of a Houston specialty-shop owner, was acclaimed the best-dressed cowgirl. She was attired from head to toe in an outfit of shimmering gold kid, relieved by a wide-brimmed white hat, white earrings, and white boots. Among the other fashion leaders, Mrs. J. Collier Hurley, wife of an oilman, appeared in a rather conservative pink ensemble featuring her three French poodles, while Mrs. Bill Williams, wife of a restaurant owner, favored a mint-green suit decorated with several pounds of silver fringe and complementary dazzling hat and boots. Her husband, who was judged "best-dressed cowboy" by the fashion editor of *Houston Town*, was elegantly turned out in an iridescent suit of white and gold, and looked, according to the magazine, "like a bright early-morning sunrise." Williams bested many other aspirants, including C. M. (Pete) Frost, an oilman, rancher, and hunter, whose outfit was notable for, among other things, a snakeskin tie imported from Italy (another somewhat unusual tie on view was made of sterling silver) and alligator boots trimmed with jaguar fur, the materials for which Frost supplied from animals he had personally killed.

The most consistently resplendent couple to grace Houston's show in recent years has been Mrs. A. B. Lawrence, a handsome brunette, and her husband, a Baytown rancher whose clothes George Fuermann has described in the Houston *Post* as "what a bashful cowboy might wear if he happened to have a fortune of several million dollars and a taste for extreme luxury," adding, "But his wife's outfits go considerably beyond that point. It would seem safe to say that she is the only woman in the world who has an off-the-shoulder cowgirl outfit. It is a fire-truck red as to color, and on Mrs. Lawrence's figure, superior to a bikini on a movie starlet." Both Mrs. Lawrence and her husband generally arrive in Houston for the show with a couple of dozen complete changes of Western costume, which they bring in a pair of Cadillacs. His is white and hers is pink.

Chapter Eight

To say, as everybody does, that Neiman-Marcus has done more than any other store to influence the dress of Texas women, especially the rich, is to speak the truth but by no means the whole truth. Neiman-Marcus long ago passed the point of being merely a famous store; it became an institution. Indeed, the Alamo excepted, Neiman-Marcus has for years been the most celebrated institution in Texas. More than that, it has gradually developed into a stylish shrine with an international following. Its roster of charge-account customers includes devotees residing in all fifty states, as well as in England, France, Italy, and thirty-six other foreign countries.

The fame of Neiman-Marcus is no accident. For half a century, it has assiduously been calling attention to itself with practically every known means of communication short of sky-writing. More pertinently, Neiman-Marcus is in fact the most noted commercial ornament in the Southwest (if not, perhaps, of "really unequalled stature . . . in the market places of the world," as a recent Neiman ad declared). George Sessions Perry, a native Texan and a gifted writer, was so bewitched by Neiman-Marcus that he lamented all his life his inability to summon words of sufficient power and glory to describe the store properly. To do so, he once said, one would have to "burn butane on Olympus' highest crag." Still, he never gave up trying. "Many folks look at Neiman-Marcus and see only a breathtakingly beautiful store," he wrote in one of his best efforts. "This is like a rancher looking at wild flowers and seeing only cow feed. Neiman-Marcus is a state of mind. Almost a state of grace." Mrs. Edna Woolman Chase, the independent-minded former editor of *Vogue*, was similarly transported. "I dreamed all my life of the perfect store for women," she once said. "Then I saw Neiman-Marcus. And my dream came true!" Outpourings such as these are accepted by the Neiman-Marcus people with admirable, if by now not unexpected, equanimity. After all, their leader, Stanley Marcus, has himself in recent years taken to speaking matter-of-factly of his place of business as "a magic land."

In its terrestrial form, at least, Neiman-Marcus provides a striking reflection of its president, who is sometimes referred to on the premises as Mr. Stanley, to distinguish him from his two younger brothers—Edward, executive vice-president, and Lawrence, a vice-president. Collectively, the three are known in Dallas as the Marci. In appearance, Mr. Stanley, who is fifty-six, heavy-lidded, and olive-skinned, is a paragon of neatness and subdued elegance—qualities that, by no coincidence, are also the chief physical characteristics of the three stores that at present make up the Neiman-Marcus operation: one in downtown Dallas, which has always served as headquarters; another in the suburb of Dallas called Preston Center; and the third, and newest, in the business section of Houston. (A fourth unit, similar to the one in Preston Center, is scheduled to open in the Ridglea section of Fort Worth in the fall of 1962.) The downtown-Dallas store, a six-story structure with an unadorned façade of terra-cotta and buff limestone, bears a resemblance in size and in its clean exterior lines to Bergdorf Goodman. Inside, Neiman-Marcus is distinguished by a feeling of spaciousness, which results from a combination of high ceilings, wide aisles, freestanding fixtures, unbacked window displays, and immaculate housekeeping. Anybody who walks around the store in the company of Mr. Stanley soon finds out why it is as spotless as an operating room. Wherever the "beady-eyed chief," as the help sometimes fondly refer to him, goes, he is constantly touching counters, merchandise, display materials, and, perhaps unconsciously, an occasional clerk with the middle finger of his right hand, which he then inspects for evidence of dust. Should any appear, the chief glowers—a sure sign that trouble impends in magic land.

Even the discovery of a particle of dust, however, does not rob the merchant prince—to use another of his appellations, and one that he rather fancies—of the obvious pleasure he derives from taking a guest on a conducted tour of the store. "Ours is not, as some people who have never been here think, a department store," Mr. Stanley explains in the course of his tour talk, "although, as a matter of fact, we do a larger volume of business than any department store in town. Actually, we are a collection of thirty-one separate but integrated specialty shops." Approaching the jewelry department—or, in Neiman-Marcus terminology, the Precious Jewelry Salon—Mr. Stanley calls attention to a diamond necklace displayed in a showcase by itself. "That is priced at a million dollars," he says. "If times hadn't changed, the logical buyer would be King Farouk. He used to be one of our best jewelry customers." At a counter a few steps from the Precious Jewelry Salon, Mr. Stanley casually picks up a thimble. "Sterling silver, imported from Italy," he says. "The price is two dollars and fifty cents. A two-fifty thimble to a million-dollar necklace—that gives you some idea of the range and of the basic idea. It's not price we care about—it's quality."

As he walks about the store, Mr. Stanley takes particular pride in pointing out what he calls specially developed merchandise, which consists of things originated by somebody connected with the store, often the merchant prince himself. These articles are then made up and sold exclusively at Neiman's. For instance, Mr. Stanley had the idea for shoes made of velvet manufactured by the Italian mills that supply cloth to the Vatican, and for matchboxes bearing on the cover an original painting by a contemporary Italian artist. The matchboxes, aiding art and commerce concurrently, are sold in the stationery department, where one may also buy a telephone stand that, should the owner be called away from the phone, plays music during his absence to the party at the other end of the line. "A bit of Southwestern hospitality," Mr. Stanley remarks.

Then, stepping through the bronze-and-silver doors of one of a bank of elevators set in a slab of Swedish marble that extends from floor to ceiling, he escorts his guest to the second floor, where the most expensive clothes are offered, and where Mr. Stanley has personally sold over six million dollars' worth of furs. His main interest here is in directing the sightseer's attention to oil portraits of two of the store's founders—his father, Herbert Marcus, and his aunt, Mrs. Carrie Marcus Neiman. In 1907, these two fashion pioneers, together with Carrie's husband, A. L. Neiman, all of whom had previously worked in department stores, launched the specialty shop bearing their names in a small two-story building in Dallas, a city on which they had rather ambitious designs. "Any fine store can dress a few women beautifully," Herbert Marcus remarked when the store opened. "Our idea is to dress a whole community that way." He pursued the idea single-mindedly until his death, in 1950, whereupon Mrs. Neiman, who had been divorced in 1928 (her husband afterward enjoyed a successful merchandising career in New York), took over as chairman of the board. She had seldom missed a day working in the store, and from the beginning had had a strong influence on the management of the business. Long before her death, in 1953, she was generally acknowledged to be the elder stateswoman of fashion in Texas. "She was a beautiful, sad-eyed woman with almost faultless taste," Mr. Stanley says, moving on toward the third floor and the Sports Shop, where both his wife and Mr. Lawrence's wife worked before they were married. Mr. Edward's wife, before her marriage, was employed as a fashion editor in New York. Besides experience in the fashion business, the wives of the Marci share extraordinary good looks.

After strolling through shops offering other kinds of apparel, as well as china, glassware, linen, and antiques, Mr. Stanley winds up the tour on the fifth floor, which houses a restaurant called the Zodiac. Across the center of this room—which seats two hundred and forty and is open every business day for lunch and tea—stretches a raised, curved promenade upon which models continuously show clothes and accessories. "The restaurant loses about forty thousand dollars a year," Mr. Stanley says, "but it's worth all that and more as a means of bringing customers into the store." Not the least of the Zodiac's attractions is its décor; it is done mainly in shades of blue, including the granulated sugar on the tables.

A woman of taste and perception who is herself the proprietor of a fashionable New York shop recently made her first visit to Dallas and, embarking on a busman's holiday, spent a good while looking around Neiman-Marcus. "Two things struck me," she said afterward. "First, the housekeeping, which is fantastic. Second, the atmosphere, which was a surprise—the store has no sense of humor." The basically sober spirit that pervades Neiman-Marcus reflects another aspect of Mr. Stanley's character. While he appreciates a practical joke, especially a complicated one, he is otherwise inclined these days to take himself as seriously as he takes life. Back in the twenties, as an undergraduate at Harvard, he impressed the home-town folks as a mildly madcap figure with an amusing overlay of pomposity; returning to Dallas for Thanksgiving vacations, he would buzz around town and sit through football games wearing a voluminous raccoon coat, despite temperatures in the eighties, and he customarily appeared at formal parties in full dress with a wide red ribbon draped across his shirt front. Little pleasantries such as these he abandoned abruptly after he graduated, in 1926, from the Harvard School of Business Administration and went to work in the store. He has since become, according to *Town & Country*, "a one-man definitive oracle on what constitutes good taste in all Texas."

The metamorphosis no doubt explains Mr. Stanley's solemnity. Oracles don't make jokes if they want to stay in business. And if they want to get ahead, it is essential that they possess a talent for that combination of art, science, and humbuggery known as public relations. To Mr. Stanley, the talent has been given in abundance. It is, in fact, doubtful whether he has a peer, when it comes to public relations, among practicing oracles. Most of his waking hours, and apparently his night thoughts as well, are concerned with publicly relating Neiman-Marcus in one way or another. To this end he employs a public relations department whose principal job, he has said, "is to sell Neiman-Marcus throughout the world as a magic land." As a first step in pursuit of its peculiar Grail, the department is prepared to furnish journalistic sorcerers and their apprentices with a kind of basic magic kit containing a bibliography of all the significant articles that have been written about the store, as well as mimeographed copies of most of them; a book titled "Neiman-Marcus Texas" by Frank X. Tolbert; and an eight-page, single-spaced, documented collection of anecdotes titled "Tales of Neiman-Marcus," prepared by a University of Texas professor as part of his doctoral thesis.

"One of the earliest Neiman-Marcus tales concerns a woman from Electra, Texas, an oil town near Wichita Falls," the scholarly work begins. "About 1927, this woman appeared in the Neiman-Marcus store barefooted and in a sunbonnet. She announced that she wished to purchase a mink coat. When she had selected a coat, she paid for it on the spot with currency. The sales force at Neiman's, sensing an exceptional opportunity, also sold her a pair of shoes." However mystical the goal set by Mr. Stanley for his public relations department, it is hardly less arcane than the one to which he has committed his advertising department. Its aim, he says, is "to translate and transmit Neiman-Marcus." Obviously, this means something to the advertising people at Neiman's; otherwise, they could not consistently turn out newspaper advertising—stylish, handsome, and often in color—that is probably more attractive than anything of the sort being produced here or abroad.

When, as frequently happens, the store feels like transmitting on the editorial wave length, it includes in its newspaper advertisements a column of opinion called "Point of View," which, according to Mr. Stanley, "gives Neiman-Marcus its own voice in things of civic, state, and national interest, and perhaps tends to humanize the concrete and brick of our buildings." The column is signed "Wales," the pseudonym of the store's youngest vice-president, a thirty-three-year-old native of New York named Warren Leslie, who reached Neiman-Marcus by way of Exeter, Yale, and the Dallas *News*. In his humanizing efforts, Leslie, who affects a long cigarette holder and an awesomely casual manner, has touched on an assortment of topics ranging from a complimentary article about a newly engaged conductor of the Dallas Symphony ("Having been away for a couple of weeks, last Monday's symphony concert was our first of the season. It is absolutely extraordinary what Maestro Paul Kletzki has done with this orchestra in less than a month"), through mood pieces on spring, fall, and Christmas, and endorsements of Red Skelton, Arthur Godfrey, the Royal Danish Ballet, and various books, plays, and other cultural fare, to an impatient chiding of the citizens of Dallas for displaying "an almost total lack of interest in anything associated with the mind."

If Neiman-Marcus were to depend only on its myriad public-relations and advertising activities, it would get attention at least as good as that enjoyed by any other enterprise of its kind, but good enough, as they say in Dallas, is not at all good enough. "We try," says Mr. Stanley, "by doing things that are newsworthy to keep our name in front of the world, not just Texas." As a result of the try, which is made in the name of sales promotion and is formidable, unremitting, and global, Neiman-Marcus takes on the aspect of a repertory theatre. Its most venerable attraction is a weekly fashion show. This has been staged without interruption for over a quarter of a century, and is now put on every Wednesday at noon (admission two-fifty, including lunch) in the Empire Room of the Statler Hilton Hotel. For a great many Dallas women, attending the show is a weekly ritual, like church.

In the first week of September, the fall theatrical season gets under way with the annual Neiman-Marcus Fashion Exposition. After a whirlwind round of pleasure, including a rodeo at Mr. Edward's ranch and a dinner dance at Mr. Stanley's house, seven hundred and fifty formally attired fashion designers, apparel manufacturers, and out-of-town customers who have paid thirty dollars each for tickets (the proceeds go to a civic or charitable organization) arrive at the Grand Ballroom of the Sheraton-Dallas to attend the Exposition Fashion Show. This is an elaborate affair at which some forty mannequins (at times augmented by Saint Bernards, leopards, and other live props) display over a million dollars' worth of apparel, including clothes bought at the Paris collections the preceding August, complete with accessories, furs, and jewels. The show is climaxed with the presentation by Mr. Stanley of what are known as the Neiman-Marcus Awards—silver-and-ebony plaques "for distinguished service in the field of fashion." With characteristic diffidence, Mr. Stanley refers to the awards as "the Oscars of the Fashion Industry." They have been presented in past years to fashion creators like Chanel, Adrian, Schiaparelli, Gardner Cowles and his former wife Fleur, Scaasi, Hattie Carnegie and Cecil Beaton, as well as to fashion consumers, as the store refers to this small group of distinguished customers, including Dolores Del Rio, Gloria Swanson, Mrs. Leland Hayward, and Dinah Shore.

Because the Exposition, which Neiman's quietly describes as "the most famous show (and week) in the world," provides the store with considerable publicity and attracts Neiman-Marcus aficionados from all over, Mr. Stanley feels that the yearly stunt is well worth its cost, which amounts to some thirty-five thousand dollars. As a man who deplores waste in any form (upon finding that the marble originally used to floor the Man's Store was too slippery for magic land, he had the slabs taken up and relaid as a terrace at his home), Mr. Stanley has in recent years allowed another business concern to share both the expenses and the promotional benefits of the Exposition. In 1957, for example, the Exposition was co-sponsored by Rolls-Royce, which sent from England a caravan of twenty-one new and ancient models, worth half a million dollars, to be used in parades and other events connected with the festivities.

The customers had scarcely caught their breath after that

year's Exposition when Neiman-Marcus whirled into a production so spectacular as to make anything they had tried before about as exciting as a January White Sale. This giant stunt, called the French Fortnight and staged in October, was the pièce de résistance of the store's fiftieth-anniversary celebration. More than two years in preparation, the Fortnight was sponsored jointly by Neiman-Marcus and the French Comité Permanent des Foires et Manifestations Economiques à l'Etranger and brought to Dallas a swarm of celebrated French citizens, sixty-five of whom arrived on an Air France flight direct from Paris. First off the plane was the Mayor of Dijon— a city that had been selected for "twinning," apparently because its name also starts with a big "D"—who kissed the Mayor of Dallas, R. L. (Bob) Thornton and made him blush. Other imported notables included the aviatrix Jacqueline Auriol; the French cover girl Marie-Hélène Arnaud; a hundred and twenty business executives, representing not only *la haute couture* but such other fields as Pommery champagne, Lanvin perfumes, Baccarat crystal, Christofle silver, and Faré gloves; the writers Pierre Daninos and Louise de Vilmorin; and the millionaire artist Bernard Buffet, who felt right at home.

To the astonishment of the visitors, not to mention any West Texas cowboys who happened to be in town, the exterior of Neiman-Marcus had been decorated for the occasion to resemble a row of French shops, and the entire first floor had been transformed into a three-dimensional replica of the Place de la Concorde, on which real French cars—Renaults, Simcas, Citroëns—were parked. Almost exact replicas of a Hermès and a Dior boutique, with both merchandise and staffs from Paris, were installed on the second and fourth floors. A group of French artists, using giant photomurals, converted the Zodiac into an imitation of Maxim's. There the Fortnight was officially opened with a twenty-five-dollar-a-plate lobster and champagne dinner, at which the principal speaker was French Ambassador Hervé Alphand. From then on, Neiman's was awash with Gallic doings. For the first week of the Fortnight, the menu of "Maxim's" offered a daily specialty flown in from the

Paris Maxim's; thereafter, it was prepared by the head chef of the Liberté, on loan for the occasion. Elsewhere, the store featured French glassware, linen, silver, textiles, periodicals, and so on. Every afternoon, the Chambre Syndicale de la Haute Couture presented a special fashion show; eight Paris mannequins modelled clothes by Balmain, Carven, Catherine Sauve, Dior, Charles Montaigne, Claude Rivière, Maggy Rouff, Nina Ricci, and Raphaël—a show that could never, of course, be found in Paris or anywhere else.

Not only Neiman's but the whole town went Frenchy. The Municipal Auditorium offered an exhibition of French tapestries; the Dallas Museum of Fine Arts featured a collection of twenty-three Toulouse-Lautrec paintings lent by France's Albi Museum; the Rotarians, Kiwanians, and Lions honored the visiting businessmen at luncheons; the supper clubs featured French entertainers; the movie houses showed French films; M. Daninos and Mme. de Vilmorin addressed the students at Southern Methodist University; Professor Lon Tinkle, the best talker of French born in Texas, worked happily around the clock interpreting; the Mayor of Dijon kept on kissing people; and the newspapers praised the enterprise in classic Americanese as "a downright inspiration in friendly relationships hitched to the legitimate development of trade." The inspiration cost approximately four hundred thousand dollars, slightly more than half of which was contributed by the French government, French industries, and Neiman-Marcus suppliers. "This is producing direct, cold-cash business," Mr. Stanley said along about the fifth day of the Fortnight, when the store had already sold most of the imported merchandise. "But," he added hastily, "it is more than just a luxury show—it is cultural and intellectual as well." On all counts, the French Fortnight proved such a success that Neiman's has gone on turning the store and parts of Dallas upside down again and again with British, South American, and Italian Fortnights, all dedicated to cold cash and hot culture.

"One of the reasons we get involved in promotions as spectacular as Expositions and the Fortnights," Warren Leslie, who has the general responsibility for putting them on, has explained, "is that we have a very different problem from that of New York stores. None of our local customers 'lives in town,' so to speak. They all live from five to fifteen miles away, even the Dallas ones. To come downtown they must fight parking, traffic, and so forth. A store such as ours would die if we depended on drop-in traffic. We must stage things as spectacularly as possible in the effort almost to force our customers to come down and shop with us." By whatever means the customers arrived, they rang up sales in 1959 of $41,507,842, giving Neiman's a net profit after taxes of $1,145,187. Nine out of ten people who shop at Neiman's are charge customers (including Abe Burrows, who refers to Mr. Stanley as "the Duveen of Texas"); some two thousand of the store's charge accounts range between two and five thousand dollars annually, four run to fifty thousand, and one to more than a hundred thousand.

Beneath the surface appeal of Neiman-Marcus as an extraordinary store lies its basic fascination—its function as a mirror that reflects the community. The primary characteristic of Neiman-Marcus customers is, to judge by the store's treatment of them, a mass inferiority complex in matters of fashion and taste. They are by no means illiterate in these respects—after all, Neiman's has been trying for over half a century to teach the whole community how to dress beautifully—but, as the store tirelessly insinuates, its customers still stand in need of constant help, which Neiman's is able to supply. In fact, according to Neiman dialectics, nobody can supply it better, because the store has all the answers—or, in its more elegant but no less forthright phrase—it is "the authority." It always has been, fortunately for Texas and its millionaires. "Many of these millionaires," Mr. Stanley explained to Frank X. Tolbert, "never had the money [in their early days] to buy fine clothes for themselves or their families—to provide comfortable, gracious décor in their homes. But because there was a recognizable authority in the form of a store a hundred miles away, they were able to avoid many of the pitfalls of the rich.

. . . They were willing to be guided, because they recognized an authority on which they could depend." The store seldom misses an opportunity to emphasize its continuing dependability as an "authority"—a word that turns up in Neiman-Marcus talk with remarkable frequency. "We expect our advertising to always underline our fashion authority," Mr. Stanley says. A newspaper advertisement assures the customers that the store is "doing everything humanly possible to fortify our fashion authority." The Exposition "underlines annually our supreme fashion authority," Warren Leslie says. He adds that Rolls-Royce, by co-sponsoring the 1957 Exposition, reaped the benefit of having Neiman-Marcus "put our stamp of fashion authority on their product."

As the chief authoritarian in residence, Mr. Stanley has explained that "all the store's communication devices are intended to make merchandise mean something to a lot of people to whom it would mean nothing until the merchandise had been authenticated. In the minds of thousands of customers we supply that authentication, and thereby we create a wantability and decision to buy." How Neiman-Marcus strives to create wantability was classically illustrated a while ago in a half-page newspaper advertisement that appeared shortly before the Metropolitan Opera opened its annual season in Dallas. "Neiman-Marcus Opera Libretto," the advertisement was headed. "Information no opera-goer should be without, concerning what to wear for each performance, the right accessories, and even what your husband should wear!" There followed a series of black-and-white drawings accompanied by text that read, "Opening Night. 'Il Trovatore,' by Giuseppe Verdi. You wear a full-length dress (here, Dior's yellow lace sheath, 495.00); your escort, white tie and tails. Saturday Afternoon, the beloved 'La Bohème,' by Giacomo Puccini. Attend it in a sophisticated print, such as this Traina-Norell dotted surah, 210.00. Your husband should wear his newest dark silk suit. Saturday Night, hear Renata Tebaldi in Verdi's 'La Traviata.' Go gala in short, flowing chiffon by Traina-Norell, 485.00 Your husband? In dinner jacket, of course.

Sunday Afternoon, the delightful 'La Périchole,' by Jacques Offenbach. Plan ahead—wear a silk ensemble like this Blotta design, 265.00. You'll shed the jacket for a final opera celebration Sunday evening." The husband apparently would be unable to take in the Sunday performance, since Neiman's neglected to tell him what to wear. Attendance at all four performances would have cost an opera-lover whose wantability had been properly stimulated a total of $1,455.00, not counting the price of admission.

Once a piece of merchandise has been authenticated, it is entitled to bear the Neiman-Marcus label, which, according to Mr. Stanley, signifies that the product is "tops in fashion, taste, and quality." But that is not all it signifies. Mr. Stanley has convinced himself, and for years has waged an incessant campaign to convince others, that the Neiman-Marcus label, like the rosette of the Legion of Honor, automatically confers distinction. Playing on the communal insecurity, he has concentrated on inculcating the idea that the Neiman-Marcus label is the equivalent of a safe-conduct, permitting the bearer to pass freely through all social lines. Customers accepting this notion are naturally relieved of the burden of exercising their own taste; they need only to make sure that everything they buy carries the magic badge. The store does all it can—especially with advertisements harping exclusively on the label— to help the community remember this comfortable concept. For example, in a recent half-page persuader showing a couple who are obviously tops in fashion, taste, and quality sitting in a restaurant that might be in Dallas or Paris or Hong Kong, attention was focussed on the label in the lady's coat, draped ever so carelessly over the back of her chair. "All the world loves a Neiman-Marcus label," the message read in full.

"Not long ago," according to a story in a recent "Point of View" column, "one of our customers received from her family a handsome birthday present, a very beautiful mink stole. As a joke, the family sewed the label of another store over our own. When the birthday girl opened the present and saw the stole, she was delighted. When she saw the label, she burst into tears and said it would have to be returned immediately. Calm was brought about only after the top label had been removed and ours exhibited." Neiman's has launched another venture designed to add still one more facet to its emblem. It takes the form of a series of advertisements offering handsome antiques—a silver wine cooler made in 1836 by Paul Storr, an eighteenth-century Meissen figurine, a silver tray, dated 1814, by William Pitts. Each advertisement features a facsimile of the maker's signature—"W.P.," for example—and next to it the store's label in script. "Twin hallmarks of excellence—Neiman-Marcus . . . William Pitts," the copy says, placing the hallmarks in what the store evidently considers the proper order. The Neiman-Marcus label is thus presumably invested with rich historical dimensions, despite the fact that when Pitts and the others were putting hallmarks on their creations, the present site of Neiman-Marcus was a rather bleak spot, where, as the Dallas *Times Herald* has remarked, "even the more cultured races of Redskins in America could have found nothing," except perhaps a few uncultured Indians turning out unsigned arrowheads.

Customers who have been trained up to the point where their faith in the Neiman-Marcus label is unquestioning form that rather sizable group who, in Mr. Stanley's words have "proudly become devotees of the Neiman-Marcus state of mind." Some customers progress beyond that; for them, Neiman-Marcus becomes a way of life. Besides buying all their clothes at Neiman's, the confirmed devotees put in a regular appearance at the weekly fashion show, lunch in the Zodiac, and drop in there for tea; they consult Mr. Stanley and members of the store's staff, including a full-time professional counsellor, on the proper dress for various occasions; they attend the Exposition Fashion Show and Grand Ball, as well as the cocktail parties, dinners, luncheons, and other events held in connection with stunts like the international Fortnights; and they seek Mr. Stanley's advice on what college their daughter should attend, what wardrobe she should take along, and what gown she should be married in, among other things. Their husbands can also participate in the full life through the Man's Store, where they will find that the clerk who waits on them is, as the advertisements say, "more than just a salesman! He's a friend . . . a welcome critic . . . an authority on proper dress . . . a mindreader . . . knows what you like (almost better than you do) . . . also knows how to get tickets, where the town's best steak is, this winter's number one resort." After a good steak, Neiman's customers can turn to the store's Travel Bureau to make their resort arrangements, or if interested in the Old World, they can sign up for the annual, month-long Neiman-Marcus Continental Tour of Europe. For tickets to Broadway's shows, they need only drop a word to the store's New York office. (It has so far supplied customers with nearly two thousand tickets to "My Fair Lady.") For some of its out-of-town customers whose football weekends in Dallas have been unusually colorful the store has obligingly furnished bail.

Because of this close, if not unique, involvement with the community, Neiman-Marcus is a reliable conversation piece—to use one of the store's favorite expressions—practically everywhere in Texas. Whereas few New Yorkers spend much time discussing, for instance, Bergdorf Goodman's influence on the city or the personality traits of its executives (if, indeed, the customers could conjure up their names), many Texans never seem to tire of talking about the Marci and the effect their glittering emporium has had on Texas. Opinion on the subject is divided. Mrs. Edgar Tobin, once described by a friend as "the Mrs. August Belmont of San Antonio," expresses the affirmative view. "Texas has a group of extraordinarily well-dressed women," Mrs. Tobin, herself a very stylish figure, has said, "and the reason is that they have been very largely influenced by Neiman-Marcus. I think the store has served a great purpose." The contrary viewpoint has been voiced by an outspoken matron who informs acquaintances that she is descended from a third-generation Texas family. "It is hard for outsiders to realize the bitter dislike that we of the Old Guard have for that store," the Old Guardswoman once informed a dinner companion. "We think they 'take on'—they try so hard to be something more than they are. It's that awful pretentiousness we cannot abide." Probably as sensible a comment as any ever made on the topic of marathon interest was contributed at a dinner party by a beautiful but astute Dallas woman whose background includes New York, Palm Beach, and Newport. "Say what you wish about Neiman-Marcus," she coolly observed, "but let me ask you one thing—what would Dallas be like without it?"

Chapter Nine

In many ways, a more interesting question than what Dallas would be like without Neiman-Marcus is the reverse: What would Neiman-Marcus be like without Dallas? Today, of course, Neiman's draws its trade from all over, but how, the speculation goes, would it have fared if the founders had originally set up shop in Houston or San Antonio or anywhere else in Texas? Even the store's oracular headman has no sure answer, but it may be indicative that Neiman-Marcus had been in business for nearly fifty years before venturing to open a branch in Houston, its first outside Dallas, and that Houstonians responded by staying away in such numbers that the branch operated in the red for at least its first two years. It took Dallas—"a place that's on the make," as Mr. Stanley has described it—to appreciate Neiman-Marcus right off, and when Dallas appreciates a thing, its success is assured. Dallas likes to be *for* something, especially something in the mode. "Dallas has a 'chic' complex," says the architect O'Neil Ford, a former resident. The city also has a compulsive attachment to growth, which it equates (as is the American habit) with progress. Dallas citizens are convinced that by putting their shoulders to the wheel, to borrow a popular localism, they can put their city so far over the top that it need take a back seat to no other, New York included. It is typical of the sky's-the-limit philosophy of Dallas that it fancies itself in direct competition with New York. That explains why the Dallas *News* made no effort to conceal its glee when commenting editorially on the results of a recent special census that showed a small decline in New York City's population. By contrast, the paper announced, Dallas is growing at the rate of two thousand new residents a month, and at present has a population of some seven hundred thousand. The editorial purveying this gratifying intelligence was titled "Rosy Dallas Outlook."

If anything about Dallas doesn't look rosy, especially compared with any other Texas city, Dallas citizens pitch in and make it so. A while back, for example, they realized that their zoo was not up to snuff. Instantly, the Dallas Zoological Society summoned its members to a "kickoff meeting," listened to Mayor Thornton explain how a bigger and better zoo would "benefit the city economically by bringing customers into Dallas stores," and pledged support of a campaign to raise three hundred thousand dollars for expanding and shining up the zoo. The campaign was a splendid success, partly because of the publicity it received under the direction of the Society's president, E. M. (Ted) Dealey, who is also president of the *News,* and whose paper for a spell printed so many animal stories and pictures that it looked as if Noah had been made editor. Dealey was also among the prime movers in a memorable civic adventure of the middle thirties, when Dallas set itself up in competition against all other Texas cities to be selected as the site of the state's centennial celebration. Dallas won, not because it had a superior historical claim—as a matter of fact, when Texas won its independence from Mexico, in 1836, Dallas, unlike Houston and San Antonio, hadn't even been settled—but because it had the wit and daring and gumption to put up the biggest guarantee.

The same tactics were used to bag the Metropolitan Opera, which in 1939, after a dozen years of persistent entreaty by a Dallas merchant and music lover named Arthur Kramer, finally offered to include Dallas in its spring tour if the city would furnish a guarantee of sixty-five thousand dollars. Kramer, after making a few phone calls to other boosters, informed the Met that Dallas would be pleased to make the guarantee an even hundred thousand. (The guarantors have never been called upon to put up a cent.) Art lovers in Dallas are also full of get-up-and-go. Three years ago, they were fretting because the city lacked a museum devoted to modern art, a deficiency more galling because no other large Texas city was so deprived. A committee was formed to rosy up the Dallas outlook on art. Today, the Dallas Museum for Contemporary Arts is housed in a modern two-story air-conditioned building, which was bought for four hundred and twenty-five thousand dollars, has eighty-four hundred square feet of floor space, and so is larger—at least in area—than anything like it in the state. Members are now busy filling the new museum with pictures. This may take another three years.

Since Dallas heroes are those who do something to make the city grow, it is no wonder that so many plaudits have been heaped on Robert Lee (Bob) Thornton, a tenant farmer's son who started work picking cotton at eleven, is now board chairman of the Mercantile National Bank (and, of course, a millionaire), and recently completed his fourth consecutive term as Mayor of Dallas. "Bob Thornton," a fellow civic leader and millionaire named Jack P. Burrus once declared, "has done more for his and our Dallas, that he loves almost more than members of his family, than any four or five men combined have ever done in its entire history. He is more than Mr. Dallas; he is Mr. Big. Every resident of the community," Burrus added, in phrases typical of community life in Dallas, "should thank his God for having had, and for being privileged to have, Bob Thornton's leadership." Although Thornton, who is eighty, declined to run for a fifth term (he was succeeded in the spring of 1961 by a millionaire businessman named Earle Cabell), he remains, according to a local Ford dealer's newspaper advertisement hailing him upon his retirement, "Mr. Bob—Mayor Forever!" The perpetual mayor's philosophy of municipal leadership reflects his own refreshingly uncomplicated nature. "You gotta build a city," he says. "The damned things don't grow like mushrooms."

It would be hard to find a more impressive illustration of the efficacy of the Thornton forced-feeding treatment than Dallas, a city that, according to the rules, should never have been created, much less have survived. It has no water transportation of any kind—the largest city in the world to hold that peculiar distinction. Though the "rat-tailed Trinity River," as Walter Prescott Webb has called it, flows, in a manner of speaking, within the city limits, it is not navigable, and is so eccentric that it has been referred to as "that often unpredictable drainage ditch." Furthermore, Dallas, at the time of its incorporation as a town, in 1856, was not at or even near the center of anything; the closest railroad was several hundred miles away. The area had none of the natural underground resources—oil, gas, sulphur—that contributed to the growth of other Texas cities. In short, Dallas was born without so much as a wooden spoon in its mouth. To what extent, one might wonder, does the almost hectic activity that characterizes the present behavior of the people of Dallas result from a haunting uneasiness, going way back, that comes from being committed to a never-ending struggle to make something out of nothing, a struggle that calls for a bold and constant mockery of both logic and nature?

Whatever its effects today, the effort proved too much for the city's founder, a native Tennessean named John Neely Bryan, who brought Dallas into existence as a city. Setting the pace early, Bryan not only designed the settlement but served as its first lawyer and postmaster, and ran a business besides. He eventually cracked under the strain, reached for the bottle, and ended his days in the state mental hospital. His successors have plainly been made of stronger stuff, endowed with vast determination and sensational loyalty. As the Fort Worth *Democrat* remarked as far back as 1872, the first thing Dallas parents teach their children to say is "Hurrah for Dallas!" The cheering has never ceased, nor has the growth of the city. Big D, as the natives actually refer to it, now ranks as the fourteenth largest city in the country. "It's the people who get the credit—nothing else," the Dallas real-estate operator B. Hick Majors has remarked. "The people who came here were daring and optimistic. They fed in first from the small towns. Then, as the city grew, they began coming in from the

North and from other parts of the South and West. These people had the energy of the Yankee and the thrift of the New Englander, and they took on the optimism of the Texan. But, most important, no matter where they came from, they right away picked up the great old Dallas tradition of go-go-go."

Being always in such a hurry, Dallas has had to develop its municipal personality on the run. As a result, its communal character gives the impression of being sketchy, not filled out, unjelled, offering no promise of hidden depths, no secrets. Everything is on the surface: youthfulness, pride, desperate ambition—a combination that naturally wells up from a community on the make. One trait above all dominates the Dallas personality—reverence for business. If, as Calvin Coolidge so trenchantly observed, the business of America is business, Dallas may well be *the* All-American city, for it is a city of the businessmen, by the businessmen, and for the businessmen. It got that way, of course, not by choice but by necessity. Short-changed by Providence, the settlement that later became known as the Athens of the Alfalfa Fields wisely pinned its hope for survival on making the most of its instinct for trade.

Today, Dallas is the banking capital of the Southwest (twenty-seven commercial banks, including two of the nation's thirty biggest); ranks as the country's third-largest insurance center; has more planned industrial districts than any other city; has expanded the number of its manufacturing establishments to nearly two thousand; has added more than fifteen thousand business concerns since 1946, thereby sparking, in the same period, the biggest office-and-store construction program (twenty-six new major office buildings in the past decade alone) of any American city except New York; has developed its municipal airport into the third-largest in volume in the Western Hemisphere; and has now become the fastest-growing city in the United States, according to the Dallas Chamber of Commerce. The Dallas Chamber, naturally, has the largest membership, in proportion to population, of any in the country.

From Mayor Cabell down, the government of Dallas rests securely in the hands of businessmen, predominantly millionaires. All eight members of the Dallas City Council are businessmen. So are the hundred and seventy-five "dydamic men," in R. L. Thornton's memorable phrase, who make up the Dallas Citizens Council, the city's most influential civic organization. Members of the Citizens Council, according to its bylaws, cannot be mere run-of-the-mine businessmen but either "presidents or general managers of business enterprises" doing business in Dallas County. Because of this stipulation, Council members are known locally as "boss men." Working behind the scenes, the Council decides what is good for the citizens of Dallas, and then sees that they get it. The boss men are equally effective when moving in the opposite direction. If the Council considers something to be not good for the local citizenry, members give it what they humorously call "the reverse application."

The consensus in Dallas is that the Council has done an admirably vigorous foursquare job of promoting the city, including the encouragement of what the *News* has described as "a wealth of cultural activities." Every boss man in town is keen about elevating the cultural tone. "I'm for the Symphony one hundred per cent," Mayor Thornton once advised an orchestra official who had called on him in connection with a fund-raising drive. "The Symphony is good for Dallas. I'll be glad to do anything I can to help it, as long as you don't ask me to attend any concerts." The boss men's united cultural and civic front, like nearly everything else in Dallas, is another manifestation of the noted American talent for enlightened self-interest. "Sure, we fight like hell with each other," Mayor Thornton has said, "but when it's for Dallas—then it's 'Line up, boys!'"

A few boys in Dallas do not believe that lining up on order necessarily represents the ultimate in civic virtue, but they are about as scarce as a sale on tombstones. Furthermore, they mind their public manners, or, as de Tocqueville said of the backstage dissenters he encountered, "they hold a different language in public." To all appearances, therefore, the existing benevolent regime has almost unanimous support; unbelievers either have been successfully rehabilitated or have willingly become expatriates, like O'Neil Ford, who gave up Dallas for San Antonio, the most cosmopolitan and attractive city in Texas and one that, its citizens proudly point out, isn't growing very fast, compared to other major cities in the state. "As for Dallas," Ford said a while ago, "the main business up there is defending the status quo. Keep in line. There is an underlying current of —well, one doesn't want to call it reaction, but it's almost that. And, of course, some of it is bound to get out and affect the whole atmosphere. They'd be the last to admit it, but the people in Dallas are ill at ease."

Perhaps nothing brings the latent uneasiness to the surface more quickly than critical comment, however slight, that a visitor may make about any aspect of the city. The residents are particularly sensitive about its appearance, and with some reason. Anthony Sampson, taking a look at the city in connection with the British Fortnight, remarked, in the London *Observer*, "It is not, on the face of it, a very promising setting. Dallas must have a claim to be the bleakest city in the world. It makes Johannesburg seem pretty." That is not quite cricket, really, but Dallas does, by comparison, enhance the beauty of (to pick a couple of places closer to home) cities like Charleston, South Carolina, and Tucson, Arizona, which lie on approximately the same latitude.

For reasons that it doesn't take a visitor long to discover, sightseeing buses do not make up the most flourishing business in Dallas, though since 1957, the Dallas Transit Company has been offering, for two dollars and a half, a daily "Scenerama" Sight-seeing Tour. It takes two hours and covers many memorable sights, such as office buildings and factories; the Public Library; Union Station; the suburbs of Highland Park and University Park, where the bulk of the millionaires live; the Dallas Theatre Center; Highland Park Methodist Church (circa 1920); Southern Methodist University; and the State Fair Grounds, the city's cultural hub, reached by traversing a slum area inhabited by Negroes, who comprise approximately one-fifth of the city's population. The permanent cultural installations at the Fair Grounds—or Fair Park, as it is officially known—include the Dallas Museum of Fine Arts, the Museum of Natural History, the State Fair Auditorium, and the Cotton Bowl. Returning to the city's center, a sightseer can take in such other attractions as the Central Expressway, the Municipal Auditorium, and both the Masonic and Scottish Rite Temples.

His tour completed, a visitor is likely to be left with the impression that Dallas is "distractingly regular," as Dickens, with considerably less reason, remarked of Philadelphia. "After walking about it for an hour or two," he wrote, "I felt I would have given the world for a crooked street." Few people except letter carriers feel compelled to spend that much time walking around Dallas, even in its showcase section, known as "the downtown." This is a surprising conglomeration of handsome skyscrapers, like the Republic National Bank and the Southland Center, which rise in the midst of a motley of parking lots, hot-dog stands, pawnshops, and other shoddy structures. Directly across Main Street from Neiman-Marcus, for example, stands a row of unsplendid buildings housing a newsstand that specializes in out-of-town newspapers and girlie magazines (with a pool parlor in the back room), a ramshackle lunchroom and beer bar called Jack's French Fries, and the Central Shine Parlor, whose bootblacks drum up trade by shouting from the entrance at passersby. On nearly all downtown streets, a stranger is likely to be impressed—particularly in view of the city's wealth—by the number of blind beggars and other mendicants in some sort of physical distress.

Dallas has recently embarked on a program not only to get the beggars off the streets and to rid the city of small-town stigmata, such as commercial signs overhanging the sidewalks, but to renovate the entire downtown area. The first stage, now under way, consists of arousing strong dissatisfaction with the area in its present condition. (Furious self-criticism, if properly inspired and directed, is encouraged in Dallas, as it is in other striving communities around the world.) Newspapers and civic leaders, tackling the initial phase of the face-lifting project with characteristic Dallas enthusiasm, have engaged in what to an outsider would seem an almost embarrassing orgy of vilification. "Dallas has beautiful skyscrapers—and dirty feet," said Angus Wynne, Jr., upon assuming the chairmanship of the newly formed Beautify Greater Dallas Association. "Dallas is beautiful from a distance, but close up there's visual chaos," said an architect imported to advise on the urban-renewal project. John Rosenfield, the music critic of the Dallas *News* and widely regarded as the cultural Pooh-Bah of the entire Southwest, also joined the knock-Dallas circle, saying, "It is a 'dead' city after nightfall, unless one knows the suburban spots, and then it is none too lively." A three-column headline on page 1 of the *Times Herald* declared, "DALLAS CALLED CITY SICK WITH SLUMS." No chance was missed to low-rate the heart of the city. "DOWNTOWN DREARY IN RAIN," read the headline on one newspaper article ("The small old buildings seem like mourners huddled together at a funeral"), while another went so far as to complain, "DALLAS SIDEWALKS LACK EYE APPEAL."

Dallas isn't as bad as all that, though room for improvement is patently not lacking. And it is just as plain to anybody acquainted with Dallas, which, as the *Times Herald* noted the other day, "is barely older than Grandma Moses," that improvement is bound to come. Still, the renovating process, regardless of its extent, is not likely to rob the city of its essential character. After all, what radical innovations need be feared in a community dominated by the philosophy of bankers and insurance men? Inasmuch as the future of Dallas, no less than its past, depends on trade, the "melancholy air of business" that Dickens found so widespread in America will not quickly be dispelled. So it seems safe to predict that when Dallas dons its new suit of clothes, its municipal personality will change no more than that of the star salesman who becomes sales manager. No matter how grand its trappings, Dallas will remain at heart a drummer.

Though only twenty-nine and six-tenths miles of new six-lane turnpike separate downtown Dallas from downtown Fort Worth, the two cities stand about as far apart in character as the city mouse and the country mouse. According to the masthead of the Fort Worth *Star-Telegram*—the larger of two newspapers in a city of approximately four hundred thousand —Fort Worth is "Where the West Begins" (Dallas, according to the old saw, is "Where the East Peters Out"), and a visitor soon encounters enough phenomena popularly associated with the West to make him think that the motto tells the truth. For one thing, genuine cowboys, something of a rarity in Dallas or anywhere else in East Texas, suddenly become a common sight. In the old days around Fort Worth, they used to say the cowboy was king; there is evidence that he has not yet really been deposed. A noticeably large share of the people in the hotel lobbies are cattlemen, easily identifiable by their ranch suits and wide-brimmed hats. Many of them have been making business trips to Fort Worth for twenty years or more without once going over to take a look at Dallas. They have seen pictures of the new, shiny, skyscraping Sheraton-Dallas and Statler Hilton, and read all about them, but they prefer to keep on giving their trade to Fort Worth hotels, like the Texas and the Worth—Texas-owned institutions not given to putting on airs. Fort Worth doesn't lack the usual physical attributes of a big city—it has the customary pyramidal skyline (distinguished by the new First National Bank Building); traffic congestion; attractive residential sections (those around the River Crest and Ridglea country clubs, where mainly millionaires live, are considered choicest); an extensive park system, which includes five large artificial lakes; and other such things—but the over-all impression created by the entire layout is that of a not very large Western town, and a rather tacky one at that. In contrast to the chromium-plated gloss of Dallas, Fort Worth has the faded silver-gray look of a weathered barn—undeniably picturesque and improbably appealing.

In nearly every outward respect, Fort Worth lives up amply to its nickname—Cowtown. Residents attend the Cowtown

Drive-In Theatre, eat at the Cowtown Grill, listen to radio station WBAP, whose identification signal is a cowbell, and so on. Whereas Dallas has at least one public restaurant that serves Continental food, Fort Worth's best-known eating place is the Cattlemen's Steak House, which specializes in steak and baked potatoes, and is situated, appropriately, near the stockyards. (A few doors down the street from the Cattlemen's is the well-known Leddy Brothers establishment, turning out handmade boots, saddles, and chaps.) The marketing and processing of livestock has long been a major Fort Worth industry, though its largest today is aircraft production, in which it ranks second to Los Angeles. While the public event that currently creates the greatest sensation in Dallas is the opening of the newly formed Civic Opera Company, starring Maria Callas, the big turnout in Fort Worth is for the old-established Southwestern Exposition and Fat Stock Show, featuring Roy Rogers and his wife, Dale Evans.

In typical contrast, too, is Fort Worth's largest and best-known retail establishment, a block-square department store called Leonards. Like Neiman-Marcus, Leonards is a brotherly enterprise, being headed by J. Marvin (Mr. Marvin) and Obadiah P. (Mr. Obie) Leonard, a pair of Texas farm boys who entered the retail business in Fort Worth shortly after the First World War with a capital of six hundred dollars and a gift for handling all kinds of distress merchandise and bankrupt stocks, from cribs to coffins. Within a dozen years, their original twenty-five by sixty-five-foot quarters, across from Court House Square, had expanded over an entire block. Then, moving slightly uptown both in location and in merchandising methods, the brothers put up on an adjoining block a three-story air-conditioned building that thereupon became Leonards (or Leonard Frères, as it is sometimes waggishly referred to), while the old, lower-priced store, continuing in business, took the name of Everybody's. Before opening the doors of the new place, Mr. Marvin gathered his managers together for an indoctrination talk on matters of policy. "A great many people say we're making the mistake of our lives, moving from our junk-store location," Mr. Marvin told the assembled employees, as one of them later recalled to the writer Neil Clark. "They say we'll lose our old customers and won't get new ones. Whether or not that's so, I believe, depends on you. I'm sure every old customer will come at least once to see the new store; if he feels at home, he'll come again. He's been used to spitting on the floor in the old store. If you see a customer looking for a place to spit on your nice new floor, walk in front of him and spit, so he'll think that it's the thing to do. If you see a woman looking for a chair to nurse her baby, get her one, or tell her to sit on the piece-goods counter."

By making the customers feel mighty to home—the carpet covering the second floor seems to be composed equally of patches and original material—Leonards has grown without interruption, to the point where it has some fifteen hundred employees and does an annual business estimated at more than fifty million dollars. Crowded and noisy, the store sells everything from common pins to tractors, likes to think of itself as the Gimbels of the Southwest, and has long since turned the founders into millionaires. Though both still come to the store daily, they now have extensive outside interests in real estate, oil, insurance, and, partly as a hobby, country clubs. Back in the late twenties, Mr. Marvin took up golf at his doctor's suggestion, and became so enthusiastic about the sport that he decided Fort Worth ought to have a championship course. He accordingly bought a hundred-and-fifty-seven-acre tract of land, and built the Colonial Country Club—the first course in the Southwest to have bent-grass greens. The National Open and many other notable tournaments have been played on the Colonial course since it was opened, in 1936. Mr. Marvin sold the Colonial layout to the members a few years later, but he has subsequently been involved in the building of a couple of other golf clubs, which have been constructed on a scale of ascending grandeur. Aside from his penchant for the links, Mr. Marvin's main extra-business interest is church work. Mr. Obie's is Scouting. He has received the Silver Beaver Award, the highest honor a Boy Scout council can bestow. Both brothers, though they are now accustomed to seven-figure wheeling and dealing, have remained plain-spoken, down-to-earth, and civic-minded. Along with many other forward-looking Fort Worth millionaires, they share a serious interest in making a municipal silk purse out of Cowtown.

"It's only recently that people here have been attracted to anything that didn't involve a high degree of manure," a native Fort Worth millionaire who also happens to be a Princeton graduate remarked a while ago. "In the past, just about everybody was a rancher, or wished he were, and about all that people cared about were cows and bulls and horses. That gave the town a definite flavor of manure. It's still around—I read in the paper the other day that Fort Worth continues to be the horse capital of the world—and it won't go away overnight. But give this place a few years—and some luck—and it'll come out smellin' and lookin' like a rose. We hope." The reason for the qualified local optimism (in Fort Worth they don't go in much for the double-your-money-back-if-not-satisfied kind of positivism so popular in Dallas) is the limited success so far achieved in adopting the so-called Gruen Plan, an ambitious scheme, devised by Victor Gruen Associates, to renovate the entire business district so drastically that it will look like Sunday-supplement drawings of the Dream City of the Future.

To enlist public support for the creation of this commercial Garden of Eden, a Chamber of Commerce committee, headed by Sam Cantey III, a banker with so many civic interests that he is sometimes spoken of as "a strictly *pro-bono-publico*-type guy," has sponsored a series of stirring illustrated lectures to scores of civic groups and to numerous other collections of two or more people willing to listen. Probably the most tireless backer of the plan is the man who initiated it—J. B. Thomas, president of the Texas Electric Service Company, "The Gruen Plan will cost a hundred million dollars over fifteen to twenty years," Thomas has said, "but what's that to a city like this?" More than small change, apparently, for bond issues to finance several components of the plan have been turned down by Fort Worth voters. Though stalled, the project continues to be pushed hard by local boosters for a variety of reasons, not the least consequential being the storied Fort Worth urge to needle Big D. "If the Gruen Plan is adopted, it will make Dallas a satellite of Fort Worth." Mrs. J. Lee Johnson III, an enthusiastic advocate of the plan, has remarked, showing the old-time spunky spirit that would have pleased her father, the late Amon G. Carter, history's most gifted Dallas-baiter.

For more than a quarter of a century before his death, in 1955, Amon Carter also enjoyed the reputation of being the First Citizen of Fort Worth—a fact not likely to escape a visitor arriving by plane at Amon Carter Field and subsequently driving past the public school, the art museum, and the numerous other memorials bearing Carter's name. Small, agressive, and supremely self-confident, Carter operated on the principle that he would do all the civic work as long as he got all the credit. "Amon was a gladiator," Mayor Thornton, of Dallas, once observed. "But this same ambition produces a weakness in city building." However that may be, Carter showed plenty of strength in keeping things stirred up. "That man," John Nance Garner said when Vice-President, "wants the whole government of the United States to be run for the exclusive benefit of Fort Worth."

Carter was a blacksmith's son who left school after the eighth grade to wait on tables and work as a "chambermaid," as he liked to put it, in a boarding house, at a weekly salary of a dollar and a half; he wound up owning the Fort Worth *Star-Telegram*, radio stations, real estate, and various other properties that brought him great wealth. This he spent with a free hand to amuse himself and to promote Fort Worth, which amounted to the same thing. He made a determined point of cultivating the friendship of the celebrated—presidents (particularly of the United States), financiers, generals, admirals, industrialists, actors—whom he entertained with other guests (often a thousand or so at a time) at his Shady Oak Farm. To let his guests know they had reached the place where the West begins, Carter liked to summon them to a meal by mounting his palomino and galloping at high speed around the premises, meanwhile letting go with a pair of six-shooters. Any advance for Fort Worth, especially the attraction of new industry, elated Carter, but the triumph was sweeter if it was gained at the expense of Dallas. So finely honed was Carter's competitive sense, the stories have it, that whenever business required him to spend a day in Dallas, he carried a box lunch in order to avoid contributing to the city's prosperity. By word and deed, he spiritedly encouraged friends and business associates to pursue a similar economic policy. As a result, a Fort Worth matron has recalled, wives of men wishing to remain in Carter's good graces made a practice of removing the labels from anything surreptitiously bought at Neiman-Marcus (in Mr. Stanley's view, the supreme sacrilege) and replacing them with labels from a Fort Worth store. (It is hard to imagine Carter's sharing Mr. Stanley's belief that Neiman's new store in Fort Worth will create what he has called "general euphoria" among the citizens there, because "it will give them a feeling they have arrived.") When, despite the exercise of Carter's notable talent for persuasion, Fort Worth lost out to Dallas as the site of the Texas Centennial, Carter turned a typically jaunty trick by engaging Billy Rose—then in his Purple Period—at a fee of a thousand dollars a day, to put on a rival celebration called the Frontier Centennial. Its main attraction was "Casa Mañana," an elaborate musical staged by Rose and John Murray Anderson on what was ballyhooed as the world's largest revolving stage, and featuring Sally Rand, Paul Whiteman's orchestra, and some of the other choicest talent that money could buy. Carter advertised his offering, a tremendous success, with the characteristically pungent slogan "Go to Dallas for Education, Come to Fort Worth for Entertainment."

Inspired nose-thumbing like that comes naturally to Fort Worth, a community that began earning a reputation for independence and boisterousness even before Ed Terrell, back in the eighteen-sixties, opened the town's famous original civic center, which went under the name of the First and Last Chance Saloon. Since then, Panther Town, as it was called with ample justification (if originally only in derision) in the old days, has been tamed, but its communal personality has suffered less disturbance in the domestication process than that of many another Texas city. Compared to Dallas, for instance, which has become, in John Rosenfield's descriptive term, "synthetic," Fort Worth has remained distinctly natural, and this probably accounts in large part for the fact that visitors often get the impression that people in Fort Worth are indeed as open, direct, and friendly as people in Texas, according to the legend, are supposed to be.

In contrast to Dallas millionaires, who appear frantically determined to prove their sophistication, Fort Worth millionaires seem to take theirs quietly for granted. They act as if they knew and were satisfied with who they are, and consequently they are considerably more relaxed. In fact, they tend to spend part of their time exploring the possibility that there may be something more important, or perhaps just more entertaining, than making a few extra millions or adding another peak with their name on it to the skyline. Not that they lack ambition or community pride; rather, with them ambition is not sleepless and the skyline is not a religion. "Hucksterism is almost unknown in Fort Worth," a local capitalist named Robert Dupree has remarked. "Not much of the social life here is oriented around business. The lives of the men I know are oriented around their families. That's why the Fort Worth Club, where you'll find the men congregating during the day, is virtually deserted at night. Everybody's home."

Not only does the city offer few nocturnal public pleasures and palaces ("After nine o'clock," a young woman recently arrived from the West Coast has observed, "you can shoot a rifle down any street with no worry about hitting anyone") but Fort Worth millionaires seem to share the poet's notion about home, be it ever so grand. At any rate, it may be indicative that at the time the establishment of a contemporary-art museum was a high-priority civic project in Dallas, people in Fort Worth were working on plans to add a wing to their Children's Museum, which is the country's largest, is considered by some experts the best, and has no counterpart in Dallas.

Fort Worth has also supported the Reeder Children's School, a private institution patterned after New York's famous King-Coit Children's Theatre and directed by the artist Dickson Reeder and his red-headed wife, Flora.

Entertaining at home—another straw in the wind—is much more frequent in Fort Worth than in Dallas, and the custom is dictated not by necessity but by choice. Though it is true that Fort Worth's leading and, for practical purposes, only public restaurant is the meat-and-potatoes Cattlemen's, it is also true that the food served at two of its country clubs—Ridglea and Shady Oaks—is prepared by French or Swiss chefs under French or Swiss maîtres d'hôtel, and is, in the opinion of some itinerant eaters, superior to any fare easy to come by in Dallas. One other hint of the difference that twenty-nine and six-tenths miles can make: While the Dallas Museum of Fine Arts was putting on a large and worthy show called "Religious Art of the Western World," the Fort Worth Art Center was offering a lighthearted and worldly exhibit called "Nudes." Thus do the contrasts multiply, all somehow indicating that the point of the fable about the wise mouse who has enough and is happy with it has not been lost on Fort Worth.

Chapter Ten

Judged by the way we live now, Texas millionaires, taken together, are quite adequately housed. Still, it must be acknowledged that their shelter, compared with that of the less repressed rich who graced the American scene at the turn of the century—the original millionaires, so to speak—comes dangerously close to substandard. Consider the living accomodations of Leo Corrigan, a Dallas real-estate operator worth something over a half a billion dollars. He lives in a neat suburban house, built in 1929 on a hundred-foot lot, that has nine rooms and two baths, and cost forty thousand dollars. That is just sixty-six rooms, thirty-eight baths, and four million one hundred and sixty thousand dollars less than went into the dwelling that Charles Schwab put up in 1905 on Riverside Drive. To be sure, Schwab's place had a few conveniences Corrigan has denied himself, such as a swimming pool of Carrara marble, a gymnasium, bowling alleys in one of the sub-basements, a billiard room with ten tables, and a private chapel containing a marble altar that cost precisely what Corrigan paid for his house and lot. Another latter-day millionaire, Jake Hamon, lives a few miles away from Corrigan in a white Colonial frame house for which he put out forty-seven thousand dollars in 1946, or approximately seventeen million dollars less than Henry Clay Frick did for his block-square marble-and-limestone quarters on Fifth Avenue. The place that Algur H. Meadows, one of the richest oilmen in Texas, calls home is an English Tudor stone-and-brick structure, set on some five suburban acres, that real-estate men figure might sell for as much as five hundred thousand—the sum that another oilman, John D. Rockefeller, Sr., spent every year to maintain his seven-thousand-acre, thirty-million-dollar spread near Tarrytown. B. G. Byars, of Tyler, lives the year round in a house of sixteen rooms, or not quite half as many as Cornelius Vanderbilt provided for servants in his five-million-dollar Newport cottage, which he used ten weeks of the year. Early in 1960, John Mecom, of Houston, picked up some cash by selling a fraction of his oil properties for an even twenty-seven million, but he has been content to stay on in his eighteen-room château-type residence, which would have fitted handily into Edward Stotesbury's hundred-and-thirty-room Whitemarsh Hall, in Philadelphia, with ample space left over to hold half a dozen other Super-Americans' residences, including the one belonging to H. L. Hunt, who is first in assets among his fellow-oilmen and lives in an outsize replica of Mount Vernon that needs painting.

In their preference for shelter that would have been considered embarrassingly modest by the original millionaires, the Super-Americans are simply reflecting the current tendency of the rich everywhere to favor the soft pedal in public performance. But here again some Texas millionaires carry the thing too far, not only in holding on to old low-cost houses but also in building new ones. At a time when the national average spent on millionaires' new houses is, according to *Fortune*, roughly two hundred and fifty thousand dollars, a substantial number of Texas millionaires are skinning by with places that cost half that much.

As a rule, the bargain hunters choose a contractor-built ranch-style house with twelve or fourteen rooms, an attached two-car garage, and a basic price of around a hundred thousand, to which twenty-five thousand is usually added for various extras, such as a swimming pool and sunken bathtubs. These unassuming structures, stretched out next to one another in suburban developments, are so similar in design that they can hardly avoid looking like de-luxe row houses. "For these people, buying a house is like buying a car," a Texas architect once said. "They want to see the finished product before they put down their money." The assembly-line quality of much Super-American housing makes a quick and puzzling impression on visitors who have a special interest in the subject, such as William Haines, the former movie star, now in the decorating business. How does it happen, he asked his Fort Worth friend Edmund Schenecker, the founder and president of one of the largest trucking concerns in the Southwest, that Texas millionaires exhibit taste in clothes, paintings, music, and many other things and yet build houses that are—especially in relation to the means available—generally quite ordinary? "Well, you've got to remember that down here we're not too far removed from the log cabin," Schenecker replied amiably.

While the majority of Super-Americans' dwellings may be as basically conventional as the log cabin, a host of others display a fine distinctive touch, the Scheneckers' among them. It was designed in the shape of a fan, and was strikingly decorated by Mr. Haines. He was later engaged by the Scheneckers' friends the Robert Windfohrs to restyle their traditional house, which he transformed into a Super-American show place by adding an enormous wing, known as the Pavilion, which is made up of a gallery, a solarium, a game room, and a bar, all with floor-to-ceiling glass windows and terrazzo floors, and all so subtly connected as to give one the feeling of being in a single airy, almost limitless room. In decorating the addition, Haines was not without the help of Mrs. Windfohr, a woman of taste and purpose who is sometimes referred to by her friends, with affectionate awe, as Anne the Great; a lifelong art collector, she had on hand a number of useful objects to set off the Pavilion, including some exquisite pieces of Oriental sculpture, and paintings by Rouault, Picasso, and others of that company.

Another remarkable Fort Worth dwelling, the Andrew Fullers' unmonotonous contemporary house, contains no square or rectangular rooms; instead, the library is circular, the dining room is diamond-shaped, and the rest of the rooms are otherwise variously formed in order to achieve what the architect considered the best use of the site. In San Antonio, Tom Slick recently built a dazzling, half-million-dollar contemporary mansion that has a number of novel features, such as a Japanese bath, and is spacious enough to inspire his friends to speak of it as the Slick Hilton. Frank Lloyd Wright is represented by two houses in Super-America; he came close to building more. At one time or another, several of the up-to-date natives toyed with the idea of having the Master build them a place and some went as far as to commission plans, but the projects always foundered. In the last decade of his life, Wright finally came upon two Texas millionaires willing to go all the way—John Gillin, of Dallas, and William Thaxton, Jr., of Houston—and each, after the customary delay of a few years caused by unexpected construction problems, such as finding the building site to be of solid rock, has moved into his new abode, content in the knowledge that he inhabits not only, as Wright put it, "the finest residential example of organic architecture" but "one of the world's most beautiful homes."

Super-America also offers many examples of beautiful unorganic homes, such as the one in Dallas that belongs to Pio Crespi, an Italian cotton merchant of aristocratic bearing who lives with his Texas-born wife in a white stone French château that was designed by Maurice Fatio and is situated in a manicured, parklike setting. Like the Crespis', the Robert Vernon Kings' residence, in Houston, is elegantly formal, full of antique furniture and crystal chandeliers (one belonged to Mme. Pompadour), and all very French, even its name—Villa Roi. At Boerne, near San Antonio, the Ralph Fairs have a traditional residence that is also imposing. "Actually, the house isn't quite as long as a football field," a frequent guest has remarked, "but it comes close. The driveway leading up to it from the road is just a mile. The house is fieldstone on the outside and all eighteenth-century on the inside, or at least that's the way it was the last time I was there. The place changes all the time, because Ralph and Dorothy won't stop working on it. They must have spent at least a million dollars on the remodelling alone."

Easily the most impressive collection of traditional houses in Super-America is situated in the River Oaks section of Houston, which dates as a residential area from the early twenties, when Will Hogg, son of the renowned Governor of Texas, and a few other prominent citizens founded the River Oaks Country Club and divided some twelve hundred acres around it into plots for members' residences. Developers subsequently built on all sides of the original tract, with the result that the area now generally known as River Oaks covers roughly five thousand acres. Wooded, intersected by wide, curving streets, and meticulously maintained, they are probably the most attractive five thousand residential acres in the country. They contain some five thousand houses, on pieces of property running from half an acre up to fourteen acres. An average-size lot sold recently for thirty-five thousand dollars. Houses in River Oaks also fetch respectable prices. The Herbert Townsends, upon moving to Paris early in 1960, put theirs—a five-year-old place with a master bathroom done in turquoise mosaic, "to match Mrs. Townsend's eyes"—on the market for three hundred and forty-five thousand dollars.

Other houses in River Oaks have cost more to build, such as the massive English Regency dwelling designed for Hugh Roy Cullen by John Staub, who was also the architect for the estimable residence of Miss Ima Hogg. An architectural reflection of its occupant, this little mansion, done in the manner of a Louisiana plantation house and situated amid fifteen acres of magnificent gardens, has great dignity and charm, and no pretension. These qualities are also apparent, and for the same reason, in the most appealing contemporary house in River Oaks—the handsome residence designed by Philip Johnson for the John de Menils. More than one guest approaching its classically simple façade of soft-red brick broken only by a pair of glass doors has found the house suggestive of a museum of modern art, and so has not, upon entering, been astonished to find that it is just that. The de Menils, both of whom are French by birth (she is from what an English acquaintance has called "the *haute-société-protestante* Schlumberger family"), are among the country's leading collectors. Not all of their pictures are in their River Oaks house, for the de Menils (along with the majority of Super-Americans) have a few other places to live, including an apartment in New York and another in Paris.

The de Menils have not, however, fully developed the knack that some indigenous wheeler-dealers have for diversifying their shelters as widely as their investments. In both respects, Clint Murchison has been a trail blazer. The place that he called home for about a quarter of a century was a comfortable twenty-five-room Dutch Colonial house just outside Dallas, which he had built by two brickmasons and a carpenter in 1936 for about a hundred and fifty thousand dollars. The house had nine bedrooms, one with eight beds—"so a group of us boys can talk oil all night," Murchison once explained. Last year, he and his elder son John, who had been living with his wife and three children in a twelve-room house, did a little interfamily wheeling and dealing and wound up trading houses. When the elder Murchison feels like getting away from it all, which is often enough so that his wife has learned how to pack up on ten minutes' notice, he has to make a choice. If he wants a very short trip, he drives out to his Bluebird Farm, about forty miles from Dallas. If he wants to fish, he climbs into his private plane and flies down to El Toro, his thousand-acre island in the Gulf of Mexico. If he wants to go to the track, he flies out to California and drops in at Del Mar, putting up in nearby La Jolla at the Del Charro Hotel, which he owns. If he hankers for privacy, he tells the pilot to head for Acuña Ranch, his seventy-five-thousand-acre ranch deep in Mexico's Sierra Madre mountains.

The Murchisons and their guests are obliged to fly into the Mexican retreat, since the nearest highway is about forty miles distant and the ranch can be reached only over trails almost impassable by cars. When Murchison acquired the property, there was nothing on it but grassy hills, trees, and an abundance of deer, quail, wild turkeys, and other game. Under his supervision, a twenty-room U-shaped ranch house was built of native stone hand-carved by Mexican artisans. Practically everything that went into the house, aside from plumbing fixtures, kitchen equipment, and plate-glass picture windows—which were shipped from the United States and carted in—was made at the ranch from local materials. After stocking it with cattle, Murchison put up a dozen or so other structures, including a school, for the ranch hands. "It sounds presumptuous," he once remarked to a visitor, "but what I've created here gives me a feeling of achievement. I feel I have really got me a place."

When, in 1953, Murchison developed an interest in using scientific methods to revive worn-out land, he wound up, not unexpectedly, with still another place, this one consisting of two thousand acres in East Texas near Athens, his birthplace. Marshalling a small army of men and machines, he cut a road system through the woods, cleared a thirty-three-hundred-foot landing strip, dammed a stream, made a lake and stocked it with fish, built a house for the manager of the property and a rambling glass-walled, cork-floored contemporary one for himself, and landscaped the place with transplanted oaks, magnolias, and pines. He also set out ten thousand pine seedlings and ten thousand strawberry plants. ("Clint does almost everything by ten thousands," one of his friends has explained.) The Athens property, which now has six privately stocked lakes, has been transformed from a sorry wasteland into a flourishing show place, and Murchison goes there often. "Some men got to have their feet in the city," he has said. "I've got to have mine in the soil." This sentiment is shared by John Murchison and his attractive wife, who have also built a contemporary house on the site, overlooking a swimming pool.

Murchison's other son, Clint, Jr., likes to keep his feet firmly in Dallas, where he recently put up a one-story house that spreads over an acre of ground; contains two dining rooms and a children's wing, among other conveniences; and, according to informed estimates, cost about a million dollars. This figure includes the expense of landscaping the twenty-five acres around the house and the installation of three swimming pools, of varying depths, connected in a cloverleaf pattern. Since the majority of second-generation millionaires make an obvious point of choosing relatively modest shelter, the younger Clint's new quarters have raised an eyebrow here and there among his contemporaries. His older friends are more understanding. "After all," one of them has said, "it's the only place he's got."

Perhaps because they have so many opportunities for practice, Texas millionaires often display an unusual talent for performing that indigenous American rite, the showing of the house. This rather formalized ceremony has been commented on by Europeans, who are likely to know people for years without once being invited to their homes, much less shown around them. "The Englishman," Walter Lionel George said, "is not accustomed to the spaciousness of American hospitality. We are not accustomed to being shown a house in detail—the labor-saving appliances at work; told the story of the pieces of furniture, of the pictures. The Americans are never weary of this, because their vitality is enormous." None are more vital than the hospitable Texas millionaires, who do a house-showing with remarkable thoroughness, even to opening closets for inspection. A Super-American in Wichita Falls invited a few hundred guests to a housewarming and, being unable to give each the usual personally conducted tour, considerately turned on the lights in all the closets and left the doors open, thus permitting a check not only on the house but on the owners' luggage. A visitor who had been treated to an exceptionally intensive house-and-grounds showing in Fort Worth was touched when his host, putting his hand on still one more doorknob, asked, "Would you care to see the basement?" (air-conditioning machinery, small gymnasium, indifferently stocked wine cellar).

It is not unusual for devotees who have witnessed house-showings in various parts of Super-America to come away with the impression of having seen, again and again, an almost identical collection of expensively furnished model rooms. The lack is not of taste, only of style. Often handsome, the houses are generally as impersonal as a calendar, and could belong to anybody with money. But not all of them, of course. The impeccable collection of Early American furniture with which Miss Ima Hogg has decorated her house expresses her innate sense of style no less than the ermine jacket she wears to the opening of the Symphony. A relaxed assurance and kind of careless grace are also implicit throughout the de Menils' house. The living room, for example, combines a modern sectional lounge; French chairs upholstered in apricot-colored leather; a large and elaborately carved black Victorian rocker, more or less reserved for the head of the household; and, on a wall adjacent to the light-flooded garden court, a huge Braque. Among the estimable pictures in the entrance hall, the de Menils have placed a weatherbeaten wooden figure of Pan that originally decorated a circus calliope. It took a sense of self-reliance for the F. Kirk Johnsons to frame the fireplace in their Fort Worth residence with a pair of enormous tusks from an elephant shot by their son. V. L. Evans, of Houston, showed an equally individualistic spirit by making a living-room rug from the hide of a prize bull that accidentally choked to death six months after Evans had bought it for twelve thousand dollars.

Yet for every house that strikes a blow for a sane decorator policy there are a dozen that look as if they had been furnished à la Conrad Hilton, to suit well-heeled interchangeable tenants. The sense of standardization stems largely from the fact that, with a very few exceptions, most Super-American women have their houses done by decorators, whose word is followed with awed obedience. In a Dallas house, a decorator set a vase on the mantel; to make sure the ornament would always be returned, after dusting, to just the right place, the hostess immediately pencilled a circle around its base. In a Houston house, a decorator installed an exceptionally long sofa and scattered along its back a great many small pillows of different colors. "But what happens if they get mixed up?" the worried chatelaine asked. She was given a color chart showing the proper position of each pillow.

The decorators' informal monopoly may also account for the fact that the interior colors in Super-American houses seem to be restricted to tones of sandy beige, like the landscape itself, and therefore hardly productive of *esprit décor*. One spot of color in many houses is provided by an oil portrait of the owner, sometimes in the direct line of sight of a visitor coming in the front door. Another feature common to Super-American houses is a hi-fi system to provide music in most rooms and around the pool—which is also standard equipment. Still another, of course, is air-conditioning. All the millionaires' houses are supplied with an air-conditioning system, and some, like the Andrew Bradfords' new pink stucco Party House, in Midland, with two systems, in case one should break down. Since efficient air-conditioning depends on it, windows are generally kept closed and, in addition, are shaded with draperies, Venetian blinds, or awnings, and sometimes with all three. The result is that Super-America, which has more air-conditioned houses than any other state, is developing a race accustomed to living in perpetual semi-darkness.

Super-Americans are also demonstrating that it is possible to sustain life over long periods while drawing only an occasional breath of fresh air, for it is not only their houses and clubs that are air-conditioned but also their cars, stores, theatres, diners and barbecue stands, garages, restaurants, hotels, banks and office buildings, museums, hospitals (human as well as dog-and-cat), and practically every other inhabitable facility. One day last August, the Dallas *News* columnist Paul Crume has reported, a Dallas matron, feeling that she had been spending too much time indoors, left her air-conditioned house, drove her air-conditioned car to the air-conditioned lodge of some friends at Lake Texoma, and spent a few days fishing from their air-conditioned pier.

Since the land, which in general is as ornery as the climate, also calls for conditioning, landscape architects come close to being Super-America's indispensable citizens. They are also apt to be among a millionaire's best friends. Marie Berger, who, with her late husband, Arthur, has probably done the most notable landscaping in the area, could, if she wished, spend all her leisure time in the company of millionaires with whom she has dealt professionally. Joseph Lambert, officially not a landscape architect ("Just a bushman," he says) but no doubt the most popular earth mover and shaker, is on friendly terms with so many millionaires that he drops their names as casually and inoffensively as he does a customer who shows a base inclination to put money before beauty. The California landscape architect Thomas Church is "Tommy" to a number of Texas millionaires whose earth he has transmuted.

It is customary for a Super-American landscaper to refer to a professional assignment as "doing a garden," a term that, in local usage, means landscaping all the property around a residence, including the walks, swimming pools, fountains, dining patios, and other usual embellishments. Thus, to do a garden in Super-America generally demands more than a green thumb. For example, when Paul Moss, a lawyer and rancher who lives in drought-prone West Texas, asked the Bergers to do his garden, he said he wanted fifty-seven acres of lawn. Easily arranged, the Bergers said, though the occasional absence of rainfall for a few years at a time might make a maintenance problem. "If you can plant the grass," Moss said, "I can take care of it." The Bergers could and did, and so, with a sprinkling system supplied by half a dozen new wells, has Moss. To complement the E. L. DeGolyers' residence (described variously as a "massive fortresslike hacienda," as a "Mexican-style palace," and, by DeGolyer himself, as "a Los Angeles architect's idea of what a Mexican rancher should have if he struck oil"), the Bergers designed a widely celebrated tropical garden, complete with producing banana trees.

The leading exhibit in the ten-acre garden of H. Lutcher Brown, a San Antonio oilman, is a large walled area planted exclusively with white azaleas. In the past, Brown has lavished time and money on the garden, even building a plant to acidize the water used in it. Recently, however, his neighbors have heard he has become so concerned about the future of capitalism in this country that he is contemplating economy measures—shutting down the acidizing plant, among others—even though, according to another San Antonio capitalist, he replenished his cash position a while ago by selling one of his companies for ninety million dollars. Thrift was not the first consideration in the assignment handed the Bergers by Charles F. Urschel, another San Antonio oilman. Urschel—who figured in the news in 1933, when he was kidnapped by George (Machine Gun) Kelly and released after the payment of a two-hundred-thousand-dollar ransom—decided a few years ago to build a new house, and picked a site that had a splendid view but was otherwise somewhat unpromising, the entire tract being sheer rock. "There wasn't an ounce of topsoil on it," Arthur Berger once recalled. "That didn't bother us—we just brought topsoil in by the ton—but the planting was a little difficult." Since Urschel had specified a rather large garden, and one that wouldn't look brand-new, the Bergers first selected a hundred and fifty trees, varying from twenty to thirty feet in height and averaging twenty-five hundred dollars apiece in price. These were planted in holes blasted out of the rock at a cost of six hundred dollars a hole. The Bergers completed the job by planting two flatcarloads of magnolias, a few flatcarloads of azaleas, and scores of camellias (at three thousand dollars a bush), and adding various other adornments. "The Urschels wanted the garden finished at the same time as the house," Marie Berger later said. "The day they moved in, the house was filled with flowers from the new garden."

Perhaps the only large Super-American garden not done entirely by professionals is the one Ted Weiner created on four and a half undulating acres around his residence in Fort Worth. Weiner's garden is a welter of Palo Pinto sandstone, twenty-one hundred tons of which he imported from Palo Pinto County, in West Texas. As the more than four million pounds of various-shaped rocks, each hand-picked by his workmen, were delivered, Weiner personally directed the placing of them, a task vaguely reminiscent of supervising the building of the Pyramids. Once the basic structure of the garden had been completed, Weiner began embellishing it with sculpture, including pieces by Laurens,

Calder, Lipschitz, and Henry Moore. "When I was in Japan, in 1960, I studied their gardens, and I also bought an old cemetery, up above Kyoto," Weiner said recently. "It was over nine hundred years old, and had about a hundred headstones. I had twenty-one of them dug up, crated and shipped back for the garden." Weiner also masterminded the garden's illumination, which consists in part of hundreds of mercury-vapor lamps partly concealed among the rocks; the construction of a stone grotto large enough to walk into; the installation of a stereo music system; and the design of a complex of streams that course over waterfalls through the rocky wonderland. In the still of the night, when the grotto exudes a bluish glow, the partly hidden lights flicker eerily among the rocks and headstones, and the air is filled with a Montavani serenade, the effect is enchantingly spooky.

One of the most interesting houses in Super-America ("one of the most interesting houses in two hundred years," according to Lambert) was inspired, appropriately, by one of the most interesting women in Super-America—Mrs. Bruno Graf, who lives with her husband in a stunning Dallas edifice that she once described, with characteristic candor and good humor, as "a monument that Edward D. Stone built to himself—with my money." Mrs. Graf's ability to joke about money, and occasionally to act as if she agreed with Gene Fowler that it is something to be thrown from the rear platform of railroad trains, sets her apart in a society that honors wealth but is afraid to be caught having fun with it. "Josephine is an original," one of Mrs. Graf's friends has said. "She likes to put on the dog, of course, but she knows she's doing it, and she doesn't care what anybody says or thinks about it. She happens to be one of those rare basic people."

A tall, handsome, high-spirited woman with blond hair and an easy smile, Mrs. Graf makes a point of being smartly groomed and impressively jewelled. Although she was annoyed when two hundred thousand dollars' worth of diamond rings, bracelets, and clips were stolen from her house a few months ago, the loss did not noticeably impair her resplendence. "When you see successful people like me," she once remarked, her fingers glistening, "you might think everybody in the oil business is successful. But more people have gone broke, by far, than have made a success." Mrs. Graf's own success can be traced to her meeting with John W. Herbert III, a New York millionaire's strong-minded son who kicked over the social traces to make a fortune of his own in the Texas oil fields. "He arrived in style, driving a white automobile, as I recall," Jake Hamon, who became Herbert's close friend, has said. "He brought along some of his daddy's money, and before long he'd put it in the ground. He was a wild Indian. If you went out with him for an evening, you had to plan on ending up fighting your way out of some place or else getting thrown out bodily. I must say this for Josephine—when she married Jack, she helped tame him. She also took good care of all of her kin. Her daddy died eating." Mrs. Graf's own recollections of this period tend to be marvellously compact. "There I was working in the oil fields," she once said, "and the next thing I knew I was going all through Europe with all my diamonds and my personal maid."

After Europe, the Herberts settled in Fort Worth, became the parents of two daughters, bought a cattle baron's mansion, and, under the direction of John Staub, remodelled it into an eighteenth-century English town house. With the help of agents operating in New York and London, they assembled such an imposing collection of desks, secretaries, sideboards, sofas, tallboys, mirrors, and other furniture and decorative accessories of the late-Georgian period that their house became a kind of Chippendale-Sheraton museum. They didn't neglect the grounds, either. The estate, consisting of two hundred acres, was developed in a semi-formal English style, with tier upon tier of natural terraces leading down to a lagoon upon which swans glided peacefully. Cowtown thought all this was putting on the dog indeed.

Soon after the outbreak of the Second World War, Herbert, then forty-two, enlisted in the Army Air Forces and was assigned to the Southwest Pacific as a captain in Intelligence. "The minute he decided to go into the service," Mrs. Graf has said, "I started sitting down next to him at his desk to learn the business. 'When I come back,' he said, 'I want to pick up the same operation I had before—no outside stockholders.' So when he left, I took over the active management of the business, and went to the office every day." Arriving home from the office on the afternoon of December 24, 1942, she sat down to look through her Christmas cards and other mail, which included a letter that began, "The officers and enlisted men of the Third Bombardment Group join me in extending to you our deepest sympathy on the loss of your husband on November 24, 1942, while on combat mission in New Guinea. Captain Herbert was one of our best officers, and we all share your sorrow." This was the way Mrs. Graf learned of her husband's death; the customary official notification by telegram was never received. Herbert's will named his wife as the principal beneficiary; she became president of the Herbert Oil Company ("I had prepared myself, so I knew how to take over") and continued to pay close attention to its management.

In January, 1947, she was married to Bruno Graf, a gray-haired, distinguished-looking European, courtly in manner and witty in conversation. Though he found the Georgian mansion congenial, he was somewhat put off by Cowtown, and Cowtown by him. He knew little and cared less about cattle, a sacred subject in Fort Worth, and his knowledge of oil was limited. Furthermore, he spoke with an accent—always a danger signal on the frontier. More suspicion was aroused when it became known that he preferred reading and piano playing to hunting and fishing. Most alarming of all, he kissed ladies' hands. As a consequence, Graf was not unduly exposed to Cowtown's usual cordiality. "Fort Worth was not a good place for Bruno," Mrs. Graf says. "They can be very rough over there. There was nobody for Bruno to talk with." In a search for a more beneficial conversational climate, the Grafs picked up and moved to Europe, where they planned to live permanently. "We had a penthouse in Lausanne, and it was all very beautiful," Mrs. Graf has remarked, using her customary verbal shorthand. "However, we missed the naturalness. We noticed it when we came back, and the bellboys would come into the room and say, 'How are you today?' It would never be like that in Europe. We were glad to get back."

While in Europe, the Grafs had decided to sell the house in Fort Worth, and upon their return Mrs. Graf did so—to an independent oilman named Ralph Lowe, for four hundred and fifty thousand dollars. To avoid paying a capital-gains tax on the house transaction, Mrs. Graf decided to build immediately a new, more expensive residence in Dallas, and chose as her architect Edward D. Stone, the designer of the American Embassy in New Delhi and the American Pavilion at the Brussels World's Fair. "When I told them what I wanted," Mrs. Graf recalls, referring to her first meeting with Stone and his associates, "they said, 'You're an architect's dream.' What I wanted was marble floors throughout, a circular dining room floating on water, an indoor swimming pool, and hi-fi all through the house." She engaged T. H. Robsjohn-Gibbings to design the interior (she had parcelled out the furnishings in the Fort Worth house between her two daughters), and Thomas Church and Joseph Lambert to collaborate on the landscaping.

During the time the house was under construction, the Grafs divided their time among their place at Southampton ("I've been going there for more than twenty-five years," she says), their twenty-second-floor apartment in the Sherry-Netherland ("From my terrace I can see the sun rise over the East River and set over the Hudson"), and a rented apartment in Dallas ("Bruno wanted to be around to learn all about the plumbing and electricity, so he'd know about maintenance. The electrical installation was as complicated as Los Alamos"). Though five or six dozen artisans worked on the job steadily, progress was not rapid, because practically everything that went into the house was custom-made—the fifty-four-inch squares of white marble veined with gold for the floors; the seventy walnut doors, all with gold-and-ivory doorknobs; and the pair of white porcelainized-aluminum gates at the entrance, as well as the furniture, the rugs, the lighting sources, and a piano for the master of the house.

In view of the talent and money poured into the project, it is not surprising that the finished job has a way of inspiring those who see it to descriptive flights: "astonishing virtuosity"; "Pompeian splendor"; "conceived in a dimension of time encompassing the past, fulfilling the present, and foreseeing the future"; "an enchanting environment of rare and timeless beauty"; "a heritage for future generations." The structure inspiring these encomiums is a large white two-story building with the superbly substantial yet light and lacy look that has become Stone's hallmark. From the street, one approaches the house through the graceful white gates, which open into a big formal courtyard enclosed by white boundary walls to provide privacy for the ground floor. The second floor is shielded with Stone's customary veil of delicate white concrete grillwork.

Walking through the double entrance doors—which, like the other doors in the house, reach from floor to ceiling—one enters a sensuous world of marble, gold, and walnut. From the foyer, one walks across a marble bridge spanning an illuminated pool of blue-green water, eighteen feet wide and forty-five feet long. In the center of the pool is the floating dining room that Mrs. Graf specified—a circular slab of marble, seventeen feet in diameter, for which Robsjohn-Gibbings designed a circular table of pale-gold walnut. Since there are no visible supports for either the dining island or the bridge, both give the illusion of floating on the water. Beyond the dining room is the living room, which, like the library, at one side, and the music room, at the other, is a dramatically handsome exhibit of hand-turned furniture, specially woven fabrics, and custommade rugs. And beyond the living room is an oval indoor swimming pool of white Venetian tile. "When you go into the pool," Mrs. Graf explains, "you push a button, and the level of the water goes down six inches—that's so it won't splash." On either side of the pool are dressing rooms, and next to each is a guest suite, consisting of bedroom, bath, and walled private garden. From the swimming pool one looks through a wall of glass onto the exquisitely planted and furnished main terrace and garden court. Throughout, the ground floor has an air of extraordinary spaciousness, resulting from the fact that no walls separate the foyer, the dining room, the living room, and the swimming pool. Instead, they are set apart by airy floor-to-ceiling walnut grilles that in themselves are works of art.

No matter which of the living areas a visitor happens to be in, he finds himself surrounded by a combination of elements that convey a sense of delight in life. The air is also charged with a feeling that the entire premises could at any minute explode into an elegant white-tie revel. A highly developed interest in comfortable living is also reflected on the second floor, which, except for servants' quarters, storage space, and a kitchenette, is devoted entirely to the Grafs' bedroom, dressing rooms, baths, and secluded terraces. The bedroom, designed and furnished for use during the day as a living room, is twenty-seven feet square, and flanked on one side by a terrace almost as large and on the other by one three times as large. "We have all this space outside our bedroom because Bruno said he wanted a lot of area for walking and exercising in the morning," Mrs. Graf has explained. Except for an early Mondrian in each guest room, the Graf house, unlike the typical Texas millionaire's residence, does not go in for modern art. "I'm not going out and buy a Braque—a dead fish on a platter—just because that's the thing being done," Mrs. Graf said when she was planning the house, and she didn't.

Mrs. Graf also followed her own inclinations in the housewarming. In place of the customary gala, the Grafs launched their house with a series of small dinner parties. Among the guests at the first were the Russian-born oilman Paul Raigorodsky and two Russian friends. While admiring the Imperial Russian crystal chandelier that hangs over the dining table, one of Raigorodsky's compatriots made a misstep and fell into the pool. Dinner was postponed while the host took his dripping guest upstairs and outfitted him with dry clothes, including a dinner jacket. Upon finishing dinner, another guest, the gray-haired Dallas banker and philanthropist Karl Hoblitzelle, pushed his chair back from the table too vigorously and went over backward into the water. As before, the host retrieved the guest and retired with him to the dressing quarters. In the interests of keeping aquatic activities confined to the main pool, the Grafs gave some thought, after the first party, to putting a railing around the dining island. "We decided against it," Mrs. Graf said later. "If anybody falls in, he can't get hurt very much. Besides, not having a railing is more chic."

Nowadays, it is also considered chic by Texas millionaires to live in houses designed, like the Grafs', to operate with a small staff. "The other house had ten servants inside," Mrs. Graf says. "Here we won't have to bother with the servant problem. You can always get cleaning help, and if we had to, we could do the rest ourselves. We have this tiny upstairs kitchen, with a three-burner stove and so on. If the servants didn't show up, we could just prepare our own breakfast."

The problem of servants—or help, as we usually say in America ("a sop to the republican conscience," Roger Burlingame has noted)—is hardly confined to Texas millionaires, though they are inclined to believe that, like everything else, it is bigger in their case. "We have always been accustomed to a more plentiful supply of servants than people in the North," Mrs. Edgar Tobin, of San Antonio, has remarked. "And so, naturally, the decline is harder for us to adjust to. At any rate, it's hard to maintain an establishment these days. Here in San Antonio we're lucky if the butler has on a white coat. It's different in Houston. People there still have butlers in livery." In the opinion of Mrs. Herbert Gambrell, of Dallas, the word "butler," as generally used in Texas, is a high-toned term for a servant who could more accurately be described as an "all-purpose houseboy." By whatever name, a man who performs varied inside and outside chores is the standard servant in a Texas millionaire's household. In addition, most millionaires also employ a colored woman who cooks and does some cleaning. The usual staff consists of two live-in houseworkers and occasional by-the-day help. For the most part, the help is colored, although Mexicans are employed as domestics in San Antonio and other sections near Mexico, and as gardeners in many areas. A couple is paid about a hundred dollars a week, a cook forty-five, a maid thirty, and a good all-purpose house-boy about sixty. A reliable nurse or governess is hard to come by at practically any price. The help are treated in the pater-nalistic tradition of the South; kindness is mixed with an im-plied insistence on the servant's knowing and keeping his place.

When they entertain, millionaires in Texas, like those on the Philadelphia Main Line and elsewhere, augment their regular help with servants hired from a floating labor supply. This practice is so widespread that nobody in Dallas is sur-prised when, for example, he is served by a colored butler named Gentry three times in a single week at different parties. "Margaret Simmons used to say that she could measure her social popularity by the number of times she saw Gentry in the course of a week," Joseph Lambert once remarked.

Chapter Eleven

In the opinion of most Texas millionaires, the scarcity of servants and the trend toward smaller houses account for the
decline in at-home entertaining that has occurred in recent
years. In the opinion of the Dallas savant Thomas Knight, the
explanation lies elsewhere. "It's all the fault of the goddam
women," Knight has said, with his usual reserve. "They've
gotten so bone-lazy they won't even spend time managing the
help who do the work." Whatever the cause, the small at-home
dinner party is going out all over Super-America. Entertaining
at home is more popular in Forth Worth than in Dallas, although the dining rooms of few Fort Worth millionaires seat
more than twelve. (However, Mrs. Robert Windfohr and Mrs.
Andrew Fuller, two Fort Worth hostesses who hold to the
older tradition, can, and frequently do, seat two or three times
that many guests at dinner.) In Houston, Miss Ima Hogg is
the most prominent devotee of the old-fashioned at-home dinner party. "She always serves champagne when entertaining
guests at dinner," Alvin Romansky, a frequent guest, has remarked, "and she also has finger bowls on little doilies. You
don't see that so much any more."

Nor does one often see intimate, stylish refreshments of the
sort with which Mrs. Rose Lloyd entertains her friends. Small,
bright-eyed, and witty, Mrs. Lloyd grew up in Louisiana, the
daughter of a banker and plantation owner. After years of
world travel (beginning at fourteen), she moved to Dallas in
1913, and built the house she has since occupied—a stately
white terra-cotta mansion, in which she installed the complete

drawing room from her family's Louisiana plantation house, including wall coverings of specially woven French brocade. Mrs. Lloyd likes to entertain eight or a dozen friends, who, after cocktails in the drawing room, move to the solarium, where, seated four at a table, they dine on one of Mrs. Lloyd's favorite menus—caviar, served on silver plates with small mounds of chopped egg and diced onion, and champagne. Two colored waiters are assigned to each table; they see to it that no guest has an empty plate or glass until he requests it. Moreover, a guest who does not down his champagne soon after it is poured finds his glass replaced by another, which is then filled with wine that is properly chilled.

In San Antonio, entertaining at home is more popular than in either Dallas or Houston, and of a noticeably different nature. "Entertaining here is likely to take the form of a big, casual buffet dinner," Mrs. Edgar Tobin has observed. "It's just another reflection of the easier kind of life we have in San Antonio." Everywhere in Texas, the outdoor barbecue, usually considered a man's province, is a popular form of entertaining, and can be managed, as Jack Vaughn does, for six or eight guests around his swimming pool, or, as R. E. (Bob) Smith does, for two or three hundred guests around the barbecue pavilion on one of his ranches.

Whether the millionaires give their parties at home or, as is more usual, at a club, they tend to be large. The cocktail party in Texas, no matter how simple, approaches an informal dinner, for, besides the usual hors d'oeuvres, guests are served such substantial fare as cold meats, slivers of hot barbecued beef on hot biscuits, salad, cheeses, dessert, and coffee; furthermore, a hostess doesn't consider such an affair a success if it breaks up before eleven. As a preface to the elaborate buffet at her cocktail parties, Mrs. A. Pollard Simons customarily serves her guests caviar and sour cream and *blinis*, washed down with ice-cold vodka in chilled glasses. Before the night-game opening of a recent Southern Methodist University football season, Mrs. Ralph Howell gave a cocktail party for twelve hundred guests in Food Hall, an exhibition building on the State Fair Grounds; drinks were served from sixty-foot-long tables attended by a dozen bartenders, and the food, consisting of barbecued beef, baked ham, ranch-style beans, hot rolls, cake, and coffee, was dispensed from two large catering trucks that had been driven into the hall.

Many Texas millionaires like to concentrate their entertaining in one big annual affair, such as the one that the J. Alvin Gardners and the John Kettles, neighbors in Dallas, jointly give each year. They combine and decorate their gardens—one year the décor was that of a French sidewalk café—and invite sixteen hundred guests for a sit-down dinner and dancing to music provided by two orchestras. Since Texas millionaires like parties, they do not mind travelling a bit to take in an event like the Gardner-Kettle entertainment, which usually draws a dozen guests from Houston, thirty from Wichita Falls, a hundred from Midland and Odessa, and a hundred and fifty from Fort Worth. The larger delegations often arrive in chartered buses.

Because of what they consider an unjustified reputation for free spending, Texas millionaires, particularly oilmen, subscribe to a kind of gentleman's agreement against letting their parties receive any public attention. Once in a while, though, a fun-loving couple like the George Gillilands, who hail from a hamlet in West Texas, put on a do, usually someplace outside of the state, and call in photographers from *Life*. One of the Gillilands' frolics was staged in Hollywood and featured, among other attractions, what appeared to the guests to be barrels of twenty-eight-dollars-a-pound caviar and a fountain that continuously spouted champagne. The cost of the freeloaders' dream was estimated at thirty thousand dollars, which is about a quarter of the sum that D. D. (Tex) Feldman reportedly spent in 1957 on what *Life* called "the nation's most lavish New Year's party." For his well-publicized affair, Feldman rented Romanoff's restaurant, in Beverly Hills, and transformed it into a kind of elegant "My Fair Lady" set; he engaged Edith Piaf to sing for the three hundred guests, who included numerous movie stars, as well as many of Feldman's

Texas friends, who disapproved of the party in principle but enjoyed it in practice. Although notable by contemporary standards, the parties of Texas millionaires are modest indeed compared with those of the original millionaires. For example, when Clarence Mackay entertained the Prince of Wales in 1924, the floral bill for the occasion amounted to a hundred and twenty-five thousand dollars, or roughly what Feldman's party cost *in toto*.

As a rule, party givers in Super-America count on their guests to amuse one another, a circumstance that no doubt accounts for the great popularity of the costume party—in particular, the *luau*, or Hawaiian-type fête. This has become a kind of standardized affair that features drinks served from a Hawaiian punch bowl, fresh fruit offered in a scooped-out watermelon, poi eaten while sitting on the floor, Hawaiian music, and an exhibition of Island dancing by one or more couples who have studied it with evident seriousness. A highlight of the Dallas social season is the Jake Hamons' annual costume party, at which the hostess once made her entrance on an elephant, and one of the most talked-about parties in Houston in recent years was the Robert Vernon Kings', at which the guests showed up dressed as Roman slave girls, gladiators, and senators (one senator wore cowboy boots under his toga), and disported themselves until dawn in ancient-type revelry, including dining on steaks served on flaming swords. A more typical masquerade party was one that the Christian Holmeses, of San Antonio, gave shortly after the publication of Nancy Mitford's "Noblesse Oblige," a copy of which was thoughtfully made part of each invitation. The society page of one local paper later reported the success of what it called the Holmeses' "You and Non-You Party."

Though all Texas millionaires are party-prone, the ones in Dallas verge on being party addicts. "Party giving is the primary avocation in Dallas," Lon Tinkle, who has nothing against festivity, has remarked. "When I came here in 1936," Joseph Lambert, a native of Shreveport, said a while ago, "the parties were all done, you might say, with loving hands. Now the usual big parties and even the smaller cocktail parties have more formality, more grace, and a greater sense of elegance." Lambert's own part in this transformation, as well as in shaping other sides of the municipal personality, has been considerable. In addition to his work in landscaping, he is active in industrial decorating, antiques, and real estate, and also figures large in the civic and cultural areas—the Museum of Fine Arts, the Theatre Center, the Symphony, the Park Board, the annual Dallas Arts Festival, and so on. Moreover, he is the busiest planner of debutante parties, weddings, and similar divertissements in Dallas.

What Lambert has described as "the largest wedding in ten years" was that of Miss Nancy Ann Smith and James Kirksmith, in 1957. Naturally, Lambert handled it. Miss Smith, an attractive, vivacious blonde with an accent that prompts New York taxi-drivers to start off by asking her how things are down in Texas, is the only niece and one of four surviving relatives of the late Sid Richardson, a bachelor who bequeathed thirteen million dollars to be divided among his kin. How much he may have turned over to Miss Smith, who was a favorite, during his lifetime has long been a matter of lively speculation. Though Miss Smith had many suitors, who came from all over, she picked Mr. Kirksmith, a tall, good-looking native who, as Lambert puts it, "is in investments." They were married at St. Michael and All Angels Episcopal Church, and Lambert was responsible for everything connected with the event except the selection of the groom.

The reception, for a thousand guests, was held at the Brook Hollow Golf Club, which Lambert redecorated to look like an eighteenth-century English garden. The winding drive from the street to the porte-cochere of the clubhouse—a distance of about a city block—was lined on either side with hundreds of hurricane lamps mounted on steel rods and spaced at intervals of eighteen inches. (Six men were assigned to relight candles snuffed out by the wind; altogether, three hundred and fifty in staff were laid on for the event.) To create a garden effect in the ballroom, Lambert used a hundred and ninety-three dozen camellias, eleven hundred and seventy Easter lilies, forty-three dozen gardenias, a thousand bride's roses, six hundred and fifty sprays of white stock, fifteen dozen white freesias, a thousand white snapdragons, a hundred strings of hothouse smilax, fifteen hundred stems of peach blossoms, five hundred bunches of violets, two thousand azaleas, fourteen dozen white lilacs, a dozen pink magnolias, five flowering white peach trees, and a dozen flowering crab-apple trees. Three thousand feet of laurel roping, intertwined with camellias, was hung around the molding of the ceiling. The flowers and trees were assembled from Los Angeles, San Francisco, Chicago, Mobile, Birmingham, North Carolina, South Carolina, and Belgium. Sixty tables were set up, each decorated with candelabra (Lambert used approximately four thousand white-beeswax candles indoors, and gave two men the exclusive chore of keeping them lighted) and a centerpiece of camellias and gardenias entwined with smilax. In addition, violets were scattered generously over the tables. "It sounds terribly sweet, but, after all, it was a wedding," Lambert remarked not long ago in recalling the event. "It pains me to have to add that the Kirksmiths were divorced last year."

The flight of entertaining from the home has stimulated the building of country clubs, where a hostess can give a party for twelve or twelve hundred by making a phone call. Perhaps the finest specimen of such a labor-saving institution is Fort Worth's Ridglea Country Club, a one-story structure that sprawls over a hundred and twenty-five thousand square feet, cost two million dollars to build and furnish, and serves as a home away from home for twelve hundred members and their families. The front doors—sheets of glass fourteen feet high and eight feet wide—open into a foyer containing lush tropical foliage planted around a body of water described by members as a fishpond. Guests are warned not to dip their fingers in the pond, as it is stocked with eighteen-inch bass that bite. The cocktail lounge, to the left of the foyer, has a walk-in fireplace, a grand piano, and an organ, and seats two hundred. To the right of the foyer is the Blue Room, used primarily as a ladies' card room and for small parties of sixty or seventy. A member who walks from the Blue Room, at one end of the building, to join a friend in the Men's Grill, at the other, covers two hundred and thirty feet, or slightly more than three-quarters the length of a football field.

A feeling of having been reduced to the size of a pedestrian in an architect's scale drawing comes over a visitor when the sliding doors that separate the various dining and drinking areas are recessed, creating an unobstructed expanse in which fifteen hundred people are often seated for dinner. A stranger can be heard laughing across this crowded room, but it takes binoculars to see her. Besides the clubhouse, which has locker rooms not only for men and women but also for boys and girls, Ridglea offers other comforts not always found at home: a Teen Room, equipped with a soda fountain, a jukebox, television, and the like; a swimming pool large enough for official A.A.U. meets; and a nursery, attended full time by two registered nurses and three assistants, where members can leave offspring from 9 A.M. to 8 P.M. daily, and until they feel up to calling for them after an evening party at the club.

While the country clubs do not put gastronomy before golf, the fare that many of them serve shows evidence of a belief that food can do more than allay hunger. This is rare in Texas, where good public eating is harder to find than oil. That Texas is a feeder's wasteland not only strikes most visitors (a survey conducted by the Texas Highway Department revealed that only three per cent of people visiting the state were "impressed" by the food) but is generally acknowledged by those of the natives who do not consider ranch-style beans the ultimate taste treat. "Texas has a black eye about food, and deserves it," Mrs. Rose Lloyd has said, with brisk authority. In a concurring but more extended opinion, Stanley Walker has written, "I used to have a theory that it was almost impossible for an honest Chinese or halfway intelligent Italian or Frenchman to cook a really bad meal. I was mistaken about this; in Texas they can botch it." The chief failings of Texas cooks,

Walker reported after long study, are that "they rely too much on the skillet . . . are too close-fisted with butter . . . ignore wine and most herbs . . . have a horror of fat meat, except salt pork, but use quantities of lard for frying . . . are not venturesome, and fear all deviations from the ordinary."

The widespread, almost morbid aversion to experimenting with food continually irritated Miss Willie (her father had expected a boy) Sterett when she was the proprietress of the S & S Tea Room, the luncheon rendezvous of the Dallas millionaires' wives. "They won't try anything new, and they won't change," she once complained, sputtering like a pinwheel. "They won't eat fish. Here we are, overnight from the Gulf, and they have no interest in sea food. It's just pure damned ignorance. They don't know what a scallop is. I had a customer ask me if a scallop was like an oyster. If I brought out a new dish, I named it after some hotel. That made it sound familiar, and then maybe they'd try it. Maybe. If these women would try to be a little cosmopolitan, you wouldn't have to practically break their arms to get them to take something they haven't been eating since they were kids." Texans, being the country's largest producers of cattle, naturally start eating beef at an early age, and as the years go by they often develop the belief, which they do not keep secret, that steak—particularly Texas steak—is slightly superior to ambrosia. Considering the tall talk, visitors are almost always disappointed and sometimes bitter when they discover that Texans, putting profit above palate, invariably ship their best steaks to Chicago and New York and retain for themselves the humble T-bones.

If Texans are cruelly limited in first-class restaurants, the fault is not so much in their chefs as in themselves, for a people gets the kind of cuisine it deserves. In recent years, however, restaurants with a cuisine in the French tradition have been established in Texas. They are two in number—Maxim's, in Houston, and La Vielle Varsovie, in Dallas. Once a traveller in Texas leaves the cities, he is, as in America generally, at the mercy of cooks and countermen who, to judge by the food they serve, are barely able to conceal their homicidal instincts.

In Texas, the roadside specialty (also widely purveyed in dismal little *bistros* in the cities) is a sort of barbecued beef that leaves on the tongue a lasting, distinctive, acrid taste, suggesting gunpowder. Another specialty is Wop Salad, the localism for a mixed green salad. A traveller becomes accustomed to picking up a menu, like the one in the Scharbauer Hotel Coffee Shop, in Midland, and being confronted with the intelligence "Wop Salad served with all entrees listed below." With any luck, a sojourner will be treated to a few native specialties, such as Mincemeat Mother-in-Law and Son-of-a-Bitch Stew. In the end, he may wind up feeling that in Texas, as Taine found to be true in England, "one is simply and wholesomely fed, but one can take no pleasure in eating."

One can drink well enough in Texas, however, even though more than half the state is legally bone-dry and nowhere is it lawful to sell liquor by the drink. Furthermore, even in wet counties it is forbidden to consume liquor between 12:15 A.M. and 7 A.M. on weekdays and between 1:15 A.M. and 1 P.M. on Sundays. Nevertheless, Texans annually get away with more than eight million gallons of hard liquor, five million gallons of wine, and a hundred and twenty-five million gallons of ale and beer. This performance appears even more respectable when one considers that it is turned in with no help from some forty per cent of adult Texans, who are teetotallers.

In getting around the legal obstacles intended to curb drinking, the bibulous majority displays the pure Super-American spirit, for, as Roger Burlingame has observed, "It has always been an American impulse, the moment a prohibition is proclaimed, to try to circumvent it." Nothing so keenly stimulates that impulse, recent history has demonstrated, than attempts to interfere with the national drinking habits, which have always been sufficiently rugged to make foreigners in our midst pop their eyes in wonder. After paying us a visit in 1902, François André Michaux returned to France all choked up over the effects of what he called the American "passion for spiritous liquors," and a few years later William Cobbett, who had plainly been shaken by his observation of the American proclivity to tie one on, went back to England convinced that "this beastly vice" was the gravest defect in the American character. It was what travellers saw on the frontier that gave them their greatest start, for there whiskey flowed almost like water and seemed to be considered nearly as efficacious, being consumed by men, women, and children.

Just as the passion for spiritous liquors has always been most evident on the frontier, so has that area always been an important battleground in the struggle between people who drink and those who don't, and don't want others to, either. The temperance strife has been going on in Texas at least since 1876, when the Texans wrote their present constitution and included a provision for local-option elections, which allow citizens in any community to decide by direct popular vote whether the sale of liquor should be permitted in their locality. The exercise of this right has produced a colorful wet-dry economy. Of the state's two hundred and fifty-four counties, a hundred and thirty-two—more than half—are legally dry; the rest are wet in degrees ranging from the eighteen that permit only four-per cent beer to the hundred and one that permit distilled spirits. To complicate the drinker's life further, certain sections of some wet counties are dry. Because of the statute making it illegal to sell liquor by the drink ("You can buy a carload," the local adage says, "but you can't buy an ounce"), the bars and cocktail lounges that are a conspicuous part of the American landscape do not exist anywhere in Super-America.

Even in wet territory, a visitor without connections is obliged to buy a bottle if he wants a nip, and he must take the bottle with him if he wants a drink before dinner at a restaurant. He soon learns that to walk about holding an exposed bottle of liquor is considered extremely bad form. A brown paper bag is de rigueur for this purpose, as a visitor discovered who approached the dining room of the Dallas Statler Hilton with a naked bottle of Scotch in his hand; at the doorway, a captain courteously but firmly relieved him of the offending article, put it in a brown paper bag (a supply of bags is kept on hand for such emergencies), and ushered him and his decorous parcel to a table. To a new immigrant, it is an arresting sight to observe a throng of people in evening dress entering a hotel en route to a party; most of the men and many of the aging, unaccompanied matrons unconcernedly display the distinctive brown badge identifying them as members of the drinking class.

The crazy-quilt pattern of prohibition in Super-America sometimes proves an inconvenience to outsiders, like the thirsty untutored traveller who, registering at the Carlton Hotel, in Tyler, asked the desk clerk where he could get a drink. "Twenty-six and a half miles from here," the clerk replied. Natives and experienced travellers avoid getting caught in such untidy situations by carrying a supply of liquor with them when heading into dry territory. Department stores and specialty shops stock a variety of containers for transporting liquor in amounts ranging from a half pint to a gallon. A Houston matron who gets around the state carries a handbag of her own design that contains a small bottle for gin, a smaller one for vermouth, and a still smaller one for cocktail onions.

As a matter of everyday practice, however, elaborate precautions to insure the availability of a drink are unnecessary, for in spite of the widespread prohibition, it is about as difficult to buy liquor almost anywhere in Super-America today as it was in the United States during those immaculate times when the Eighteenth Amendment was counted among the national treasures. For one thing, a preponderance of the population live in the wet areas—which include all the important cities except Tyler and Lubbock—and so can buy as much liquor as they wish from package stores. People living in dry areas make occasional visits to the nearest oasis or, if that is inconvenient, patronize the bootleggers who abound and in many places compete quite openly for trade. In Lubbock, whose population of a hundred and fifty thousand makes it the largest of the dry cities, some four thousand bootleggers, according to Jim Mathis, of the Houston *Post*, do an annual business estimated at fifteen million dollars. They solicit trade by distributing business cards that carry their phone numbers and such reassuring slogans as "Never More Than Fifteen Minutes from Your Door," or "We Can Satisfy Your Every Need," or simply "Don't Fuss, Call Us." Those who call must be prepared to pay fifty cents for a can of beer and anywhere from eight to fifteen dollars for a fifth of whiskey.

With the bootleggers have come, not unexpectedly, the hijacking of rival stocks, the machine-gunning of competitors, moonshining (this last, though, is on a relatively small scale; "Texans," the Houston *Post* remarked, "prefer their illicit liquor bonded"), the bribing of sheriffs, and all the other stigmata, including wholesale public approval of lawbreaking, that characterized national prohibition. "We drink wet and vote dry," the natives remark. This dissembling attitude toward prohibition is nicely reflected in its enforcement. Although the state annually takes in nearly thirty-five million dollars in taxes on alcoholic beverages and in similar revenue, the legislature refuses—despite an almost comically obvious need for additional men and equipment to cope with the bootleggers alone—to appropriate more than a million and a half dollars to administer and enforce the whole prohibition enterprise. Consequently, the enforcement of the liquor laws is handled by a hundred and thirty-five liquor-control agents (known locally as L-men), or less than one per county. They are paid three hundred and fifty-six dollars a month and are obliged to supply an automobile for use in their work. On their present salary, which hasn't been raised in years, few L-men are able to drive a new Cadillac, Chrysler, or Oldsmobile—the cars preferred by the bootleggers. "Despite the fact that our men are beaten up and shot at," Coke Stevenson, Jr., Administrator of the Liquor Control Board, has said, "their greatest danger is from automobile accidents when they are chasing bootleggers. Quite often, the insurance companies won't even insure their automobiles." If caught, a bootlegger can be charged only with committing a misdemeanor; if convicted, his punishment is limited to a fine not exceeding fifty dollars, or roughly the profit on a half dozen bottles of whiskey.

However fanciful Texas-style prohibition may seem to out-siders, the natives have become accustomed to its Alice-in-Wonderland quality, and never seriously discuss the possibility of repeal. Maintenance of the status quo is a matter of pas-sionate concern to several groups, including the bootleggers and many of the churches. A Baptist dry leader named O. F. Dingler, testifying before the Texas House Liquor Committee in 1959, was asked if he thought members of any religious group who drank a glass of beer on a Sunday picnic could be Christians. "I think the wet and dry issue pretty well divides the Christians from the unsaved," Dingler replied.

The legal ban on selling liquor by the drink has resulted in the creation and wild proliferation of an indigenous local institution known as the private club, the main function of which is the serving of liquor by the drink to the unsaved. In their utility, abundance, variety, and atmosphere, the private clubs are reminiscent of the old speakeasies. Since the statutes contain no provision specifically authorizing the incorporation of organizations that serve intoxicants, the clubs for many years sought to secure a semblance of legality by being chartered, for a fee of fifty dollars, under Subdivision 9 of Article 1302 of Title 32 of the Business Corporation Act, which gives permission "to support and maintain bicycle clubs and other innocent sports." Furthermore, because Texas corpora-tions are indexed in the state's records by name and not by the purpose for which they were organized, nobody knew exactly how many private clubs were in operation until January, 1961, when the Liquor Control Board required them to get a permit, issued by the Board without charge. As of the first of the year, six hundred and thirty-one permits had been granted. Since then, a law has been enacted that assesses private clubs a minimum annual membership fee of five hundred dollars.

Though the Board's records do not reveal how the private clubs are distributed around the state, there are, according to the informed opinion of Coke Stevenson, Jr., approximately three hundred registered private thirst-slaking clubs in Houston, two hundred and twenty-five in Dallas, thirty in San Antonio, and twenty-five each in Fort Worth and Austin. Smaller towns and cities, including some in dry territory, usually support a club or two. As a convenience, many hotels maintain their own clubs, in which guests are automatically enrolled upon registering, and several of the more expensive restaurants have installed a similar facility on their premises.

The private clubs come in all prices and sizes. The Meadowbrook Club, in Fort Worth, which charges an initiation fee of fifty dollars and monthly dues of two, is a one-room spread accommodating about sixty members; the International Club, in Houston, which charges an initiation fee of twelve hundred dollars and monthly dues of eighteen, consists of a cocktail lounge, a grillroom, a private dining room, a cardroom, and a to-all-intent-and-purposes night club seating three hundred and fifty and featuring entertainment by performers like Lisa Kirk, Joe E. Lewis, and Herb Shriner. The same quality of entertainment is provided by Glenn McCarthy's Cork Club, the most famous of them all, and by the Tidelands Club, which both share with the International Club the distinction of being the headquarters of Houston's cafe society. It is customary for convivial millionaires to belong to private clubs in all the major cities they visit regularly on business or pleasure. In Dallas, their choice is apt to be the Cipango Club, which occupies a mansion located a couple of miles from the center of the city and is very aggressive about keeping poor people away from its door. A more typical institution is the University Club, which occupies the two upper floors of a three-story building in downtown Dallas, and is presided over by a former boxer named Bennie Bickers. "In this club," Bickers has said, "everybody knows everybody else, and everybody's real relaxed."

The atmosphere in a private club naturally gets tense when L-men kick in the door and stage a raid, as they often do if undercover work has revealed evidence of curfew violation or the serving of drinks to non-members. As a rule, only the smaller places get into trouble with the L-men. However, club life in Dallas took a lively turn in April, 1960, when the 3525 Club, referred to locally as "super-swank," was raided twice within three weeks. On both occasions, not only the managers, waiters, and entertainers but all the members present were stashed in paddy wagons and police cars and hauled across town to night court. Some things in Super-America would make Jay Gatsby feel right at home.

Chapter Twelve

Society in Texas has been widely represented as such a gaudy affair that it suggests, as someone has said, "a latter-day alliance of Dogpatch with the Court of Louis XIV." For this gay deception, Texans can, once again, thank the sentimental tourists—the kind described by Constance Rourke, in another connection, as those who carry "the amiable light luggage of preconceptions." It was one of that carefree crowd who sought to sum up the social structure in Texas with the taut remark that crude oil naturally produced a crude society. Travellers of a similar disposition have helped to circulate many kindred fancies, one of the most widespread being that Texas society is about as hard to get into as the telephone directory. "Texas aristocracy," Robert Ruark once remarked in a thoughtful essay, "is not based on how long you lived there, and pinched nostrils, and the thin blue-blooded lines of some long-dead ancestor. Texas is what you are, not what you *were*, or might yet be." Up to a point.

However, Ruark's view is shared by most visitors to Texas in the beginning. The reason has been explained by a wealthy, prominent, self-made Houston lawyer whose wife comes from one of the state's old and well-to-do families. "The French Ambassador could visit Houston and never come into contact with the real society of this city," the lawyer has said. "He would be picked up at the airport by the Mayor, and on the way into town the Mayor would brag about how much money he'd just made in a real-estate deal. Our distinguished guest would spend the rest of his time with the Chamber of Commerce group and the members of our synthetic society. When he got ready to leave, he'd very likely think that that was all there is to Houston society—just those people who are always out in front, pushing. The truth is, of course, that the real society here—the entrenched group—doesn't seek the limelight. They stay in the background. They keep pretty much to themselves."

The same situation obtains in other Texas cities, whose entrenched groups are not known for going out of their way to seek new members. "If Dallas has the reputation of being a place where it is difficult for an unsponsored stranger to become a part of its inner social life," John William Rogers, a native whose old-family credentials are in order, has said, "it is simply because so many strangers have been arriving for so many years that it has long been a physical impossibility for old families to occupy themselves with the newcomers." This idea was put more succinctly by Mrs. Edgar Tobin when asked how newcomers are apt to be received in San Antonio, whose society is considered the most aristocratic in the state. "If they don't know somebody when they come here, I feel sorry for them," she replied.

In its appreciation of the principle of exclusiveness (if not of its inflexible application), Texas society resembles any other, but at the same time it differs in some ways from, say, Philadelphia society. In fact, to some social critics, like Green Peyton, an Easterner who became so fond of Texas that he made his home in San Antonio for some years, Texas society is so different that it does not, as Peyton has written, "constitute society in the ordinary sense of the word." He adds, "For society consists of something more than an amiable set of people with money and a respectable background. It presupposes, in the first place, that its members belong to an acknowledged group of leaders who set a conspicuous example of dignity and good manners. It imposes certain civic obligations, too. The social leader may not belong to any business-luncheon clubs or benevolent fraternities, but he takes an active interest in the welfare of his town and the less favored people in it. No group of citizens in San Antonio fulfills all these conditions—not even the cattle families. They are dignified enough, and no one would criticize their manners. But they are just one of several isolated groups of well-to-do, well-dressed, well-educated people who are obsessed by the fear of being noticed and disturbed in their tranquil enjoyment of their wealth and cattle."

Whether or not the people regarded as the social leaders of Texas meet Peyton's or Philadelphia's or even Webster's (6b) definition of society, they meet that of Texans, who have never taken what could properly be called an idolatrous view of society in the East—or, as they sometimes say, when in a cutting mood, the *Far* East. Nor do they show any signs of being downcast because no Texas city is among the fourteen in the country graced with an edition of the *Social Register*. "Down here we know who's who without being told," Jesse Jones once said, with enduring accuracy.

Nevertheless, in 1950 a Houston public-relations man and former United Press sportswriter named George Kirksey started publishing the *Social Directory of Houston,* a yearly volume with a *Social Register* format and containing some thirty-two hundred listings. "It's not a hard book to get into," Kirksey, who has got into it himself, has explained. "Almost the sole reason for its existence is to provide a handy list of the decent people in town. Also, it makes a good address book, something people like to take along when travelling." A similar work, titled the *Fort Worth Social Directory,* which made its initial appearance in 1957, provides an additional service by including three and a half pages of "Ready Telephone References"—hairdressers, jewellers, department stores, reducing salons, and such, all apparently in good social standing. Both directories are notably inclusive, listing the socially impeccable along with what a Proper Houstonian would call the socially illiterate. The fact that the twain meet, if only in print, suggests that society in Super-America has been affected, to the usual exaggerated degree, by the common-man complex—the twentieth-century tendency, as it has been put, "to raise the low and to lower the high." In addition, society in Super-

America still retains a kind of built-in automatic leaning toward the democratic, derived from the influence—diluted but discernible—of the frontier. To be sure, social hierarchies were established in Texas, as in Philadelphia, with the arrival of the first settlers, but it takes time for class lines to rigidify, and it was only yesterday, as things go, that Texans of every rank were obliged by circumstances to be more concerned with preserving their scalps than with improving their station. For several reasons, therefore, Super-American society probably comes closer than any other to representing the "open society" that has always been considered typical of America.

Being the most typical, Super-American society should also, according to the logic of some Europeans, be the most comic. "The real trouble," D. W. Brogan has explained, "is that American society has never developed indigenous standards of its own, except in small areas. It has been parasitic on Europe, especially England, for its ideas as well as its butlers. . . . So it is that in any faithful chronicle of American society, comedy must prevail." In a sense, all society, whether English or Super-American, is intrinsically comic, since its raison d'être is to favor those whose essential—though, of course, not necessarily only—accomplishment consists in having had forebears who were good at making money and willing to stay put.

At any rate, it is true that neither in England nor in Texas will the mere possession of money unlock the door to society— an immutable fact of life that the ingenuous everywhere are forever breaking their hearts trying to disprove. "It happens all the time," the well-known Texas artist Cynthia Brants has remarked. "Newly rich oil people move in from West Texas, buy a big house or build one, and start giving ten-thousand-dollar parties. This doesn't get them in, of course. After a while, quite a few pack up and leave, but more arrive, and the process never ends." Talk about money, to say nothing of its ostentatious display, is more or less taboo among the entrenched group. Conversation at a small and rather proper dinner party in San Antonio was interrupted by an expressive flash of silence when a beautiful young matron, fresh from

New York, gaily remarked, "I don't care how *nouveau* I am, just so long as I'm plenty *riche*." The knowledgeable Fort Worth banker Sam Cantey III has observed that "money isn't really important, even when it comes to moving in from the outside. There just happens to be so much of it around that it doesn't have much significance socially." But if wealth may not be a prerequisite for admission to society in Texas, or elsewhere in America, its possession by members and aspirants is generally taken for granted.

A slightly different value is attached to descent from a so-called old family. In Texas, a genuine old family is usually defined as one that settled in the state about a hundred years ago, but the span need not be that long to assure a solid social position. "I'm from an old Houston family—my father came here in 1905," one of the city's social leaders likes to announce, with a mixture of jocularity and belligerence, after a drink or two. Upward social mobility, as climbing the social ladder is now known in Texas, can be managed with no old-family connections. A past president of Houston's most exclusive social organization is a self-made millionaire who arrived in Texas in the early twenties. Cases like that, however, are exceptions proving the rule that in Texas, as in Florence or Forest Hills, long residence contributes to social standing. Consequently, Texas society, like most, is customarily classified according to chronology.

The top layer is composed of what may be called the Ante-Oil Group; that is, families who accumulated their fortunes before the discovery of Spindletop, in 1901—usually in cotton, rice, cattle, timber, or commerce. In the social scale, cotton money, because it is older, takes precedence over cattle and timber money, and rice money, for the same reason, has a slight edge even on cotton money. The distinctions are fine and of interest mainly to devout ancestor worshippers. Cattle money, though not the oldest, is the most plentiful source of what are regarded as the aristocratic fortunes. The social prestige associated with the raising of cattle (but not sheep; cattlemen have always looked down on sheepmen, because, apart from more important economic reasons, the latter worked on foot, the former on horseback) no doubt helps to explain why a ranch is often one of the first acquisitions of the new rich. The ideal situation, socially speaking, is to belong to an old ranching family on whose property oil was discovered.

The second stratum of Texas society is the Post-Oil Group, whose wealth dates from around the turn of the century and stems in large part from oil. Some students have been tempted to subdivide this group into Old Oilers, who made their money before 1930, and New Oilers, who made it after that, and to declare that while Old Oilers are accepted by society, New Oilers are not. This is a rank over-simplification, of course, but not without a certain rough validity. "Some people in the oil business are accepted and some aren't—that's about all you can say for sure," Joseph Lambert, who functions in some ways as the Ward McAllister of Dallas, has remarked. "However, you will find that the best clubs have a minority of oil people on their membership lists and a conspicuous scarcity of oil people among their officers. For instance, oil has never played a part in Idlewild, the club that presents Dallas débutantes. No officer of the Steeplechase Club, a similar organization in Fort Worth, is in the oil business. The same thing is true of the Allegro Club, in Houston. And so on. It still happens, too, that a hostess, in the course of issuing an invitation, will say, 'There are going to be a few oil people present—I hope you won't mind.'" "You have no idea how the Old Guard resents the oil people," a Dallas Old Guardswoman once informed a dinner companion. "You can be sure we do all we can to keep them out of everything worthwhile, especially our really top organizations, such as the Shakespeare Club. Why do we do it? I'll tell you why. We consider oil money the same as gambling money, and we just don't care to associate with gamblers. As for their wives, they're what I call the monkey-fur set. The Old Guard simply won't have anything to do with them, and oh, how they would like to get into the inner sanctum!"

Such rancor, however, is rare among the entrenched group. They keep the oil people out of things, it is true, but they don't see that as anything to get worked up about, since they always have. They are accustomed to a state of affairs in which people who accumulate money in practically any legal way other than oil—real estate, merchandising, banking, law, and dry cleaning—have an easier time than oilmen making the social grade. Dallas society even includes an undertaker, whose unfailingly cheery presence at parties has scarcely ever been commented on, except in a lighthearted way by one elderly *grande dame*. "Always, when he bids me good night, he says, 'Be seeing you,'" she told a friend. "You know, I really don't like for him to say that." The fact that several public-spirited oilmen rank among the state's leading citizens does not detract from the essential accuracy of an offhand and not unkindly intended remark by a socially fortified San Antonio financier, who said simply, "Oil people as a group are a little out of it."

The accepted method of getting in, or trying to, follows the contemporary American pattern of doing good works; this requires giving not only money (the easy part, and expected) but much time and hard work to the Symphony, the Community Fund, children's hospitals, mental health, and a myriad of other community enterprises, ranging from the art museum to the zoo. All provide ambitious newcomers with a chance to meet, and try to make a favorable impression on, the old families, who, despite the withering away of class lines, still decide the composition of the in-group. Probably no activity in the civic-social arena, where the climbing game is played nowadays, attracts a more eager following than the charity ball, the all-purpose, income-tax-incubated substitute for the big, expensive private party. A booming institution throughout the country, the charity ball has a distinctly Super-American quality, for it enables participants not only to help the less fortunate, to have a good time, and (the costs as a rule being deductible) to enjoy the satisfaction of having made a good deal but also to have a chance at getting something for nothing in the form of a door prize, which, at these affairs, is seldom a bagatelle. At a recent Crystal Charity Ball, in Dallas, a then unmarried millionaire named Bill Moss won the grand prize, a Cadillac convertible, but he didn't need it, so he gave it to his date.

Though the entrenched group in Texas smiles on the moneyed up-and-comers to the extent of mingling with them at social events like charity balls, Texas bluebloods are not markedly less remiss than their counterparts anywhere else in exercising the sweet privilege of exclusion. Every Texas city, therefore, naturally has social organizations that, it is tacitly understood, are reserved for the local aristocracy. These restricted preserves, which are most plentiful in Houston, are generally small, like that city's Tejas Club, situated atop the Petroleum Building, and the Eagle Lake Rod and Gun Club, whose headquarters, a rather ostentatiously unpretentious structure, is located some fifty miles from town; the Tejas limits its membership to one hundred men, the Eagle Lake to sixty, and each maintains its particular character by giving preference in the election of new members to sons of old ones. The Tejas is known for its exceptional food, as is the Ramada, another downtown men's club, which, according to John Blaffer, a founder, "compares largely with any of the better New York clubs, such as the Racquet Club and others, where business associations and family background and individual personalities play an important part." Like the Ramada, whose monthly dues are thirty dollars, the other exclusive clubs adhere to the genteel practice of keeping the fixed charges low; it costs a thousand dollars to join the Tejas or Eagle Lake. In line with the prevailing pattern, the fees of a club tend to vary in relation to its age; for example, a membership in the Houston Country Club, founded in 1908, costs twenty-five hundred dollars, while one in the River Oaks Country Club, founded in 1923 and therefore the runner-up socially, sells, when available, for around ten thousand.

Among the more colorful of the exclusive groups that take pride in their remoteness from the general social hurly-burly is the Paul Jones Dancing Club, the oldest social dance group in Houston. It gives four dances a year, all at the Houston

Country Club, where these functions have been held for more than four decades. Along with the rollicking Paul Joneses, members gambol through a folk-dance series, beginning, as a rule, with "Put Your Little Foot Down" and winding up with "Herr Schmidt," a number so strenuous as to make even the fittest on the club's roster welcome the intermission that follows. According to past-president John Staub, the members of the Paul Jones, slightly less than a hundred in number, are "people who have been here years on end." The complexion of the membership is not apt to change radically in the near future, since new members, admitted only to fill vacancies caused by death and selected by a secret committee consisting of the current president and four former holders of the office, generally turn out to be relatives of old members.

Of the first-rank family clubs in Houston, the Bayou would no doubt be the pick of a socially alert newcomer if he had the choice, which he hasn't, since the Bayou Club has only a hundred and twenty-five select members, and taps more of the same to fill rare vacancies. Its clubhouse, set in a wooded area away from the center of town, is a two-story structure designed by architect-member John Staub and has the appearance of a small, elegant country house. It is comfortably and handsomely furnished, overlooks a swimming pool, and is surrounded by towering pines. Originally founded as a polo club, the Bayou now offers facilities for riding, swimming, and tennis, as well as for small receptions and entertainments, such as the popular Sunday buffet lunch. "The Bayou Club people are the ones who are interested in the cultural things in the city," a member has said. "It is a set unto itself. You feel at home there."

A sense of the familiar is even more pronounced in several women's organizations of the more elect sort, such as the Hesitation Club, in Dallas, which a member has proudly described as "a very related club—just about everybody is a daughter or daughter-in-law or cousin or related in some other way to a past or present member—and that accounts for our really splendid *esprit de corps.*" The club puts on one dance a year. "It's not what you would call a fabulous affair," one of the less hesitant members has said, "because most of our ladies are a little too—what shall I say—provident, perhaps, to splurge." The Hesitation's membership is limited to one hundred. To make possible keeping it at that number, the ladies changed the bylaws a while ago to require five, rather than two, adverse votes to reject an application for membership; the liberalization was considered necessary to counter the tactics of a pair of rather unbending members who for years blackballed just about everybody who applied. A possibly even more exclusive, and certainly more active, social group is the Dallas Shakespeare Club, which was organized in 1886 by Mrs. Henry Exall, Sr., who served as its president for the ensuing fifty-two years. The club, whose membership is limited to fifty-five actives and a handful of honoraries, meets every other Friday afternoon from November through April, devoting the first half of the season to the study and reading aloud of a Shakespearean play and the second to oral reports on contemporary theatrical matters. Some members take the preparation of their reports so conscientiously that they avail themselves of professional assistance. "Belonging to this club carries kudos," Mrs. John William Rogers, a member who has been a successful novelist, has remarked. "It is such an honor that members are very anxious to have their daughters accepted. Of course, we let no oil people in."

And so the social wheel in Texas turns, in the big cities and in the smaller ones. "There is a Four Hundred here," a Fort Worth matron whose family has been one of them for three generations has remarked, "just as there is in Dallas and Houston and San Antonio, and they all exclude people they don't like. The natives know who and what everybody is and has been. If the newcomer has built up his capital in a conservative way—hasn't speculated or engaged in any sharp practice—his chances of being accepted are good. But he can't count on it. After all, human nature can be just as cussed here as anyplace—in some things, I guess, maybe more so."

It is the male side of human nature that has customarily been regarded as dominant in Texas, and still is. "Down here," a believer in the natural superiority of the Texas male once advised a foreigner, "men are in charge of everything, and I mean everything. Why," he added, producing what is apparently regarded in some circles as a clincher, "the men even pick out the débutantes." In most Texas cities, it is true, débutantes are presented by male clubs—the Bachelors, in Austin; the Idlewild, in Dallas; the German, in San Antonio; and so on. The practice is not, of course, uniquely Texan but, rather, is in the tradition of the South, where the males of the family serve as its young ladies' social mentors. Furthermore, in several Texas cities there are, as elsewhere, what have been called "degrees of débutantes"; it is, for example, more prestigious for a young lady in Houston to bow at both the Assembly, a women's organization, and the Allegro, a men's club, than at the latter alone. The reason is that the Assembly presents only daughters and other close relatives of members, while, as John Staub has remarked, "the Allegro is more conglomerate." Last season, the Assembly presented four young ladies, the Allegro nineteen. One recent season, the Assembly Dancing Club, in San Antonio, which Mrs. Edgar Tobin has characterized as "the nearest to the old-time kind of society here," presented one débutante.

Regardless of locale, Texas débutantes engage in the customary whirlwind round of balls, luncheons, dinners, and receptions, which for the young ladies of Dallas and Fort Worth in the season just past added up to some six dozen. Probably the most elegant affair of this kind was the ball that Mr. and Mrs. Robert Windfohr gave in 1959 for their daughter Anne. It was held at Fort Worth's Ridglea Country Club, where, under the direction of a New York decorator, a parquet dance floor was specially built over the club's Olympic-size swimming pool and illuminated by some eighty thousand blinking lights arranged to simulate three tents. Music was provided by three bands, including Louis Armstrong's, flown in for the occasion. At three o'clock in the morning, a tremendous fireworks display was set off, but the bands played on until long after dawn, the guests having been thoughtfully provided beforehand with sunglasses. The cost of the affair—a hundred thousand dollars or so—was considerably more than that of the usual Texas debutante party, which since the Second World War has ranged from ten to twenty-five thousand.

In expense, décor, procedure, and punctiliousness, the functions that present débutantes in the large Texas cities are quite indistinguishable from those in older sections of the country. However, in addition to making their local bows many Texas débutantes also find time to be presented at such affairs as the Neches River Festival, in Beaumont; the Fiesta San Jacinto, in San Antonio; and the Rose Festival, in Tyler, and these are all distinctively Texan. Being in the nature of pageants, they call for both expensive costumes and time-consuming rehearsals. In Tyler, for example, out-of-town débutantes are presented in the course of the coronation of the queen of the festival, an event held in the high-school auditorium and constructed around a rich and romantic theme —"Splendor of Light" being, in the opinion of many experienced observers, the most memorable in recent years. In that one, the ceremony began as the curtains parted on a softly illuminated stage with tiers of stairs extending from one side to the other. An orchestra struck up "Three O'Clock in the Morning," and an off-stage, mellow-voiced narrator, speaking over a public-address system, announced a production "re-creating nature's mood from the first rays of dawn through evening's dazzling grandeur."

As the narrator went on to tell of "Majestic Sun unfolding the secret splendors of the day," there appeared at the top of the stairs a young lady wearing a voluminous hoop-skirted gown with a train large enough to carpet a fair-sized room and on which was embroidered an elaborate sunburst design. The music faded to allow the narrator to present "Miss Mary Winn, Duchess of the Tyler Rose Growers, portraying Majestic Sun." As the music swelled, Majestic Sun slowly descended the stairs, and at the foot made a full court bow, her forehead nearly touching the floor. So nature's mood wore on, until some twenty-five young rays of light, each appropriately costumed, had been presented, ending with "Her Gracious Majesty, Gail of the House of Hudson, Empress of Celestial Light." To the strains of "Pomp and Circumstance," Miss Hudson, in a stunning gown of white lace encrusted with mirrored jewels and sequins, accepted a jewelled sceptre, bowed to the applauding audience, and made her regal way, drawing a tremendous sparkling train, to the top of the stairs, there to witness the royal entertainment. This was provided by a male quartet that enthusiastically rendered "Without a Song" and several other numbers, after which the lights dimmed and the curtains closed on the queen and her court.

The social position of the American woman, particularly in reference to her place in the national design for living, is a subject that has endlessly fascinated foreign observers. Their consensus, though usually expressed in more stately phrases, is that until America, women had never had it so good. As usual, de Tocqueville said it first, when he declared that "although the women of the United States are confined within the narrow circle of domestic life, and their situation is in some respects one of extreme dependence, I have nowhere seen woman occupying a loftier position." He had not, of course, seen Texas. The position of the millioned women there is even more sublime, for they not only enjoy the independence stemming from community-property legislation but have been released from the customary confinements of domestic life. Also, without a known exception, they have been freed from what Henry Ford III has called "the thralldom of the one-car family." As far as transport is concerned, the wives of some Texas millionaires have been liberated to the extent of having their own private plane, though the majority, like Mrs. Clint Murchison, have to be satisfied with simply having one or more in the family. When the wanderlust mood strikes, Mrs. Murchison collects five or six similarly inclined millionaires' wives, loads them aboard "The Flying Ginny," a luxuriously outfitted DC-3 named by her husband in her honor, and takes off for a few days, dropping in perhaps at the Murchisons' thousand-acre island in the Gulf or at their imposing ranch in Mexico.

Much the same kind of impulse to get away from it all struck Mrs. James Abercrombie, of Houston, a few years ago, and in no time, accompanied by four friends, she was aloft in one of her husband's planes headed toward the Caribbean and a gay spell of island-hopping. That jaunt turned out so successfully that The Flying Five, as those who made the trip began calling themselves, thenceforth took up impromptu travelling as a hobby. "We have a pilot and a co-pilot, and the object is sightseeing—nothing else," Mrs. Abercrombie said recently. "No collecting of antiques, souvenirs, picture postcards, or lugging of cameras. We travel, we look, we enjoy ourselves." Enjoyment is also the basic aim of the excursions that Mrs. Ralph Fair, of San Antonio, arranges periodically for herself and a handful of women friends at the Fairs' ranch in Montana, a spread that includes a landing strip big enough to accommodate the owners' DC-3. To enable her guests to vary their vacation routine, consisting mainly of cardplaying and relaxing, with a certain amount of beautifying and conditioning, Mrs. Fair always includes in the party a hairdresser and a masseuse. "It's a grand two weeks," a veteran of the outings has said. "Sort of like Maine Chance Farm, only with Martinis."

Activities closer to home take up a larger share of the abundant leisure of Super-American women, who tend to pursue their pastimes *en bloc*. Reading is usually for the purpose of preparing a report to a literary club; painting is customarily done in a class; even gardening involves spending a good deal of time in the company of other women, for garden clubs abound in Texas (over seven hundred in Dallas alone) and members thrive on frequent meetings. Since the daily round of civic and social activities gets under way early, the well-organized woman tries to complete her housekeeping duties, shopping, beauty-parlor visits, and the like by ten-thirty or so, when she may attend an informal "coffee," usually in connection with some community enterprise. Lunching in groups—ordinarily at a club or a restaurant, and frequently to meet an out-of-town guest, who is known as the honoree—takes care of the midday hours.

The next order of pleasure for many Super-American women is attendance at a meeting of a so-called investment club, like the Girls' Investment Group, in Dallas, whose members contribute to a common fund that they use to buy and sell securities of their own choosing. But the real business of these clubs, like so many other ladies' organizations in Texas, is to engage in the most popular of all pastimes—cardplaying. Card clubs flourish in Texas, and to insure a maximum opportunity to play, a large percentage of Super-American women belong to two or three. Most meet weekly and make an afternoon of it, though some get under way before lunch. For example, Mrs. Jake Hamon, of Dallas, a talented and dedicated player, occasionally collects the members of one of her clubs early enough to transport them in a chartered, air-conditioned, bar-equipped bus to the Shady Oaks Country Club, in Fort Worth, for lunch, which is followed by a long afternoon at the card tables. Other devotees, like Mrs. Donald Lee, of Houston, are willing to travel even farther to find a congenial site for playing. A while ago, when Mrs. Lee and three of her friends simultaneously felt the need for a bridge-playing vacation, they boarded a train for Colorado Springs, taking along a maid to minister to their needs en route and thus insure no interruption of their game, which went on until dawn.

To provide their wives with a certain extra amount of money and leisure is no more than what is expected of Texas millionaires. Were they to act otherwise, they would be considered not only un-Super-American but plain un-American, for everybody knows that the men of this country, as the English traveller George Warrington Steevens some while ago reminded us, "furnish a shining example to all the world in their devoted chivalry toward their women. They toil and slave, they kill themselves at forty, that their women may live in luxury and become socially and intellectually superior to

themselves. They do it," Steevens continued, the chaff beginning to show, "without even an idea that there is any self-
sacrifice in it. Whether it is good for the women might be
doubted, but it is unspeakably noble and honoring to the
men."

Chivalry in contemporary Texas, as in the olden times, makes
few demands on women, but the few it makes are strict.
The first is an at least ostensible acknowledgment of male
superiority—or, as it was put by one Texas woman, whose
career has made her more cosmopolitan than most, "The role
of women down here is not to appear smarter than men. For
a woman to act as if she thinks she's as bright as a man—
that's fatal." Of course, there are few women anywhere in the
country who have the daring to pursue a contrary course in
public, but whereas implied deference to men is, to a certain
extent, voluntary elsewhere, in Texas it seems to have the
oppressive status of law. As a matter of fact, Texas laws relating
to married women are based in part on the Spanish code, and
consequently make a husband, in effect, the custodian of his
wife and her property. Thus, she cannot make a contract, sell
or give away a piece of property, even if bought with her own
money, or do any number of similar things without obtaining
her husband's signature.

While many business and professional women in Texas have
been agitating for a so-called equal-rights amendment to the
State Constitution, few other Texas women would think of
bringing up this subject or any other so potentially displeasing
to a male. In consequence, conversation with women in Super-
America tends to be agreeably undemanding. Rather than risk
offense, they normally shy away from talk about politics or any
other controversial subject, but on topics like golf, television,
and travel they can be torrentially responsive. Their *expertise*
in the aim-to-please role stems from what appears to be an
uncanny, intuitive comprehension of the place that women
have traditionally occupied in the hearts of Texas men—a place
implicitly staked out in the affectionate declaration of W. T.
Waggoner, one of the great old-time cattle kings: "A man who

doesn't admire a good steer, a good horse, and a pretty woman
—well, something is wrong with that man's head."

Though an almost Oriental courtesy toward men comes
naturally to Super-American women, coquetry does not. The
kind of "sparkling and amusingly flirtatious little woman" that
Taine found to be practically nonexistent in England is equally
rare among wives of Texas millionaires. In the normal course of
social events, they avoid anything resembling flirtation as carefully as if there were a law against it. In effect, there is, according to the Dallas psychiatrist Dr. Perry Talkington. "There
was a time in this part of the country when women were at a
premium—far and away the most valuable import," Dr. Talkington has explained. "As a consequence, men put their wives
under bell jars, so to speak. In those days—sixty years ago or
so—if you asked a man his name, he might very well have
shot you, and if you flirted with his wife, you can be pretty
sure he'd have shot you. Furthermore, he would then have
gone about his business with no concern about being punished.
The situation hasn't changed entirely. Today, if a man finds his
wife being unfaithful and kills her lover, he doesn't have to
worry about being tried. What it comes to is that when this
was the frontier, flirting was rather unhealthy, like cattle rustling, and those days aren't too far in the past."

The relative proximity of the frontier also serves to explain
why love and sex are taken even more seriously in Texas than
in the country as a whole, if that is possible, and it is. A Super-
American suspected of harboring anything as radical as "the
French point of view that love is very often an exceedingly
comical affair," to quote Raoul de Roussy de Sales, would be
considered a clear and present danger to the community. In
showing disapproval of their local Don Juans, Texans reveal
not only a sectional reverence for the puritan tradition but the
effect of changing national customs. Fifty years ago, many self-
respecting American millionaires took much pride in showing
off their mistresses; the current fashion is to be surreptitious.
Whatever the style of such arrangements, however, the institution of marriage in Super-America, as in the rest of the

country, has remained constant in one respect—in the rate at which it ends in divorce.

On the basis of actual performance, Texans can prove that they believe even more deeply than most Americans in divorce as an instrument of marital policy. That is, admittedly, a large claim, since approximately every fourth American who marries is divorced at least once. But Texans do better than that, as witness the contribution of Tarrant County, taking in Fort Worth and environs, where, in 1958, filings for divorce outnumbered applications for marriage. While not quite up to that mark, figures for the state as a whole show that in marital, as in traffic, fatalities, Texas ranks second only to California— and it must be remembered that the Texans' score in both areas is accomplished with a population handicap of some six million. In achieving their divorce record, Texans, together with other Americans, have the obvious advantages that result from belonging to the only known civilization to embark, Denis de Rougement has observed, "upon the perilous enterprise of making marriage coincide with love . . . and of making the first depend upon the second." In addition, Texans have the special regional benefit of the frontier spirit, which invites the squandering of resources at hand in the belief that better is to be had beyond the horizon.

All things considered, it is not hard to understand why Texas millionaires regard divorce, like daybreak, as an everyday fact of life, and take note of it only when it becomes a kind of hobby with one of their members, as with the late Guy Waggoner, who had seven wives. The acceptance of serial monogamy, as Margaret Mead refers to the American system, is indicated by the fact that the acknowledged social leader of Fort Worth has been married three times, while a popular hostess in Dallas has now settled down with her fifth mate. The heavy local demand for professional aid in dissolving the marriage contract has brought into play the American genius for mass production, which has had the usual result of reducing the unit cost. Indeed, at the Gala Ball of the Houston Museum of Fine Arts last year, Percy Foreman, one of the city's most colorful and high-priced lawyers, offered to donate a divorce as a door prize; his generous gesture was not accepted, although, as the knowledgeable columnist Bill Roberts later remarked, "there was more than one at that affair who would have liked to win that gift."

The steadily increasing reliance on divorce to resolve marital difficulties has disturbed some Texans, and for truly Super-American reasons, which were brought out in a letter written a while ago by a West Texas matron to a friend. The subject was a contretemps involving, as the lady put it, "a gun-totin' rancher, very rich and pretty violent, and his wife, who lives in the city." Her account went on, "She's very handsome, and lives in very high style. One day, big, handsome hubby comes in from the ranch and discovers he has been cuckolded—not once, but numerous times. He wastes no time finding out, by threatening the little woman, who the varmints are, and they turn out to be four of the Four Hundred, each with a wife, kids, etc. Well, he naturally decides to shoot all four of the interlopers—and he meant it—but then he had another idea. He arranged a dinner party, the guests being none other than his wife's gentlemen callers and their wives. (I understand he issued *very* firm invitations to the affair.) After what must have been a rather tense meal, the guests and our host and hostess retire to the living room, and while coffee and brandy are being served, our host walks over to a desk, takes out his trusty Smith & Wesson .38, and proceeds to load it. He then announces that the evening's entertainment is going to consist of a little game of true confessions. He explains the rules—each of the male guests will be called upon to tell the whole story of his skylarking with his evening's hostess. This caused some commotion, of course. After it had died down, our rancher friend, twirling the barrel of the revolver, made it clear that anybody who refused to play the game wasn't going to *walk* out of the house. Fortunately for the name of our fair city, everybody did finally walk out, but the party didn't break up until the early hours of the morning, our host being the fussy type. What with the late hour and all, I understand everybody went home fair tired. Several weeks later, the paper carried a tiny story announcing the divorce. Quite a few people around here have stopped shaking, at last."

Though the case is closed, debate about it goes on. Some of the rancher's fellow-millionaires endorse his choice of divorce, despite the quite extraordinary provocation. Others argue that by not shooting the trespassers he let down the state and sullied one of its finest traditions. Together, the two factions demonstrate once again the sure grasp that Texans have of both the American way and the Super-American way.

Chapter Thirteen

In their talent for self-deception, Americans have few peers. "Nowhere, surely, is the superiority of American know-how more evident than in our use of hypocrisy," William S. White, veteran Washington correspondent, Pulitzer Prize winner, and native of De Leon, Texas observed a while ago in beginning a *Harper's* essay straightforwardly titled "The American Genius for Hypocrisy." Though this form of know-how is hardly an American monopoly ("There's nothing commoner in life than hypocrisy," another Texan, J. Frank Dobie, has said), we have turned the practice of conning ourselves into an art. And Texans, being Super-Americans, have perfected it. Thus, when the poet George Cabot Lodge asks, "Was there ever such an anomaly as the American man?" the answer is, "Yes, the Super-American man." Consider his love affair with the doctrine of states' rights, a term that, like "Mother" or "The Alamo," can make moist his eyes. To listen to his passionate public utterances, one would think he not only originated the doctrine but stood as its sole and beleaguered protector. Thus, when Governor Nelson Rockefeller made his swing through the region in 1959, the Houston *Post* headlined its story of his visit "ROCKEFELLER BACKS STATES' RIGHTS HERE," and the Dallas *News* reported "ROCKY VOWS BELIEF IN STATES' RIGHTS." Like everybody else outside Dixie, he had been suspected of being against them.

Free whiskey, it has been said, will draw a crowd anywhere; in Texas free talk about states' rights will do the same. It did in December, 1958, after an advertisement in the Houston papers announced, "Believe in States' Rights? . . . Don't Fail to Hear Hon. Orval Faubus, Governor of Arkansas. . . . Tonight at 7:45 P.M. . . . Music Hall . . . Admission Free . . . Governor Faubus, Outstanding Defender of States' Rights, Will Speak Under the Sponsorship of the Sons of the American Revolution in Observance of Bill of Rights Day. . . . His address will be on 'States' Rights.'" As the ad hinted, the Governor did touch on the topic of states' rights, which is locally interpreted to mean that there must be absolutely no interference whatever by any non-Texas agency or person in the domestic affairs of what former Senator William A. Blakley and other stalwarts refer to as "Texas, a sovereign state and once-sovereign nation." In the light of this interpretation, a rumor, for example, that Walter Reuther has endorsed a Texas candidate for Congress is apt to stir up about as much public alarm around the state as a report that the Premier of the U.S.S.R. has taken up residence in Austin.

While fiercely opposing interference in their sovereign state, Texans think it all right for them to interfere in the domestic affairs of other sovereign states. Their specialty is influencing the election of Congressional candidates with contributions of cash. For instance, Clint Murchison, as ardent a states'-righter as ever came out of Athens, Texas, contributed ten thousand dollars to help defeat Senator Millard Tydings, of Maryland, and another ten to unseat Senator William Benton, of Connecticut—both among the few outspoken Senatorial critics of Murchison's friend the late Senator Joseph McCarthy. Texas millionaires have also put money into the campaign funds of candidates in Arizona, California, Idaho, Illinois, Indiana, Michigan, Missouri, Montana, New Mexico, New York, Nevada, North Dakota, Ohio, Utah, Virginia, Washington, and Wisconsin, to mention those states where their contributions are on record.

As dedicated believers in states' rights, the Super-Americans take the logical position that the wickedest interference in their affairs is the federal government's. Consequently, terms like "social security," "federal aid to education," "welfare," and "medical care for the aged" are dirty words to Texas millionaires. They hold with a recent editorial in the Dallas *News*, which declared, "When our forefathers stepped on the west bank of the Mississippi and headed West to carve an empire, did they look back over their shoulders to the national government for 'welfare' and help? No—with an axe and a Bible and a wife, the pioneer did it himself." One difference between the pioneers stepping on the riverbank and the Texas millionaires stepping into their swimming pools is that the millionaires *won't* do it themselves; they refuse to support tax measures that would give the state enough money to meet its expenses, and, as a result, Texans are obliged to swallow their pride and ask for federal aid.

Taking a deep swallow, Texas, which stands sixth in population among the states and seventh in the amount of federal taxes paid, ranks third in the amount of money it takes every year from the federal government. An indication of the Texans' skill at getting into the Washington trough is the fact that their state is first in taking federal handouts for agricultural-experiment stations, child-welfare services, cooperative agricultural-extension work, hospital construction, primary-highway funds, secondary-highway funds, watershed protection and flood prevention, and services for crippled children; second in taking federal funds for old-age assistance, aid to the blind, airport programs, and wildlife restoration; and third in taking money for interstate-highway construction, general health assistance, and the maintenance and operation of schools. By dipping its hand ever deeper into the federal till, Texas has now reached a point where a fourth of the state's annual income is derived from the United States government. Texans talk less about this than about their fiscal skill in getting by without either a state income tax or (until 1961) a state sales tax. Such is their pride in this accomplishment that they suffered no visible humiliation when, in the spring of 1959, the sovereign state and once-sovereign nation was completely flatpocket, and was forced to pay its employees with hot checks.

Even though Texas takes a highly disproportionate share of

federal funds, it lags in the services it provides its citizens. For example, in 1959 Texas was first among the states in the amount of federal money accepted for child-welfare services but forty-fourth in the amount spent for child-welfare services; in other words, Texans will not part with enough of their own money to bring the level of care for their dependent children even up to the national average. The pattern is consistent: Texas is second in the amount of federal money it takes for old-age assistance, fortieth in the amount spent; second in the amount accepted to aid the blind, fortieth in the amount spent; and so on.

Texans make no secret of the fact that they lead the nation in cattle production; at the same time, the state ranks forty-seventh in the amount of money the legislature provides for animal-health work. "That's not very much money to do the job right," the director of the State Livestock Sanitary Commission has said of his budget. "It's like trying to paint the Capitol Building in Austin with a pint of paint." The director of the Texas prison system has some concern about his budget, too; he told a legislative committee in February, 1959, "We are absolutely broke. We don't have a dollar. We are the most understaffed of any prison system in the country." The prisons, he added, are so overcrowded that two or three men occupy space designed for one, and some five hundred men are obliged to sleep on the floor. Things had not improved by the early part of 1961, when the director told the legislature that he could not even pay his outstanding bills. "We're running on borrowed time," he said. "We need help."

Texans take justifiable pride in their industry, which has skyrocketed to tenth place in the nation; little is heard of the fact that the industrial-accident toll in Texas is one of the highest, if not the highest, in the country. Nobody knows for sure, because Texas, alone among the large industrial states, has no state industrial-safety program and therefore no state agency charged with collecting statistics on industrial injuries. In unemployment benefits, Texas is tied with Alabama for next-to-last place. In public-school enrollment and in number of teachers employed, Texas ranks third among the states, but in total spending for education it ranks sixth, in teachers' salaries twenty-eighth, and in spending per pupil thirty-second. It is able to do this well only because it accepts more federal aid for schools than any other state except California and Virginia. And still more could be used, since Texas, whose young men stood fortieth in Selective Service mental tests during the Second World War, has some eight hundred thousand illiterates over the age of twenty-four, thereby placing eleventh among the states in rate of illiteracy. Yet, to judge by their words, Texans are in uncontested first place in opposing federal aid to education.

While thundering continuously against this and every other federal grant, the Dallas *News* from time to time prints stories like a recent one headlined "UNCLE SAM'S BUSINESS FILLS IMPORTANT ROLE FOR DALLAS," which reported that the city has more than ten thousand federal employees, with a combined payroll exceeding thirty-five million dollars a year. "That's the federal government in Dallas," the article said. "Big, busy, and vitally important to the city's economy, it ranks as a major 'industry.'" It went on to quote Chamber of Commerce officials, who said, "We are just as interested in attracting new federal offices and keeping the ones we already have as we are in getting and keeping industry and business." There was, therefore, considerable disappointment when, in May, 1960, the House Public Works Committee refused to approve the construction of a new twenty-six-million-dollar Federal Building in Dallas. Nobody was more upset than Representative Bruce Alger, the only Republican member of the House from Texas, who declared that the Committee's action was an attempt by the Democratic leadership "to punish the citizens of Dallas for daring to elect a Republican congressman." He has made it clear that he intends to keep right on fighting not only for the Federal Building in Dallas but against federal aid in every form. He is so unalterably opposed to it in principle that in 1958 he had the desolate distinction of being the only member of Congress to vote against free milk for school children. He keeps his constituents informed on how he is saving the taxpayers' money, in this and other ways, in a weekly newsletter, which, alone among congressmen, he has printed in the *Congressional Record*, at a weekly cost to the taxpayers of a hundred dollars a page.

The ambivalence that colors some aspects of life in Texas often puzzles outsiders, especially Europeans, such as the Italian industrialist who remarked after a sojourn in Texas, "They treat your Uncle Sam as if he were a complete stranger. You listen to them, and you think he doesn't protect them with an Army, a Navy, and Air Force; he doesn't make any missiles; he doesn't build any dams; he doesn't build any roads; he doesn't support a Foreign Service, an Intelligence Service—he doesn't do anything for them. They just want to forget him. It's fantastic." Not, however, to an American accustomed to the dualism in the native grain, but even he might be moved to wonder how much federal aid Texans would be willing to accept if they approved of it.

Apart from its ambivalence toward Washington, the state government of Texas is itself quite generally free of hypocrisy. The principal reason for this refreshing state of affairs has perhaps never been more succinctly stated in public than it was in 1947, by Robert W. Calvert, then chairman of the Democratic State Executive Committee. "It may not be a wholesome thing to say," Calvert told the Lions Club of Hillsboro, "but the oil industry today is in complete control of the state government and state politics." This being so, there is little need for sham by members of the legislature and other elected officials. Since they—as well as the voters who put them in office—know that their chief allegiance is to the state's largest industry, it is understood that their support of the oil companies is simply the performance of a duty. There is also a sensible understanding of the fact that the oil companies will show their appreciation for work well done, or to be done, by supplying members of the legislature and other state officials with free food and drink on the job. In addition to the free-loading in Austin, the legislators are provided with such amenities as transportation in company-owned planes and gala all-expenses-paid outings to hunt ducks, deer, quail, and whatever else may suit their fancy. There are, of course, more tangible gestures of gratitude, such as the highly popular "retainer fee," paid on a year-round basis.

The acceptance of favors by lawmakers is scarcely unique to Texas, but the nice thing about it there is that nobody has to be sneaky about it. As Ronnie Dugger, a contributing editor of the *Texas Observer* and one of the handful of native journalists who take an interest in the local political morality, has pointed out, "The rich think they can buy stock in the legislature or an executive agency as they can in a corporation, and they can." The result is that lobbying is to Austin roughly what gambling is to Las Vegas. When the legislature convenes, more than three thousand acknowledged lobbyists—or nearly twenty lobbyists for every lawmaker—take up their work in behalf of oil companies, gas companies, naturopaths, highway builders, unions, brewers, temperance movements, and scores of other worthy principals, including the insurance companies, which conduct a lobbying operation in keeping with their position as the state's second largest industry.

Texas has shown insurance companies such hospitality, in the way of low capital requirements for their establishment and a passionately laissez-faire attitude toward their regulation, that the industry expanded steadily to the point where, in 1955, nearly two thousand companies were registered in the state. That, of course, was not counting some five dozen Texas insurance companies which had gone bankrupt in the previous fifteen years because of comically bad management or outright fraud. Altogether, an estimated half-million Texans have lost money through the failure of insurance companies. One of the more enterprising was the Texas Mutual Insurance Company, which was organized with five hundred dollars in cash and a loan of nineteen thousand five hundred; it went bankrupt, owing a million two hundred thousand dollars in claims. Another that went out with a bang was the General American Casualty Company, which was so imaginatively managed that in the year before its demise it took in six million dollars in premiums and yet wound up a million dollars in debt. Perhaps the most resounding failure was that of the U. S. Trust & Guaranty, in which a hundred and fifty thousand people had invested.

After this collapse, some of the stuffier legislators began an investigation of the industry. It developed that the companies had not been remiss in looking after insurance commissioners and examiners, as well as legislators. The U. S. Trust & Guaranty, for example, had paid the chairman of the State Board of Control ten thousand dollars for "legal work" in its behalf, besides passing out cash to nine members of the legislature in amounts ranging from a hundred and fifty dollars to ten thousand. The largest sum went to a state senator who for years had successfully stymied legislative efforts to check up on the company's operations. Among many other disclosures that came as a surprise to few people acquainted with Austin was the intelligence that the Texas Mutual Insurance Company, before going broke, had kept a state senator on its payroll, paying him thirteen thousand dollars over a three-year period. The so-called "insurance scandals" brought about legislation revamping the state organization that was charged with administering and regulating the industry. But though the new legal machinery was a notable improvement, it did not operate well enough to keep a smooth-talking manipulator named W. L. Bridges, after serving a sentence in a Kansas prison for violating the state securities laws, from moving into Texas and acquiring a complex of eighteen solvent insurance companies, which, with the help of his son, he systematically drained of assets and sent to the wall in June, 1960, leaving fifty-three thousand policyholders and scores of creditors holding the bag.

The air had scarcely cleared after the insurance scandals when, in 1956, the Texas Land Commissioner was convicted of agreeing to accept seventy-four thousand dollars in bribes and of conspiring to steal tens of thousands of dollars from the state through his administration of the Veterans' Land Board, set up to enable veterans to buy a little place of their own with long-term, low-interest loans. The Commissioner worked in cahoots with shady promoters whose legal work was handled by a state senator for a fee of some twenty-eight thousand dollars. So aroused were the legislators by the land scandals that at their next session they passed what they called a Code of Ethics Bill, which "requires any legislator who serves as a member, or represents, or has a controlling interest in any firm under state regulation to reveal such connections in a sworn statement filed with the Secretary of State." Putting teeth in the measure, the legislators included a provision making "failure to comply to any section of the code grounds for expulsion from the legislature." Extracting the teeth, they set no date for filing such reports.

In the same crusading spirit, the legislature went on to pass the Lobby Registration Act, which requires any person who undertakes to influence legislation to register with the clerk of the House, giving his name, the organization he represents, and the legislative measures with which he is concerned; he must also file, between the first and the fifteenth of each month after the legislature goes into session, a sworn statement showing how much money (minus a fifty-dollar-deductible arrangement) he has spent for "direct communication" with the legislature. "Of course," the San Antonio *Express* commented in an editorial, "that part of the law is as loose as your maiden Aunt Minnie's kimono. How direct must the communication be?" After the law went into effect, in January, 1959, the lobbyists apparently started to work almost entirely by indirection, for of nearly nine hundred then registered, less than an eighth felt called upon to file an expense report for that month. Few students of Texas politics take these figures to mean that the legislators are not dining and wining as well as ever. In the most recent regular session, they were the objects of massive attention by a horde of lobbyists interested in defeating a bill to outlaw loan sharks, who operate in Texas (contrary to the practice in forty-five other states) without regulation and are accordingly able to charge interest ranging from a hundred to twelve hundred per cent. "There's been some 'lettuce' floating around," Senator Culp Krueger said during debate on the measure, gesturing toward the Senate gallery, where the loan-shark lobbyists had forthrightly seated themselves to keep an eye on the proceedings. Whatever was floating around was sufficiently influential to keep the bill from becoming law, thus prolonging the reputation of Texas as "The Loan Shark State."

The state treasury, meanwhile, has become steadily more emaciated. When the legislators convened for the session beginning in January, 1961, they were faced with the necessity of passing new tax measures not only to erase a sixty-three-million-dollar deficit but also to provide for three hundred million dollars' worth of proposed new spending. Not a dollar of the needed funds had been appropriated by the time the session ended. The lawmakers had, however, found time to vote themselves a comfortable raise in pay. They took care of that the second day they met. On the last day, they celebrated the windup of their hundred-and-forty-day meeting—which had been so fruitless that Governor Daniel had to call a special session to convene two months later—with a variety of high jinks in the legislative chambers, including the rendition by an impromptu barbershop-type quartet of "You Tell Me Your Dream, I'll Tell You Mine" and a wrestling match between a couple of legislators who disagreed over a fine point of parliamentary procedure.

A genial, rough-and-ready spirit; a willingness, born of the conviction that only the future counts, to let bygones be bygones; an air of sprightly casualness—these are some of the things that give a sense of Texas. The easy-does-it approach to work and play that is one of the attractions of life there has been ascribed by the Dallas psychiatrist Dr. Perry Talkington to the comparative youthfulness of the region. "As a culture grows older, life becomes more ritualistic," he has remarked. "There is much more ritual in Boston, for example, than in Dallas. And more ritual in London than in Boston. The relative absence of ritual tends to make life here more casual." J. Frank

Dobie, the distinguished freelance analyst, has suggested that the pace of Texas life reflects the Texas character, which, he has observed, contains such tranquillizing elements as "the leisureliness of the Old South, the *mañana*-ness of Mexico, and the waiting quality of the Indian."

The first hint of easygoingness that a visitor from the North or the East is apt to notice in Super-America is the language, which, compared with what he hears at home, is softer, spoken more slowly, and, being less aggressive, easier on the nerves. Words are often slurred, and little energy is wasted on sounding the final "g" of participles. The tide of immigration in recent years has resulted in a modification of the local accent, especially in the cities, and even in out-of-the-way places one is no longer apt to hear any of the old-time indigenous expressions, such as "knee-weakener," for a pretty girl, or "windmill-fixer," for a know-it-all. However, a gift for the laconic, another quality long associated with Texas speech, still turns up in remarks like that of James A. Elkins, Sr., the Houston lawyer and banker, whose favorite maxim is "Remember, you never learn from talkin'. Every fish ever caught on a hook had his mouth open" (Sid Richardson had a similar mot: "You ain't learnin' nothin' when you're talkin'"), and in Clint Murchison's haunting declaration, "Cash makes a man careless."

The usual form of greeting in Texas, which tends to establish a tone of informality, is "How y' doin'?"—sometimes put more specifically as "You all right?" In either case, the salutation implies a warmer interest in one's welfare than the curt Northern "Hi" or "Good morning." People meeting on the street have time for joshing. Sam Cantey III, walking out of the First National Bank of Fort Worth, of which he is a vice-president, is not surprised to be greeted on the sidewalk by the president of another bank with "Why, if it ain't old Sam! Who let you out?" In Texas, you call a friend "old" if you are really fond of him, and you never give offense by addressing him or introducing him by his nickname. The use of nicknames is so common that one gets the impression that all Texas millionaires are called Jim, Joe, Billy, Ted, Ed, Mike, Kip, Dutch, Slats, or something equally breezy, and the value attached to them is so generally recognized that some millionaires have incorporated theirs into their given names. For example, Robert E. Smith, the Houston oilman and civic leader, is always referred to in the newspapers as "R. E. (Bob) Smith," and in Midland the firm of J. P. (Bum) Gibbins is listed in the telephone directory as "Gibbins, J. P. Bum, Inc."

The soft-sounding language, the penchant for joshing, and the wide-spread use of nicknames and affectionate terms like "honey" and "sweetie" combine to give Texas talk an easy, friendly tone. That it also seems calm and unruffled arises in part from the preference for such polite-sounding phrases as "I'm not about to," to convey a sense of determined opposition. If a person says, for example, "I'm not about to go to that party," he is, in effect, saying, "You couldn't drag me to it." However, putting the thought with a whim-of-iron expression keeps the conversational surface placid.

If, as foreigners keep telling us, the habit of conversation does not exist in the United States, nobody should be surprised that what generally passes for conversation among Texas millionaires—aside from the anecdote, usually risqué and often told in dialect—is a mélange of talk about sports, television, bridge, gin rummy, poker, movies, parties (past, present and future), cars, cooking recipes, travel plans, gossip about friends, and similar matters, which are touched on so pell-mell that anybody who wants to participate must be ready to jump in quickly whenever he sees an opening. It is perhaps a commentary on the state of social discourse in Texas that probably nowhere else does one so often hear the term "conversation piece." Salespeople at Neiman-Marcus use it to develop interest in merchandise ranging from cigarette lighters to mutation-mink coats. A handbag is advertised as a "conversation starter," and an art show is recommended as a "conversational leader." The food editor of the Dallas *News*, in presenting a recipe for "*hors d'oeuvres délicats*," gives it the nod as a "conversation

piece, a spread which will have the sophisticated group raving."
If a visitor finds his group talking irrationally about the hors
d'oeuvres and the conversation, accordingly, somewhat unre-
warding, he cannot deny that it has the charm of being neither
stodgy nor taxing, and usually seems aimed to please.

In addition to their gift for communicating more easily than
people in the North, the Super-Americans are a more favored
nation in their management of the simple mechanics of living.
This accomplishment results in part from their sense of courtesy. Terms like "please," "thank you," "pardon," and "sorry"
are still in common usage. Men and boys, and even younger
women, give their seats on buses to the elderly. Children are
taught manners. Men tip their hats. Women acknowledge
having a door held open for them. Men do not grab taxis ahead
of ladies, even when it's raining.

Courtesy also prevails among those who serve the public.
When, for example, Mrs. E. Pollard Simons goes to the supermarket, as she sometimes does, in her Thunderbird, she need
not be burdened carrying her purchases to her car. Every
supermarket has a corps of men and boys who, summoned
by the checker with the familiar cry of "Package out!" perform
this service cheerfully and without expecting a tip. Sales clerks
are not against smiling. Bus drivers do not growl when spoken
to. Except in some private clubs, waiters generally act as if they
believed that their first duty was to serve food and their second
to collect tips. By and large, the natives still adhere to the
ten-per cent rule in tipping, and, to the astonishment of outlanders, are not snarled at but smiled at. No gratuities are
expected by the squad of men who descend upon a car entering
a filling station, one to fill the gas tank, another to "check under
that hood," as it is put, and still another to wash all the windows; if the day has been dusty, an attendant brushes out the
floor. Upon paying for his purchase, a customer—in a gas station
or anywhere else—receives not just a nod or a grudging "Thank
you" but usually a smile and a remark such as "Come back
and see us," "You hurry right back, now," or simply "Come

back," and always delivered as if they were meant. Trivial though such gestures may seem, they contribute to a net gain in living by diminishing, to a certain extent, the abrasiveness of existence.

The quality of Super-American bonhomie varies from city to city, a discovery that could hardly be avoided by even the most sentimental tourist who visits, for example, San Antonio and Houston. The two cities are separated by some two hundred miles in space and by an immeasurable distance in character. "In Houston, women think mainly about their homes, and in Dallas they think mainly about their clothes," Mrs. Edgar Tobin once remarked. "But here in San Antonio, they just think about having fun." This objective seems to be shared by most of the nearly six hundred thousand people of both sexes in San Antonio, which, despite steady growth, has dropped during the past half century from first to third in size among Texas cities. Instead of being cast down by this un-Super-American development, the residents of San Antonio have taken their demotion in stride, thereby incurring the disapproval of their more patriotic countrymen. In a recently published analysis of the San Antonio economy, the Federal Reserve Bank of Dallas felt called upon to scold the unrepentant municipality for its "attitude of complacency with respect to the city's growth."

Except for up-and-coming bankers, visitors to San Antonio have always been charmed by its complacency with respect to just about everything, an attitude that has given the city what Walter Prescott Webb has called its "joyously relaxed and playful" spirit. The slowed-down tempo is in part a product of maturity. San Antonio, the oldest city in Texas, was settled in 1730 by sixteen families who had been transplanted from the Canary Islands by the King of Spain. Since then, sizable migrations of Germans (local débutantes are still presented by the German Club), Swedes, Irish, Poles, French, Norwegians, and Mexicans have contributed to the city's cosmopolitan atmosphere, which provides a suggestion of Europe to many visitors. "The various objects that create this comforting sensation," Ludwig Bemelmans wrote, "are a canal which reminds one of the Belgian city of Bruges, a tower which looks as if it had been taken from Sienna, a zoo that is like the one in Hamburg, and a Spanish cathedral." It took the Dallas *News* to point out that San Antonio also has "too many rows of commercial structures that have the dinginess of Des Moines or Jersey City." In addition to its many other sights, such as the Alamo, the Menger Hotel, and the numerous military installations (the city has long been a favorite retirement spot for generals, a hundred and twenty of whom were in residence at last count), San Antonio has an agreeable climate and an even more agreeable style of life. "There is an urbanity about the people here," the San Antonio architect and Dallas emigrant O'Neil Ford has remarked. "The thing you come to notice about them is simply their nice behavior."

The thing a visitor notices immediately in Houston is that it is a big city, not only the biggest in Texas but the biggest in the South. In 1960, census takers counted 938,219 residents in Houston—enough to rank the city seventh largest in the country, and only 806 short of enough to beat Baltimore for sixth. "It is frustratingly disappointing, any way you look at it," the Houston *Post* observed, accurately reflecting local sentiment, which, with reason, is oriented toward bigness. Houston's metropolitan area is not only the largest in Texas in both expanse (1747 square miles) and population (1,215,000) but is also first in, among other things, retail sales, construction, petrochemicals (eighty-five per cent of the nation's productive capacity), heavy manufacturing, cotton marketing, crude-oil refining, cattle, and skyscrapers. The city has also reached what the magazine *Houston Town* calls "super-city status" in other fields, such as culture. The art critic of the *Post* remarked a few months ago that "the reputation of Houston as a city of extraordinary spirit and achievement in the cultural arts is now large. No city in the United States or the hemisphere is better known in this light today." Houston's reputation in the sporting arts received a boost from the recent announcement that in 1962 the city will have a National League baseball team—the only city in Texas or in the South to boast a major league team. Apropos of that news, the Houston columnist Bill Roberts remarked, "We ARE in the big league now."

Houston has other big-league aspects. At its municipal airport, for example, direct flights can be booked to Europe. Being a port city, it is visited by large numbers of foreign businessmen, whose passage lends an extra dimension to the local commercial life, and for the same reason it is the residence of a consular corps consisting of representatives of thirty-two countries, whose presence adds an international grace note to the city's social life. Perhaps partly because of access to the sea, the municipal personality of Houston is largely free of the claustrophobic fretfulness that is found in some inland Texas cities, notably Dallas. Compared to that land-locked city, Houston has a feeling of spaciousness; its streets are wider; its trees more plentiful; and its lawns and foliage greener. Palms and banana trees thrive, and Spanish moss drapes the trees. The generally lush effect is the result of the climate, which is semitropical and is not bragged about by the natives. The man who described Houston as the "Riviera of the Southwest" was no doubt visited by that soaring thought when under the influence of air-conditioning, which, in Houston, is carried to the point where a hostess who wishes to give a garden party can make her yard comfortable by renting a sixty-ton mobile air-conditioner.

Along with its big-city overtones, Houston has a few small-town undertones, such as the fact that there are some three thousand grade crossings within the city limits; it is not unusual, when driving about town, to be obliged to stop while a train goes by. A visitor also soon sees evidence that Houston (alone among major American cities) has never had zoning laws. As a result, it has become an example of what a local architect calls "pure American Motley." Houston has the widest variety of restaurants and night spots in the state; at the same time, it is an early-to-bed town. "Houston," the owner of one of the city's best-known clubs has explained, "is the only metropolitan city in Texas with a midnight curfew. At least, Houston is supposed to be a metropolitan city."

Exactly what Houston is supposed to be eludes visitors and natives alike. "There is no particular pattern to Houston life," the *Post* observed a few months ago in its special seventy-fifth anniversary issue. "There is no particular mood, no atmosphere, and no particular frame of reference by which a person in Houston can feel any identity. No one came to Houston because of scenery, weather, or atmosphere." Instead, everybody came to make money, as did the brothers Augustus C. and John K. Allen, a pair of upstate New York real-estate promoters, who laid out the original settlement, consisting of some twenty-two thousand acres purchased for five thousand dollars, in 1836. "The city was born lucky, and for a century and a quarter has led a charmed life," Hubert Roussel remarked the other day. In the last decade alone, more than a third of a million people, mostly young (the average age of Houstonians is slightly less than twenty-nine years), have flocked to the charmed city, changing it both physically and temperamentally. "Houston used to be a truly Southern city," J. Frank Dobie said a few months ago. "And it once was a cowtown. Now it's neither. It's cosmopolitan—mostly midwestern." A local sage and newspaperman named Hubert Mewhinney, who once called Houston "a whiskey and trombone town," was asked not long ago how he would describe it today. "Hell, I don't know what it is now," he said, "and I don't believe anybody else knows."

One thing that native Houstonians do know is that the influx of outlanders has brought about a blurring of what was once a local individuality, not only in speech and dress but also in attitude. "The easy, slow-moving graciousness that once marked Houston has all but disappeared," the *Post* has said. "Its people are not brusque and snappish, as they sometimes are in New York, but they are not nearly so prone to unsolicited helpfulness as they once were, either." However, to immigrants like Mrs. Gerri Gilbert, who had lived in Ohio, Illinois, and New York before moving to Houston with her husband and children in 1960, the spirit of the city seems very attractive indeed. "If people are different at all in different places," she said a few weeks after her arrival, "the people in Houston have got something different and better—an openness, a friendliness, a straightforwardness. We want to be like them, a part of them."

The ease of manner that lubricates life in Texas goes hand in hand with another quality characteristic of the frontier—hospitality to strangers. Americans have so often been told that they are the most hospitable people in the world that they are now almost ready to believe it; Texans have never needed any convincing, as witness their state motto: "Friendship." Texans like to do favors for strangers and then turn aside expressions of gratitude. On whatever scale it is offered, Texas hospitality is a fact, and its manifestations are many. The essence of its spirit was touched on by Thomas W. Blake, Jr., a fourth-generation native, in his casual remark: "If your car breaks down at night somewhere out on the highway, the chances are ninety-nine out of a hundred that somebody will stop to help you." This ready willingness to put oneself out for strangers —American hospitality in its most noticeable form—is, of course, a holdover from pioneer days, when loneliness and the need for reinforcements assured newcomers of a warm welcome.

There is more to it nowadays. Other sentiments that have been added to the amalgam include a measure of pride and ostentation, an honest desire to oblige, and, above all, a craving to be liked. One reason for this has been suggested by the British anthropologist Geoffrey Gorer: "The signs of friendship, of love, are a necessity for the American. . . . There is no occasion, however trivial or however important, which brings two or more people together in which such signs are not desired. The smallest purchase should be accompanied by a smile and by the implied assurance that the vender is delighted and privileged to serve you. . . . There are no alternatives to these signs; unsmiling subservience produces discomfort, unsmiling arrogance, fear and hostility. The emotional egalitarianism of America demands that all relationships bear some resemblance to those of love and friendship." Our determination to win the approval of everyone in sight—and even out of sight—is so fierce that, according to Louis C. Jones, executive director of the New York State Historical Association, even American ghosts, on whom Jones spent twenty years of research, "display definite tendencies of wanting to be liked, like the rest of us."

The essential nature of American hospitality, which is perhaps more interesting than its surface indications, has not changed much since Francis and Therese Pulszky remarked about a century ago, after a trip here, "The Americans are cordial, frank, anxious to oblige, and ready to make friends. In the fullness of their hearts, they generally promise more than they can keep." There is a curious echo of this observation in a letter written recently by a New York woman who has been living in Texas for the past three years. "On the social side of things," she said, "it is exceptionally hard to make friends here, and quite deceptive. People take to you most cordially, but they practically never follow up on it. They mean to, but they never get around to it. They make overtures, which rarely materialize. Nor is this just my experience. It is a common complaint among newcomers. Yet, everyone wants to be a good guy, which I find far more unkind than being less affable and more dependable." This sort of disappointment arises from, as it were, a hasty reading of the Texas social contract. With their easy "How y' doin'?" in the streets, their spontaneity and informality, their native courtesy and kindliness to travellers, and their general dukes-down approach, Texans indicate their willingness to make the acquaintance of practically any stranger. It is down in the fine print that they reserve the right not to make him a friend.

The ancient European animadversion holding that Americans have hundreds of acquaintances but no true friends may not be wholly without foundation, even in Super-America. But Texas hospitality, whatever its motivations and shortcomings, is a thing to take pleasure in, after the fashion that Caitlin

Thomas, widow of Dylan Thomas, recommended for the enjoyment of American hospitality. "To us of the frozen north, as I always think of our chilblained island," she has written, "it is very hard at first not to suspect such a basketful of warmth, generosity, and hospitality; but whether it springs pristine from the heart, or is a cultivated college art, it is equally pleasant; and should be taken at face value: appreciated, and responded to; not carped at, as some nasty people do."

Not far below the frontier ebullience that dominates the surface of life in Texas, a visitor soon becomes aware, there exists a bed of conservatism as expansive and unyielding as the rock that underlies Manhattan. The flourishing of fierce intellectual resistance to change in a land that is changing physically by the minute strikes some newcomers as a peculiar dissonance, but the seeming incongruity is really very American. The conservative impulse came over in the Mayflower and has been the central influence in our politics, economics, and culture from Cotton Mather to Clint Murchison. If the conservative streak is broader in Texas millionaires than in others, it is because the Super-Americans are more fearful that their money, which most of them made fast and recently, will be taken away from them by the machinations of "the Communists," the Super-Americans' habitual designation for all persons and institutions of which they disapprove. High on their blacklist, of course, is the federal government, which in the Super-American view is an insidious apparatus made up mostly of traitors, misfits, fools, and knaves bent on ruining the millionaires by socializing the country. The prevailing opinion was voiced a while back by William Fleming, a Fort Worth millionaire and prominent lay Baptist leader, in the course of an address to the Baptist Brotherhood Convention. Departing from his prepared text, entitled "Christ and the Brotherhood of My Church," Fleming said, "There are good men in Washington—you can find them if you look hard enough—but most of them are rotten. All they think about is getting enough votes to be elected. I spent fifty thousand dollars on lawyers going to Washington to defend my companies on this infernal income tax when I could have sent a mink coat or a silk petticoat and got the job done cheaper. Free men are just not free any more."

According to the consenus of Texas millionaires, the country has been going to the dogs since McKinley was shot, and was damaged beyond repair by Franklin D. Roosevelt. On the day of Roosevelt's death, a San Antonio millionaire hastily improvised a cocktail party to celebrate the event. An Army Air Force captain who was stationed in San Antonio at the time found himself briefly at the macabre affair and recalls how his host raised his glass and said, "Let's drink to the son of a bitch, now that he's dead." Long before that, a Fort Worth millionaire offered to donate a pair of gorillas to the local zoo, provided they were named Franklin and Eleanor. The Zoological Association refused the offer. There was a precedent; another wealthy citizen had been rebuffed in his effort to present the zoo with a rare and expensive female baboon on condition that it bear the name of the donor's ex-wife.

Though the majority of Texas millionaires have traditionally been, and still call themselves, Democrats, their money and votes for the past quarter of a century have been going to Republican candidates for President. Adlai Stevenson was considered so dangerous that during the 1956 campaign the San Antonio chapter of the Minute Women, an extremely right-wing national organization that thrives in Texas, put a watch on the local Catholic archbishop, who had been reported endorsing the Democratic candidate, and on the First Unitarian Church in Dallas, for having permitted the Young Democrats to hold a meeting on its premises. In the special election held in 1961 to fill the Senate seat vacated by Vice-President Johnson, Texans were offered a choice, as Gladwin Hill put it in the New York *Times*, "between two candidates [Republican John G. Tower and Democrat William A. Blakley] as alike in their conservatism as Tweedledum and Tweedledee." Though Texas had not sent an acknowledged Republican to the Senate

233

since the Reconstruction era, Tower convinced a majority of the voters that he would represent them even more ultra-conservatively than his opponent, and therefore won.

Organized labor has also always been looked on with suspicion in Texas. When the State Capitol was being built, in the eighteen-eighties, a strike of the International Association of Granite Cutters was broken by importing sixty-two scabs from Scotland. The Texas attitude toward organized labor has remained consistent. For example, in Texas today such measures as the union shop, the closed shop, and maintenance of membership are illegal. So is picketing, if the picket line has more than two demonstrators every fifty feet. A union demonstrator who gets into trouble on a picket line can be known thereafter under the law as a felon, and the law prohibits felons from holding office in a union. Officers and organizers of unions are compelled by law to register with the state and to carry special identification cards. A union official who uses violence in dealing with a non-striker can count on receiving a penalty more severe than that customarily imposed in Texas for murder. In these circumstances, it is not surprising that of some two and a half million non-agricultural workers in the state, only slightly more than fifteen per cent are union members.

Much of the anti-union legislation was enacted during the regime of Governor Allan Shivers, who in 1954, with the backing of many of his fellow-millionaires, pressed for a law making membership in the Communist Party a crime punishable by death. He felt that a rather strong deterrent was needed, even though he acknowledged that Texas had been troubled with so little Communistic activity "that it can't be called a problem." To the Governor's disgust, the legislature chickened out and made the maximum penalty for Party membership merely a fine of twenty thousand dollars and twenty years in prison.

Measures such as this reflect the Super-Americans' overriding interest in fighting Communism at home rather than abroad, where it costs money. The fact that Senator Joseph McCarthy was a tireless espouser of this bargain-basement

234

concept of dealing with Communism helped him become the hero of the Texas millionaires. Though not all went as far as Hugh Roy Cullen, who said, "I think Senator McCarthy is the greatest man in America," his prestige among Texas business-men was, Charles J. V. Murphy reported in *Fortune* in 1954, "higher by a considerable margin than *Fortune* found in any other section of the U.S. business community, with the possible exception of Chicago." The Texas businessmen bought the whole McCarthy package—allegations of "twenty years of trea-son," the villainy of General Marshall, the homosexuals in the State Department, and all the rest. In the days when McCarthy was their anti-Communist candy kid, Texans not only helped him out financially in a substantial way but showered him with other tokens of esteem: a six-thousand-dollar Cadillac sedan as a wedding present; a scroll signed by Governor Shivers proclaiming that "Joe McCarthy—a real American—is now officially a Texan"; making him guest of honor at a hundred-dollar-a-plate Republican dinner (the sec-ond ever held in Texas) and principal speaker at the San Jacinto Day exercises, an honor fraught with emotional signif-icance; and so on.

When his star began to dip, following the Army-McCarthy hearings, the enthusiasm of Texas millionaires for what they liked to call their "third Senator" began to wane. And when, toward the end, McCarthy was ailing and desperately anxious to accumulate enough money to buy a ranch where he could retire with his wife and daughter, his Texas patrons seemed to evaporate—even the big Dallas wheeler-dealer who in earlier days had habitually wound up his letters to McCarthy with the promise "I'm with you Joe, to the bitter end." In death, however, McCarthy became something of a martyr in Super-America, and many Texas millionaires now talk about how "old Joe" is needed to bring Khrushchev, Castro, and other latter-day foreign devils to heel. No one seems able to take his place, although the John Birch Society—whose aims, accord-ing to a letter to the editor of the Houston *Press*, are "as Ameri-can as apple pie" is making a try.

Since Super-Americans have, to the usual exaggerated degree, the built-in American suspicion of Europe and the rest of the world, they believe that we ought to cut loose from all foreign entanglements. In May, 1960, a Church of Christ preacher named Wayne Poucher, visiting Dallas on a speaking engagement as the guest of H. L. Hunt, said that our salvation lay in breaking off diplomatic relations with Russia and all other Communist countries. "If we did that," he remarked confidently, "I believe Communism would collapse within twelve months." In the popular Super-American view, foreign aid is the most demoniac scheme yet invented to ruin the country. "I don't know much about all these world affairs," a Texas millionaire remarked at the time of the Hungarian uprising, which generated about as much public interest in Super-America as a run-of-the-mill football game, "but one thing I do know: Uncle Sap always picks up the bill."

Ten years ago, another Texas millionaire, named H. Neil Mallon, seeking to encourage a somewhat broader view of Uncle Sam's role, founded the Dallas Council on World Affairs, which weathered a Texas-size campaign of slander and vilification, and now, with some twenty-five hundred members, is generally considered one of the top organizations of its kind in the country. Credit for the Council's flowering is unreservedly given to Mallon, board chairman of Dresser Industries, Inc., which supplies equipment for oil, gas, and chemical industries around the world, and to his foresight in having originally elicited support for the Council from numerous other leading businessmen, who, though not wild-eyed one-worlders, saw the organization as a possible civic asset. That possibility has been realized. The Council, which has brought (usually in private planes belonging to Mallon's company) Henry Cabot Lodge, Jr., John Foster Dulles, Herbert Hoover, Lewis M. Douglas, Alfred M. Gruenther, and scores of other world figures to speak in Dallas, has, as the *News* said a while ago, "spotlighted this metropolis as a visiting center for the world's policymakers."

Serving as a counterbalance to the Council is the Public

Affairs Luncheon Club, whose speakers may seldom be luminaries on the international scene but are nevertheless colorful in their opinions. In recent months, club members have heard that "international Socialists still control the State Department"; that "the United Nations is the springboard from which the great Communist movements are coming"; that "the U.N.'s illegitimate child is UNESCO, and UNESCO is the fountainhead carrying the main line of the Socialist front"; that "the internationalists have all but completely destroyed U.S. national independence"; that we should "give Red China a seat in the United Nations—our seat"; and many similar arguments. In the spring of 1960, Texas newspapers announced that a group of fourteen businessmen from Houston, Dallas, Midland, Wichita Falls, and other Texas cities, alarmed over "the possibility of Texas becoming another liberal state," had launched a campaign to "carry on the fight to maintain conservatism." And so they are at work, figuratively carrying timber into a wood.

Chapter Fourteen

"Like one huge children's party, endless fun and games and expensive presents for all." So the British traveller Lord Kinross recently wrote of Texas, and so—the patina of life there being what it is—Texas appears to the fast-moving visitor. Unfortunately, the fly-by-night disciples of Herodotus, as Stanley Walker describes swift observers of his country, miss many of the values of the Super-American way of life, such as the latent violence expressed covertly in the uglier manifestations of the conservative spirit and openly in the nonchalant attitude towards the taking of human life. An example: Shortly after eleven o'clock on a recent February evening, Mrs. John Smith (as she will here be called), an attractive, twenty-seven-year-old bride of three months, broke off a quarrel with her husband, a former assistant district attorney in Houston who was fifteen years her senior, by packing a bag and walking out of their apartment. She drove her car to the Luxury Motel, registered, left her bag in her room, and drove on to the Club Kohinoor. There, by chance, she met a twenty-three-year-old securities salesman, here called Richard Baker, with whom she had had dates before her marriage. They each downed a beer, and then, since it was closing time, Mrs. Smith bought half a dozen cans to take out. "Richard asked me where I was going," she later recalled, "and I told her I was going to have a beer. He asked me where John was, and I told him he was at home. Richard then told me he would go with me to have a beer and asked me where I was staying. I told him the Luxury Motel."

Mrs. Smith and Baker proceeded to the motel in her car, went to her room, and locked the door. While Baker sat on the bed and removed his shoes, Mrs. Smith opened two cans of beer. Before they had taken more than a couple of swallows, there was a knock on the door. After affixing the safety chain on the door, Mrs. Smith opened it and discovered the caller to be her husband, who had been scouring the area and had found her car in the motel's parking area. There was a bitter argument, and Smith, upon learning that Baker was also in the room, abruptly left and started walking toward his car. Mrs. Smith, evidently sensing what was in the wind, opened the door and ran after him. "I asked him not to be stupid," she said later. "I told him what he was thinking was not true, and I knew he was thinking there was something between Richard and me." Her protestations did not convince her husband, however. He went to his car, took a .25-calibre automatic pistol from the trunk, returned to the room, and shot Baker five times in the chest, killing him. Then he called the police.

When they arrived, Smith readily admitted murdering Baker, adding that he had only done what any other man would have done in the circumstances, and turned over his pistol, together with another one, which he had found in his wife's handbag. He was taken before a justice of the peace, charged with murder, and released on his own recognizance. He was never brought to trial; the grand jury, after hearing testimony from Houston's chief of police and two of his subordinates, handed down no indictment. The grand jury evidently took the same understanding view as Mrs. Smith, who remarked after the shooting that she still loved her husband, and added, "I don't blame John for thinking what he did. Although there had been nothing between Richard and me, it looked bad from where John was standing." The incident aroused no particular public interest, because it was just a standard murder—the kind that happens all the time in Texas.

The prevalence of this type of casual killing and capricious punishment, if any, has enabled Texas to maintain a crime rate that is consistently imposing, even by American standards.

That takes some doing, for, as everybody knows, we are the most lawless of all the so-called civilized peoples. We lead the world in homicides, in other violent crimes, and in juvenile delinquency; we have a burglary every forty-six seconds and a murder, rape, or assault to kill every four minutes; and, according to F.B.I. Director J. Edgar Hoover, crime costs the nation approximately twenty-two billion dollars a year. While foreigners find our crime rate at least astonishing—it was one of the things that Kipling said made us "the scandal of the elder earth"—we fail to find the subject of much interest; head-hunters don't see anything novel in head-hunting. Our attitude seems to be that crime statistics, like those for the population, the gross national product, and everything else in an expanding economy, should show a steady upward trend, and we are never disappointed.

"We make more laws and break more laws than any other people on earth," an American judge matter-of-factly told the English traveller William Dixon in 1876. More than a century before that, our Colonial ancestors, who were not keen on many kinds of social restraint, had set the pattern by thumbing their noses at British customs regulations. Contempt for law, part of our national heritage, has always been most powerfully illustrated on the frontier. "In the new states of the Southwest, the citizens generally take justice into their own hands, and murders are of frequent occurrence," de Tocqueville recorded. "This arises from the rude manners and the ignorance of the inhabitants of those deserts, who do not perceive the utility of strengthening the law, and who prefer duels to prosecutions."

While the Texans' manners have noticeably improved since that observation was made, their ability to appreciate the usefulness of strengthening the law has not kept pace. "You get in law enforcement what the people demand," John Crooker, Sr., of Houston, remarked a couple of years ago when he was chairman of the Texas Law Enforcement Study Commission. The state of the demand in Texas is suggested by the fact that in all categories of violent crime Texas ranks, in proportion to population, in the Top Ten among the states. An incident reflecting the Super-American attitude towards strengthening the law occurred in August, 1958, when some citizens of Boyd, a town twenty-eight miles north of Fort Worth, became so angry with their chief of police for enforcing the law, in their opinion, too zealously that they shot him and sent him to the hospital in serious condition.

With assists like this, it works out that a major crime is committed in Texas every three and four-tenths minutes. In the past two years, Texas, while ranking sixth in population, walked off with third place in aggravated assault (otherwise known as attempted murder), non-negligent manslaughter, and burglary. (No cash is kept in the vault of the state treasury, a policy dating from June 11, 1865, when the treasury was burglarized by bandits, who rode off with the swag.) In the past ten years, youthful crime in Texas has increased more than fifty per cent, and the number of inmates of Texas prisons has increased more than a hundred per cent.

However, nothing indicates the low state of the demand for law in Texas more clearly than the figures on homicides. Of all crimes, murder, as W. H. Auden has pointed out, is alone in being an offense against both God and society. Murder is, therefore, *the* crime, the main event in the criminal sweepstakes. Here Texas wins handily. In each of the last four years, more murders have been committed in Texas than in any other state, regardless of population. In 1959, a thousand and ninety-four persons were shot, stabbed, clubbed, or otherwise snuffed out in Texas; that was more than twice as many as in New York, which has seven million more people. Put another way, more people killed other people in Texas in 1959 than in all the New England states together, plus Iowa, Kansas, Minnesota, Nebraska, North Dakota, South Dakota, Montana, and Utah. To make an international comparison: Every year there are more murders in Dallas alone than in England, which has approximately forty-five million more people. And every year Houston has more murders than Dallas. Any way you look at it, Texas is tops in murder.

The pinnacle was not reached overnight. Back in 1879, a correspondent who had travelled through Texas reported in *Harper's* that "Texas is charged with some three hundred murders within the past twelve months, against which is credited eleven executions." He seemed to find both the number of murders and the ratio of executions to killings, which was 3.6 per cent, impressive. Visitors still do. In 1960, a thousand and eighty murders were committed in Texas, but executions for murder under civil authority dropped to five, thus reducing the ratio to less than half of one per cent. In those early days, Walter Prescott Webb has pointed out, travellers from the East were ill-equipped to understand the Westerners' extralegal custom known as the Code of the West and the place that killing played in it. "Under the social conditions," Webb has written, "the taking of human life did not entail the stigma that in more thickly settled regions is associated with it. Men were all equal. Each was his own defender. His survival imposed on him certain obligations which, if he were a man, he would accept. If he acted according to the code, he not only attested his courage but implied that he was skilled in the art of living. Murder was too harsh a word to apply to his performance, a mere incident, as it were. But how could the Easterner, surrounded and protected by the conventions, understand such distinctions?"

Quite a few Easterners still have trouble regarding murder as a mere incident, even in Texas, where they are surrounded by signs that homicide is a casual act. One sign is the use of the word "fuss." In Texas, a fuss can lead to murder. A recent headline in the Dallas *News* read, "HOME FUSS ENDS WITH MAN'S DEATH," and an equally even-tempered one in the Houston *Post* read, "THIRTY-THREE-YEAR-OLD FATHER OF SIX KILLED AFTER FUSS." In February, 1960, the wealthy owner of a chain of restaurants in Dallas was rubbed out by his brother-in-law, who had been employed as manager of one of the restaurants. Explaining his action, the brother-in-law said that the restaurant owner "started fussing at me and told me to get out," so he took a .38-calibre revolver out of a paper bag behind the cash register and shot the boss to death. In July, 1960, a forty-year-old-woman living in Farmers Branch shot her husband in the head with a .22-calibre rifle because he refused, she said, "to leave me alone and quit the fussing."

If a fuss goes on for a long time, it becomes a feud, and a feud can lead to what is known in Texas as folk justice. An expert on this subject, Dr. C. L. Sonnichsen, Dean of the Graduate Division of Texas Western College, has explained, "You won't find a better laboratory for the study of feuds than the State of Texas. The roughest kinds of people sought refuge in this frontier state. The only way the good settlers could deal with them, in order to protect their families and possessions, was to resort to folk justice. Nobody feuded for fun. These were mostly good people, 'no hands for trouble,' but sometimes a man had to fight, and when he had to, he did. Even today, if a man's life and his livelihood are endangered and he has no recourse to law, he will resort to folk justice, as did his ancestors." A fairly recent instance of the operation of folk justice occurred in June, 1960, when the secretary of the school board in Brownsboro punctuated years of bitter feuding over local school affairs by shooting and killing a fellow-townsman after a free-for-all at a school-board meeting.

How extensively folk justice is practiced in Texas nobody knows for sure, but the Texas Society of Pathologists believes it is meted out so freely that for every murder on record nine go undetected. The reason for this uncertain state of affairs is that of the two hundred and fifty-four counties in Texas, only three—those in which Houston, Dallas, and San Antonio are situated—employ a pathologist as a medical examiner to determine the cause of questionable death. The rest give this responsibility to justices of the peace—elected officials who need have neither medical training nor experience in scientific crime detection. In March, 1960, Justice of the Peace H. M. Newman, of Wichita Falls, decided to change his verdict that a local resident had died of natural causes when the undertaker reported he had found a bullet hole through the dead man's heart. If the Texas pathologists' suspicions are true, it would turn out that in 1960 the state chalked up a total of 10,800 murders, or one every 48.7 minutes, day and night. However, on the basis of recorded figures, a murder occurred in Texas only once every eight hours around the clock.

Perhaps because Texas's frontier-type coroner laws make getting away with murder easier in rural than in urban areas, the preponderance of recorded homicides occur in the large cities and are distributed roughly in proportion to population, although Fort Worth, slightly smaller than San Antonio, sometimes surpasses it in homicides. Still, there is always enough action in San Antonio to make it worthwhile for Alex's Reweavers, at 319 North Main Street, to keep in its window a large sign reading, "We Weave Bullet Holes and Knife Cuts." The proprietor, Alex Martinez, says that he averages about four such jobs a month and can usually spot patrons seeking this type of service by their bandages—the wound stripe of civilization in Texas.

Of all the contributions to the state's impressive murder record, Houston's is the most generous. "The murder capital of the United States," as Billy Graham describes Houston, has not only more murders annually than any other city in Texas but, on a per-capita basis, more than any other big city in the country. Dallas, the *Times Herald* recently noted, "doesn't fall far short of being the nation's murder hot spot." It had ninety-one killings last year. However, for at least the past eight years, Houston has averaged slightly more than a hundred and fifteen murders annually. In 1952, a strong year, the number climbed to a hundred and thirty-four, but even that was topped in 1957, when the total went to a hundred and thirty-six. The record-setting murder occurred late in the year, just under the deadline, on December 29th. That day, a thirty-year-old resident of Brownsville named Richard Roe arrived in Houston to pay a Christmas visit to his mother, who operated an inn. It seems that Roe walked into the inn, pointed his finger at a customer named Harry Smith, and said to his mother, "Why do you serve these wore-out people?" Smith, who was forty-seven at the time, told police that he objected to being called "wore-out," and consequently took out his .38-calibre revolver and shot Roe to death.

For a while after the vintage year of 1957, murders in Houston declined—a development that the city's chief of police, Carl L. Shuptrine, attributed simply to an increased budget, allowing him to hire more men, including a number of Negro recruits. "It has been a fact," Shuptrine said, "that seventy per cent of our murders were committed by Negroes, who comprise only twenty-two per cent of our population. Now we have thirty-eight Negro officers. Our figures on murder decrease as we give the Negro people better police protection." (Murders involving Negroes exclusively, whether in Houston, Dallas or elsewhere in Texas, are reported in the newspapers very briefly, if at all.) Though the number of Houston police has increased more than fifty per cent in the past four years (the force still needs at least a thousand more members to bring it up to the national average of the larger cities), murders have not dropped proportionately or even, for the period as a whole, perceptibly. In fact, killings during the first five months of 1961 were being carried out at a rate, which, if maintained through the year, promised to bring the city a new record. At present, Houston's homicide rate per hundred thousand inhabitants, which stood at 24.4 in 1946, has been cut to 10.9 —that is, only two and a half times the national rate, three and a half times the New York rate, and nine times the Massachusetts rate.

"Murder without motive"—the phrase used by a Houston police official to describe the local situation—occurs widely in Texas, as it did in San Angelo in November, 1959, when a twenty-two-year-old former Waf shot her daddy to death, as she later told police, "for the hell of it." Just two years earlier, a sixty-six-year-old native of Houston was playing dominoes with a friend half his age when an argument arose, and the elder man took out a .38 Colt revolver and shot his opponent between the eyes. "I didn't have anything against the boy," the hot-tempered player told the police. "I just killed him. That's all."

However, there is usually some fairly sound reason behind the shootings. For example, in July, 1959, a sixty-three-year-old Houston grandmother, having become exasperated with her son-in-law, who was arguing with his wife about some furniture, brought the argument to an end by firing eight shots into the young man. An equally good motive lay behind a shooting in Dallas the same month. A thirty-three-year-old interior decorator returning to his apartment house about midnight found a number of youths, who had been drinking beer at a party nearby, milling around his driveway. After telling them to move on, he went to his apartment, called the police, armed himself with a .22-calibre pistol, and went downstairs, where he opened up on the youths, shooting a seventeen-year-old schoolboy above the heart and killing him instantly. "I felt they might start ripping my convertible top," he explained to the police.

A similarly valid motive caused another bit of gun-play in the summer of 1959, in San Leon, where a father and son had a falling out at the dinner table. The father, getting ready to sprinkle salt on his mashed potatoes, found the shaker clogged, and grumbled about it. His son got up, walked to the kitchen, and returned with a full box of salt, which he set down next to his father's plate. For some reason, this infuriated the older man. He and his son began to argue, and the ladies of the house, wanting no part of the trouble, went outside to wait until peace was restored. When they heard shots, they rushed inside, to discover that their menfolk had engaged in a duel; the father had been cut down with eight slugs from a .22-calibre pistol in his heart and neck, and the son had been killed with a single shot in the heart from his daddy's .38-calibre pistol. A while ago, a short-tempered Houston contractor resolved an argument with one of his workmen over a matter of thirteen dollars and fifty cents by shooting him dead—an action apparently in accord with the Code of the West, since the murderer was no-billed by the grand jury. In March, 1960, a Houston woman eliminated her husband because he had made her very angry by spitting out some black-eyed peas she had cooked specially for him.

In contrast to murders with such understandable motives, others are committed inadvertently, as it were; participants in these often explain that the shootings were really just a mistake, growing out of a desire to have a little fun or to scare somebody. In June, 1960, a forty-eight-year-old San Antonio man killed his wife with one shot from a .22-calibre pistol, and explained later to the police, "I was only trying to scare her." In May, 1958, a former infantry officer showed his displeasure with his estranged wife by turning a German burp gun on her while she was sitting in her car. Although a dozen bullets were found in the car, and one had torn through her handbag, which was lying on the seat next to her, the woman was unharmed. This, the husband said, was what he had had in mind. "I didn't intend to kill her," he told police. "I just wanted to scare her." That was also what the wife of a drugstore manager in San Antonio said she was trying to do when she let her husband have it with a .32-calibre revolver. "Come in, Officer," she said when the police arrived. "I just shot my husband. He's in the bedroom." She added confidently, "He won't die—I know, because I'm a nurse. I aimed above the heart." She was wrong. In May, 1960, a Houston woman stabbed her seventeen-year-old son to death with a kitchen knife by mistake; she had planned to stab her husband. "I didn't mean to hurt anyone," she said. Sometimes both parties to a murder explain that they didn't plan to have it turn out that way. The woman who shot her husband over the black-eyed peas told the police, "I did not intend to shoot him," and her nine-year-old daughter testified that after her daddy had been plugged, he had said, "Mama shot me, but she didn't mean it."

The fact that Texans prefer folk justice is no proof that they are inherently mean; after killing somebody, they often express regret. In the spring of 1958, a young Dallas father of three children became angry with his wife, who had left him and

247

refused to return, so he looked her up and shot her three times. "I wish I hadn't done it," he told reporters afterward. "I'd give anything if it hadn't happened." Somewhat more specific remorse was voiced by a young Dallas man who, in September, 1958, shot and killed a packing-plant employee in the course of an argument. "I'd give all the money in the world if it hadn't happened like this," the young man said. The Dallas restaurant manager who shot his brother-in-law to death said, "I wouldn't have done it for the world." In July, 1960, a Dallas bride of two months shot her husband, but said soon afterward, "I didn't want it to happen this way." In August, 1959, a young Houston woman, who had been married the preceding June, became angry with her husband because he turned the garden hose on her while they were washing the car. She shot him to death, but later regretted it. "I don't care what you do," she said. "I just wish I could bring Bob back. I loved Bob very much." The Dallas interior decorator, after killing the schoolboy, said, "I'm awfully sorry it had to happen this way."

According to the so-called paramour statute in Texas law, a husband is permitted to shoot any man if "he has reason to believe the man is committing adultery, has just committed adultery, or is about to commit adultery on his wife." As a consequence, there is a tendency among men who live by the Code of the West to resolve marital troubles by the use of firearms, a habit that produces a surfeit of newspaper stories bearing headlines such as "HUSBAND KILLS 'BEST FRIEND' IN 'TRIANGLE'" and "MAN GIVEN 2 YEARS, SUSPENDED, IN SHOTGUN SLAYING OF WIFE'S LOVER." Actually, there is seldom serious prosecution or punishment of any mate who does in a spouse because of a real or suspected wayward romping on the counterpane. In August, 1959, the owner of a nursery in Houston was acquitted of murdering a man whom he had discovered sitting in a parked car with his wife. He was later asked what he would do if he were ever again confronted with such a predicament, and he said, "I believe I'd be a little more tolerant.

I didn't hate Bill, and I don't hate him now, but I hate men who set forth examples as Bill did."

Apparently, a sizable number of men in Texas are setting forth Bill's kind of example, for in October, 1958, the sheriff's office in San Antonio received an unsigned letter saying that the writer planned to kill his wife and her paramour the following day, at 3 A.M., and within a couple of hours after this information was printed in the newspaper the sheriff's office received telephone calls from fifteen women demanding protection. Texas juries habitually show a nice gallantry toward women who dabble in homicide, especially if they plead that they have been badly treated. "I like to defend women in murder cases," Percy Foreman, the busy Houston criminal lawyer and millionaire, has said. "Juries will turn a woman loose on the same evidence they'd convict a man on." Perhaps Foreman's finest hours were reached in the year when he defended thirteen high-spirited women, accused of murdering their husbands. His record was not perfect—one of the women received a suspended five-year jail sentence—but the twelve others got off without even an unkind word from the judge.

It is not only wronged wives and husbands who are not penalized for murder; lenient punishment for wrongdoing is the rule in Texas. The minimum sentence for assault with intent to murder without malice (cases where the party involved says, "I didn't mean to" or "I was only trying to scare him") is one year, and the maximum is three. The maximum sentence for murder with malice is death—a penalty seldom assessed by Texas juries. (In Texas courts, juries impose sentence.) Of Houston's hundred and thirty-six murders in 1957, seventy-two went to trial; two defendants received the death penalty, two received life sentences, and the rest got prison terms of varying length, ten being given five-year terms that were suspended. Last year, grand juries in Dallas no-billed one of every three persons charged with murder. In January, 1959, a man pleaded guilty to murdering an acquaintance during an argument in a restaurant and, in a fight that followed, inadvertently shooting and critically injuring a woman bystander; the murderer was given five years for killing the acquaintance and two for shooting the woman. In March, 1958, a woman who shot and killed her husband and pleaded guilty to a charge of murder without malice (she said the deceased had threatened to kill her, so she took a pistol from under his pillow and beat him to it) drew a five-year sentence, which was suspended. In February, 1961, a man in Houston was given a three-year term for his second murder; this was harsher than the punishment for his first, which drew a five-year suspended sentence.

A murderer who has the bad luck to land in prison can take comfort in the fact that the Texas parole system is marked by Southwestern openheartedness. According to J. C. Roberts, chief of the Records Bureau of the Texas Department of Correction, a person sentenced to ninety-nine years in prison in Texas spends, on the average, about ten calendar years behind bars. Many spend a good deal less; a person sentenced to ninety-nine years can be considered for parole in five and a half. Shorter sentences are reduced proportionately. The disinclination of juries to assess penalties elsewhere thought appropriate to the crime, along with the liberal parole system, often tend to discourage the more zealous district attorneys. One of this group, recently prosecuting an A.W.O.L. soldier for a particularly vicious crime, asked for a ninety-nine-year sentence; the jury settled on ten. "Ten years!" the prosecutor exclaimed later, adding an expression common among his colleagues: "He'll beat the jury home."

If Texas justice is not always majestic, it can, on occasion be awesome. The case of Miss Candy Barr is one in point. Miss Barr, an accomplished exotic, or strip-tease, dancer, played such an important role in the popular cultural life of Dallas in recent years that she was once favorably mentioned in the chaste editorial columns of the Dallas *News* and for a time became something of a Texas institution. A native Texan with the given name of Juanita Dale, she moved to Dallas in her teens and, after working for a while as a waitress, enrolled in an institution sometimes referred to locally as Strip-Tease University. This is actually a night club called the Theatre Lounge, which features strip-tease entertainment and also serves as a school for aspiring exotic dancers. The owner of the club and dean of the school, a thoughtful Texan named Barney Weinstein, founded his unique contribution to the halls of academe some ten years ago when faced with a scarcity of performers who had sufficiently mastered the indigenous American art form to meet his exacting standards. "A lot of girls think they can succeed in this business just because they're willing to take their clothes off," Weinstein says. "That's not it. They've got to have character." Qualified applicants enroll in the undergraduate course, which lasts six weeks and includes instruction in music, singing, makeup, and, as the dean puts it, "undressing with finesse." The school charges no tuition, but its graduates, in return for their education, are expected to engage Weinstein as their manager and agent, and if they succeed when they go out into the world, his philanthropy and investment are rewarded in the form of commissions. (Weinstein also offers what he calls a "special course," a session lasting three days, for students who wish to learn the technique as an adjunct to professional skills they have already mastered. Carol Channing recently completed the cram course.) Commencement exercises at the school occur when the students, bearing stage names concocted by Weinstein, make their initial appearance before an audience in the Theatre Lounge.

Since its establishment, Strip-Tease U. has turned out more than three hundred graduates, including several who have made a name for themselves, such as Holly Day, Black Velvet, Nikki Joye, and Honey Bare, but perhaps none climbed higher than Candy Barr, whose professional name Weinstein regards as one of his happier inspirations. (As a connoisseur of such matters, Weinstein has nothing but praise for whoever named a West Coast stripteuse Norma Vincent Peel.) Miss Barr not only became the best-known artist of her genre in the Southwest (she received considerable free publicity in 1956 when she shot her husband in the stomach, because, she said, he tried to break into their apartment after a fuss; she was not, of course, indicted) but showed marked versatility by modelling lingerie, posing for calendar art, and starring in a Little Theatre production of "Will Success Spoil Rock Hunter?" Though Miss Barr's memorable figure, blond hair, and baby face became familiar to aesthetes in New Orleans, Las Vegas, and Hollywood, they were most often on view in a downtown Dallas night spot called the Colony Club, where she found employment after graduation from Strip-Tease U. The towns-people showed a warm appreciation for her act, which wound up with some terpsichorean high jinks that left her wearing little to speak of except her native modesty. To acknowledge applause, she would return attired in nothing noticeably more substantial than white cowgirl boots and a white cowgirl hat. After taking a bow, she would remove her hat and hang it over her heart, where it remained—an insouciant gesture showing great poise, her admirers felt.

Miss Barr's career was speeding swiftly upward until ten-thirty in the evening of Sunday, October 27, 1957, when, upon answering the doorbell of her apartment, which had ostensibly been rung by a Western Union messenger, three detectives from the Dallas Police Department burst in, and, flourishing a search warrant (which did not state the reason for the search), started to give the premises a going over. They later testified that they had found a marijuana cigarette on the floor and were looking for more when a man walked into the apartment. The detectives announced that they were going to arrest him, whereupon Miss Barr said, "If you let him go, I'll give you the rest of the marijuana." She thereupon produced from her bosom a bottle containing three hundred grams of marijuana —enough to make some seventy-five cigarettes. Miss Barr's friend was released, and she was taken off and charged with possession of narcotics. Her trial, held some three months later and lasting four days, was a civic event; as the Dallas *News* put it, in a headline over a year-end-review article, "CANDY'S TRIAL LED '58 SCENE." The courtroom was filled to capacity every day, and the proceedings were widely covered by both radio and television. District Judge Joe B. Brown, who presided, did some of the camera work himself; during one recess, he borrowed a movie camera from a television photographer and shot considerable footage of "the shapely defendant," as she was customarily called, who smiled sweetly for the Judge as she obligingly sat, stood, and walked about the courtroom.

As the trial proceeded, it developed that the detectives who made the raid had acted on a tip from an unnamed informant; that it was staged shortly after another young exotic dancer, presumably a friend of Miss Barr's, had paid a quick visit to the apartment and asked Miss Barr to keep the bottle containing the three hundred grams of marijuana; and that some time before the raid a Dallas detective had rented an apartment under an assumed name in the building where Miss Barr lived. A telephone-company repairman, testifying for the defense, said that when he inspected the telephone equipment in the apartment building twelve days before the raid, he found what he called a "jumper tieup" linking the detective's phone with Miss Barr's apartment and enabling him to listen to conversations on her line. In their final argument, Miss Barr's counsel, acknowledging that she had been "stupid" to hold the marijuana for her friend, tried to convince the jury that she had been "trapped" by the use of illegal wire-tapping.

However, the prosecuting attorney declared that the wire-tap claim had not been proved, and that the detective who had taken up residence in Miss Barr's building was working "on another case" at the time. "They caught her with the goods, and she's got to be punished," the prosecutor concluded. The Judge, in his charge to the jury, which was composed of eleven men and one woman, said that Miss Barr should be acquitted if the jurors thought that any evidence in the case had been collected through wire-tapping.

After deliberating for two hours and forty-five minutes, the jury convicted Miss Barr and sentenced her to fifteen years in prison. ("CANDY BARR GETS FIFTEEN-YEAR WRAP," the San

Angelo *Standard-Times* reported.) Around the same time, a man convicted in Dallas on six separate counts of transporting and selling heroin received a five-year term, and a former airline stewardess who had pleaded guilty to possession of narcotics—the same charge made against Miss Barr—received a five-year sentence, which was suspended. Miss Barr also encountered unusual difficulty in getting released on appeal bond. While a third-generation Dallas police character, convicted for the second time of possession of narcotics, received a five-year sentence and was released from jail minutes after his conviction on a twenty-five-hundred-dollar appeal bond, Miss Barr spent eighteen days in jail before she was released on a fifteen-thousand-dollar bond.

In January, 1959, the Texas Court of Criminal Appeals upheld her conviction in a two-to-one decision. In his fourteen-page dissenting opinion, Judge Lloyd W. Davidson, holding that the conviction resulted from an illegal search warrant, remarked, "So the time has come in this state when peace officers can kick in the door of one's home and search and ransack it at will and without any lawful authority to do so and in total disregard of the law, and the owner of that home, upon trial for possessing property found therein, must submit to such outrage and deprivation of her constitutional right against unlawful search before she can show that she was innocent of any unlawful connection with the property so found. If that is equal justice under law, I want no part of it. If a conviction obtained under such circumstances is due process of law, then there is no due process of law."

Miss Barr's attorneys next undertook an appeal to the United States Supreme Court, but in October, 1959, the court unanimously refused to hear it, and, the following month, wiped out any chance of changing her conviction and sentence by denying without opinion her attorneys' motion for rehearing. On November 25th, Miss Barr was divorced in Dallas from her husband, to whom she had been married for six years, and a few hours later she married a Los Angeles beauty-salon operator in Las Vegas. A justice of the peace performed the ceremony after two ministers had refused to do so on the ground that it might bring them bad publicity. On December 4th, after parting with her four-year-old daughter, her stepmother, and her husband of nine days, Miss Barr was taken to the Goree Prison Farm for Women, in Huntsville. If accorded the treatment given other prisoners under the Texas parole system, she could be released toward the end of 1964.

Though out of sight, she was not out of mind. In its 1959 year-end-review article, the Dallas *News* again put Miss Barr in the headlines, and her name continues to crop up in conversation. To many out-of-state visitors, the severity of her sentence is a matter of some astonishment, but not to knowledgeable local analysts. "Why, there's no deep mystery to the matter at all," a native of Dallas who is possessed of a philosophical cast of mind and a family pedigree going back to Sam Houston recently remarked. "That girl was framed like a window in a church, because she was endangerin' the morality of our fair city. She was takin' money to let menfolks come look at her dance around when she wasn't wearin' so much as a petticoat. That was enough to rile up the women's chamber of commerce—not an official organization, you understand, just a group of middle-aged-and-over ladies bound together by a common aim to stamp out dancin', drinkin', and enjoyin' the company of women.

"Besides Candy Barr's fancy dancin', the chamber-of-commerce ladies were disturbed by what they called her gross impudence. I never knew Candy Barr, but I used to have coffee in the hotel where she lived. She was exceedingly shapely, but there was this downright impertinent air about her. I guess she was just about as impertinent as she could be to everybody, includin' the cops. The worst of it, as far as the chamber-of-commerce ladies were concerned, was that she was gettin' away with it. She was showin' her bosom and bein' snippy to anybody she pleased, and all this time she was goin' up in the world—gettin' her picture and write-ups in the paper and makin' a fat lot of money. She wasn't sufferin' at all, the way the chamber ladies thought she should, and they began sayin', 'That Jezebel has got to go.' Pressures got to movin', and pretty soon the cops were after her, and they took her away. The jury gave her a sentence five or six times what's usually given for doin' what they said she did. There were eleven men on the jury and one woman. We won't worry about the woman. But those eleven men, they got a chance to go home that night and say to their wives, 'Well, Maude, you can brag on me for what I did today. We put that shameless creature away for a good long spell.' Texas isn't the only place where you find people who act mean and hypocritical, but some of ours, they've got a genius for overdoin'."

No doubt the most important circumstance promoting the gunplay that enlivens existence in Texas is the fact that anybody there can buy a pistol as easily as a fishing rod. To be sure, the law provides a mild penalty for selling a pistol to "a minor, or any other person under the heat of passion," and requires, furthermore, that anybody buying a pistol present the dealer with "a certificate of good character" secured from a judge or a justice of the peace. How much attention is paid to this provision of the law is indicated by the experience of a former mental patient who, in August, 1959, went to a pawnshop in Dallas; bought, after haggling, a fourteen-dollar-and-ninety-five-cent pistol for thirteen dollars and ninety-five cents; and, four days later, used it, as he had planned, to shoot to death an Air Force sergeant. Aside from the purchase price, the murderer had furnished the pawnbroker with nothing more than his name, address, and telephone number. As a Houston *Post* reporter named John Davis wrote, after an intensive shopping tour in Houston for firearms, "All you need to buy a pistol is money." The same is true everywhere in Texas.

Though anybody can buy a deadly weapon, the law says that "any person who shall carry on or about his person, saddle or in his saddlebag, or in his portfolio or purse, any pistol, dagger, dirk, slungshot, blackjack, hand chain, nightstick, pipe stick, sword cane, spear, knuckles made of any metal or hard substance, Bowie knife . . . or any other knife manufactured or sold for the purposes of offense or defense, shall be punished by a fine of not less than $100 nor more than $500 or by confinement in jail for not less than one month nor more than one year." It has been quite a spell since anybody in Texas was fined for carrying a hand chain in his saddlebag, or, for that matter, a sword cane in his portfolio.

The fact that, in practice, nothing prevents any adult from not only buying a pistol but carrying it accounts in large part, in the opinion of many officials connected with law enforcement in Texas, for the state's championship standing in murder. "The critical factor in most of the tragedies seems to have been the accessibility or availability of a weapon," the Houston Law Enforcement Commission said in a report in December, 1959. "Even though a person is seriously provoked or is not completely stable to begin with, the availability of a weapon can be critical; if there is no weapon, there usually is no murder." The Commission has steadily recommended that Texas adopt legislation similar to New York's Sullivan Law, but so many Texans still seem to feel they need a gun to defend themselves that the legislature has never taken action to deprive them of one. Any suggestion for the control of firearms brings an outpouring of indignant protest that such a measure would violate what its opponents ringingly call "the citizen's basic constitutional right to keep and bear arms for defense of self and property." Texans are nearly as zealous about this right as they are about states' rights. The young man who put a dozen bullets from a German burp gun into his wife's car, and was sentenced to five years in prison for assault with intent to murder without malice, appealed his conviction on the ground that a state law banning possession of machine guns violated his constitutional right to bear arms. Though his appeal was rejected, things worked out so that he served no time for having given his wife such a good scare.

The merchants, anxious to be of assistance to citizens exercizing their constitutional rights, advertise their lethal wares conspicuously in the newspapers. The Outdoor Stores and Oshman's, in Houston; A. J. Anderson's and Morris Jewelry, in Fort Worth; and United Pawn Shop, in Dallas, among others, regularly offer in their newspaper ads a variety of hand guns ranging from a six-shot vest-pocket .22-calibre German revolver ("Reg. $29.95 Val."), at $13.95, to the S. & W. .38 Military & Police, at $64.95, for fancier work. Perhaps the most accommodating gun supplier is Montgomery Ward, which not only offers "sensational gun scoops" but also advises, "No money down—ten months to pay!" And, in case of emergency, there is a further advantage, pointed out in the ad: "Open every night till 9."

If a person doesn't own a gun, he can usually go next door and borrow one, as he would a quart of milk. In June, 1958, a former ace high-school quarterback had a falling out with his fiancée, who returned his engagement ring and refused to allow him in the house. He sat outside in his car until the young woman called the police, who made him drive away. Worried lest he return, she went next door to a neighbor's house and borrowed a .22-calibre pistol. Consequently, she was prepared when, later that night, the former football player smashed his way into the house. The young lady came down the stairs and fired six shots, of which four struck and killed him. The two others were stopped by the young lady's mother, who was taken to the hospital in fair condition. No charges, of course, were filed against the young woman, and the unfortunate consequences of her bad marksmanship brought her considerable sympathy. That was also the fate of the woman who shot and killed her seven-year-old son by mistake. She explained to the police that she had borrowed a .22-calibre automatic pistol in order to kill her husband, and was, in fact, aiming at him when the boy ran into the line of fire. She said she was sorry about the mixup.

All things considered, it would certainly not be fair when the Dallas *News* says "Life is cheap in Texas" to accuse the paper of bragging.

Chapter Fifteen

Poor people take comfort in the thought that, unlike themselves, rich people do not know how to have a good time. "We may not have much money," those without it tell one another in quiet desperation, "but we sure have a lot of fun." The view that fun and money are mutually exclusive has also been sedulously documented by the non-poor. In his masterwork, de Tocqueville, who never had to worry about the rent, flatly declared that in democratic countries like America "the rich do not know how to spend their leisure." The millionaire George Bernard Shaw had one of his characters in "The Millionairess" ask, "Why is it that people who know how to enjoy themselves never have any money, and the people who have money never know how to enjoy themselves?" More recently, Sloan Wilson, the author of "The Man in the Gray Flannel Suit," whose income is now comfortably beyond that of the average man in that uniform, consoled the poor with this contribution to their folklore: "No matter what praises are sung of leisure, those who have the most of it in the United States seem to be the most miserable." If Texas millionaires, who probably have more leisure than any other group in the United States, are miserable, they are devilishly artful at concealing it. Indeed, to observe them not only confutes the opiatic notion that people with money do not know how to enjoy themselves but raises the question of whether they know how not to.

Texas millionaires work even harder at having fun than most Americans, who, of course are famous for wearing themselves out having fun. They can hardly do otherwise, for they are obliged to run faster and faster just trying to stay abreast of their ever-increasing leisure, or "discretionary time," as the sociologists call the hours left over from eating, sleeping, and earning a living. It is the cross we have to bear as the most leisured civilization yet. The average wage earner in this country, according to a recent study, has at his disposal, aside from time to sleep, the awesome equivalent of two hundred and thirty full sixteen-hour days off a year. Texas millionaires are in a more ticklish situation, since they could, if they cared to, dispense with all activity involved in making a living, and wind up with every day off. To avoid this fate, most keep some kind of office hours, ranging from those of Kay Kimbell, who says, "I'm passionately devoted to work" and proves it by arriving at his office at seven-thirty in the morning and not leaving it until twelve hours later, to those of E. E. (Buddy) Fogelson, who is interested in the higher things of life and manages to polish off his offices chores in about three hours, beginning at five in the afternoon.

Even taking into consideration occasional hard days at the office, most Texas millionaires have an extraordinary amount of discretionary time on their hands, and it is a tribute to their energy and ingenuity that they have learned how to use it by steadily expanding ways in which to pleasure themselves. At home and abroad—at Maxim's in Houston or Maxim's in Paris, at the Four Seasons in New York or the Seven Small Houses in Copenhagen, in the Cotton Bowl in Dallas or the Colosseum in Rome, at the Fat Stock Show in Fort Worth or the running of the bulls in Pamploma, at the Fiesta in San Antonio or the Mardi Gras in Milan, on the beach at Corpus Christi or the sand of the Riviera, shooting ducks in the Gulf, elephants in Africa, tigers in India—wherever the most amusing action is, there are Texas millionaires, following the fun.

The gaiety begins at home, where discretionary-time activities, apart from civic undertakings, parties, and the like, are as various as the millionaires who pursue them. Robert Windfohr cultivates orchids; Karl Hoblitzelle collects antique silver and theatrical memorabilia; Clint Murchison studies migratory birds and can talk as knowledgeably about roseate spoonbills as about monthly allowables; R. E. (Bob) Smith takes an interest in planning and financing expeditions to recover cargo from ancient ships sunk off the Yucatan Peninsula. Thomas W. Blake, Jr., an oilman by profession, is an architect by preference. Pursuing his hobby, he bought a thirty-six room stone cottage in Newport from his wife (she had acquired it before their marriage) for sixty thousand dollars, and spent some thirty thousand more remodelling it into three separate apartments, which he leases for the summer at rents ranging from fifteen hundred dollars to five thousand. Like a great many other Texas millionaires, Blake enjoys his hobby more when it shows a profit; the Newport project, which he undertook four years ago, is now returning about ten per cent on the investment.

Backing Broadway shows is currently becoming a chic hobby of Texas millionaires, and though the profit motive also plays a part in these ventures, other considerations, such as the chance to share the glamour of it all, have proved better bait for Texas angels. Among them have been Stanley Marcus, and a couple of dozen other Dallas residents, who each put a few thousand into Leonard Bernstein's musical interpretation of "Candide," which closed after a few performances, and Michel Halbouty and several other Houston millionaires, who invested some three hundred and fifty thousand in the doomed musical "Happy Town." "One good thing about this business is that it doesn't take long to know whether you've hit a dry hole," Halbouty remarked to a companion during intermission on opening night. He knew what he'd hit about three hours later. Many other rich Texans have taken up the angel pastime (the wives of two San Antonio millionaires, Mrs. Carolyn Negley and Mrs. Jean Kuntz, tried their hand in 1960, with investments in three Broadway productions), but none has shown such durability as Harris Masterson, a Houston millionaire who does well in oil, cattle, and art treasures but so far has been unable to cut the mustard in the theatre. Since making his début with his wife, Carroll, as a Broadway producer in 1959, Masterson has been the principal backer of four costly failures, ranging from the serious dramatic work "God and Kate Murphy" to the beatnik musical "Beg, Borrow or Steal." They had an average run of seventeen performances. His fellow-angel Edgar W. Brown, Jr., of Orange, Texas, has had smoother sailing with his substantial investment in the hit musical "Bye Bye Birdie." Brown followed the form expected of Texas angels by flying a couple of dozen friends up from Texas to attend opening night.

Eugene McDermott, another show-business buff and leading contributor of time and money to community theatrical enterprises, is by nature a scholar who believes that the proper hobby of mankind is man. A native of Brooklyn, McDermott was graduated from Stevens Institute, took his Master's degree in physics at Columbia, and then decided, before continuing his studies, to spend a year seeing the world. Stopping off in Texas, he and an associate named J. C. Karcher founded, in 1930, a firm specializing in the reflection-seismograph method of exploring for oil and gas. Later, they formed a manufacturing subsidiary called Texas Instruments, which outgrew the parent company and was incorporated as an independent organization in 1951. Since then, Texas Instruments has not only become the largest employer in Dallas County but, with other plants in the United States and abroad, has mushroomed into one of the world's important manufacturers of electronics equipment. In the past seven years, the company's stock has climbed from five dollars a share to two hundred and fifteen, turning it into a star among the so-called glamour stocks. At present, McDermott's Texas Instruments stock is worth sixty-five million dollars; that of Erik Jonsson, the company's board chairman, eighty-two million; and that of Patrick Haggerty, the forty-seven-year-old president, who journeyed from Milwaukee to Dallas to seek his fortune in 1945, twenty-six million.

Although McDermott is not without pride in his professional accomplishments, he appears to find them quite pedestrian compared with his chief amateur interest—a long-standing collaboration with Dr. William H. Sheldon, of Columbia University, in exploring a field Sheldon has named constitutional psychology. This is intended to demonstrate, Dr. Sheldon has explained, a "correlation between man's structure and personality." The Sheldon method classifies people, according to their physical construction, into three main categories—endomorphs (fat types), mesomorphs (medium), and ectomorphs (thin); these are further subdivided into eighty-eight so-called somatotypes. The essential raw material for research in constitutional psychology consists of nude photographs of various somatotypes; after the pictures have been collected (mainly from universities that photograph students as part of the enrollment procedure) and analyzed, case histories are made of the photographees, and these materials are then used to show a relationship between physique and behavior. Dr. Sheldon has published several volumes of his findings, the most recent and ambitious of which is the "Atlas of Men," an endomorph-type book measuring twelve and a half by nine and three-quarter inches, and tipping the scales at nearly five pounds. In discussing the work, Dr. Sheldon is inclined toward the poetic: "The somatotype is therefore a groping for a reflection in man of the orderly continuum of nature, and in a more specific way it is also an attempt to identify the music of one's own particular dance of life." McDermott, on the other hand, tends toward plainer talk: "This is just so goddam fundamental you can't escape it. Psychologists are all wrong if they think they can get anywhere studying the nervous system alone. That's like trying to understand an automobile by studying only the engine and paying no attention to the chassis." In his office, McDermott keeps a supply of the "Atlas of Men," and generously passes out copies to interested callers. While he discourages inquiries about the extent of his outlay in the project (an "Atlas of Women" is now in the works), his friends believe it to be in the neighborhood of two million dollars.

The pastimes that have a wider appeal among Texas millionaires involve a large element of luck. Of these diversions, none exert more fascination than bridge, poker, and gin rummy. The last, for many Super-Americans of both sexes, amounts almost to a way of life. Upon arriving at a dinner party, these addicts greet the host and hostess, and proceed directly to the card tables, where they spend the entire evening playing gin, taking time out only to eat right at the table. The card tables at the various Petroleum Clubs begin filling up with gin players at noon; quite a few stay on for the rest of the day. Devotees keep on the alert for every chance to pick up an impromptu game. B. G. Byars and Roy Woods took their wives one afternoon to call on a friend; while the women talked, the men slipped into the library for a quick game, and when it was time to leave, about twenty minutes later, Byars had won six hundred dollars. "I think a good gin game is for twenty-five cents a point," Byars says, although he often makes a game two or three times that good. According to Mrs. Jay Simmons, considered one of the most accomplished as well as most attractive gin players in the state, the ladies favor a game at five or ten cents a point.

Poker is played for sums large enough to hold the players' interest. Those who sit in on the games that John Mecom and John Blaffer often organize in Houston feel that they have had an average evening if they win or lose in the neighborhood of twenty thousand dollars, and a good one if they go home with fifty thousand; when, as happens not infrequently, their winnings amount to twice that much, they know they have been living right. An outsider unaware of the typical oilman's passionate attachment to gambling is likely to be surprised, when first lunching at a Petroleum Club, to note the number of members who, before going in to eat, pick up a telephone and place a few thousand dollars in bets on horse races, football games, or whatever other contests are in season.

It is no doubt proper that H. L. Hunt, the biggest oil man in Texas—who, according to legend, started his career in a gambling house in El Dorado, Arkansas, and won his first oil well in a poker game—should also have the reputation of being the biggest gambler. Hunt modestly denies the distinction. "If you play a little gin, bridge, or bingo you are about as much a gambler as I am," he said a couple of years ago. With an income estimated at two hundred thousand dollars a day, Hunt can get but pale satisfaction from playing cards for conventional stakes; he prefers instead to bet on the horses (the story is that he employs a graduate of M.I.T. as a statistician to figure the odds) and on other sporting events. In the opening game of the 1956 World Series, according to a Dallas friend, Hunt favored the Yankees over the Dodgers—a mistake that cost him three hundred thousand dollars, or a day and a half's income. He customarily has better luck, especially at the race tracks, to most of which he has special communications facilities from his office. A friend visiting there a while ago suggested that Hunt's gambling pursuits added up to a rather costly pastime. "Well, no," Hunt replied. "I made a million and something out of it last year."

Another Texas millionaire who has long been fascinated by the ways of chance is Ralph Lowe. "He'll bet on anything," a friend has remarked. "He'll bet you fifty thousand dollars on whether it's going to rain within the next hour. One way or another, it seems as if his wins and losses average out." Not always, as Lowe acknowledged a few years ago when he was subpoenaed to testify at the trial of a St. Louis bookmaker. "In 1949," Lowe genially told the court, "I placed $248,593 in bets, mostly on horses and ball games, and I got back $107,775. I sort of quieted down after figuring my losses at the end of the year."

Lowe has never been quiet very long since his birth, in 1902, on a Missouri farm. "I grew up there, the oldest of four children," he has recalled, "but left when I was twenty-one, for Casper, Wyoming, where I worked in a machine shop. Four years later, I went back to Kansas to work in the oil fields. Then I came to Texas. My first stop was in Fort Worth. I remember the date well—January 1, 1928—but the next day I went on to Wink, where a field was opening up." He began his career in Wink as a filling-station attendant, later acquired a station of his own on the site where the Midland Tower Building now stands (possibly as a sentimental gesture, he subsequently bought all the stock in the structure), and eased his way into the producing side by po'-boying his first well on a highly unpromising farm-out from the Texas Company. He struck oil then, and has kept on doing it since. "He's got a nose to find it," a Fort Worth friend has said. "Back in the early fifties, he made a couple of real big strikes. He's got really important production now."

Soon after making his extraordinary strikes, Lowe decided to go into big-time racing and spent more than a million dollars buying horses, including (for two hundred and twenty thousand dollars) nine yearlings from the Aly Khan stables. Among them was the colt Gallant Man, whom Lowe entered in the 1957 Kentucky Derby, with Willie Shoemaker up. Gallant Man was neck and neck with Iron Liege going into the stretch; then, about seventy yards from the finish line, Shoemaker, to the consternation of Lowe and a hundred thousand other spectators, stood up in his stirrups and brought Gallant Man off stride. He had mistaken the sixteenth pole for the finish line, and Iron Liege won by a scant nose in the tightest Derby finish in twenty-four years. The Churchill Downs stewards, calling Shoemaker's error "gross carelessness," suspended him for fifteen days. (In the 1959 Derby, Shoemaker rode Tomy Lee, owned by a Midland oilman and rancher named Fred Turner, Jr., to victory.) Lowe's disappointment was not made any easier by the fact that in a dream two nights before the Derby he had seen Gallant Man winning the race handily until the jockey pulled him up. Lowe told his trainer, John Nerud, about the dream, and Nerud repeated it to Shoemaker over dinner on the night before the Derby. "Whatever you do, Willie," Nerud said, "ride the horse out around the turn. He's fit. Ride past the wire."

Despite the cheerless outcome of seeing his dream come true, Lowe was a good sport. "I won't criticize Shoemaker's riding," he said after returning to Texas. "I was pleased with the race. It was a big thrill for me." Though robbed of the top Derby money, Gallant Man went on to increase his earnings to slightly more than half a million dollars by September, 1958, when Lowe sold a three-quarter interest in him to a syndicate headed by Leslie Combs II for an even million. Shortly afterward, the colt developed a foot injury and was retired to the stud at Combs' Spendthrift Farm. "That's the way it is with Lowe," an acquaintance said. "He keeps getting these tough breaks that make people cry every step he takes on the way to the bank."

Because thoroughbred racing is still dominated by Easterners, owning a stable, though an acceptable leisure-time activity among Texas millionaires, retains a slight foreign taint. Owning a ranch, on the other hand, is above suspicion, if not, indeed, a patriotic duty. "The first thing an oilman does after amassing a few million," J. Frank Dobie has remarked, "is buy a ranch where he can get away from oil—and on which he can spend some of his oil money." The casual way in which a Texas millionaire may acquire a ranch is illustrated by the experience of Daniel W. Varel, president of a drilling-equipment manufacturing firm, who for a while owned a spread of fourteen thousand acres. "I don't know why I bought it," Varel said not long ago. "A guy came in one day and said he was going to lose it, couldn't keep up the payments, so I took it over. As a matter of fact, I never once saw the place in all the time I owned it."

In most cases, oilmen go into ranching with somewhat more forethought, if no more experience. "I don't know a thing about it, but we'll make it go," R. E. (Bob) Smith said when he took the customary step a few years back, and he has. So has John Mecom, who owns three ranches—in Louisiana, Colorado, and Texas. While it is perhaps not necessary to go that far, it is de rigueur to own at least one, because ranching, the occupation associated with the older families and fortunes, confers status. That consideration is quite incidental to the operation of many of the larger ranches—such as the fifty-one-thousand-acre Lambshead Ranch, the one-and-a-quarter-million-acre King Ranch, and those owned by the Waggoners, the Scharbauers, the Cowdens, the Burnetts, the Armstrongs, and other descendants of old families—which have always been run to confer profits.

For the majority of Texas millionaires, however, a ranch is

in the nature of a hobby, worthwhile because it enhances social position and also because it provides wonderful relief from tax oppression. "A man with a large outside income," Charles Pettit, who is one of that group, has pointed out, "can make many ranch improvements at literally no cost to himself, because the government allows a charge-off on income tax for ranch development." Pettit, who set out to be a schoolteacher but switched, after oil had been discovered on his property, to a more remunerative line of work, has devoted his time almost exclusively in recent years to transforming some seventeen thousand acres, called Flat Top Ranch, from a virtual wasteland into a model of scientific ranching. "Of course, the ranch has never made any money," he remarked to a visitor recently as they tooled smoothly along the ranch's hundred and fifty miles of gravelled road in Pettit's chauffeur-driven Chrysler, "but the value I have created here has given me more satisfaction than trying to become a second Standard Oil Company."

Pettit also takes pride in having turned Flat Top Ranch into a wildlife preserve that supports antelopes, doves, ducks, wild turkeys, some ten thousand quail, and hundreds of deer. Once a year, Pettit sells deer-hunting privileges on his ranch, at twenty-five dollars a day, to about a hundred and fifty sportsmen. For safety's sake, they are transported by station wagons in the early morning to various positions on the ranch—usually a comfortable perch in a tree—and are not allowed to leave their assigned places until they are picked up at nightfall; a box lunch is brought to each deerstalker at noon. On the average, about half the hunters willing to rough it in this fashion kill a deer. Quail hunters are also welcomed, for a fee, at the ranch, and Pettit picks up some additional change by selling small trees on his tract to the Lambert Landscape Company. "Whatever I do on the ranch," he says, "I would like for there to be a little profit in it."

Dear though the classic goal of mingling pleasure with profit is to all millionaires, the majority of those in Texas spend their discretionary time just having fun. Among the active sports, golf is the most popular. A few players, including W. E. (Bill) Grace, of Fort Worth, president of the Fruehauf Trailer Company, go around the links carrying a putter with a fourteen-carat-gold head, sold by Tiffany for fourteen hundred and seventy-five dollars, including federal tax. Skiing, perhaps because it is the only sport Texans cannot pursue within the borders of their state, appeals to a sizable and growing number of natives (the Dallas Ski Club has over two hundred members), who fly to Colorado or Switzerland when the slalom mood comes over them. Bowling is also booming in Texas, where two of H. L. Hunt's sons, in association with other sports-minded millionaires, are planning the construction of, naturally, the world's largest bowling center, a five-million-dollar circular structure containing a hundred and thirty-two lanes and some other attractions, such as a swimming pool, a miniature-golf course, a restaurant, a private club, and an ice arena. Cockfighting, though outlawed in Texas, has such a considerable following there that a Texas millionaire named Bobby Manziel, who was one of the country's leading breeders of gamecocks before his death, in 1956, used to say that he was willing to bet that pits for cockfighting outnumbered movie theatres in Texas.

To millionaires with a preference for legitimate pastimes like sailing, boating, and fishing, Texas offers more than six hundred miles of tidewater coastline and roughly two and a half million acres of inland-water area. According to the Texas Game and Fish Commission, the state has no fewer than one and three-quarter million fishermen; of these, the élite are the hundred and forty who make up the membership of the Koon Kreek Klub, an organization of millionaire anglers whose private playground is an eight-thousand-acre tract of swampy woodland near Athens, some seventy-five miles east of Dallas. The determination of the members, who pay an initiation fee of twenty-five hundred dollars and annual dues of two hundred and forty, to keep their retreat simple at all costs becomes evident to a visitor upon approaching the Klub's property, the entrance to which is marked by a weather-beaten wooden sign supported by two unpainted poles. A dirt road leads to the Klubhouse, a long, one-story, tan-colored building that has the architectural distinction of a temporary Army barracks. The same note of resolute unpretentiousness is struck by the interior décor as well as by the Klub's food, which is the best quality that money can buy, simply prepared and served boarding-house style.

Though members do some duck-shooting in season and, in bad weather, play a good deal of gin, the main purpose of the Klub is fishing, primarily for black bass, white perch, and many varieties of bream (pronounced "brim" around the Klub), a kind of sunfish usually no longer than a man's hand but, in the opinion of Clint Murchison and other Klub members with extensive angling experience, unmatched in fight per ounce. Members go down to the Klub's chain of lakes, kept amply stocked from the Klub's hatchery, in fishing skiffs equipped with swivel chairs, powered by outboard motors, and operated by guides, who bait the hooks, remove the fish, and later clean and pack them in ice to carry home. Once a year, the Klub puts on a stag party that gets under way on a Wednesday and winds up the following weekend. Guests at a recent do included, besides a number of oil-company presidents, lumbermen, and ranchers, O. M. (Red) Mosier, an executive vice-president of American Air Lines; Pete Kriendler, one of the owners of "21," and General Emmett (Rosie) O'Donnell, of the Air Force. The festivities began with a meal that included ninety gallons of crayfish and four large roasted pigs. A guest sitting near Sam Gladney, an executive of the Sun Oil Company and then president of the Klub, asked whether he thought it true, as somebody had said, that there would be no trouble raising five million dollars on short notice from among the Klub members who happened to be there at the time. "Why, I wouldn't want to guess," Gladney replied, "but they say just two or three of them have a billion or so between them."

If, as Stephen Potter has suggested, "the basic gambit of U. S. Manship . . . is to be just that one degree *more so*," the basic gambit of Texmanship, or Super-Americanship, is to be just those two degrees more so. This proposition is demonstrated with Euclidean logic by the game of football, which, as Ralph Barton Perry has remarked, is "peculiarly American in its mixture of physical force with elaborate strategy and the opportunism of the 'huddle,'" and in the fact that, as the game is played, "sportmanship means not scrupulous observance of the rules but acceptance of the penalty, together with team work and a spirit of camaraderie." For these and other reasons, Americans have made football a kind of national ritual, getting so worked up over it as to appear at times quite unhinged. This goes double, of course, for Super-Americans. They are ahead of all other states in number of football players (approximately 120,000), number of teams (roughly 975 in high schools and colleges), cash receipts (in excess of five million dollars a season), and in generation of lunacy in the fans. This last manifestation of the football mania can be seen to advantage in the so-called pre-game rallies, staged the night before a big game in the larger cities, where the faithful show their allegiance by gathering in mobs to cheer, sing, drink, and mix it up with partisans of the other team. During a recent football season, at least ten such merrymakers in Dallas alone wound up in the hospital.

Demonstrations of loyalty on this scale are culminations of a cultural conditioning that begins among Super-Americans in pre-puberty, when they are introduced to the mysteries of the gridiron. Unlike many other societies, which postpone this rite, and whose young members consequently play football only in college and high school, Super-Americans start teaching their children to handle the pigskin in junior high and even in elementary schools. Those having an enrollment too small to produce an eleven-man team carry on with one made up of eight or six. In backward areas, where football indoctrination is not provided in the elementary schools, the gap is customarily filled by a Y.M.C.A., service club, or parents' organization that sponsors teams made up of students in the fourth, fifth and sixth grades. The neophytes receive intensive coaching, wear regulation uniforms, and elicit such demonstrative support that referees in the so-called Peewee League are frequently permitted to penalize teams whose members' parents excitedly rush onto the field to whisper strategy hints or to reward a good play with a kiss.

Games in the Peewee League are usually played on Wednesday afternoons or nights; this enables the players' parents and other rooters to take in the high-school games, customarily played on Friday nights under lights; junior-college games, on Thursday nights; and major college games, on Saturday afternoons or evenings. The staggered schedule permits a football enthusiast, on an average weekend, to attend three or four games, though meeting the full quota—especially in the sparsely populated sections of West Texas—usually demands a few hundred miles of travel. This is done with pleasure. On weekends, the skies of Texas swarm with private planes (one Saturday last fall, some three hundred landed at the Dallas municipal airport) carrying alumni—or "exes," as they are known—to the big games. The exes, besides giving their moral support through attendance, take an active part in what a Fort Worth *Star-Telegram* editorial referred to straightforwardly as "the recruiting wars." The battles waged among the Texas institutions of higher learning to enroll talented football players are so spirited that many a high-school ace has to consider a dozen deals before picking the one he feels offers the most in scholarship money, summer employment, and other fringe benefits, including educational opportunities.

The competition for topnotch football coaches is, if anything, even livelier. When, in 1957, the coach of the University of Houston was lured away by Southern Methodist University, a Houston oilman named Francis Blair dispatched a telegram to the athletic director of the bereft institution urging him to "get the best coach in the nation." Blair added, "If you will bring Bud Wilkinson [the conspicuously successful coach at the University of Oklahoma] here as coach of Houston University, I will give him an oil well and a seagoing yacht. This offer is made in all sincerity." It failed to move Wilkinson from Oklahoma, which also has oil wells.

Because Texas football requires Super-American support on the field as well as in the bursar's office, the art of cheerleading is also taught at an early age. Young people with a desire to improve themselves can study baton-twirling and cheerleading at summer sessions—or clinics, as they are referred to locally— held at Texas Woman's University, Sam Houston State Teachers College, and half a dozen other institutions. The most popular is the five-day Cheerleaders and Twirlers School at Southern Methodist University, which yearly teaches some fifteen hundred high-and junior-high-school students the rudiments of tumbling and twirling and a variety of other useful skills. For students seeking a kind of graduate school, Trinity University provides an annual Music and Baton Camp, conducted by Mrs. Pat Hooker, famed throughout the country as the originator of the Dixie Strut; the Trinity seminar is open only to bona-fide majorettes, who are offered, the announcement states, a "week-long course in intermediate and advanced baton-twirling."

Since the Cotton Bowl and other post-season games are played in January, and since spring training starts in February, Texans are able to read about football in their newspapers practically the year round. As a result, they have become so familiar with the vocabulary of the gridiron that they are ac-customed to its use in other areas, such as in the headline over a Dallas *News* story concerning the space achievements of the United States vis-à-vis the Soviet Union; it read simply, "RUSSIANS AHEAD AT THE HALF TIME." When the football sea-son is in full swing, a great deal of social life revolves around it. A typical entertainment consists in inviting forty or fifty guests for cocktails and what is called brunch, after which all hands are transported to the game in a chartered air-conditioned bus. As a rule, the buses are equipped with a bar, and waiters keep liquid refreshments flowing en route. Whether because of Texas law, which provides a fine ranging from twenty-five to two hundred dollars for anyone convicted of carrying "intoxicating beverages into any athletic field or enclosure where athletic events are being held," or because of local custom, the excessive drinking observable at football games in the North is not much in evidence in Texas. Even nipping is guarded. Some of the more imaginative students at Texas Technological College use hypodermic needles to inject vodka into oranges, thus creating clandestine screwdrivers that they carry to the games.

Since stadiums in Texas are roughly as important as they were in ancient Greece, they are usually impressive structures, carefully maintained and abounding in conveniences: spectators in the stadium of West Texas State College are provided electric outlets for their electric blankets. Before the kickoff at all Southwest Conference games, the players, spectators, officials, and attendants stand with bowed heads as a clergyman recites an invocation. "Lord," said a minister before the start of a recent game in Waco between Baylor University and the University of Texas, "we thank You for the many privileges You have bestowed upon us. We thank You, Lord, for the privilege of football."

Following their favorite football teams around the country gives Texas millionaires an opportunity to indulge in what is perhaps their chief leisure-time activity—travel. It is, one might say in the words that Taine used of the English, "the occupation of their holidays, a habit, a pleasure, and almost a mania." Born with the wanderlust, Texans exert themselves to the customary extra two degrees in upholding our national reputation as a race of gadabouts. Most Texas millionaires have diversified and scattered holdings and are accordingly obliged to do a great deal of travelling in the line of duty, but even when they could be still they are not. For example, one Saturday morning last fall, three Dallas millionaires and their wives boarded a twin-engine Beechcraft and flew down to Austin, where they had lunch and took in a football game. Returning to Dallas, they changed into evening clothes and flew off again, this time to Wichita Falls for a dinner party and the night; on the way home Sunday afternoon they dropped in at Fort Worth to have cocktails with friends, and then flew on to Dallas to wind up a weekend that to them did not seem out of the ordinary. Nowadays, the term "to travel" is properly used only to describe a journey to a place that is remote, hazardous, or exotic, and preferably all three. Texas millionaires understand the current usage, and consequently seldom bother to inform anybody but their servants when flying to New York to take in a show or to Paris to buy a dress. However, they do tell their friends when going on a safari; that is good form, for the safari is at present considered the most fashionable gambit in the travel game.

The African hunting trip—which had a large following among Texas millionaires long before attaining its present status as a major industry with such frilly innovations as all-girl safaris and the like—suits Texans to perfection, because it combines travel with hunting, and hunting has always been the favorite outdoor sport of the native males. In his novel "Home from the Hill," William Humphrey, who grew up in Texas, wrote, "For a Texan the names of guns and calibre numbers are magic: Winchester and Colt and Remington and Smith & Wesson; .30-30 and .22, .44 and .45 and .32 and .38-Special. You could speak of a Texas boy's growth and manhood as his .410, his 20, and his 12 gauge years." No gift is more acceptable to the average Texas millionaire than a new firearm to add to his collection; Sid Richardson's wedding present to Clint Murchison and his bride consisted of a matched set of Remington rifles inlaid with mother-of-pearl. Mrs. Murchison is an expert shot, as are the wives of many other Texas millionares, including Mrs. Alfred Negley and Mrs. Richard Kleberg, who score higher than many male contestants in wild-pigeon-shooting tournaments, an exacting sport recently imported into Texas from Europe by way of Mexico.

Another accomplished huntress, Mrs. A. B. (Lu) Wharton, is the first and, as far as is known, the only American woman to slay a bongo antelope, a rare and elusive African animal, which she bagged in 1959. It took three expeditions—which she made with her husband, who is known as Buster and used to amuse himself with a private polo team—to satisfy what she once said had been her "determination that one day I would have me a bongo." Though many other Texas millionaires and their wives have recently made a point of getting to Africa while the supply of animals lasts, few have been so keen about bringing home the bongo; most, like Mr. and Mrs. Toddie Lee Wynne, Jr., the Wilson H. Browns, the Frates Seeligsons, the Herbert Gibsons, and many others go for the general fun of it. Getting there has been made as easy for them as buying a mink coat. During the Neiman-Marcus British Fortnight, a representative of White Hunters (Africa), Ltd., set up shop on the store's fourth floor amid an exhibition of stuffed big game, and did a brisk business booking safaris. They can now be arranged through the store's travel bureau. It is no wonder that of all the people on safari in Africa in 1959, nine out of ten were Americans, and a conspicuous share of the nine were Texans.

As hunters, probably no Texas millionaires have gone farther out than F. Kirk Johnson, of Fort Worth, and Tom Slick, of San Antonio, who have jointly spent considerable time and money in recent years trying to bag an Abominable Snowman. For Johnson—an independent oilman with a wide range of business holdings and a past president of the Fort Worth Zoological Association as well as its chief angel—the quest for the legendary creature of the Himalayas has been a logical extension of a lifelong interest in animals and hunting. For Slick—a second-generation millionaire, a Phi Beta Kappa with a degree in science from Yale, and the founder of the Southwest Research Institute—the hunt for the Snowman has been a logical extension of a lifelong interest in science and an acquired interest in the occult. In 1956, with the assistance of Tensing Norkay, Sir Edmund Hillary's companion in the conquest of Mount Everest, Slick formed a search party consisting of himself as leader; the director of the New Delhi Zoo; a Nepalese-speaking Irish journalist, hunter, and explorer named Peter Byrne; seven Sherpa guides; and some seventy porters. Off they trudged into the wild Himalayas, which they scoured for a month without catching sight of a Snowman. However, after coming out of the mountains Slick told reporters that he considered the expedition a success, because it had discovered three sets of footprints thirteen inches in length and thirty-one in spread; found a clump of black hair believed to have been shed by a Snowman; come upon some droppings; and talked to fifteen Nepalese who claimed to have seen a Snowman. "I'm ninety-five per cent certain that it really exists," Slick said, "but I want to see one before I'm a hundred per cent sure."

Back in Texas, Slick found in Johnson a most receptive listener to his Snowman theories and stories, and early in 1958 the two men announced their decision to co-sponsor the Slick-Johnson Nepal Snowman Expedition, which was to be equipped with, among other innovations, a pack of hounds trained as bear and cougar hunters, and an air gun, developed under Slick's direction, that could shoot a bullet containing a temporarily paralyzing but harmless drug. The strategy called for the hounds to corner a Snowman, whereupon it would be immobilized by means of the scientific airborne Mickey Finn. After the searchers had been four months in the field and had again found, in addition to footprints, what they considered promising hair and droppings, Slick cabled instructions to call off the dogs and come home. Far from being disappointed, Slick said that the results strengthened his belief that in time three or more types of Snowman would be found in the Himalayas and in other places, such as Burma and Cambodia. "It may even be found on this continent," he added. "Some very plausible reports have come out of British Columbia." Slick and Johnson have since sponsored expeditions to look for the Snowman's North American cousin, who is familiarly referred to in scientific circles as Bigfoot.

The existence of the Snowman also seems reasonable to H. W. (Herb) Klein, the most renowned hunter in Texas and, according to his friend and fellow-sportsman Kenneth Foree, "probably the world's greatest." A rugged, amiable independent oilman, Klein has hunted on four continents and has taken, as hunters say, twenty-seven of the twenty-eight North American animals classified as big game by the Boone & Crockett Club, of New York. "What's missing is a lousy caribou," Klein said the other day. "There's nothing to getting one—the caribou is a very stupid animal—but you've got to go to Newfoundland for it, and the season conflicts with all other North American hunting seasons, besides the Asian and African. I've just never wanted to waste the time." When not hunting animals or oil— sometimes in tandem—Klein lives in Dallas in a house that consists primarily of an enormous trophy room containing a hundred and thirty-five exhibits and that accordingly bears a certain resemblance to the Museum of Natural History. In the past few years, he has journeyed from the Bering Sea, where he shot a mammoth polar bear (fourth on the Boone & Crockett Club trophy list) and a one-ton walrus (tenth on the list), to French Equatorial Africa, where he bagged a white oryx (third in the world record book), as well as a Barbary sheep and a dama gazelle, both the largest ever killed by a hunter.

To add yet another exhibit to his collection, Klein set out a couple of years ago for the kingdom of Hunza, a remote piece of real estate some sixty miles long and from four to thirty miles wide lying in a valley beyond the Himalayas in northern Kashmir—the only habitat, outside Russia, of Marco Polo's sheep, celebrated for the size and spread of their horns and considered by many hunters the world's greatest trophy. To get to Hunza, Klein and a fellow hunter named Elgin Gates trekked through deserts in Pakistan in temperatures averaging a hundred and twelve degrees, and, because a flood had washed out the jeep road they planned to use, completed the journey on foot, climbing a hundred and twenty miles to an altitude of fifteen thousand feet over an ancient mountain trail faced with sheer rock on one side and with sheer nothing on the other. "It was the roughest trip I ever made," Klein has said. "By the time we reached our destination, my left leg must have been at least two inches shorter than the right one."

Hunza is one of the world's two remaining absolute monarchies (the neighboring state of Nagar is the other), and Klein and the king—His Highness Mohammed Jamal Khan, who is known as the Mir of Hunza and rules over some thirty thousand subjects—hit it off from the start. Tourism has never caught on in Hunza, and the Mir, whom Klein came to regard as "one of the most generous, hospitable, humble, and sincere persons I have ever met," was so pleased to have visitors that he overwhelmed them with kindness, at times even personally waiting on them at meals. The Rani, or queen, though able to speak little English, also strove to please. "She gave me the use of her private yak," Klein says. "All those people are just wonderful. Anything you want, they'll give you." While the Mir's scouts were out scouring the kingdom for sheep, Klein and his host engaged in conversations that ranged from crime and punishment in Hunza (it has not had a major crime of any kind in the past century) to death and taxes (the Mir levies the equivalent of a thirty-three-per-cent tax on income but keeps only enough for a modest living and returns the rest in social services to his subjects, many of whom live to eighty or ninety on a diet that consists mainly of fruit and grain).

When sheep had been sighted, Klein and his companion bagged several prize specimens and then packed up for the journey home. "The hardest thing I had to do on the whole trip was to say goodbye to the Mir," Klein has recalled. "We had become real good pals. He refused to let me leave until I'd promised that one day I'd return. Tears gathered in his eyes as I climbed onto my yak. When I turned to wave a last goodbye, darned if I wasn't having the same trouble." Although Klein took his leave of Hunza most reluctantly, he departed with the feeling that he had made at least one contribution to the well-being of the kingdom; he had taught the Mir to play gin rummy.

Chapter Sixteen

In line with Ida Craven's tenet that it is not the quantity but the quality of a society's leisure that largely determines its tone, Texas millionaires, putting aside their guns and cards, work indefatigably at making culture in Super-America hum. "Texas," William H. Lowe, Jr., a former editor-in-chief of *House & Garden,* was once moved to remark, "may lay an understandable claim to being the most civilized state in the Union today." He went on to say, "And if Texas is not in every respect a microcosm of our national culture, it is at least a most worthy model." This last tribute is an interesting reflection of a current international phenomenon, for just as Lowe and many other Americans have recently taken to singing high about Texas culture, once thought hardly worth serious notice, so have many Europeans lately been giving the nod to American culture, not so long ago considered in the Old World good mainly for laughs. For example, André Maurois recently contributed to the French magazine *Réalités* an open love letter entitled "Why We Like the Americans" ("Because they are kind and generous. . . . idealists," and so on). His countryman Father Robert Léopold Bruckberger, after eight years' residence in this country, published his thoughts about it in "Image of America," a heady verbal bouquet ("The American economic and social revolution is the only revolution in modern times to have achieved its aim"). Patrick O'Donovan, for five years the United States correspondent of the London *Observer,* began an appreciative essay in *Vogue* by remarking that "it takes a scholar to write adequately about America," which, he went on to say, "is a far more exacting and genuine democracy than any other in the world." Furthermore, said O'Donovan, it is no longer considered clever to be aloof about the workings of our political system. "Now," he declared, "it is academically and politically fashionable to know and appreciate the American system. It is accepted as one of fantastic subtlety, as one of the supreme products of human genius, [and to understand it] is a new art of sophistication."

All these kind words, inconceivable fifty years ago, seemed to diminish into little more than grudging, halfhearted compliments when the London *Times Literary Supplement* published, in the fall of 1959, a special thirty-nine-page, three-quarter-pound section titled "The American Imagination—Its Strength and Scope." In the introductory editorial, the *T.L.S.*, which has never been chaffed for indiscriminately approving all American cultural efforts, declared, "We in Europe take the vitality of the arts in America so much for granted that we seldom pause to assess it for the remarkable phenomenon it is . . . but in fact it is true to say that the flowering of the American imagination has been the chief event in the sphere of living art since the end of the First World War."

After collecting a certain number of these European posies, one might begin to think that not knocking American culture had become positively chic. One would have another think coming. While the younger, more daring outriders have commenced sending back favorable reports on the state of American culture, these estimates do not carry much weight with the senior group at headquarters. Generally, the old, forthright downgrading of American culture *en bloc* has given way to a new, sleight-of-hand approach, which bestows praise while at the same time taking it away. The British writer Kingsley Amis has called this sort of legerdemain "non-overt anti-Americanism." The European detractors of American culture, as André Visson has written, "ask the same questions the Greeks of Athens were asking in the third century B.C., when the rising Roman Empire was imposing its leadership on the peoples living around the Mediterranean: You say that you have philosophers; but where is your Plato and your Socrates? You say that you have statesmen; but where is your Pericles? You certainly have superiority in military power and you are much wealthier than we are, but all your power and all your wealth cannot take away from us our cultural and intellectual superiority." This, Visson added, became known as "the Athenian complex."

The recognition of historical antecedents for European criticisms of our culture, though edifying, does not make such criticisms much more fascinating to Americans, nor is it likely that Texans would be soothed to realize that the Athenian complex plays a large part in the outsiders' view of their culture. In keeping with the present national tendency toward non-overt anti-Texanism, Texas culture is for the most part regarded not with hostility but with levity. Foreigners are inclined to express their opinion of it in terms of anecdotes like the one about the oilman who built a handsome new home-office building, complete with a patio designed to resemble an enormous hanging garden. Upon its completion, an art dealer told the oilman that the beauty of the garden would be enhanced by a piece of sculpture—perhaps, to carry out the garden's floating motif, a statue of Icarus. "Sounds good," said the oilman. "What does Ike Harris get for his stuff?"

In covering the field of music, non-overt anti-Texans usually refer to Hugh Roy Cullen and his annual gift of twenty thousand dollars to the Houston Symphony Orchestra, which reciprocated by including in every concert Cullen attended a rendition of his favorite work, "Old Black Joe." As for musical composition, smart-alecky foreigners hold up as a model the former Texas Governor and Senator Wilbert Lee ("Pass the Biscuits, Pappy") O'Daniel, whose vast production of musical numbers includes "Marvelous Mother," "Your Own Sweet Darling Wife," and "The Boy Who Never Gets Too Big to Comb His Mother's Hair." The Neo-Athenians also like to give the impression that O'Daniel stands first among Texas poets, and cite as proof his haunting composition:

A mother is a mother
Wherever you find her
Be she a Queen
Or an organ grinder.

All such frivolous exhibits are naturally resented by Texans, who are even worse than Russians or ordinary Americans in their sensitivity to being thought uncultured. They have yet to recover from what they consider the unkindest cut of all—the careless assertion of the character in Edna Ferber's "Giant" who says, "You'll never hear a word of talk about books or music or sculpture or painting in Texas. . . . They never speak of these things. They have a kind of contempt for them." Such assaults on their culture have caused Texans to become almost morbidly preoccupied with it, and, lately, to strike back with vigor. "TEXAS IS, TOO, CIVILIZED," proclaimed the headline over a San Antonio *Express* article written by the paper's art editor, Gerald Ashford. An out-of-town guest invited to a meeting of the Shakespeare Club, in Dallas, was approached after the session by one of the officers, who said earnestly, "Now you see there's no truth to the stories that we are not cultured."

The most obvious sign of the Texans' preoccupation with what the art critic of the Houston *Post* calls their cultural setup is their tendency to be the first to say a good word about it. "Texas," declares the Fort Worth *Star-Telegram*, "once famous for oil and 'brags' and beautiful women, is gaining national prominence for another product—music, drama, and the general field of entertainment." "It is impossible," says the director of the Southern Methodist University Press, "to refrain from optimism about the current state of literature in Texas—and the outlook for the next twenty-five years." "It is now an acknowledged fact that the Casa Mañana," states the director of the Fort Worth theatre bearing that name, "is without a doubt the finest theatre of its kind in the United States." Brags about the cultural setup seem most often to take the form of counting the state's cultural blessings. "We have symphony orchestras operating in nearly twenty cities," writes Jim Mathis in the

Houston *Post*. "At least a hundred and fifty Texans can conscientiously be called artists," says the director of the Dallas Museum of Fine Arts. Other native authorities periodically inform their fellow-citizens that they now have this number of museums, that number of theatres, and so on down the cultural line.

The Texans' attempt to measure the level of their culture by quantitative standards is thoroughly and joyously American. It is the old cultural numbers game, a national pastime that appraises our cultural attainment according to dollars spent on classical phonograph records, square feet of museum space, and other numerical standards. No matter where one looks, one is apt to see scores of the game. The New York *Times* reports that "as against 600 museums serving the American public in 1932, there are now 2500," and that "twice as many people played musical instruments in 1957 as in 1938." *Fortune* announces that "Americans are buying some 630 million books a year . . . up from 330 million ten years ago." The *Saturday Review* states that "of two thousand symphony orchestras in the world, fourteen hundred are in the United States. Of the twenty-three with annual budgets in excess of a quarter of a million dollars, we have fourteen."

As these various scores prove, we have been going great guns in the cultural numbers game. The indications are that we are about to do even better, for, as *Look* recently pointed out, "America has gone culture-crazy. We have sculpture in our shopping centers, concerts in our banks. . . . Music is even piped underwater in swimming pools. . . . Bookworms read some $2 billion worth of paperbacks a year. . . . Painting exhibits are now held in banks, supermarkets, political clubs, and department stores. . . . Two new apartment houses are named the Van Gogh and the Picasso. . . . Extra kicks for bibulous art lovers: liquor bottles packaged in prints of paintings by Gauguin, Renoir, Cézanne, and other famous artists." Along with tippling art lovers living in the Picasso, there are, inevitably, a few spoil-sports, like Joseph Wood Krutch, who not only have not been rocked by the recent cultural explosion but even go around taking the fun out of the cultural numbers game. "To prove that ours is the most cultured nation which ever existed will constitute a barren victory if we must, to prove our point, use nothing but quantitative standards and reconcile ourselves to the common denominator as a measure of excellence," Krutch has written. Another unreconstructed observer, Ralph Barton Perry, showed his colors by remarking, "When men are encouraged to believe that the great and good things of life are within the reach of all, they are inclined to invert the principle and to believe what lies within the reach of all is great and good."

Texas also has to put up with a few people, like the Dallas lawyer Thomas Knight, who are given to saying things that make their cultural patriotism suspect. "I don't think half a dozen people in Texas would buy the Sistine Madonna if it were up for sale at a bargain-basement price," Knight once remarked. "They'd think there was some wop propaganda behind it." However, such rude noises disturb the cultural scene more rarely in Texas than in America as a whole. Thus, while a certain number of Americans may fret about our cultural homogenization, the advent of *Kitsch,* and allied woes, Texans are able to remain, culturally speaking, serene.

In its once-over of American culture, the *Times Literary Supplement* took a look at education in this country, and found amusing what it called our "childish infatuation" with the subject. "A cynic," said the *T.L.S.* "may suggest that a constitutional amendment making all American citizens A.B.s at birth would meet the case." The fact that we do indeed believe a college education to be every American's birthright could hardly fail to strike the British (though scarcely less than other Europeans) as somewhat comic, considering their centuries-old conviction that it is preposterous to maintain that everybody is equipped to benefit from higher education. That advantage (despite a doubling of British university graduates since the Second World War) is still accepted by the British as the special province of the minority. Six out of ten children in

Great Britain leave school and start work at fifteen, and only six per cent go on to the universities. This state of affairs is considered peculiar in America, where more than thirty-three per cent of all young people between eighteen and twenty-one now attend institutions of higher learning. Our boast that of every million persons in America 16,670 are university students, compared with 1185 of every million in England—not to mention our eighteen hundred colleges and universities, as against her fifteen—is put down by the British as just one more proof of the American preference for quantity over quality. While we are sometimes willing to acknowledge that our novel educational experiment may have some defects, we would much rather talk about the fact that no society has ever spent as much money on education as ours. This kindles in the national bosom a warm glow of self-satisfaction, which is only slightly dampened by the realization that we spend only one-half of one per cent more on education than we do on alcohol.

The school situation reaches its acme, of course, in Texas, where the verbal worship of education is rampant. In spite of that, Texas stands thirty-second among the states in spending per pupil in the public schools. Gifts to local colleges and universities are a favorite philanthropy of Texas millionaires, but even with this largess Texas, according to a recent study of twenty-one states comparable in population and income, ranks next to the bottom in the average amount spent per student in state-supported institutions of higher learning. In education, as in other areas of life in Texas, the conservative spirit reigns. "Texans approve of education so long as it consists of handsome buildings, vast endowments, and hosts of bright-eyed, sturdy youths studying such harmless subjects as trigonometry and Chaucer," Green Peyton has written. "But if education means the development of free minds, equipped to examine the strange forces let loose in the world, they are against it."

A classic example of the Texas distrust of anything that resembles free inquiry is the Board of Education in Houston, which, under the domination of an extreme right-wing faction led by a lady vigilante, has for the past dozen years been firing teachers and administrators on charges of being "controversial," banning textbooks it considers "anti-capitalistic," and engaging in other antics of similar design. "God, it's still the funniest thing in town," remarked the magazine *Houston Town* in 1958. (There may be less of this kind of comedy in the future, some Houstonians feel, because of the resignation last fall of the board's star performer, after a revolver she was holding accidentally went off and shot her husband.) Dallas, on the other hand, has well-regarded public schools, especially in the prosperous residential section, Highland Park. During the past three years, approximately ninety-seven per cent of the Highland Park High School graduates have gone on to college, and last year two of its alumni—Ensign Alton Thompson and Second Lieutenant Charles Otstott—led their classes at Annapolis and West Point, not only as president in each case but in both academic and military standing. This unprecedented event stirred up local chauvinism. Neiman-Marcus took a half-page newspaper ad showing pictures of the two men under a headline reading, "TOP THIS, ALASKA!"

While Texas millionaires have increasingly tended to send their sons to Eastern schools and colleges, the vast majority of them prefer to have their scions get their education from Texans in Texas, and there they can choose among a hundred and thirty-five universities and colleges. Eighty-three of these, including three of the largest universities, are privately supported—for the most part by churches. Southern Methodist has fifty-five hundred students, Baylor (Baptist) has over five thousand, and Texas Christian (Disciples of Christ, an offshoot of the Presbyterian and Baptist Churches) has slightly more than six thousand. Rice University—until recently called Rice Institute—the top-ranking institution of higher learning in Texas and among the best in the country, is also privately supported; its income is derived from an endowment established by a Massachusetts grocer who emigrated to Texas in 1837 and prospered. Situated in Houston, Rice has a distinguished faculty, a handsome campus, air-conditioned buildings, a student-teacher ratio of eleven to one, and it charges no tuition. Rice can afford to be selective, and is; the enrollment is limited to fourteen hundred men and four hundred women. Rice has the distinction of being one of the five universities and colleges in Texas that require applicants to take College Entrance Board examinations; the others are Southern Methodist, Austin College, Trinity University, and, starting last fall, the University of Texas.

The generally relaxed entrance standards of Texas colleges, have naturally induced a tremendous and—as elsewhere in America—rapidly mounting enrollment, which in the fall of 1960 reached a peak of 165,000 students. Of these, 18,442 were enrolled in the University of Texas, at once the state's largest university and its richest. Its endowment ranks in size after the endowment of Harvard, and is, like many other accumulations of cash in Texas, more the result of good luck than of good management. When the university was established, in 1883, the legislature gave it two million acres of land in West Texas, the grazing rights from which yielded an annual income of approximately five hundred dollars. In 1923, the Big Lake oil field was found on land owned by the university; since then, oil has enriched its endowment by three hundred and fifty-four million dollars. Despite this comfortable nest egg, the university has a hard time making ends meet, since a third of the income from its endowment must be given to Texas A. & M. (enrollment 7100), which is constitutionally a branch of the university. Once operating expenses have been paid, there is very little money left for the expansion of facilities in order to keep up with the times. To fill this gap, Harvard relies on the generosity of its alumni ($18,981,227 contributed in 1960); the University of Texas, short of generous alumni ($169,389 contributed in 1960), relies on the state legislature, a frail reed indeed, since it is unwilling even to pay the university president's full twenty-five-thousand-dollar salary; of this sum, forty-four hundred comes from a grant bequeathed the university by one of its first alumni.

The effects of the legislature's parsimony have not gone unnoticed by Texans less driven by the economy demon. A couple of years ago, a committee appointed to appraise the university and measure its progress toward its orginal goal—which, as the writers of the Texas Constitution put it, was to establish and maintain a university "of the first class"—reported that the university, far from having reached the point of being first class, ranked as "barely satisfactory." Two years after being given this rather cheerless word, the university's Board of Regents announced a ten-year, eighty-million-dollar plan to upgrade their institution. The project appears to have some chance of success, since it does not place primary reliance on the legislature but plans instead to secure over half of the required funds from private gifts—not necessarily by the alumni.

Whatever happens at the University of Texas in the future, the state's educational system as a whole is at present distinguished by quantity rather than quality—a condition abundantly demonstrated a few months ago by Jim Mathis in the Houston *Post* with a spate of statistics showing, for one thing, the comparatively infinitesimal sums granted for research to educational institutions in Texas by the Atomic Energy Commission, the Public Health Service, the Defense Department, and other agencies that demand top-grade standards of scholarship. Other figures revealed that of 166,000 scientists and technicians listed in a register of the National Science Foundation, slightly more than five per cent live or are employed in Texas. Furthermore, in 1958, only 263 persons were awarded doctorates by Texas universities, compared with 1379 in New York; in the same year, Texas conferred 3721 Master's degrees and New York 9917. "By almost any measuring rod you can find," Mathis remarked after finding several more, "the state has a brain-power shortage, and is suffering from the lack."

It is not easy to make up this lack by attracting the best-qualified teachers to state-supported colleges and universities, Dr. Logan Wilson, until recently chancellor of the University of Texas, has pointed out, since they offer salaries thirteen per cent below the national average. "In no instance," he added, "has a Texas college or university been categorized as equal to the best of its kind anywhere." One result has been a flight of native talent; less than one out of five honor students who leave the state for graduate work ever return. Another result was revealed in a recent large-scale sampling of Texas industry, which showed that sixty-five per cent of the employees being paid more than ten thousand dollars a year were graduates of out-of-state colleges, while an equal proportion receiving lower salaries were products of native institutions. (To do something about this intellectual lag, commercial and educational leaders are setting up the Graduate Research Center of the Southwest, a sixty-million-dollar "brain factory," as it is sometimes referred to locally, that its backers hope will develop into a regional facsimile of M.I.T.) Quality and money are not the only problems confronting Texans in charge of their state's higher education. In a survey conducted a while ago at the University of Texas, faculty members were asked the single question "What do you regard as the university's most perplexing problem?" The preponderant response was "Parking."

The reaction of Texans to the 1954 United States Supreme Court decision declaring school segregation unconstitutional has been typically American, and then some. Depending mainly on the section of the state, it has run all the way from anger, resentment, and all-out opposition, through calm detachment and resigned acceptance, to reluctant approval and, here and there, genuine endorsement. In contrast to other Southern states, where the decree was everywhere met with open defiance, sixty-five school districts in Texas voluntarily ended segregation within a year after it became illegal. However, the strong segregational sentiment that predominates in Texas had been stirred up, and in 1957, when sixty-nine additional school districts voluntarily abolished segregation, Governor Price Daniel, to impede further moves in that direction, called a special session of the legislature, which enacted a law providing for the withdrawal of state aid and accreditation from any school district that desegregates without approval of its voters, and for fines of up to a thousand dollars for school-board members who permit desegregation without a local referendum favoring it.

Thanks to this disingenuous legislation, attorneys arguing before federal courts on behalf of segregationist Texas school boards were able to present their clients as innocent bystanders caught in a legal crossfire; if they obeyed federal law, they were liable under state law to be penalized personally and also to bring great hardship to their schools by depriving them of state aid. When the attorneys had exhausted their variations on the conflict-of-laws theme, the school boards in Houston and Dallas, where the N.A.A.C.P. has concentrated its pressure, were obliged to draw up and submit to the federal courts actual desegregation plans. Further delays were accomplished, but finally Federal Judge Ben C. Connally ordered the Houston school system, then the largest segregated school district in the country, to integrate its first grade in September, 1960, and to complete the desegregation process by integrating one additional upper grade each year thereafter for eleven years. After making unsuccessful appeals to a higher court and to the Governor to postpone or nullify the court decree, the board agreed to obey it. At the same time, the board announced that a Negro child, to be eligible for acceptance in a white school, would be required to file an application; present a doctor's certificate attesting his good health; be immunized against smallpox and diphtheria; have no brothers or sisters attending an all-Negro elementary school; be six years old; and if a former kindergarten pupil in a Negro school, obtain a transfer slip from the principal of the school. Altogether, twenty-two such applications were made; twelve were accepted. Thus, six years after the Supreme Court desegregation decision, twelve of Houston's forty-six thousand Negro schoolchildren were benefiting from it.

In Dallas, desegregation, even to the limited extent adopted in Houston, was not undertaken until the fall of 1961. In fact, no integration at all has been attempted in East Texas, which prides itself on its strict adherence to the segregation customs of the Old South and contains ninety per cent of the state's

Negroes. As for Texas colleges and universities, the majority, including large ones like Texas A. & M., Texas Tech, and the state teachers' colleges, are completely segregated. A few, such as Texas Christian and Southern Methodist, accept Negroes only in their graduate schools; in 1960, Southern Methodist had a dozen Negro graduate students. However, more than forty other Texas colleges and universities—in addition to two state-supported and eight privately financed all-Negro institutions—now accept Negroes as undergraduates. In the desegregated colleges, Negroes, though accepted in the classroom, are still at least partly segregated in housing, in off-campus eating facilities, and in various ways socially. "What we have," a Negro student at the University of Texas said recently, "is desegregation without integration."

Though non-Southerners are given to criticizing Texans for their "ingenious procrastination," desegregation in Texas can perhaps be correctly appraised only in context—in relation, that is, to the other states that made up the old Confederacy. As of the fall of 1960, five of these states—Alabama, Georgia, Mississippi, South Carolina, and Louisiana—were still flatly refusing to recognize the Supreme Court edict, and in none was a single Negro child attending class with whites. Five other onetime Confederate states—Virginia, North Carolina, Arkansas, Florida, and Tennessee—also opposed the law with massive resistance but by the fall of 1960 had accepted desegregation to the extent of permitting a total of 807, of their combined school population of 982,822, to attend mixed classes. At the same time, in Texas, 3511 Negroes were attending public schools with white students. That was more than four times as many as in all the other former Confederate states together.

Chapter Seventeen

"Somewhere in this broad land, many people read books as daily nourishment," wrote Lon Tinkle, book critic of the Dallas *News*. "This must be in the cold climates, where you have to stay indoors, or maybe in the sophisticated cities. If the latter, this leaves Dallas out in the cold, or at least outdoors. In the sophisticated metropolis of New York, for example, thirty-seven per cent (or more than one copy out of three) of the total sales of Boris Pasternak's Nobel Prizer 'Doctor Zhivago' were made. You know what percentage was bought in Texas? Texas, plus the entire South put together, consumed only four per cent of the national total." In this gentle chiding of his compatriots, Tinkle was simply noting one more area in which Texans outdo other Americans—non-reading. The same is true of television; while the majority of Americans spend approximately twenty per cent of their waking hours watching television, forty-two per cent of adult Texans, according to a survey by Belden Associates, spend "most" of their leisure in that pursuit. Television is not, of course, responsible for the unpopularity of books in this country. Before television, it was radio, and before that the phonograph, pinochle, whittling—anything but the comparatively hard discipline of reading.

Many people in this broad land, as Tinkle has said, do read books for daily sustenance, but more, to judge from the best-seller lists, prefer non-books, as *Time* has termed the confections turned out by, among others, Dr. Norman Vincent Peale, Dr. Smiley Blanton, Arlene Francis, Bishop Fulton J. Sheen, and Art Linkletter, the jovial author who is also in oil and supermarkets in Texas. Despite our heavy consumption of non-books and comic books (we spend a hundred million dollars a year on the latter), we remain the world's greatest non-readers.

Though this fact has been known to all for a couple of centuries, we continue to act surprised every time we learn it has been rediscovered, as it was, for example, in a recent issue of the *Saturday Review*, which printed excerpts from a speech by Robert Kenyon, president of the Magazine Publishers Association, who spoke of "some rather shocking readership figures compiled by the Gallup people. Of the English, fifty-five per cent said 'Yes' when asked whether they were reading a book at the time of the survey. Of the Germans, forty-five per cent said 'Yes.' For Australia and Canada, the results were thirty-three per cent and thirty-one per cent, respectively. Only in America, among the nations surveyed, was the figure really low: seventeen per cent." Putting it precisely, Kenyon said that, except for compulsory reading of textbooks, less than half of the American people *ever* read a book and that less than one in five *ever* buy a book. He ignored at least one encouraging sign, however. In 1954, a Gallup Poll found that sixty-one per cent of adult Americans read no books except the Bible, whereas in 1958, the figure had dropped to sixty per cent. So there has been improvement, even though we still spend only three times as much on books as we do on chewing gum.

How far this new interest in literature has progressed in Texas can be seen, to a certain extent, by contrasting the visit W. H. Auden made to Dallas in 1954 with the one made by T. S. Eliot in 1958. Auden appeared as an attraction of a cultural program called the Community Course, and was introduced by Dallas's cultural attaché, Lon Tinkle. "You would have guessed the audience had never heard a British accent before when Auden got up and started talking," Tinkle said later. "The consternation at hearing a British poet speak the King's English did in a dozen right away. For their money's worth, they heard only one sentence before they were gone. This was a contagion. People got up in packs, as though a posse had been summoned to find Billy the Kid, Jesse James,

294

or Pablo Picasso. Whole rows emptied with the machinelike precision of a Rockette chorus. Finally, only Auden and we and a polite handful were left. Out of twenty-five hundred at the start." Tinkle was also instrumental in bringing T. S. Eliot to Dallas, and in skillfully publicizing his admission-free lecture, given in the nine-thousand-seat Coliseum, at Southern Methodist University. The event, Tinkle noted in one of several newspaper articles he wrote about it, was one in which "the vaunted cultural interest of Big D is put to a severe test." To hear Eliot read for an hour and a half from his works, some seven thousand people turned out in a downpour so heavy that two or three times during the evening Eliot was obliged to stop reading until he could be heard above the noise made by the rain on the roof. The audience not only stayed for the whole performance but, at the end, gave Eliot a standing ovation.

Though one poet does not make a trend, other signs indicate that literature is catching on in Texas. In 1959, the first Book and Author Luncheon held in the state was put on in Dallas. The event, with Moss Hart, Kay Thompson, and the Duke of Bedford as the honored authors, drew precisely one thousand and three guests, or, as the newspapers proudly announced, about four times the number who generally attend similar affairs in San Francisco and Philadelphia. Even more book and celebrity lovers turned out for the second Luncheon, the following year. The prime mover in arranging these outlets for the growing interest in books and authors has been Lon Tinkle, a handsome, mustached Dallas native who has been described by the London *Times* as "the arbiter of Texas letters." A product of Southern Methodist University, Columbia, and the Sorbonne, Tinkle started writing book reviews for the Dallas *News* in 1942, combining this activity with his regular work as a professor of French and Comparative Literature at S.M.U. The *News* book page, which appears once a week, usually in the women's section of the Sunday edition, has long been considered the most professional exhibit of its kind in the Southwest.

Other large Texas newspapers also have book editors—Diana

Hobby, of the Houston *Post,* and A. C. Greene, of the Dallas *Times Herald,* are among the better known—and once a week devote space, usually about a page, to reviewing new books. The Fort Worth *Star-Telegram*'s Sunday edition carries a page headed "Books and Hobbies," which contains four or five book reviews, a column about coins, one about stamps, and a third titled "Canine Comments." Books are also occasionally discussed in the Houston *Post* columns written by Bill Roberts and George Fuermann. "Only since World War II have we begun to honor the creative minds," Fuermann, who is also the author of two works about the state, said a while ago in a panel discussion of Southwestern literature. "Creative writing is now beginning to bud and shoot for the first time, and it could be said that the state's intellectual life is in the springtime."

Another harbinger has been the notable success of the *Texas Quarterly,* a venture of the University of Texas Press, launched in 1958. The state now has two literary quarterlies, the other one being the *Southwest Review,* founded in 1915 and published by the Southern Methodist University Press. The *Southwest Review* devotes more space to material of a regional nature than does the *Texas Quarterly,* whose contributors have so far included not only natives like Lyndon B. Johnson and Katherine Anne Porter but such varied outsiders as Robert Graves, Allen W. Dulles, Joyce Cary, Alexander Kerensky, Karl Shapiro, and even Walter Reuther. Though the presses at both universities, as their catalogues reveal, have a predominant interest in works like "Recollections of Early Texas," "The Legumes of Texas," "Texas Range Grasses," and "Tornadoes Over Texas," they are gradually becoming less parochial. The University of Texas Press, for example, is the only American publisher to have printed a complete English version of "Platero and I," the best-known work of the Spanish poet Juan Ramón Jiménez, who was awarded the 1956 Nobel Prize.

Though no Texas author has won a Nobel Prize, or even a Pulitzer Prize, there is no doubt a winner in the making, for, as Frank Wardlaw, director of the University of Texas Press, has put it, "Texas is bursting with creativity." The most famous writer Texas has produced is J. Frank Dobie, who has been variously—and accurately—described as "a Texas institution, loved by thousands," "both the prophet and the conscience of Texas letters," and "one of the few untamed geniuses still roaming free." A handsome, white-thatched, rugged figure of a man, Dobie was born on a Texas ranch, took up teaching after graduation from Southwestern University, and wound up as a professor ("*full* professor," he says mockingly) of English at the University of Texas, where he became known as "the best professor who ever got on a horse," and where he had his headquarters for thirty-three years. During a leave of absence in 1943–44, he served as visiting professor of American history at Cambridge. He found the experience, like everything else he encounters, exhilarating, and wrote about it in "A Texan in England." "The dons don't do so bad," he noted, "when they retire from their high table to the combination (club) room and drink port and other wines." After Cambridge, Dobie stayed on leave for three more years, and when he was asked to resume his teaching post, he refused, on the ground that he had hay fever and wanted to finish writing a book. This provided the Board of Regents of the University of Texas with an official reason for dismissing him; in 1944, Dobie, an enemy of sham and a believer in individualism and plain talk, had pungently supported Homer P. Rainey, president of the university, in his losing fight with the regents over having strayed from the straight and narrow path of Texas conservatism.

Over the years, Dobie has written close to a score of books and is full of plans for more. "There are a dozen books I still want to write," he told a friend a couple of years ago. "I want to finish my bear book. It is a book I'm fond of, and is probably what I will finish first. Then I want to write down all I've collected about rattlesnake lore and do a rattlesnake book. And I want to write a book about cow people I have known, some of them extraordinary characters, and, of course, there is my autobiography, which I work on from time to time."

Since 1939, Dobie has also written a column published in the Sunday editions of several Texas newspapers, and in this forum has expressed himself on a variety of subjects, including contemporary school textbooks ("stuffed with banal tripe that would bore the brain of a hard-shelled terrapin"), Dwight Eisenhower ("makes no pretense to a cultivated mind"), John Kennedy ("a gentleman"), Richard Nixon ("a blackguard"), Adlai Stevenson ("a great mind"), college departments of education and journalism ("mostly departments of shysterism"), high-toned terminology ("I am so old-fashioned that I still call a memorial park a graveyard"), his superior officer in the First World War ("as common as pig tracks"), and the American Legion ("an organization of petrified minds"). On his seventieth birthday, in 1958, Dobie was asked by a visitor if he cared to comment on the occasion. Opening a bottle of Scotch that a friend had sent in honor of the day, Dobie poured a drink for his visitor and one for himself, and said, "It's a diverting farce, and I'd like to play my little part in it a little while longer."

Another eminent Texas man of letters, the historian Walter Prescott Webb, has been playing his part as long and as notably as Dobie. Not only was Webb born in the same year and on a ranch but he has also spent most of his adult life as a professor at the University of Texas, with leaves to serve as a visiting professor at Oxford and at the University of London. In 1958, Webb, the state's most distinguished scholar and a historian in the tradition of Frederick Jackson Turner, became the first person from west of the Mississippi to be elected president of the American Historical Association. His best-known works, "The Great Plains" and "The Great Frontier," have made him, as *Time* recently noted, "his generation's foremost philosopher of the frontier, and the leading historian of the American West." Small, leathery, and shrewd (he has done very well on the side in real estate), Webb shares Dobie's predilection for straight talk. That and mutual high regard are among the reasons the two men have remained staunch friends for so many years. Perhaps the compliment that Webb, as a Westerner, most appreciates is Dobie's plain remark that Webb is a man who "will do to ride the river with."

A close and deeply respected friend of both Webb and Dobie, the naturalist and philosopher Roy Bedichek was, until his death in 1959, at eighty-one, customarily grouped with them as one of the Big Three of Texas literature. Bedichek, who earned his living as director of a state agency that arranges athletic, debating, and other competitions among the public schools, did not begin his writing career until he was seventy. His literary output was accordingly small, consisting of four volumes. The best known, "Adventures of a Texas Naturalist," besides being a book about Texas flora and fauna, reflects what Dobie once called "the most richly and variously stored mind I have ever associated with." In the course of reviewing Bedichek's last book, an extraordinary work titled "The Sense of Smell," Stanley Walker, for many years one of the author's close friends, said that Bedichek's death was mourned throughout the state and that it had moved an unnamed rancher he knew to remark, "This is the worst loss to civilization Texas has ever received. We could afford to lose our tidelands and a lot of our skyscrapers. We can't afford this." The deliverer of that discerning judgment might well have been Walker himself, a loyal, if non-chauvinistic, Texan who in the course of twenty years spent in New York earned a reputation as one of the country's most prominent and respected newspapermen. In 1945, he returned to his native land, and has since made his headquarters at Black Sheep Retreat, in Lampasas County, where he combines ranching and writing with civilized conversation and—as might be expected of a man who does not object to being called "the Brillat-Savarin of the Plains"—good eating.

Besides Walker, other well-known Texas writers include Tom Lea, Fred Gipson, the late George Sessions Perry, and a dozen or so younger men, who have made their reputations since the Second World War, among them John Graves, a teacher of creative writing at Texas Christian University (his first book, "Goodbye to a River," published last year, was likened by

Lewis Gannett to the work of a twentieth-century Thoreau), William Humphrey, Walter Clemons, Terry Southern, Lon Tinkle himself, William Goyen, George Fuermann, John Howard Griffin, Frank Tolbert, and Warren Leslie. At thirty-three, Leslie not only has published two successful novels but has risen to a vice-presidency of Neiman-Marcus; the latter intelligence is sometimes included in advertisements in Texas of his written works, thereby inferentially giving them the N.-M. seal of approval.

The direct contribution of Texas millionaires to literature has been less abundant than varied. In 1952, after many years of secret toil, the late Madison Cooper, an eccentric, public-spirited native of Waco, published "Sironia, Texas," a novel distinguished by its length (seventeen hundred and thirty-one pages) and, in the opinion of many residents of Waco, by the similarity of its characters to actual persons, both living and dead. In the field of non-fiction, the Houston oilman Michel Halbouty collaborated a few years ago with the newspaperman and public relations consultant Jim Clark in writing "Spindletop," which sold fifteen thousand copies, and they are at present busy with a new book, to be called "The Last Boom."

A Houston millionaire who has made a considerably larger mark in letters is Dillon Anderson, a senior partner in the city's oldest law firm and a resolute doer of good works on the national and international scene. Anderson started taking a serious interest in writing after the Second World War, during which he became acquainted with Edward Weeks, editor of the *Atlantic*. In 1948, Weeks received Anderson's first offering, a story about a pair of raffish characters named Clint Hightower and Claudie Hughes, and, after sending it back to the author ten times for revision and rewriting, bought and published it. That gave Anderson the encouragement to go on, which he did with such success that in 1959 he was named a Fellow of the American Academy of Arts and Sciences. A somewhat different approach to letters has been taken by the San Antonio millionaire Tom Slick, who has directed his writing efforts less toward entertaining than toward edifying the masses, especially on disarmament and world peace; he has presented his ideas on these topics in two books, "The Last Great Hope" and "Permanent Peace: The Checks and Balances Plan," both earnestly conceived and carefully composed.

To improve the world, though along slightly different lines, has also been the abiding ambition of H. L. Hunt, who spent a fortune trying to do it with the now defunct radio-and-publishing enterprise called Facts Forum, and is currently back at the Far Right stand with a similar undertaking called Life Line. To carry his message to an even wider audience, Hunt composed a book titled "Alpaca," which he personally published (the printing was done by a firm that puts out telephone directories) in 1960, in a paperback edition selling for fifty cents. Cast in the form of a love story, the work takes as its title the name of a "little six-province nation" long run by dictators. Its hero is a young Alpacan named Juan Achala, who, after pondering "the troubled past and inscrutable future of his unhappy country," decides to present his people with a new system of government, based on a synthesis of the ideas of wise men all over Europe. It is clear from the way he talks that Juan, whose "proud athletic bearing, his air of inborn courtesy unmarred by hauteur, his flashing eyes beneath shapely brows, and his magnificent even white teeth, accenting a ready smile, exerted a magnetic attraction even upon strangers," is a deep thinker: "It seems to me, sir, that we must begin with the individual before we can benefit society, which consists of individuals. And the crux of all that, I can't help thinking, is the protection of the individual's mind from becoming slanted toward acceptance of totalitarian government and from the great danger of having his mentality arrested or destroyed completely, not only by sly propaganda but by the evil drugs and psychic pressures of unscrupulous despots."

In the course of consulting the European wise men, Juan meets a beautiful young Alpacan diva named Mara Hani, "a slim, erect vision of femininity with exquisite coiffure above an oval face, and long-lashed eyes that were limpid pools of mystery and witchery unparalleled." She is travelling with her Aunt Arifa, who is being courted by a middle-aged gentleman identified as "Sir Gerald Ripney of Cobbles Court, in the South of England." While Sir Gerald keeps company with Aunt Arifa, Juan loves Mara ("He held her close and murmured: 'We were made for each other. It was foreordained that we should be united. You know that, don't you?'"), and tells her about his plan for reforming the government. "I can help you put it over, my darling," Mara says. "As soon as I can get this début out of the way, we'll make a Team. Oh, what a Team! We'll perfect the details here and then go back home and show the people what's good for them." Juan and Mara are married, and quickly go to work perfecting what they refer to as their dream government.

The constitution devised by the Team has many enlightened features, such as no trial by jury, a plan whereby the "rank-and-file voters" can delegate their voting power to those better qualified, an income tax limited to twenty-five per cent, and a depletion allowance on natural resources. Perhaps the most arresting idea in the dream constitution is the one giving the most votes to the biggest taxpayers; the ten per cent who pay the largest taxes automatically receive seven extra votes apiece and can buy more by paying poll taxes. Rejecting the notion that this would create a plutocracy, the author explains, "It's like a corporation: the greatest stockholders have the greatest votes." When Juan and Mara present the new constitution to the people of Alpaca, they are so delighted with the prospect of having so many things that are good for them that they promptly exchange the dictator for the dream government and give a royal welcome to its chief architects. In the midst of all this good fortune, Mara tells Juan that she is going to have a baby, and the story ends before they have decided whether to name the child Marajuana.

To promote his book, advertised as a work of "permanent importance," Hunt broke his habit of avoiding interviews and public appearances by serving as guest of honor at an autographing party at the Cokesbury Book Store, in Dallas, which, despite bitter-cold weather, was attended by some six hundred book lovers. After the author had briskly signed a couple of hundred copies of his book, he was joined by his second wife, an attractive woman whom he married in 1957, and her two daughters—Helen, eleven, and Sewanee, ten. The girls broke into a song, to the tune of "Doggie in the Window," which began, "How much is that book in the window? The one that says all the smart things. How much is that book in the window? I do hope to learn all it brings." And, four stanzas later, ended, "How much is that book in the window? The one which my Popsy wrote. How much is that book in the window? You can buy it without signing a note." After which, the girls shouted in unison, "'Alpaca'! Fifty cents!" Asked by a reporter if he expected to make money on his book, Hunt replied, with more candor than most authors, "Certainly. The profit motive is deeply embedded in me. Everything I do, I do for profit."

Though autograph parties in Texas do not always attract a crowd as large as Hunt's, they are a standard ritual for native authors, who also whoop it up for literature in many other ways, such as attending the Annual Southwest Writers Conference, which, like similar gatherings elsewhere, provides an occasion for writers and writing buffs to get together and talk big about writing. Another annual event, the Texas Writers Roundup, is put on in the fall in Austin to pay homage to native authors. The governor customarily gives a fillip to this affair by proclaiming the day on which it is staged Texas Writers Day.

When winter comes, the Texas Institute of Letters, which has about a hundred members, and was once compared by an exuberant devotee to the French Academy, holds an annual meeting to discuss literature, dine, and preside over the awarding of more, and bigger, prizes, the oldest of which is named in honor of Carr P. Collins, whose family gained fame and fortune marketing Crazy Water Crystals and who does very well himself as board chairman of the Fidelity Union Life Insurance Company. Since 1946, Collins has provided a thousand-dollar award for "the best Texas book of the year," and, as a devout and active Baptist, has stipulated only that it not be given to a book that knocks Christianity. Other prizes for native authors distributed by the Institute include the Jesse H. Jones Award (a thousand dollars), for the best fiction; the Friends of the Dallas Public Library Award (five hundred dollars), for "the most important contribution to knowledge"; the McMurray Book Shop Award, for the best first novel; and smaller sums, for the best juvenile, poetry, and book design. The Institute's biggest plum is matched by the Sons of the Republic of Texas, who annually pass out the Summerfield G. Roberts Award, named in honor of the Dallas oilman who puts up the cash, for "the best book of the year about early Texas." Texas poets, though not in the way of the big prize money, do not go unhonored. The Poetry Society of Texas annually distributes nearly a thousand dollars in forty-one separate awards, including the Vida Pifer Prize, the Green Thumb Prize, and the Horse in Poetry Prize.

As a result of the large-scale proliferation of belles-lettrists in Texas, it is somewhat easier to encounter a published author than a first-class bookstore in which his works can be bought. Though the telephone books of all major Texas cities list a dozen or more bookstores, they usually turn out, with a few agreeable exceptions, to be either greeting-card-and-wrapping-paper emporiums or church-supported establishments specializing in religious books. Every large city in Texas has one or more Baptist bookstores, a Presbyterian bookstore, and a Catholic bookstore, and several of the cities have stores supported by other denominations as well. Though the church stores handle some books of a general nature, if wholesome, their stocks as a rule are severely limited by their special interest and bias; a Baptist bookstore once returned to a publisher a landscape-gardening book because it contained a photograph of a monastery garden. A remarkable exception is the Cokesbury Book Store, which is owned by the Methodist Church and devotes the major share of its profits to the care of superannuated ministers. Calling itself the Cultural Department Store, Cokesbury's is the state's largest bookstore, and carries a stock of sufficient range to compare with nearly any in the country.

Unlike Houston, which, as J. Frank Dobie has remarked, "is the only city in America claiming a million inhabitants that doesn't have a decent second-hand bookstore," Dallas has the Aldredge Book Store, which does about eighty per cent of its business in second-hand books. The store, which occupies a converted residence a couple of miles from the center of town, has a conspicuously relaxed atmosphere, owing perhaps to the fact that its proprietor, Sawnie Aldredge, who comes from one of the older Texas families, takes a quiet, realistic view of the part that books play in the local culture. "Old Dallas doesn't buy books," Aldredge says. "Some of the new rich do, especially the generation now in their thirties and forties. But if Dallas had as many bookstores, in proportion to the population, as San Francisco does, we'd all starve. This is a boom town. People here are too busy doing other things to have time to read. They prefer to collect pictures instead of books. And there are a couple of good reasons for that. For one thing, it is a simple fact that there is more wall space in Texas than in, for example, New York, and, in the second place the ownership of a book implies an obligation to know what's in it. It's different with pictures. You buy them and put them up, all your friends see them, and you have proved your interest in culture without putting in too much time on it. When it comes to acquiring a culture rating, pictures are quicker than books."

Chapter Eighteen

The chief cultural interest of Texas millionaires is art collecting. It could hardly be anything else. "Collecting today in America is a sickness," the eminent New York art authority Sam Salz recently observed, and if that is so, it is in the nature of things that Super-Americans should come down with the worst case of it. The malady, which has been compared with the Children's Crusade and with the tulip mania that swept over Holland in the seventeenth century, is, like those phenomena, of European origin, but it now rages throughout the world, taking perhaps its heaviest toll among Greek shipowners. However, it appears that nobody is immune, as a visitor discovers on dropping into the Parke-Bernet Galleries, in New York, or Sotheby's Auction Rooms, in London, especially on days when Impressionist and Post-Impressionist paintings are up for sale. Seven of the latter were snapped up at Sotheby's a couple of years ago by hectic bidders of several nationalities, who paid $2,186,800 for the lot, including $616,000 for a Cézanne that the artist orginally sold for $340. In this country, the art sickness is reaching epidemic proportions. "In America," the London *Times* has flatly declared, "everybody buys art"—a statement that does not seem wide of the mark in the opinion of dealers, who now sell about half of their paintings on the installment plan and have adopted practically all other mass-merchandising techniques except passing out S. & H. green stamps.

The art market today is reminiscent of the stock market in the late twenties, with the bulls again on the loose. "No Recession in Painting," proclaimed a recent article in the English-language edition of the French magazine *Réalités*, which painted a rosy picture of the investment opportunities in art and provided the novice with a list headed "A Few Market Tips," such as "Portraits of women are worth more than those of men. . . . A painting in red sells better than one in any other color. . . . Flowers sell better than vegetables or fish. . . . Portraits of military personages sell badly." On the art scene today, as on the securities scene in the twenties, there is an occasional bear, like A. Wilfred May, executive editor of the *Commercial & Financial Chronicle* and a collector, who recently explored art as an investment in an essay titled "Does Rembrandt Pay Dividends?" After noting that at present "the ownership of a Seurat is as good as a triple-A rating in Dun & Bradstreet," May reviewed the fads and fancies that have affected the art market in the past and arrived at the cautious conclusion that "any material gain from art is windfall." Ignoring this kind of counsel, buyers have made the art business, once a relatively quiet pursuit for the knowledgeable few, into a multimillion-dollar industry, with such a swelling consumer demand that a dealer in Paris remarked a while ago, "The difficulty is not selling paintings but finding enough to sell."

For this novel state of affairs Americans are mainly responsible, since they are the leading buyers of both modern art and Old Masters. In their acquisition of the art treasures of Europe, our current crop of millionaires is carrying on the pattern set years ago by the Morgans, Fricks, Mellons, and other so-called American Medicis whose ruthless enterprise, though naturally deplored by Europeans, resulted in endowing this country, until then practically barren of significant art, with collections that are now comparable to any in the world. After a tour of America in 1960, Sir John Rothenstein, director of the Tate Gallery, reported ruefully in the London *Observer*, "Works of art are to be seen everywhere in a profusion unparalleled in the world outside. As one visits collection after collection, one cannot but speculate about how little there is left in Europe, and how long even this little can remain there."

The prognosis, from the European side, is not good. The art sickness, not unexpectedly, is incubated in the endlessly entertaining American tax structure, which encourages millionaires to accumulate art by largely blunting what H. L. Hunt customarily calls the tax bite. If he or one of his art-minded friends buys a work of art and presents it to a museum or other tax-exempt institution, he can enter a delightful deduction on his tax return and yet retain custody of the work during his lifetime. It is possible to reap even greater rewards by buying a painting for, say, two hundred thousand dollars and keeping it for a couple of years, while its value—in the opinion of a hired expert—increases to two hundred and fifty thousand dollars; thereupon the art lover donates the painting, keeps it on his wall, and benefits from an even higher tax deduction for being a public-spirited citizen.

The pleasures of art are by no means all pecuniary. Collecting on an important scale today confers a cachet that in other times was awarded for owning a yacht or a string of race horses, or for giving elaborate entertainments. To be a collector is to be marked as not only a man of means but a man of taste and civic virtue, worthy of notice—perhaps even of being taken up—by desirable new friends. "Art has become a social thing," Alvin Romansky, a Houston lawyer and art patron, said a while ago. "For a great many people, the interest is only superficial. When they go to a show, they're really interested only in seeing their friends and meeting people and having drinks. It's not just here. All over the country, people are using art to promote themselves socially."

In addition to the social thing, the skyrocketing prices that pictures have recently been fetching have introduced into collecting the always fascinating element of profit-taking possibilities. Discussing his preferences in art, Jack Vaughn, of Dallas, once said, with enthusiasm, "My passion is for the Impressionists, and dollarwise they are also great." (Vaughn prefers to buy pictures on the installment plan. "A painting is a luxury item," he has explained, "and if I buy it on time, I'm not taking the money out of the business all at once. It's all relative, whether you need ten dollars or ten million. I have my cash problems, like everybody else.") One of the most discerning art patrons in Fort Worth was once joshed by his Dallas friend William Kittrell for collecting Picassos. "Those paintings make you a Communist, the way some of our local patriots see it," Kittrell said. "If you come over to Dallas, they'll have your scalp." "Bill," the collector replied, "you can tell those sons of bitches over there that I've made a quarter of a million dollars on these paintings so far. That will shut them up, because that's the kind of language they understand." Besides conferring these benefits, collecting entices the busy millionaire because it requires the least discipline of all cultural pursuits, especially when done under the guidance of an expert. It helps if a collector knows what he likes, but even that is not essential. All that is really required is money.

Since money is not in short supply in Texas, and since wealth has always been the handmaiden of the arts, Texas millionaires are just doing what comes naturally in assuming the role of Big Daddies of Culture. Mainly through their largess, established museums in Texas are expanding and new ones are springing up. In Houston, the Museum of Fine Arts recently completed a million-dollar building program, including the addition of a spectacular wing designed by Mies van der Rohe and donated by the daughter of Joseph S. Cullinan, a founder of the Texas Company. In Dallas, the Museum for Contemporary Arts, founded in 1957, now has seventeen hundred members and is established (thanks to a group of local millionaires, including Edward Marcus, Algur Meadows, Waldo Stewart, and Thomas Blake, Jr., and their wives) in a handsome half-million-dollar building. In Fort Worth, the Art Center, opened in 1954, now has more than twelve hundred members, and the Amon G. Carter Museum of Western Art has just taken up quarters in a million-dollar edifice designed by Philip Johnson. Many smaller cities, like Corpus Christi (pop. 150,000) and Beaumont (pop. 100,000) have also recently established their own art museums.

Though all Texas cities, small and large, have partaken of the bounty of their art-oriented millionaires, none has struck it richer than San Antonio, which was willed a museum complete with pictures, building, and endowment by a local millionairess named Marion Koogler McNay. A colorful woman who was divorced a few times and remained throughout her life a devout Catholic and a good friend of the local archbishop, Mrs. McNay came into possession of millions from her father, a physician who had good luck in oil. Her interest in modern art was aroused when she visited the Armory Show in Chicago in 1913; she later studied painting at the Chicago Art Institute, and then began her collection, which she installed, after moving to San Antonio in 1925, in a large, rambling Mediterranean-type residence built to her specifications. At her death, in 1950, she had formed what is considered the foremost collection of modern paintings in the Southwest and one of the best in the country; there are major works by the first generation of Post-Impressionists—Gauguin, Cézanne, Redon, van Gogh—to which she added during the last fifteen years of her life, an El Greco "Head of Christ," and a superb group of Dufys. Being also interested in American water colors, she acquired, among others, paintings by Winslow Homer, John Marin, Maurice Prendergast, and Mary Cassatt. All these and more—some three hundred paintings altogether—Mrs. McNay left to what is now the McNay Art Institute, together with funds to convert her residence into a museum and a basic endowment of one million dollars. In addition, she arranged for the museum to receive income from a considerable amount of San Antonio real estate and, more important, the proceeds from what the Institute's director, John Leeper, describes as "about a county" of oil-producing properties, which net the Institute approximately a thousand dollars a day.

As a privately administered organization, the McNay Institute has not been obliged to trim its activities to suit the self-appointed custodians of public morality who are at work in Texas and have been notably successful in protecting the citizens of Dallas from painters whose work is not confined to bluebonnets or geese. In 1956, the Dallas Public Library, housed in a handsome new structure, opened an exhibition of works by a number of modern artists, including Picasso, who was represented by a rug and a painting—but not for long. Complaints started pouring into the library within minutes after the display opened. "This group—I don't know just who it was, but people who were against it—began calling to protest," the librarian, James D. Meeks, said at the time. "Various people called the library, members of the library board, friends of the library, and members of the City Council. I talked to Councilman W. C. Miller, and then we just took the Picasso rug and the picture down, rather than stir up a lot of controversy."

The incident passed with little public notice except by John Rosenfield, the acknowledged cultural czar of the Southwest, who began his column in the Dallas *News* a few days later, "This would be as good a time as any for our fair city to arrive at a clear and simple code to govern the exhibition of paintings, the performance of music and drama, the circulation of books, or any other expression of mankind's creative spirit or mental processes. This should be: If anybody objects, yank it down or ban it from the halls or burn it up." Continuing, Rosenfield recalled that the Dallas Museum of Fine Arts had also received the attention of the volunteer guardians of public morals, who had campaigned vigorously against its exhibiting either modern art or "undraped female forms," and that only the nimble footwork of the director, Jerry Bywaters, "saved us from brassieres for the Venus de Milo." Rosenfield wound up by saying, "Eastern dealers have a word for us, which has brought us a measure of 'little D' immortality. One declined to lend a painting because he didn't want it 'dallased.'"

As recently as ten years ago, Eastern dealers enjoyed a near-monopoly on the sale of art in Texas; no gallery worthy of the name existed in the state. Now there are ten galleries in Houston alone. In Dallas, where Mrs. Thomas Blake, Jr., pioneered in purveying modern art, there are thirteen, including Valley House, a handsome establishment run by the versatile

Texas artist Donald Vogel, and an interesting new gallery launched by an enterprising young dealer named Haydon Calhoun. According to the latest count, Fort Worth now has three galleries, Amarillo two, and San Antonio one, and more are opening all the time.

Most dealers feature both European painters and a number of Texas artists, whose work sells briskly. "Buying local people is quite the thing to do," Cynthia Brants, one of the most widely collected Texas painters, has remarked. "It's chic. If you have a Cézanne, you should also have a Bomar—or perhaps a Brants." The support given native painters and sculptors by Texans is on the same epic scale as their pride; the latter, of course, accounts in large part for the former. Art made in Texas is on view not only in practically every private collection (the Edmund Scheneckers' consists of Texas artists exclusively) but in banks, clubs, churches, motels, supermarkets, office buildings, and manufacturing plants; the new headquarters of Texas Instruments contains no fewer than fifty paintings, prints, hand-carved screens, and other pieces of domestic art.

After taking a close look at all this local artistic activity, Jacob Getlar Smith, an editor of the *American Artist* and a well-known painter himself, came to this carefully optimistic conclusion: "Despite the prevalence of what local wits term the Emily Post-Impressionist School of Bluebonnet Painters, serenely delighting in the state flower; despite the horde of carpetbagging portrait painters waxing fat on the vanity of the *nouveau riche,* evidence is multiplying everywhere that the arts, in all their profound significance, have an unbreakable grip on the imagination and emotions of the natives. The jokester may jest, the sophisticate may sneer, but bigness in the largest state of the Union is no longer to be reckoned exclusively in terms of physical dimensions. Its gifted are endowed with sizable proportions, too, and it would be more than folly to minimize their ultimate significance in the artistic expression of our country."

As of today, however, Texans have more standing as collectors than as creators of art. The high quality and remarkable uniformity that characterize private collections everywhere in America—"so astonishingly uniform," the London *Observer* has noted, "that one cannot help imagining they receive and act on regular taste-slogans sent out from some undercover temple of fashion"—strike the sojourner in Texas with such force that he is apt to feel after a while that having seen one collection, he has seen them all. Take a Manet, Pissarro, or Delacroix, add a large quantity of Impressionists and Post-Impressionists, season with a few Chagalls, Buffets, Picassos, Klees, de Staels, and Rouaults, add local artists to taste, hire an expert to frame, hang, and light, and the result is a typical Texas collection—fashionable, safe, and almost completely devoid of any reflection of the owner's personality. The best private collections in Texas are, of course, the exceptions—those that have been put together with taste and scholarship and with no reference to the recipe book. Four of these were made available to delegates to the convention of the American Federation of Arts, held in Houston in 1957 (the first A.F.A. convention held in Texas and the best attended): the John de Menils', the Robert Strauses', and Miss Ima Hogg's in Houston, and the Robert Windfohrs', in Fort Worth. All are distinguished not only by their quality and variety but by a sense of informality and warmth and by a certain attractive impulsiveness reflecting the owners' personal style.

One of the largest collections in Texas has been assembled by the Fort Worth millionaire Kay Kimbell, whose greatest artistic yearning, his friends say, is to own "The Blue Boy." Though that has so far escaped him, Kimbell has bought a number of other Gainsboroughs, as well as Corot landscapes and a variety of other pictures by, to name a few of the more prominent, Frans Hals, Sir Thomas Lawrence, and George Inness; all have in common a restful, no-nonsense quality exhibited in, for example, the one called "Romantic Landscape," which shows a rosy-cheeked young woman and a well-fed young man reclining on the grassy bank of a stream that flows peacefully through a forest, while stretched out nearby is

313

their dog, apparently asleep. Kimbell has accumulated so many pictures that they now take up practically all the available wall space in both his home and his office and overflow in large numbers onto the walls of the Fort Worth Public Library. His collection, in one respect, is typical of art in Texas: there is so much of it that merely contemplating it is apt in time to induce what Henry James called an aesthetic headache.

Nor is there any scarcity of music. Thanks largely to support from local millionaires ("Some presidents and general managers of Big Business may like music personally," John Rosenfield has remarked. "Whether they do or don't, they recognize the fact that a highly developed symphony orchestra is one of the best means of civic advertising, worth three pages of special pleading in any expensive national periodical"), every major city in Texas has a symphony orchestra, as have many smaller ones—Tyler, Midland, Lubbock, to mention a few of the state's total of fourteen. In the metropolitan centers, the orchestras are made up of resident professional musicians; in the smaller communities the nucleus of the orchestra usually consists of local teachers and students and other musical townspeople, who are joined for concerts by members of one of the large symphonies.

By general agreement, the Houston Symphony is foremost in the state; Leopold Stokowski, who was appointed the orchestra's conductor in 1955, has described it as one of the great musical organizations of the world. Upon his resignation, at the close of the 1960–61 season, Stokowski's place was taken by another distinguished musician, Sir John Barbirolli, who, at thirty-seven, succeeded Arturo Toscanini to become the youngest conductor of the New York Philharmonic, and since 1943 had conducted the renowned Halle Orchestra of Manchester, the oldest symphony in England and third-oldest in the world.

Other symphony organizations in Texas, though less exalted than Houston's, have distinctive qualities of their own and are equally dedicated to making good music available to a large public. When the baseball season opened a few seasons ago, the Abilene Symphony graced the local ballpark and made music while the players warmed up. The San Antonio Symphony, which considers itself the oldest in the state and is as quietly capable and unpretentious as the city itself, wound up a recent season with a concert that opened with the rendering by Dorothy Kirsten and the orchestra of "A Mighty Fortress Is Our God." "Everyone in the audience," the program said, "is invited to join the orchestra for the performance of this wonderful hymn." Most did. The program concluded with a specially arranged interpretation of Ravel's "Bolero," at the climax of which a player in the tympany section picked up a revolver and fired off a blank cartridge. Nobody in the audience paid much attention to this innovation. The music critic of the San Antonio *Express*, though making no reference to the shooting in his review of the concert, did note that the orchestra got through "Bolero" in thirteen and one half minutes, whereas Ravel had timed it at seventeen. "It must be the faster pace of modern life," the critic wrote.

Grand opera also figures in the Super-Americans' non-stop *Kulturkampf*. Houston, Fort Worth, and San Antonio each support a group that annually puts on three or four operas (the leading roles are customarily performed by imported singers, the other parts and the chorus by local talent), and Dallas is not reticent about the fact that since 1939 (except this year and three years during the Second World War) the Metropolitan has annually played a three-day, four-performance stand there. Scores of people from Fort Worth, Big Spring, Tyler, Muleshoe, and other large and small communities pour into the city for the Met weekend, which is filled not only with music but with a continuous round of cocktail parties, dinners, and other entertainments, reaching a peak at the Opera Ball, held after the opening to honor the members of the cast. "All cultural events here are primarily civic occasions for staging self-satisfied parties and celebrations," a close observer of the Dallas scene has remarked.

While continuing to brag about the Met, Dallas opera lovers

have taken to showing what seems to be even more enthusiasm for the Dallas Civic Opera, a local venture organized in 1957 by an enterprising young impresario named Lawrence V. Kelly, who had previously been a co-founder of the Chicago Lyric Theatre and had managed the American debut of his friend Maria Callas. With "the captivating darling" (to use a local critic's pet name for Miss Callas) as its centerpiece in productions that have included "Medea," "La Traviata," and "Lucia," the Civic Opera has, as *Theatre Arts* remarked not long ago, "put Dallas on the country's opera map."

It cost something to get there. Unlike other opera organizations in Texas, the Dallas enterprise has made a practice of using regional talent very sparingly and of importing—mainly from Italy and Greece—not only the principal artists and directors, but also the costume and set designers, and even, for "The Daughter of the Regiment," the entire physical production. Largely because of its taste for expensive foreign wares, the Dallas Civic Opera sets local music lovers and civic boosters back about two hundred thousand dollars a season, but as the citizens of Dallas see things, the money is well spent, for it has brought them an added measure of culture, social stature, and glitter.

Civic pride in Dallas is also served by a twelve-week season of musical comedies presented at the State Fair Grounds, and Fort Worth has a fifteen-week season of similar productions. "Consider the fact," the Fort Worth director said a while ago, "that our recent production of 'Annie Get Your Gun' featured a cast of sixty-five, thereby constituting a larger, and in many ways a better, company than the Broadway original."

As for the non-musical theatre in Texas, it is everywhere full of bounce, vigor, and stage-struck millionaires. Texas has, naturally, more of the country's thirteen thousand nonprofessional local drama groups than any other state, and is thus in the vanguard of the civic-theatre movement, which in recent years has become the rage in America. Also as might be expected, amateur theatrical companies in Texas ordinarily do not do things in a small way. Shunning converted barns and church basements, they like to perform in style in their own modern theatres. (The Midland Community Theatre, for example, which has a thousand regular subscribers in a city of sixty-seven thousand, opened its new hundred-and-eighty-five-thousand-dollar quarters in 1958, and it has prospered ever since.) Theatrical talent is in such demand that the universities scout the high schools looking for it, somewhat after the manner of football recruiters. The Drama Department of the University of Texas, which has turned out Pat Hingle, Kathryn Grant, Fess Parker, and Jayne Mansfield, among others, sponsors an annual one-act-play contest for high schools that draws close to six hundred entries; the department also presents awards to a dozen outstanding theatrically inclined high-school seniors, on condition that they pursue their dramatic training at the University of Texas.

The observation of *Saturday Review* critic Henry Hewes—"Texas may no longer be the largest state, but when it comes to theatre experimentation it can certainly claim to be the most courageous"—was inspired largely by collegiate dramatics, particularly at Baylor University, and also at Howard Payne College, which attracted considerable attention a couple of years ago with a production of "A Midsummer Night's Dream" staged as a Western. The action in this work takes place on a Texas ranch in the eighteen-eighties; Hippolyta is represented as an Indian princess wearing a white buckskin outfit, Puck as a Davy Crockett figure in a coonskin hat, and all hands join in rendering songs like "Home on the Range" and "Don't Fence Me In." A hit at the college, this adult-Western-type Shakespeare went on to greater success at the Texas State Fair, and was later tapped to appear as the United States exhibit in the International Festival of the University Theatre in Bristol, England. After fulfilling this engagement, the production was presented at professional theatres in seven British cities and collected generally good notices. "Must be classed as unusual, even in these days of Shakespearean experiments," said the *Daily Telegraph*.

On the professional level, Houston's Alley Theatre, founded in 1948, is widely regarded as the outstanding theatrical organization in Texas. Described by Brooks Atkinson as "a theatre of distinction," the Alley was one of four theatres in the country (the others being the Phoenix Theatre, in New York; the Actor's Workshop, in San Francisco; and the Arena Stage, in Washington, D.C.) selected in 1959 by the Ford Foundation to receive a grant of a hundred and fifty-six thousand dollars to hire a resident ensemble of professional actors. Nine months earlier, Mrs. Nina Vance, the Alley's director since its inception, was one of ten theatre directors given a Ford Foundation grant of ten thousand dollars for study and travel. The Alley, an arena theatre seating two hundred and fifty, occasionally produces an original script but has had it greatest success with works like "A View from the Bridge," "The Glass Menagerie," "Death of a Salesman," "Waiting for Godot," "The Skin of Our Teeth," and other solid, serious Broadway hits. Though the work of Mrs. Vance generally draws praise ("One of the most brilliant directorial talents in the country today, bar none"—Hubert Roussel, in the Houston *Post*), the quality of the acting in Alley productions tends to be as unpredictable as that in most regional theatres.

A zestful unpredictability also characterizes the recently completed Dallas Theatre Center, the Texas theatrical enterprise that has generated the greatest number of superlatives among both native and foreign drama lovers. The Center combines a permanent repertory theatre, facilities for child and adult education, and a graduate drama school under one roof. The roof caused the most enthusiastic initial comment. Frank Lloyd Wright designed the building, which is, like the Guggenheim Museum, *sui generis,* though structurally the two monuments have many exterior resemblances. The Center, situated on a hilly one-acre plot in a residential area some three miles from the business district, is made of white concrete, has no right angles, and is dominated by a shimmering forty-foot round cantilevered tower. Approached over a steep concrete ramp from a parking area at the rear, the exterior of the building has the aloof and somewhat forbidding aspect typical of the Master's edifices, but the interior is inviting, light, and airy.

The auditorium itself—called the Kalita Humphreys Theatre, in honor of the late Texas actress, whose mother donated a hundred thousand dollars to the Center—is yellow and gold and has an expansive air. The view is not obstructed by a single pillar or column. Eleven rows of comfortable seats, capable of accommodating four hundred and forty persons, are arranged in the pattern of an amphitheatre and slope down to the apron of a spectacular stage; this is seventy feet from end to end, has no footlights, and juts far out into the audience, from which it is separated in height by an elevation of one foot. Almost literally, the actors are in the audience's lap. Ground was broken for the building, which cost a million dollars, in September, 1958; exactly one year later the Center was in business, with Paul Baker—a native Texan and a graduate of the Yale Drama School whose work in the Drama Department of Baylor University has achieved international recognition for theatrical daring—as its director.

The chef-d'oeuvre of the season was a presentation of Baker's production of "Hamlet," which he had been perfecting for some five years at Baylor. In this "Hamlet," the result of what Baker calls his "rethinking" of the play, the Dane is portrayed simultaneously by three actors, who are intended to represent the "human," the "courtier," and the "matricidal" sides of his character. Dressed all in black and with dirty faces to match, the three Hamlets talk, argue, and wisecrack among themselves, inducing in some observers an emotional impact similar to that produced by the Three Stooges. Besides being quite merciless in improving the text, Baker added a new visual dimension to the play by presenting it for the most part on a wooden ramp installed at a forty-five-degree angle across the center of the stage. The angular platform produced, as the Houston critic Raymond Lankford noted, "the spectacle of the King and Queen holding a royal audience while apparently lounging on bathmats on a ski slope." No mishaps occurred (the players, listing precariously, wore sneakers for traction), and though John Rosenfield found the work "the worst theatrical miscalculation since some producer cast Eva Le Gallienne as a very girlish Hamlet," it was accorded the customary favorable reception by the paying customers; in fact, before the end of the first season, the Center's more enthusiastic backers were casually talking about it in the same breath with the Old Vic, the Comédie-Française, and Sweden's Royal Dramatic Theatre. While no Texas theatrical venture has achieved quite the shine and technique of those Old World troupes, the state's ubiquitous dramatic organizations are making their offerings more widely available than those of any other similar regional groups—a considerable accomplishment in a country like America, where the majority of adults have never seen live theatre.

"It is better for all communities to have a try at artistic expression than to have none at all," John Rosenfield recently observed in an essay in the *Southwest Review*. Therefore, he added, "local criticism should not produce an uncongenial atmosphere for the best art life a community can afford." Rosenfield himself may occasionally stray from this dictum, as he did in the case of the Dallas "Hamlet," but the majority of Texas critics evidently agree with it, for in appraising native artistic expression they are, more often than not, sympathetic to a fault. They might as well be. Rosenfield recalls hearing a hostess say to her departing guests, "We'll see you all on Wednesday at the theatre. I hear the play is lousy." Any community with such a congenial atmosphere, it is clear, does not provide ideal conditions for a flowering of the critical spirit, the *sine qua non* of civilized society. "The life without criticism is not worthy to be lived," said Plato, stating a doctrine that is all Greek to Texans, who stand first in the enshrinement of the power and the glory of positive thinking.

As a result, when a Texas critic fails to lift his voice in praise of the native arts, whatever their quality, he incurs the resentment not only of the artists but of the public in general, who tend to react to professional criticism as if it were personal insult. Because of Rosenfield's limited enthusiasm for some of the Dallas Theatre Center's offerings, his name was mud among the city's more ambitious workers for culture, and Hubert Roussel did not sound the note his readers wanted to hear when he wrote in the Houston *Post* that the opening concert of the 1960-61 season of the Houston Symphony, conducted by Leopold Stokowski, "amounted in general to a bag of musical mush," and that the first production of the Alley Theatre, after its eagerly awaited upgrading as a result of the Ford Foundation grant, was a play that "could hardly have left anyone doubtful of its positive hold on insignificance."

The Texan tendency to find all criticism so unbearable that it is dismissed without reflection stems from a communal need for constant reassurance that all is well—a desire that is heightened in a frontier society, where the emphasis is by necessity on creation, not criticism, and where the doers are the heroes and the kibitzers the dispensable men. Since, as V. S. Pritchett, the English man of letters and travel, has said, "A new country or regime regards examination, interpretation, or criticism—anything but the official view—as antisocial," it is remarkable that Texas critics of the arts ever express the unofficial view, or, in other words, are critical. Most of the time, however, they perform their duty as they see it. In Fort Worth, William J. Marsh writes in the *Star-Telegram* that the local opera association's production of "La Bohème" "can be highly praised and recommended for all opera lovers who may wish to see only the best." And even Rosenfield after musing on the entertainment attractions of Dallas, concludes, "They are the best the market can offer anywhere."

Judgments of a similarly welcome nature are not rare on the book pages. Although Lon Tinkle occasionally dissects a non-Texas writer, he customarily treats native authors with avuncular generosity. A favorite device enabling him to maintain his critical equilibrium and at the same time give the author a boost is to suggest a connection, however imprecise, between the book under review and a somewhat better-known one. For example, in giving the nod to "One Touch of Ecstasy," the first novel of "a well-known and much admired Dallasite" named Gwynne Wimberly, Tinkle said that the work (which seems to have gone unnoticed by the New York critics) "has the integrity and the honesty" that make it deserving of mention in the company of Tennessee Williams, John O'Hara, Saul Bellow, Sartre, Sagan, Camus, Robert Penn Warren, Eudora Welty, and William Faulkner.

If the critical spirit does not always burn brightly in the newspaper columns devoted to criticism, and seldom even flickers in the others, the reason is that the newspapers in Texas, almost without exception, are bound to the genteel tradition. Consequently, while not averse to printing unflattering things about non-Texans, they tend to muffle unedifying news about local people, especially prominent ones. Genteelism in the Super-American press approaches a pinnacle in the personality sketches of leading citizens, which are printed in departments called "Honor Roll," "Headliner Portrait," "Titled Texan," or something else showing suitable respect. Reading these "honeysuckle lives," as Dr. Johnson referred to fulsome biographies, one soon discovers that the Super-American newspapers are devoted to "man-worship," that ancient ritual which the Greeks, according to Arnold Toynbee, "inherited from their barbarian sires," and passed on to succeeding societies.

Probably in no society has man-worship flourished more lushly than in ours. "The ruling power in the United States is not to be made game of," said de Tocqueville. "The smallest reproach irritates its sensibility, and the slightest joke that has any foundation in truth renders it indignant; from the forms of its language up to the solid virtues of its character, everything must be made the subject of encomium." And as a result, "The majority lives in the perpetual utterance of self-applause."

This becomes deafening in Super-America, where, to judge from the newspapers, successful businessmen are "most astute, as well as dynamic in both thought and action"; successful lawyers are "master artists in the courtroom"; successful clergymen are "great spiritual leaders," often "radiant and joyful" and always possessing "a glowing sense of humor"; and successful bankers are not only "hardheaded leaders gifted with financial acumen" but "as solicitous as marriage counselors." No matter what his calling, the typical successful Super-American is projected in the newspapers as a citizen having "strong, mobile features," "a dew-fresh smile," "an imposing build," and "a persuasive and richly flexible manner of speech," whose "polished mind of near-photographic quality" and "inexhaustible talents in the civic field" and "personality as instantly radiant and warm as a room heater" are topped off with "age-ripened serenity combined with advance-minded determination." "How delicate," said Carlyle, "how decent is English biography, bless its mealy mouth."

Yet, as everybody knows, accentuating the positive is a foolproof countersign of Americanism. Our perpetual national love affair with Little Mary Sunshine has left us neither time nor interest to cultivate criticism, her mature rival, at once more demanding and rewarding. It is no wonder that despite the fact that criticism, as Admiral Hyman Rickover recently remarked, is "the very mainstay of democracy," hardly anything in this country is cherished less than the critical spirit. It gets the cold shoulder because it engenders doubt about things as they are, and anything that does that—including humor in nearly every form, and especially satire—is a luxury that can be afforded only by civilized societies that feel themselves to be secure.

"When Texans become as civilized as the French are," J. Frank Dobie has remarked, "they will enjoy rather than feel indignant at satire of their own foibles. This country needs satire as badly as the Sahara needs rain." When the need in Texas will be fulfilled Dobie has not tried to forecast. There are no strong indications that it will be soon, for, as de Tocqueville noted, "People who spend every day in the week making money, and Sunday in going to church, have nothing to invite the Muse of Comedy."

Chapter Nineteen

In Texas—that other America, where everything appears in extra-high relief—there are probably more millionaires than anywhere else in the country who have achieved that nice balance between worship of the golden rule and of the golden calf that is the hallmark of the American rich. Spiritually, Texas millionaires derive from a distinguished line of money-making churchgoers originating in the sixteenth century. Their inspiraton was John Calvin. According to the historian Herbert J. Muller, Calvin "made the pursuit of wealth and preservation of property a Christian duty, calling for the same arduous discipline as the warfare against the temptations of the flesh. He exalted the acquisitive virtues of enterprise, diligence, sobriety, frugality, thrift. He invented an ideal type hitherto unknown to religion and culture, a type neither humanistic nor ascetic—the God-fearing businessman." Two centuries later, this novel type came under the shaping influence of John Wesley, who also labored hard to justify the economic ways of man to God. "We must exhort all Christians to gain all they can and to save all they can; that is, in effect, to grow rich," Wesley proclaimed.

Nowhere has this punchy doctrine been more enthusiastically embraced than in America, where, as we have more than once been told, a profit has never been without honor. "Let your *Business* ingross the most of your time," Cotton Mather advised the Puritan merchants. Their successors have never wanted for similar welcome encouragement from latter-day shepherds. "The American ministers of the Gospel do not attempt to draw or fix all the thoughts of man upon the life to come," de Tocqueville remarked, adding that "it is often difficult to ascertain from their discourses whether the principal object of religion is to procure eternal felicity in the other world or prosperity in this." The difficulty lingers on. For the benefit of reporters meeting him at the Dallas airport last year, Dr. Norman Vincent Peale delivered a sermonette in which he said, "Success isn't the thing we should aim at—not material success. But if we become a success with ourselves, then material success may follow as a result of our changed outlook." Though the object of our religion has often induced perplexity in visitors, none has failed to be impressed by its ubiquity. "On my arrival in the United States, the religious aspect of the country was the first thing that struck my attention," wrote de Tocqueville, who went on to note that in this country religion is "mingled with all the habits of the nation and all the feelings of patriotism, whence it derives a peculiar force."

Anybody who thought we had religion back in those days ought to see us now, when we are enjoying what Dr. William Franklin (Billy) Graham has called "the greatest religious revival in American history." The so-called "surge of piety" began during the Second World War, and at present a hundred and twelve million Americans, or better than three out of every five, are church-connected, to use a trade term. That is the highest ratio to population in our history; a hundred years ago it was about one in five. A Gallup Poll taken in 1960 revealed that although only fifty-five per cent of us believe that Christ will return to earth, we are considerably more optimistic about our ultimate personal future. Of those who were asked the question "Do you believe there is, or is not, a life after death?," seventy-four per cent answered affirmatively and only fourteen per cent negatively; the rest replied, with a certain air of reasonableness, "Can't say." It is likely that believers in the life to come will increase in the next generation, since our Sunday schools now have an enrollment of forty-two million and are steadily expanding. In an effort to keep pace with the piety explosion, Americans in 1960 poured a billion dollars into the construction of new churches—more than thirteen per cent of the total spent on public building in the country.

Yet the statistics, however engrossing, can barely indicate the dimensions of the religious boom, which has become so much a part of daily life that we tend to overlook its scope and excitement. By now, we have become accustomed to best-sellers written by ecclesiastics; to the monthly distribution of suitable volumes to members of the Religious Book Club; and to the popularity of titles like "Peace of Soul," "Peace of Mind," "Go With God," "Go to Heaven," "The Day Christ Was Born," "The Day Christ Died," "God Our Contemporary," "God Keeps an Open House," "Pray Your Weight Away," "The Power of Prayer on Plants," and other inspiring works. The author of the last-named volume, now in its fifth printing—the Reverend Frank Loehr, Director of Prayer Research of the Religious Research Foundation, located in California—explained on a recent visit to Texas, that "four persons out of six can help plants by prayer."

We expect to find clergymen performing on radio and television, pious tunes in the jukeboxes (Eric Goldman has noted such favorites as "Big Fellow in the Sky" and "The Fellow Upstairs"), and billboards and other mass media being used to urge us to stay together by worshipping together. "Walk in," says the caption under the photograph of a family entering a church in a full-page magazine advertisement. "Life looks better when you walk out." The copy begins arrestingly in bold-face: "Follow the leader"—an imperative that the socially ambitious nowadays ignore to their peril. "In today's resurgence of religion, the churches are more important to the rising socialite than ever before, and clients are usually advised to become active in theirs," a New York woman who specializes in press agentry for social aspirants is quoted as saying in "The Private World of High Society: Its Rules & Rituals," a new handbook by Lucy Kavaler, who supplies chapter and verse: "The only note I must add to her advice is that it presupposes membership in the 'right' faith. North, South, East, West, members of the Episcopal Church are best—in terms of social ranking. Next come the Presbyterians, Congregationalists, Unitarians, Methodists, Lutherans, and Baptists, in just about that order. . . . In New York, public-relations firms guide their clients to such top-ranking churches as St. James Protestant Episcopal Church, St. Thomas Protestant Episcopal Church, St. Bartholomew's Church (Episcopal), Holy Trinity Church (Episcopal), Brick Presbyterian Church, Madison Avenue Presbyterian Church, and Central Presbyterian Church (not so widely known as the others, but extremely fashionable)." The relatively low social standing of the Baptists in New York has not proved an insurmountable social barrier to the Rockefeller family, whose best-known living member even takes time off from his gubernatorial duties to do some lay preaching in Baptist churches. "The world needs faith and hope," the Governor said during a recent appearance in the pulpit, "but most of all it needs love. We've got to make love a reality in our own country."

In coming out unequivocally for love, the Governor took no serious political risks. Thanks to the religious renaissance, love is In—so much so that one can open a New York newspaper and find a full-page advertisement, paid for by a private citizen, boosting what the headline calls "Love . . . the Greatest Gift." The message is direct. "He Who Understands Love Understands God, for God *Is* Love," reads the copy, which also carries endorsements of love by Matthew and John. The sponsor of the advertisement resides in Washington, D.C., which has seen a sharp upturn during the past decade in religious action; for instance, President Eisenhower's first inaugural parade was headed by an exhibit called "God's Float." On Broadway, religiously oriented plays like "J. B." and "The Sound of Music" are hits, and religion has become so important in Hollywood that the fan magazine *Modern Screen* was able to please its readers with a series of articles soberly titled "How the Stars Found Faith." Piper Laurie, it was revealed, has reached the place in her spiritual development where she refers to the Almighty as "Good Old God," said Jane Russell has a similar crush. "I love God," Miss Russell has declared. "And when you get to know Him, you find He's a Livin' Doll."

If Americans are the world's "churchgoingest" people, as the Reverend Granville T. Walker, pastor of the University Christian Church, in Fort Worth, said in 1960 after returning from a tour of Europe, they must give an extraordinary share of the credit for the achievement to Texans like those in Reverend Mr. Walker's own flock. "On any average Sunday," he has remarked, "I have more people in my congregation than worship in Westminster Abbey or Notre Dame." The same statement could be made by scores of other clergymen throughout the state, and would not be doubted by any visitor who has tried to reach Texans at home between around ten o'clock and one o'clock on Sundays. During those hours, crowds and traffic jams mark the sites of churches, which are, as elsewhere in the United States—only, as might be expected, more so—predominantly Protestant.

In Texas, eighty per cent of the churchgoers belong to one of several Protestant denominations, nineteen per cent are Catholic, and one per cent are Jewish. The Baptists, with thirty-nine per cent of all adult church members, are by far the largest faith in Texas. They are also the richest. The Baptist General Convention of Texas conducts its far-ranging affairs on a yearly budget of some thirteen million dollars, which is approximately three times as much as the state spends annually to operate its judicial system. Whereas most Texas communities have but one courthouse, the churches seem as plentiful as filling stations. Waco, for example, has some hundred thousand residents and a hundred and twenty-two churches—a ratio between population and places of worship that, Séan O'Faoláin was surprised to discover, is even higher than in his native Ireland. Waco is no exception; Tyler, with fifty thousand citizens, and Midland, with sixty-eight thousand, have ninety-four and eighty-two churches, respectively. Though Fort Worth is thirty-eighth in size among American cities, it ranks thirteenth in number of churches.

Appropriately, Dallas, the banking capital of the state, is

also its religious capital. In addition to being a diocesan seat of the Roman Catholic and Episcopal Churches, Dallas supports the largest Southern Baptist, Methodist, and Southern Presbyterian congregations in the United States. Citizens of Dallas can choose among some eight hundred churches. The biggest—the First Baptist Church, situated in the downtown area—has twelve thousand members, including Billy Graham; employs a staff of fifty; maintains a Sunday school of eighty-seven departments and more than six hundred classes; owns, in addition to its edifice, a seven-story parking and recreational building, containing a university-sized gymnasium, four bowling lanes, and a skating rink; and has an operating budget for the current year of a million one hundred and ninety-five thousand dollars. "This is probably the most stupendous financial program ever undertaken by any church in the history of Christendom," the Reverend Dr. W. A. Criswell, pastor of the church, told his congregation in presenting the 1961 budget. Undismayed, they promptly oversubscribed it, thus recording their customary annual vote of confidence in Dr. Criswell, a firm-jawed, fifty-one-year-old native of Oklahoma who was called to the ministry at the age of six. During his student days, he served as minister in the small Texas community of Pulltight, and for the past seventeen years has been making a name for himself by rapping Roman Catholicism (the election of John F. Kennedy, warned Dr. Criswell during the campaign, would "spell the death of a free church in a free state"), integration ("a thing of idiocy and foolishness"), and evolution ("a hoax perpetrated by the wild imagination of blind, misguided scientists"), and in other ways fighting the good fight, as he sees it.

The Highland Park Presbyterian Church of Dallas, though small by Baptist standards, has some five thousand members (making it the largest Southern Presbyterian congregation in the country) and uses a card-indexing system to record vital information about each parishioner, including talents and hobbies. On a typical Sabbath in Dallas, around seventy-five thousand people turn out for Sunday school. They are by no means all youngsters, since in Texas attendance at Sunday school ceases only with death, and classes for grownups are taught by many of the state's leading citizens, including the Governor.

In addition to the abundance of churches, which provides the most obvious evidence of the importance of religion in Super-American life, exhibits of a similar nature, large and small, steadily confront the visitor from the moment he enters the state. Driving in from the west on a summer night, he may pass, on U. S. Highway 62, near El Paso, an illuminated sign of the dimensions used by drive-in movie theatres, which asks, courtesy of the Assembly of God Church, "YOU THINK IT'S HOT HERE?" As he proceeds eastward, he is everywhere struck by the number of church-supported colleges, universities, hospitals, and bookstores, as well as by the amount of new-church construction and old-church expansion, to say nothing of religious installations of a more novel nature. Perhaps the most attractive of these is the Chapel in the Sky, a small oratory, complete with vaulted ceiling, stained-glass windows, eight pews, and non-denominational altar, situated on the thirty-ninth floor of Southland Center, the newest skyscraper in Dallas.

In Houston, the visitor, if he still feels in need of spiritual uplift, can pick up the phone any time between nine-thirty and five-thirty and dial Jackson 2-2928, the number of a unique institution called the Telephone Ministry. Unlike the Dial-A-Prayer service in New York, which was originated by the Fifth Avenue Presbyterian Church and provides callers of Circle 6-4200 with a thirty-second recorded prayer, the Telephone Ministry is completely live. It is sponsored by the Houston Christian Businessmen's Committee and is conducted by Mr. and Mrs. L. E. Showalter, an elderly, religiously inclined couple who spend most of their waking hours on the telephone, listening to problems and giving Christian counsel to callers who have been urged, in newspaper advertisements, to ring up the Ministry "if troubled—burdened—discouraged." If one is not feeling all that bad when he goes to a bowling alley in Houston, he may feel some discouragement when he finds the lanes taken over by several of the seven hundred church teams participating in the Inter-Faith Bowling Tournament, sponsored by the Houston *Post*. "Religion will definitely be an issue," the paper said in announcing the mammoth contest, which the *Post* describes as "a tournament with a mission—to promote fellowship through the mushrooming family sport of bowling."

In Houston, or wherever else in Texas one turns on the radio in the early morning, he is sure to find a rich offering of devotionals, gospel singing, and other religious fare, featuring, for example, the Dallas minister who calls himself Your Radio Friend and Pastor, Reverend J. C. Hibbard; Sister Jack Coe (widow of Brother Jack Coe); and dozens of other members of the clergy who use the ether waves, as they sometimes say, to bring the Gospel to their vast flocks of sinners in Radioland.

If, as the British novelist Walter L. George once remarked, "the newspaper exhibition of the national character is the national character seen under a magnifying glass," the newspapers in Texas might be expected to bring out, perhaps better than anything else, the religious temper of the community. They do, daily and Sunday, in the news and editorial columns and also on the advertising pages. On Saturdays, the newspapers usually contain, in addition to notices placed by individual churches, full-page institutional-type spreads bearing a Biblical message and an exhortation to go to church. ("A Church-Going Family Is a Happier Family"—Tyler *Telegraph*.) These are jointly paid for by a number of local business concerns and individuals, whose names are listed but, as the sentiment is phrased in the Waxahachie *Daily Light*, "Who Want as Their Only Return to See a Greater Church Attendance." From time to time, religious matters are discussed in editorials, such as a recent one in the Dallas *News* titled "Pulpit Technique" ("Results come from simplicity, sincerity and inspiration . . . the Bible has few six-bit words"), and obituaries in Texas newspapers give prominence to the religious affiliation of the deceased by stating it near the beginning of the story.

The Saturday edition of the Houston *Chronicle* carries an eight-page supplement devoted entirely to religious advertisements and news, including a recent story about a local Episcopal rector whose method of stimulating church attendance was summarized in the bleak headline, "STAY-AT-HOMES WON'T GET FULL BURIAL RITES."

It is the columns of general news, however, that offer the most rewarding coverage of the religious front, concentrating on men of the cloth, both local and national. Among the latter, perhaps none enjoys greater popularity in Texas than Dr. Norman Vincent Peale, whose books and weekly column are syndicated in many Texas newspapers and who is also in wide demand as a speaker before large groups, such as the convention of the Southern Gas Association. On his latest speaking trip to Dallas, eighty-five hundred people turned out to hear "the internationally known author, philosopher, and humanitarian," as Dr. Peale is customarily referred to in the local papers, who stated positively that the world's chief problems today stem from a lack of enough "tough-minded" people to solve them. "A man with fifty problems is twice as alive as a man with twenty-five," he explained. "If you haven't got any problems, you should get down on your knees and ask, 'Lord, don't you trust me any more?'"

Whereas Dr. Peale is ordinarily news in the Texas papers only when visiting there, Billy Graham, another newspaper pet, is seldom out of print, even when out of sight. When he went to Africa last year on a two-month "Safari for Souls," the papers reported his progress in almost daily stories and photographs, including one showing him being kissed by a camel. It is not essential to be a full-fledged minister to capture the fancy of Texas newspapers, but it helps to be at least a lay preacher, like Howard Butt, Jr., a Corpus Christi millionaire in his early thirties whom Graham has designated as worthy of inheriting his mantle. Besides serving as executive vice-president of a supermarket chain doing an annual business of a hundred million dollars, Butt has found time, according to a Houston *Post* story about him titled "Groceries and Gospel Mix Well for Texan," to make more than twenty-five hundred appearances as a preacher, occasionally as a substitute for Graham, in twenty-five states and seven foreign countries.

After professional or part-time preachers, the newspapers favor other interesting people, like Van Cliburn, who also mix the Gospel with their profession. The winning of the International Tchaikowsky Contest made Cliburn a favorite with Texans, but they have subsequently turned him into something of a hero upon learning through the newspapers that he carried a Bible with him to Moscow and, in fact, never travels without it; that before a performance he likes to pray "with the conductor that God give them power to make good music together"; that when at home he never fails to join in daily devotionals with his parents; and that it was they who gave him an admirable philosophy by bringing him up to believe, as he has put it, "Everyone has to work. No one can sit on the tracks and pray. That won't start the train."

The efficacy of combining work and prayer to get the steam up is frequently endorsed in one way or another by other subjects of feature stories. Eugene McElvaney, a Dallas banker who modestly admits to having "only three or four million," put the notion succinctly in the Dallas *News:* "When you get off your knees [from prayer], start hustling, and you simply can't fail." The minimum qualification, it seems, that must be possessed by a person who wants to make the grade in a Texas newspaper story is the habit of reading the Bible. A standard sentiment expressed in stories written about people on the occasion of their retirement is their happy expectation of using their new leisure to spend more time with the Good Book. Readers of George Fuermann's column in the Houston *Post* were pleased to learn of a retired local secretary who had recently completed the unique feat of transcribing the Bible into shorthand, a project that kept her steadily engaged for fourteen months. She then had the work bound and presented it as a Christmas gift to her former employer, a retired minister. The story, combining the elements of minister, Bible, hard work, devotion, generosity, and even Christmas, might serve as a model for journalism students in Texas.

To supplement the straight religious news, Texas papers print an imposing volume of syndicated religious columns and similar features, including, besides Dr. Peale's "Confident Living" and Billy Graham's "My Answer," the commercially marketed works of such nationally known churchmen and part-time writers as Father Keller and Bishop Fulton J. Sheen. Other popular syndicated features include "The Power of Faith," "The Shepherd," "Children of the Bible," "Bible Digest," and "The Country Parson," the last consisting of a drawing of a bespectacled clergyman in a broad-brimmed hat, a frock coat, and a string tie who makes pithy comments, such as "Two half-truths don't make a truth," or "We live in an age of plenty—plenty of goods and plenty of bads." A feature that appeals to the local cognoscenti, "Instant Bible Quiz," gives them a snappy mental workout: "Stunned by the refusal of his queen to appear at his royal cocktail party, what Persian king, sent out a decree against 'henpecking'? Esther 1:2–22."

Complementing the syndicated features is an impressive amount of locally produced religious material. The Houston *Post*, for example, every day prints a boxed item on page 1 called "Today's Prayer." Contributed by readers, the prayers as a rule are quite simple ("O Lord, help me to understand that You're not going to let anything come my way that You and I together can't handle"), though some are quite stylish ("The sky is blue, the sun is bright, Thou, Lord, has kept me safe all night. Help me, by all I do or say, to make today a happy day"). The high seriousness with which readers regard "Today's Prayer" is revealed in a recent exchange in the *Post*'s letters-to-the-editor department. A reader named Mrs. Earl Davidson complained, "I have sent in twice two original prayers and one copied, with my name and address; but they prefer to print those sent in by unsigned readers who are ashamed to admit that they believe in God or prayer." She received this soothing reply: "The prayer editor says he prefers to believe that some prayers come in unsigned because of Christian humility rather than shame. He says prayers are used in the order received."

To round out their religious coverage, the leading Texas newspapers publish a weekly column by a local clergyman with a flair for writing. Probably the most consistently arresting of the ministerial offerings have been those composed by Dr. John F. Anderson, Jr., who, until being called to a pastorate in Florida, was the leader of the First Presbyterian Church, in Dallas and the author of a column called "Down to Earth," an extremely popular front-page feature of the Saturday edition of the *News*. One of Dr. Anderson's columns that is vividly remembered by many of his following explored the value of explaining religious thought through the use of slang. "For example," he wrote, "repentance sounds stodgy and old-fashioned until it leaps to life in the explanation that we must 'come clean' with God in order to become clean before God. . . . Salvation in the Cross is a mysterious stumbling block to many a man on Main Street until it is pointed out that Christ 'took the rap' for us. . . . Another way of putting it is that He 'went out on a limb for us.' . . . Such jargon may jar the saint, but it evokes keen interest in the sinner. When he at last understands what the Son of God really did for him, he might exclaim, 'Now, isn't that the limit!'"

In addition to the great spiritual progress implicit in the religious boom that has swept Texas and the rest of the country, the movement has brought a mundane but not unwelcome increase in religious giving, which, according to a report of the National Council of Churches, has now reached the record peak of four billion dollars a year. This sum, substantial though it is in the aggregate, represents, as church people like to point out, a per-capita contribution of only forty-three cents a week, or less than the price of a movie. The national average would be noticeably more modest were it not for the God-fearing millionaires of Texas, who are possibly more stalwart in their financial support of religion than any other group to be found here below. A great many of them make a habit of tithing. For example, when Toddie Lee Wynne, a Dallas oil-man and Presbyterian, sold his American Liberty Oil Company, in 1957, for a net profit of twenty million dollars, he promptly gave the Texas Presbyterian Foundation a check for two million. Like many other Texas millionaires, Wynne not only tithes but enlarges his religious philanthropy with gifts, such as Wynne Hall, donated to the Presbyterian Theological Seminary, in Austin, and a chapel presented to the First Presbyterian Church in Dallas, where he has his membership. Another member and oilman, D. H. Byrd, recently gave the church fifty thousand dollars to construct Fellowship Hall, a building for banquets and other entertainments. The Presbyterians have also benefited from the generosity of Charles McGaha, an oil-man and banker of Wichita Falls, who donated a hundred thousand dollars toward the construction of a new church in his home town. In 1958, a Houston builder and subdivider named Fred McManis, Jr., who was then thirty-six, and his wife presented to the Presbyterian Foundation property worth approximately a million dollars. "I'd rather build up something for the Presbyterian Church and for religious and educational facilities than for my personal gain," McManis said at the time.

Many other Texas millionaires—notably the late W. W. Fondren, an orphan who as a boy went to work in an Arkansas sawmill, entered the oil business as a driller, and later became one of the founders and the first president of the Humble Oil & Refining Co., and his widow—have been just as interested in building up something for the Methodists. The Fondrens' donations to Methodist institutions may have already exceeded twenty-five million—more than eight million to Southern Methodist University alone—and are continuing. "Tithing alone isn't enough if we're to get this job done," James Willson, another stalwart Methodist benefactor, recently remarked. "Somebody has got to put up more." Willson puts up a third of his income. In 1959, a Houston millionaire and his wife anonymously donated seven million dollars to build that city's first Lutheran hospital. Owing to the size of the gift—probably the largest single charitable donation in the history of Houston—the Lutherans have been able to proceed on the project without the bother of a fund-raising campaign. A prominent benefactor of the Catholic Church has been George W. Strake, of Houston, who was also an orphan and made his fortune by finding oil—the fabulous Conroe Field—where experienced geologists said it couldn't be. "If we had drilled fifty yards away, we would have missed the field," Strake recently told Jim Clark. "I didn't even know what I was doing, but the Lord did."

As for the Baptists, they plainly did not achieve their comfortable financial situation without a sizable army of benefactors, of whom perhaps none has been as consistently generous for close to half a century as the Fort Worth oilman William Fleming. At the close of services at the Broadway Baptist Church, in Fort Worth, on the first Sunday of 1939, Fleming arose and announced that he was giving his entire income that year to the church. "Mrs. Fleming and I have been thinking about this thing for some time," he remarked offhandedly. What "this thing" would come to in actual cash was not suggested, but, considering Fleming's resources, the congregation had reason to rejoice. Since then, Fleming has given the Baptists so many more millions that, his associates say, he has probably lost track of the total. Like his close friend Billy Graham, Fleming has a strong evangelical streak; no visitor leaves his office without being asked whether he has made "a personal acceptance of Christ as Saviour."

No doubt the most unusual of Fleming's contributions to the religious culture of Fort Worth was made in 1956, when he presented "as a gift to all Christians" a permanent exhibit consisting of life-size wax figures of Christ and the Twelve Apostles as depicted in Leonardo da Vinci's "The Last Supper." Every year, several thousand Christians make a pilgrimage to the exhibit, which is housed in an air-conditioned store in the Ridglea shopping center. The vividly clad figures, arranged against a background corresponding to the one in the painting, are startlingly lifelike, a result achieved in part—as visitors learn from a recorded commentary spoken by a woman with a mellifluous voice against a background of organ music—by the fact that "human hairs were used in the scalps, beards, and mustaches" and that "untold hours were spent placing the hairs, one at a time, in each head—some forty thousand individual strands in each."

Notable and varied though the religious philanthropies of Fleming and many other Texas millionaires have been, perhaps none quite measures up to those of the earth-moving-equipment manufacturer Robert G. Le Tourneau, of Longview, who is known as "God's Businessman." Le Tourneau's version of tithing is novel: he keeps ten per cent of his income and gives ninety per cent to spreading the Gospel through the Christian and Missionary Alliance, a religious organization that supports missionaries throughout the world. The Alliance has benefited rather handsomely from many of Le Tourneau's business operations, such as the sale, in 1953, of one of his companies to the Westinghouse Air Brake Company for twenty-six million dollars. After a five-year absence from the field, required by the terms of the Westinghouse transaction, Le Tourneau is again going strong in the manufacture of heavy-duty equipment. He stops work at his plants for an hour twice a month so that employees may attend chapel services held on the premises, devotes one or two nights a week to serving as a lay preacher, and spends practically every weekend travelling to all corners of the North American continent "to give his testimony for Christ," as he describes the speeches he delivers before various groups. Le Tourneau's explanation of his religious giving is matter-of-fact. "It's not how much of my money I give to God," he says, "but how much of God's money I keep."

Chapter Twenty

To affix the epithet "materialistic" to a people as indefatigably religious and as abounding in examples of latter-day Christian stewardship as the Super-Americans would seem, on the face of things, downright preposterous. Yet it is done all the time, and not only by alien journalists. "People here are a little more materialistic, I suppose," the Dallas psychiatrist Dr. Perry Talkington said not long ago. "But that's just a phase. All great civilizations—the Egyptians, the Greeks, the Aztecs—passed through a similar period." If Texans, in the present state of their civilization, are indeed more materialistic than their countrymen, that's going some, for Americans are materialists beyond compare—or so, at least, we have long been told. It is doubtful, in fact, whether any other aspect of the American character has got the wind up in foreigners as often, or foxed them as frequently, as materialism on the American plan. "It would be well, there can be no doubt, for the American people as a whole if they loved the Real less and the Ideal somewhat more," Dickens observed a century ago, and every once in a while since then something has come along to make his spiritual descendants think he was right.

In 1959, for example, Raymond J. Saulnier, chairman of President Eisenhower's Council of Economic Advisers, came along and told the Joint Economic Committee of Congress, "As I understand the economy, its ultimate purpose is to produce more consumer goods. This is the goal. This is the object of everything we are working at, to produce things for consumers." Immediately, it became stylish among foreign and domestic

340

intellectuals to pick on Saulnier, as if he had said something wrong. Though the national goal, in his words, may not sound like one to stir men's souls, it has the solid underpinning of historical necessity; the American passion for things is a natural result of the fact that in this country there are plenty of things to be had, and have been since the beginning. When the rest of the world had been plundered, said de Tocqueville, "North America was discovered, as if it had been kept in reserve by the Deity and had just risen from beneath the waters of the Deluge." An unexampled and seemingly inexhaustible natural bounty combined with a conspicuous skill for developing it have continued to make us, in David M. Potter's phrase, a "people of plenty," a factor that in itself has had a profound effect on the shaping of the national character.

Though signs of our unparalleled abundance are hard to miss, we apparently require constant reassurance that nobody else has it so good, for it is next to impossible to read through a popular American periodical without being reminded of some aspects of our solid-gold state of grace, as when the *Saturday Review* reports, "We Americans own 50 per cent of the world's wealth, yet we account for little more than 6 per cent of its population. We own 29 per cent of the world's railroad mileage, 71 per cent of its automobiles, and 52 per cent of its radios." The *Wall Street Journal* contributes the pleasing statistic that between 1949 and 1959 the number of swimming pools in this country increased from eleven thousand to two hundred and fifty thousand. "Second cars, of course, are already commonplace," says *Look* matter-of-factly. "Some 7.5 million families now own them."

Our diet, we are regularly informed, has the highest calorie count of any in the history of man. "If you were an average American," the Dallas *Times Herald* reported early in 1961, "you consumed an estimated 1488 pounds of food last year." The cost of simply storing this country's food surpluses in 1960 came to three and a half million dollars every day. Anxious as patriotic Americans are to ease that awesome burden, they are apt to be dissuaded by daily warnings that they are already eating themselves to death. This, in turn, induces what the New York *Times* has called "the great American obsession with excess weight," and that, typically, leads to the production of more things, such as Metrecal and the several dozen imitative nine-hundred-calorie liquid diets, on which, the *Wall Street Journal* says, Americans will this year spend more than a hundred million dollars. If the abundant way of life is now taken for granted by most Americans (who, thanks to Professor Jessie Bernard's new terminology, can be conveniently classified into two groups, the Haves and the Have-Mores), our spectacular plenty continues to make a strong impression on visitors, among them the urbane French author and consular official Romain Gary, who said, shortly before being transferred from his post here, "I will be sorry to leave America. This is one place where you don't have the feeling you have taken the food you are eating from somebody else's mouth."

This is also the place, according to that earlier French visitor de Tocqueville, "where the love of money has taken stronger hold on the affections of men" than in any other country he had known. It could hardly be otherwise; men brought up to treasure things are apt to develop an affection for what it takes to get them. Furthermore, as the British lawyer and journalist Edward Dicey noted a hundred years ago, "The absence of all social distinctions and the fact that there are no established positions to which birth and rank and station give an acknowledged entrance render wealth the chief standard of distinction. In consequence, the natural ambition of every American is to acquire wealth, and thus distinguish himself in the only career which is practically open to the vast majority."

In saying "every American," Dicey was guilty of an unusual lapse of precision, but the slip is excusable, considering how exceedingly few have refused to play what Parrington called "the great American game of money-chasing." So far, the most famous holdout has been Henry David Thoreau, who, shunning work in his father's pencil factory, made something of a reputation by taking his ease around a pond and making up sayings, like "Money is not required to buy one necessary of the soul" and "A man is rich in proportion to the number of things which he can afford to let alone." Thoreau may have established himself as the patron saint of the malcontents, but he had small influence on the young, whose ideas on what makes a man rich had already been formulated along more positive lines. "The only principle of life propagated among the young people," the Colonial scholar Cadwallader Colden wrote, in 1748, "is to get Money, and men are only esteemed according to . . . the Money they are possessed of."

Never since has there been a letdown in the propagation of this principle among members of the oncoming generations, many of whom on the contemporary scene have had it expounded to them by the novelist Ayn Rand, creator of the philosophy she calls "Objectivism," the core of which is the glorification of selfishness. "If any civilization is to survive," Miss Rand told a group of six hundred students at Yale a few months ago, "it is the morality of altruism that men have to reject. Capitalism and altruism," she explained, "cannot coexist in the same man or in the same society." While enlarging on the need to stamp out altruism, Miss Rand wore, as she generally does, a large gold brooch shaped like a dollar sign. "The cross is the symbol of torture," she said. "I prefer the dollar sign, the symbol of free trade, therefore of the free mind." She left her audience with the distillation of her thought, put into a single aphorism: "Money is the root of all good." Philosophical messages of that nature receive a respectful hearing in our institutions of higher learning, because Americans, as Jacques Maritain has remarked, "are neither squeamish nor hypocritical about the importance of money." On the contrary, he adds, in this country "money is cared for openly."

Nowhere more so than in Texas, where the very sight of money apparently provides aesthetic pleasure. The most prominent piece of furniture in the lounge of the Dallas Petroleum Club is a long, custom-made ebony table, the surface of which is inlaid with coins from all over the world. As one arrives by escalator on the executive floor of the First National Bank, in Dallas, the first thing one sees is the "Money Tree," a twenty-foot-wide, three-dimensional mural depicting a tree whose branches bear 7819 pieces of currency, ancient and modern. When the First State Bank, in Port Lavaca, celebrated its fiftieth anniversary a couple of years ago, its president decided that the most crowd-catching attraction the bank could display in its lobby to commemorate the occasion would be a ten-thousand-dollar bill, the largest in public circulation. He was right. Early this year, the thirty-one sixth-graders at the William B. Travis School, in Dallas, completed an absorbing class project, which consisted of cutting a million pieces of paper in the size and shape of dollar bills. Whatever else the exercise, which took a year, may have accomplished, it showed the students in graphic (if simulated) form what they were after. As a reward for their industry, they were invited by the president of the Republic National Bank, who had learned of the estimable project, to visit his premises, where he arranged for them to have a look at the real thing—one million dollars' worth of genuine bills.

The Super-Americans' frank regard for money, besides finding expression in the actual viewing of it and in the traditional forms of Cadillacs, mink coats, diamonds, and other necessaries of the soul, is also pointedly reflected in the loving care they lavish on the places where money is kept and changed. In size, cost, architectural excellence, interior elegance, and over-all commanding grandeur, no group of structures in Texas can compare with its bank buildings—in particular the new ones, which may be useful to archeologists of some future civilization trying to discover what was worshipped in Super-America.

What is honored in a country will be cultivated there, said Plato, and it is therefore appropriate that all Americans feel, if not reverence, at least respect for money. In our country, dollars are the patent of success. As we use the standard inch to denote length, so we use the standard dollar to appraise accomplishment. The beauty of this system is its adaptability; it can put a dollar value on practically everything. On knowledge, for instance. "In terms of money, a college education is worth $113,000 more in lifetime earnings than a mere high-school diploma, the United States Department of Labor has calculated," the New York *Herald Tribune* said not long ago. Other calculators, working in broader fields, have succeeded in putting a price tag on human beings. "'The economic value of a man in the United States,' says the Institute of Life Insurance, 'has reached the $200,000 level,'" the Dallas *News* recently reported. (That figure, the article explained, applied to the average man; others may be worth up to $350,000. "And, of course, there are the exceptions—the millionaires.") Actually, as all but a few soreheads recognize, these standards are as democratic as death. In this country, everybody—painter, lawyer, businessman, poet, architect, scientist, athlete—has to prove himself in the market place. That, of course, is the essence of the American Way, and it imbues life in the United States with such a pervasive and refreshing simplicity that an American can tell how good he is by just counting his money.

If "poverty now makes a man ridiculous," as Juvenal remarked after the triumph of money in Roman society, wealth, in ours, makes him sublime. That is the reason that millionaires have in recent years become our national heroes. Their sharp upgrading in this respect has been notable. John D. Rockefeller, Sr., was an object of national loathing, yet his grandson (in a contest with still another millionaire, but one only two-fifths as well off) was elected Governor of New York; the metamorphosis in esteem took less than half a century and about a billion dollars. The fact that the richer man won is a sign of the American times. In choosing Rockefeller, the richest American ever to hold high public office, a majority of the voters of the most populous state in the nation demonstrated that they had matured to the point where they could identify with an unself-made millionaire, who has, after taxes, between six and seven thousand dollars a week spending money.

We like our heroes rich. Of all the revered leaders of all nations involved in the Second World War, General Eisenhower is probably the only one whose countrymen, by way of showing their regard, passed a special law conferring tax benefits that enabled him to become a millionaire. Ty Cobb won admiration for his ability on the baseball diamond, but he won everlasting fame for acumen in investing in Coca-Cola stock, which has made him a millionaire many times over. Gene Tunney was never a truly popular heavyweight champion, but when he left the ring, he achieved the respect of his countrymen by becoming a millionaire who can now identify himself in *Who's Who in America* as a "corporation exec." and prove it by listing eight banks and corporations of which he is a director. Joe Louis, who was a wildly popular champion, failed to hold on to enough of his winnings to pay his taxes, and has never been tapped for *Who's Who*. No matter what a man's profession, getting the million endows him with a special cachet. A couple of years ago, Toots Shor, the ebullient restaurateur who used to sum up his philosophy by saying, "I don't want to be a millionaire—I just want to live like one," actually became one. Before that, Shor's friends customarily referred to him as "meathead," "crumbbum," or "balloon-head." They don't any more.

Although wealth has never kept a man from the White House (George Washington left an estate of five hundred and thirty thousand 1799 dollars), it is only in the past century that we have developed an appreciation of its importance in the Presidential scheme of things. The trouble with President Grant, we see now, was his lack of money, a lack that led to his ruin. We are not likely to make that mistake again. Of all the candidates for the 1960 Presidential nomination, only two—Vice-President Richard Nixon and Senator Hubert Humphrey—were without substantial private means. Of the Democratic candidates, only Humphrey was not a millionaire. The defeat of Nixon, who referred constantly during the campaign to his humble ancestry, by Kennedy, who had a million dollars in the bank while in his teens, may spell the end of the log-cabin tradition and the beginning of the mansion tradition in American political life. In fact, never before has America had so many millionaires in all walks of life, to say nothing of that band of élite (two hundred and forty-four at last count) who have annual *incomes* of a million dollars or more.

The mere acquisition of a million dollars is but the first and simplest step toward becoming an American hero. The next consists in adopting the proper attitude toward money. In America, only one such attitude is socially acceptable. This requires that money be regarded as nothing more than a convenience for measuring success. To a properly adjusted millionaire, dollars are simply counters in a national game. The more he collects, the higher he is scored in intelligence, power, and success. The classic American view of money has probably never been more succinctly stated than it was by one of the richest of all Texas millionaires, H. L. Hunt, the first time he was ever interviewed. "Money is nothing," he said. "It is just something to make bookkeeping convenient." A couple of years ago, he elaborated on the subject in talking to the writer Saul Pett: "There are times when I've wished I'd wake up stonebroke. It would be a great adventure—to see how good I was, to see if I could create lots of wealth again."

To see how good he is—that sums up the purpose of money to an American. However, it is one thing to understand the correct attitude, as Hunt does, and quite another to adopt it, as Hunt does not. He exhibits his rejection of the appropriate philosophy by retaining his dollars. He prides himself on holding on to his money, and makes his view clear in his careless dress, ramshackle automobile, and in many other ways, such as personally trimming his own hair and carrying his lunch to his office. A guest invited by Hunt to lunch is apt to be served an egg sandwich, a glass of milk, and a piece of white typewriter paper to use as a napkin.

By his penuriousness, Hunt has disqualified himself from becoming an American hero. To reach that state, a man must not only make his million and comprehend the American theory of money but, taking the third and final step, put it into practice. This demands that he show as much enterprise in giving away his money as in making it. That is materialism on the American plan.

"In works of active beneficence, no country has surpassed,

perhaps none has equalled, the United States," James Bryce wrote in 1888. Today, nearly three-quarters of a century later, the United States is still the most actively beneficent country in the world. Russia may give the underdeveloped nations more theory, but we give them more money. According to the Organization for European Economic Coöperation, the average annual contribution of the United States in capital assistance to underdeveloped countries during the years 1956–59 amounted to three and a half billion dollars, whereas that of Russia and the other eight Communist-bloc countries put together came to a hundred and forty million. For all of its foreign-assistance programs since the end of the Second World War, the United States has put up more than seventy-eight billion dollars. No country has ever acted like that before. Noting our postwar aid to Europe alone, the eminent British Socialist Harold Laski, who seldom faltered in controlling his enthusiasm for things American, was moved to remark that "nobody is entitled to speak of the material-mindedness of Americans unless he can produce an instance of comparable and continuous generosity from European experience." It is in our blood, apparently, to seek the world's good will, and all signs indicate that our pursuit will continue to be based on the belief that generosity is conducive—or at least not alien—to friendship. In fact, we are at present on the verge of putting an unprecedented wager on that notion by adopting a plan to allocate annually one per cent of our gross national product— five billion dollars—for the aid of underdeveloped countries. When it comes to giving, Americans are the jubilee plungers.

Probably the main reason we have so easily acquired the habit of giving overseas is that we are so used to doing it at home. In 1960, Americans donated more than eight billion dollars to domestic philanthropies. That puts philanthropy among the nation's ten leading businesses. Furthermore, it ranks first after money-making in the respect it is accorded. Consequently, the surest and quickest way for an American millionaire to improve his public image is to give away money. Openhandedness in this country is by no means confined to the higher financial echelons. In his report on life on the Bowery, Elmer Bendiner has written, "Lodging-house keepers tell me that many men, when plunking down their seventy-five cents for a night's lodging, will toss in a twenty-five-cent tip. The calculating man who measures his pennies is a tourist on the Bowery and forever a stranger."

The achievement of popularity through philanthropy exerts such a magnetic force on American life that it even induces people to steal money in order to give it away. Early this year, Mrs. Burnice Geiger, the fifty-eight-year-old assistant cashier of the Sheldon (Iowa) National Bank, was found to have helped herself, over the past thirty-five years, to more than two million dollars of the bank's money, which she had spread around among those who were less well off. "It would take every page of an entire day's newspaper to print the good this woman has done," a neighbor told a reporter after the source of Mrs. Geiger's charity funds had come to light. The Good Samaritan impression of Mrs. Geiger held by the pastor of her church was also abiding. "She simply had a lot of goodness and expressed it without limit to anyone, particularly those in need," he said. The rich person who is able to put a limit on the financial expression of his goodness has, of course, been a standard fixture in every society, and we naturally have a few in ours. No doubt the prize exhibit is J. Paul Getty, an oilman worth about two billion ("I don't know anybody who could sell out for more than I could," he says), whose parsimony has made him, in the eyes of his countrymen, a figure of fun. It is probably as well that Getty chooses to make his home in Europe, for the calculating millionaire, no less than the close-fisted denizen of the Bowery, is a stranger in America forever.

Like so many of his other traits, the American's instinct to look out for the other fellow was developed on the frontier, where the problems, Merle Curti has noted in his study "American Philanthropy and the National Character," "did not merely favor neighborly cooperation in time of need and trouble—they made it necessary." To whatever degree necessity has diminished with changing times, it remains true that, as Jacques Barzun has remarked, "our first impulse is to help, because the memory of give-and-take, of mutual logrolling in building the continent, is with us still." It follows, in theory, that the nearer the frontier, the greener the memory, and, in practice, that the greener the memory, the greater the tendency to help. Thus, the millionaries in Texas, being more materialistic than other Americans, have, according to the correct definition of the term, an extra-lively interest not only in bringing in the dollars but also in passing them out.

Naturally, the philanthropic pudding in Texas, as elsewhere, has always been seasoned by a few provident millionaires, such as the San Antonio oilman who not long ago sold one of his companies for over thirty million dollars and who makes an annual contribution to the Community Fund of twenty-five dollars, and the late W. T. (Tom) Waggoner, a cattle baron enriched by oil, who once expressed his views on thrift in a Fort Worth barbershop.

"Well, what do I owe you?" he asked the barber as he rose from the chair.

"I'll leave that up to you, Mr. Waggoner," the barber said. "Your sons generally give me five or ten dollars when they come in."

"Is that so?" said Waggoner. "Well, I generally give two bits for a haircut, and here it is. No need to look so slack-jawed. My boys got a rich daddy, but I ain't."

While there is some truth in the *Wall Street Journal*'s recent assertion that "oilmen, with a few exceptions, never have been known for great generosity," it might properly be added that the main reason is the oilmen's conviction that they need to hold on to all their chips during their lifetime to provide maximum resources for playing the oil game. Once it is over, they often leave their whole stack to charity. Robert A. Welch, of Houston, enjoyed a deserved reputation as the closest millionaire in town (he refused to give *anything* to the Community Fund); however, he left his life savings, now worth some fifty million dollars, for scientific research and similar purposes. Sid Richardson confined his charitable impulses during his lifetime to occasional handouts to a Fort Worth drugstore proprietor and a few other friends who had helped him during what he called his "rabbit-eating days," but he left nearly all of his multimillion-dollar fortune to a philanthropic foundation. Michael L. Benedum, the famous wildcatter who discovered the Permian Basin, in West Texas—the country's largest petroleum reserve—varied the pattern a bit. Though he left his hundred-million-dollar fortune to a foundation, and restricted his personal extravagances to such things as making a five-cent bet on a television prizefight, he personally gave away a great many millions (four and a half of them, at one clip, to his West Virginia birthplace for some civic improvements), and he also made a practice of cutting his employees in on good deals. Benedum's chauffeur left an estate worth seventeen million dollars.

If a certain number of flinty Texas millionaires have been satisfied with a posthumous reputation for generosity, most of the present crop prefer to enjoy—or at least to seek—the accolade while here below. As a result, the doing of good works in Texas takes on a brisk, almost competitive air. In this field, a millionaire like Michel Halbouty, who made his fortune himself, contends on more or less equal terms with a millionaire like Tom Slick, who inherited his. Slick, who is forty-five, prematurely gray, and personable, fell heir to approximately fifteen million at the age of fourteen. After graduating from Yale and serving in the Navy during the Second World War, he returned to San Antonio, where he began devoting a significant portion of his legacy to the benefit of others. On some five thousand acres outside the city, he established a research center (now the fourth-largest in the country) that consists of the Southwest Research Institute, the Southwest Foundation for Research and Education, and the Agricultural Research Institute—all non-profit enterprises devoted to improving the human lot through industrial, medical, and agricultural studies. Although he has put money into a variety of other worthy interests, such as world peace, Slick has managed his business affairs successfully enough so that his assets today exceed his inheritance. He likes profits as well as Halbouty does, but both agree that the only proper use of profits is to do some good.

"If I made a *billion* dollars, I wouldn't quit work," says Halbouty, who is fifty, trim, brisk, articulate, and apostolic in temperament. "I'll admit that at one time I did think seriously of giving it all up. I wasn't even forty. I'd worked ever since I started selling newspapers as a kid, and then suddenly I found I had enough to live on comfortably the rest of my life. So I called a meeting of my top personnel and told them about my decision to quit. But after they'd left, I sat back and asked myself, 'What were you put on this earth for? To live like a fat cat? No!' I decided I didn't want to be a grape ripening on the vine and finally shrivelling up like a dried-out raisin. I decided to go ahead, expand my enterprises, and so do something for my fellow-men. Whatever the good Lord has done for me, I figure I should try to do something in return." Besides spending an average of four hours a day on a wide range of civic and charitable undertakings, Halbouty likes to engage in personal philanthropies, such as making a gift (as he did in 1960) to St. Luke's Episcopal Hospital, in Houston, of a completely equipped nursery for premature babies, and providing (as he has done for many years) fellowships for three graduate students at Texas A. & M.

The alumni of institutions of higher learning in Texas are generally pretty chary about contributing to alma mater, but among Texas millionaires, as in the country at large, education ranks after religion as the chief beneficiary of philanthropy. It is, accordingly, unusual to glance through a Texas newspaper without noting that, for example, B. G. Byars has given five scholarships to students at Texas A. & M.; D. H. Byrd has put some five dozen boys and girls through college; John Blaffer has presented an auditorium to the Kinkaid School, in Houston; George Strake has donated over a quarter of a million dollars to the University of St. Thomas, in Houston; Eugene McElvaney has done another good turn for S.M.U., which he has been aiding since the age of twelve, when he contributed twenty-five dollars from his newspaper route earnings to help establish the institution; J. Newton Rayzor has given a million to Rice and three hundred thousand to Baylor; Eugene McDermott (one of the most indefatigable philanthropists among Texas millionaires) has presented another new building to St. Mark's School of Texas; Erik Jonsson has donated a million dollars to Rensselaer Polytechnic, his alma mater; Cecil Green has given securities worth about three million dollars to M.I.T., *his* alma mater; and so on and on.

Aside from education, the philanthropic impulse finds many other forms of expression among Texas millionaires. For example, James Abercrombie, of Houston, annually stages the nationally-famous Pin Oak Horse Show, and gives the proceeds, which have amounted over the years to several hundred thousand dollars, to the Texas Children's Hospital. Several of the most active philanthropists in Texas have been women—notably, the late Mrs. William L. Clayton, wife of the co-founder of the world's largest firm of cotton marketers, and two residents of Houston, Miss Ima Hogg and Miss Nina J. Cullinan, both daughters of remarkable men who were associated in the creation of the Texas Company. Joseph S. (Buckskin Joe) Cullinan, one of eight children whose parents came from Ireland, also served for several years as president of the Texas Company, and meanwhile found time to indulge many other interests, such as travelling in Europe with his family and collecting paintings. "He was full of oats as far as temperament was concerned," Miss Cullinan has recalled, "and he really was a romantic about America. He was always passing out copies of the Bill of Rights and the Constitution to people. He never ran for office, but he was always promoting causes or opposing anything he felt would hurt the machinery of democracy." Miss Cullinan is herself a dedicated cause-promoter, and though she prefers not to discuss her contributions, there is scarcely a good work in Houston that she has not aided with time and money.

The general welfare has also been the primary lifelong interest of Miss Ima Hogg, as it was of her father, James Stephen Hogg, the first native-born governor of Texas and, by general agreement, the most illustrious. A mountainous man of aristocratic ancestry, he combined a dedication to championing the underdog with a gift for making money—"the perfect blend," Stanley Walker has observed, "for the making of a Texas hero." The immense fortune Hogg accumulated from oil was passed on to his three sons, Tom, Mike, and Will, who have since died, and to his only daughter, who is named after the heroine of a romantic Civil War poem titled "The Fate of Marvin," written by her uncle. As a young woman, "Missima," as she is spoken of by her intimate friends, attended the University of Texas and afterward studied piano in New York and Europe before returning to Houston to take up a life of public service that has perhaps been unmatched in duration, variety, and extent by any other Houstonian, even by her brother Will. He took after his father in his feeling for the underdog, and spent his life and fortune translating his sympathy into action. "If I knew just when I was going to die," he once said to his friend John A. Lomax, "beyond my funeral expenses, I wouldn't reserve enough money to buy a bowl of chili." They don't make Texas millionaires just like Will Hogg any more (he was so fond of chili that, to make sure of having it when visiting Paris, he established a talented Southern Negro cook in a restaurant there), but, as far as giving is concerned, quite a few of the contemporary group are modelled along roughly the same lines.

Whatever the extent of their philanthropy, practically all Texas millionaires dispense it through a foundation—a device enabling them to divert into good works of their own choosing money that would otherwise be paid in federal taxes. Though foundations have of late become a vogue among the American rich (having, as *Fortune* has said, "replaced the race horse as an expression of wealth"), they have been around since Benjamin Franklin used some of the pennies he saved to set one up in Philadelphia to permit "young married artificers" of reputable character to borrow up to three hundred dollars at five per cent on their signature only. Today, according to the Foundation Library Center, a national clearing house of information on the subject, the United States has more than twelve thousand private foundations, with combined assets of eleven and a half billion dollars. Each of the five largest— Ford, Rockefeller, Duke, Hartford, and Carnegie, in that order —has assets exceeding two hundred and fifty million; at least a hundred and twenty-four others are worth ten million or more apiece.

According to F. Emerson Andrews, director of the Center, "great wealth and smart tax lawyers" are the two chief factors in the proliferation of foundations, which in the past decade were created at the rate of a hundred a month. It does not take a lawyer of exceptional brilliance to explain to a client—that is, a client who has an annual taxable income comfortably above two hundred thousand dollars, and a desire to get into the philanthropic swim—the inspired provisions of the tax laws that allow him to have his own foundation at a cost of as little as nine cents on the dollar. If the explanation results in the establishment of a foundation, the donor can thereafter give it twenty per cent of his annual gross income tax-free. Should he wish to enlarge what lawyers call the corpus of his foundation with donations in the form of stocks, real estate, oil properties, and other holdings that have appreciated in value during his ownership, he can not only avoid the twenty-five-per-cent capital-gains tax (payable if the properties had been sold) but also deduct twenty per cent of the current value of the donated assets from his gross income. "Persons in any income bracket, therefore, secure a tax advantage through giving an appreciated asset rather than cash," Mr. Andrews has pointed out, "and in the highest tax brackets we reach those examples, dear to the heart of tax consultants, where a wealthy donor can give an appreciated asset and have more money left than if he himself had cashed the asset and given nothing away."

Perhaps because foundations, as a lawyer wise in their ways

has suggested, provide "the answer for the man who has everything," their rate of growth has been more rapid in Texas in recent years than in any other state. Unlike New York-based foundations, which generally spread the contents of their cornucopias across the country, and sometimes across the world, the Texas foundations customarily dispense their gifts only in Texas. "The goddam Texans just won't give money to anything outside the state," the Dallas lawyer Thomas Knight, whose family has been in Texas for a few generations, has said. "That doesn't apply to Gene McDermott and some others, like Erik Jonsson—they're transplanted Yankees—but it's true of the natives. A while ago, the Harvard Law School, of which I'm a graduate, undertook a fund-raising campaign, and I was put in charge of collections in Texas. So I got Mrs. Allen [his wife, whom it amuses Knight to call by her previous married name] to drive me around to Houston and San Antonio and a few other places. When I got through passing the hat, I had collected the sum of five thousand dollars, and out of that I'd put in twenty-five hundred myself. S.M.U. was running a campaign about the same time to pick up some money for *its* law school. They got three million or so without straining a muscle. It just proved that you can't get a Texan to do anything that is not, shall we say, self-improving. Texas law encourages this proclivity by giving tax exemptions to foundations established by wills and to testamentary bequests only if the money is used right here in the state. Keep it all in the family—that's what the goddam Texans want to do. So be it."

This being the case, Texans were no doubt greatly relieved to learn that the Galveston financier William Lewis Moody, Jr., who died in 1954, had left nearly all of his worldly possessions to a foundation to do good "among the people of Texas." Their relief is understandable, for while the assets of the Moody Foundation have yet to be announced officially, they are estimated at approximately four hundred and forty million dollars, making it potentially the largest in Texas and ranking it nationally right behind the Ford and Rockefeller Foundations. Because of extensive litigation over Moody's will, the Moody Foundation has been rather reluctant about distributing largess; so far, its grants have amounted to just four hundred and twenty-two thousand dollars.

Like the men behind the two bigger foundations, W. L. Moody, Jr., was a singular figure whose life is a luminous testament to the romance of American business. The only son of a Virginia lawyer who moved to Galveston and made a fortune as a cotton trader, Moody from childhood had the mercantile touch, which he demonstrated upon taking over the family business after his father's death and branching out into many other fields, including banking, insurance, hotels, ranching, and newspapers. In everything, he prospered. "All he had in the way of business ability was a knack for making four out of three," a former associate once said. It was enough to put him, in time, in possession of what was generally calculated to be half the wealth of Galveston. Meanwhile, he had married and become the father of two sons and two daughters, none of whom was spoiled. "My earliest recollection is of a little penny bank," the younger daughter, Libbie, who is married to Congressman Clark Thompson, once told Elizabeth Carpenter, of the Houston *Post*. "I got fifteen cents a week for allowance, but I always saved some of it. When I was raised to twenty-five cents a week, I thought I was wealthy." Another of her happy reflections concerned her father's establishment of what is now the Moody National Bank. "Daddy had me out trying to get accounts for his new bank," she has said. "I had good luck. Of course, I didn't do anything fabulous, but I helped. When I look back at the things I was asked to do—well, I just never would ask my children to do them."

The family lived comfortably in a Victorian mansion with a large front porch, where a night watchman habitually sat from sundown to sunrise. Aside from sleeping and eating, Moody—who never used coffee or tobacco, seldom touched liquor, and kept regular office hours six days a week—wasted little time on anything except an occasional hunting or fishing trip. A British businessman who once visited Galveston and

357

was invited by Moody to go duck hunting at his private reserve discovered that at the end of the day's shooting all the ducks were brought to Moody, who divided them among the guests, keeping the largest birds for himself. Nearly everywhere he went during the last twenty-five years of his life, Moody was attended by his Negro valet, Enoch Withers. Such was Moody's fondness for his faithful servant that he secured his promise never to leave. True to his pledge, Withers was at Moody's bedside when the old gentleman died, at eighty-nine. Later, Withers learned that his former employer had left him a bequest of one thousand dollars. Today, Moody's elder daughter, Mary, who was his favorite child, watches over her father's empire, demonstrating her loyalty to his philosophy even in her dress, which is exceedingly plain and frequently includes cotton stockings that she has darned herself.

Unlike the foundation, which fosters public charity, the trust fund—the other favorite instrumentality of Texas millionaires—allows charity to begin at home. As most commonly used, the trust enables Texas millionaires, during their lifetime, to pass on wealth to their children at a tax saving. Though neither new nor unique to Texans (President Kennedy receives about a hundred thousand dollars annually, after taxes, from trust funds set up by his father), the device has always been extraordinarily popular among farsighted Super-Americans. "It is my surmise," Thomas Knight, an expert on the subject, once told a group of trust officers, "that of the oilmen domiciled in the mid-continent area who are worth a million dollars or more, nine out of ten are settlors of such trusts. Irrespective of the verbiage used by the scrivener," Knight concluded, using some of the rounded phrases he picked up at the Harvard Law School, "the purpose of such a trust, intended by the settlor, is not so much the protection of the beneficiaries as it is the convenience of the settlor in making money for him and his to keep, and the most of it that can possibly be kept." When millionaires reach the point where further additions to their children's trust funds would be taxable at an ornery rate, they frequently begin setting up trusts for their grandchildren.

In Super-America, trusts are so closely threaded through the background fabric of everyday life that one runs across references to them in the newspapers, such as this typically Super-American item recorded by Bill Roberts in the Houston *Post*: "The estate of the late Oil Operator Maurice Grubbs is buying Jeweler Sam Becker's ranch near La Grange (appraised at $150,000) for the trust held for his grandchildren, Maurie and Wayne Ankenman, Jr., dtr and son of Wayne Ankenman. The ranch will be leased to their Mom, Jackie Grubbs Ankenman, for income purposes." In this manner are the wins of the fathers visited upon the children unto the second and third generation, but most bountifully upon the second, which in America is the chosen one, being, according to folklore, the generation that avoids shirtsleeves.

Chapter Twenty-One

"There's a difference in the second-generation rich in Texas," an unsentimental self-made Houston lawyer said not long ago. "Down here, they feel they've got to do it themselves. Not that family money doesn't count in getting them started. But they're not content to just sit back with it." An equally unsentimental self-made Dallas oilman, surveying the second-generation rich in Texas, has said, "Not one of them would be worth a tinker's dam without the old man's money. By themselves, they couldn't count up to a hundred." While both appraisals have a measure of validity, neither does justice to the second generation of Texas millionaires, a group that is distinguished, for one thing, by its short supply of career playboys. "Being a playboy is not looked on with favor down here," Jack Vaughn, a Dallas workboy who was known in his carefree school days as Cadillac Jack, has said. "Besides, the surroundings aren't conducive to it. A man with no occupation is a lost human being in this section of the world. There just aren't enough other people around with nothing to do for him to associate with."

There are, however, enough workboys around to keep one another company. Fairly representative of this group are the two sons of Clint Murchison—John, thirty-nine, and Clint, Jr., thirty-seven. After watching them in action, a financial writer for the New York *Times* reported that each works "as earnestly as a bank teller bucking for a three-hundred-dollar-a-year raise." As partners in Murchison Brothers, the operating entity created for them by Clint, Sr., they own oil, insurance, real-estate, construction, publishing, and other interests worth about a hundred and fifty million dollars. Bucking to increase it, they recently waged a successful proxy battle against the seasoned financier sixty-eight-year-old Allan Kirby for control of the Alleghany Corporation, which controls companies with assets of more than six billion dollars. John Murchison has estimated that the victory cost only about half a million.

As a rule, the workboys follow in their fathers' footsteps. Waldo Stewart, of Dallas, carries on the automotive and allied interests that he inherited; the two sons of O. P. Leonard, co-founder of Forth Worth's largest department store, are rapidly forging to the top in that business; in Midland, Clarence Scharbauer, Jr., is expanding the ranching empire founded by his father; Amon G. Carter, Jr., has assumed his father's mantle as publisher of the Fort Worth *Star-Telegram;* William P. Hobby, Jr., has become managing editor of his parents' Houston *Post;* and throughout the state sons of oilmen have taken their fathers' places in playing the oil game.

Some careers are taboo for healthy young Super-American sons—particularly in the arts—but no parental injunction forbids their entering new fields of a practical nature. W. C. Windsor, Jr., and Angus Wynne, Jr., who are sons of an oilman and a lawyer, respectively, enjoyed familial blessing when they embarked on careers in industrial real estate, and Lamar Hunt, one of H. L. Hunt's four sons, had his father's approval when he set out, in 1959, to make his mark in the sports world by founding the American Football League, consisting of eight new professional teams. The younger Hunt is not only president of the new league but the sole owner of its Dallas team, known as the Texans, who wound up their first year, in 1960, with a deficit of about half a million dollars. "I'm very encouraged about our first season," Hunt said after it was over. "Of course, we didn't win the title [the Houston Oilers, who did, ended the year, according to their owner, a second-generation Super-American named K. S. (Bud) Adams, with a loss exceeding seven hundred thousand dollars], and we have a goal to reach there, but I believe we're on our way. It will probably be the third or fourth season before we make a profit." Until then, Hunt will get along on his share of the profits from the complex of family enterprises, including eleven million acres of oil land in Libya, which have started to return what the elder Hunt, who is not given to superlatives, has called "fantastic production."

Between the workboys and the playboys stands that sizable group of second-generation Super-Americans whose counterparts in an earlier day were described by de Tocqueville as "young men of wealth personally disinclined to all laborious exertion, but who have been compelled to embrace a profession." Of the ones he met, he wrote, "Their disposition and their fortune allowed them to remain without employment; public opinion forbade it too imperiously to be disobeyed." Since public opinion has not changed much in this respect (a century after de Tocqueville, Geoffrey Gorer found that with almost negligible exceptions, "there is no place or position in American life for the young man of inherited means who is not gainfully employed"), second-generation Super-Americans who are willing and able to avoid working feel obliged to go through the motions.

Generally, the members of this in-between group are married, thoughtful parents, members of the best clubs, responsive to civic and charitable undertakings (in contributions of money, if not so much of time), seldom guilty of breaking any of the canons of respectability, and, in a general way, rather unobtrusive figures on the landscape. To hold the social franchise, they maintain an office (often one in the city where they live and another in a town near their oil properties or where, as frequently happens, they own a bank), and they do some wheeling and dealing, occasionally on a large scale, but, having been endowed with sizable resources, their business transactions are seldom marked, as their fathers' almost always were, by enough risk to make them exciting. Not infrequently, a member of the second generation disinclined to exertion keeps on his payroll a trusted employee who had worked long years for his father and who, without the existence of any formal arrangements, quietly holds responsibility for the general management of the business.

Though averse to maintaining regular business hours, the second-generation millionaires who are dedicated neither to work nor play usually spend some time at the office five days a week when they are in town; however, the occasions are not rare when they stay up until the small hours playing poker and engaging in quiet conviviality with friends, and, arising late the following day, decide to spend it on the golf course. They also spend a good deal of time out of town on hunting and fishing trips, and even longer periods on travel. Quite a number of the second-generation millionaires maintain a house in California or an apartment in New York, where they take to passing so much time that their Texas residence becomes of importance only for legal and sentimental reasons. At home or abroad, the predominant characteristic that marks both their private and professional lives is a curious lack of involvement, a kind of harmless indifference. "Could it possibly be that the present generation, enjoying the fruits of the labors of others, can afford to take things easily and to take each other more easily?" the South African novelist Dan Jacobson asked in a recent issue of the *Texas Quarterly*.

It could, in the opinion of some members of the first generation, including the Dallas real-estate operator Leo Corrigan, whose son and son-in-law are now in business with him. Corrigan, the second of eight children born in a low-rent neighborhood of St. Louis, availed himself of what economists call the advantage of an early start by leaving school at ten to go to work in a department store at three dollars a week. Moving to Texas when he was seventeen, Corrigan boosted his weekly pay to ten dollars as a classified-newspaper-advertising salesman, specializing in real estate. Within five years, by making some breaks for himself, he had accumulated five thousand dollars, which he used to construct a modest commercial building in South Dallas, a modest part of town. From there he went on to develop a real-estate empire that now includes shopping centers, hotels, office buildings, and other holdings, with a total worth of about half a billion dollars.

At sixty-six, Corrigan, who believes that the first requisite for getting ahead is "a hell of a lot of nerve," is adding to his reputation as a top-echelon wheeler-dealer (he is now completing the twelve-million-dollar Marco Polo Hotel in Hong Kong and planning others in Bangkok and Bombay), to the not infrequent consternation of his younger associates. When considering proposed big deals with them, Corrigan finds that the younger men are inclined to look for pitfalls and to emphasize the value of caution. "Hell, if I'd used that kind of yardstick we'd still be in South Dallas," Corrigan often tells his second-generation colleagues.

The emergence of a younger generation enticed by security, that stealthy mistress whose charms have hitherto mainly allured the middle-aged, is a conspicuous and typical feature of the changing scene in Super-America. There, as in the rest of the country, the style of life has been affected not only by the waning of audacity but by the simultaneous waxing of today's two great levellers—industrialization and urbanization. In Texas, these processes have operated, as might be expected, with excessive speed, changing the state's economy in a mere twenty years from predominantly agricultural to industrial, and meanwhile moving the population from farm to town in such numbers that at present three out of four Texans live in a city. In fact, one-third of all Texans now live in the state's four largest cities. The texture of Super-American life has also been colored by immigration, which has been on such a booming scale that one out of every four contemporary residents was born outside the state.

Inevitably, these interlocking phenomena have resulted in introducing into Super-American culture the wonders of homogenization—manifested, for example, in the subtle erosion of Texas pride in the Texas heritage. It used to be that San Jacinto Day, celebrating the most important event in Texas history, was the occasion for a gala statewide explosion of patriotism, but now schools and stores stay open, the day passes everywhere in a business-as-usual atmosphere, and nobody appears to be much upset by the withering away of interest, except perhaps a few sentimental newspaper editorial writers, like the old-timer on the Houston *Post* who found it "sad to think that the spirit of San Jacinto, which is the mainstem of Texas character, seems to be burning so low." Nor does the spirit of the Alamo seem to be burning at its old height. Time was when any projected tampering with that hallowed shrine would have been met with a storm of public outrage, and yet scarcely a voice was raised in anger following the announcement a short while ago that the Alamo is to be air-conditioned.

The rousing individuality and robust independence that have also long distinguished the Texas character have likewise shown a gradual diminution in intensity—a development perhaps nowhere more tellingly revealed than in the new rapprochement between Dallas and Fort Worth, whose fiery and incessant rivalry, sparkling like a perpetual Catherine wheel, kept the scene sparkling in years past. "Back there when I was a kid, it was practically as serious as the Holy Crusades," Bill Cunningham, the talented sportswriter, who was brought up in Dallas, once recalled.

The same fine patriotic fervor was still ablaze in the nineteen-forties, when the two cities, situated just under thirty miles apart, decided to cooperate on the construction of an airport, to be placed midway between them. All went well until Dallas discovered that the plans called for the airport administration building to be placed three-tenths of a mile closer to Fort Worth, and, worse, to face Fort Worth. The Dallas city fathers, wounded and angry, protested to Amon Carter, then the city father of Fort Worth, who replied, "I see no reason for changing the plans. And no goddam reason for the administration building being one goddam inch nearer Dallas than it is to Fort Worth." That was the end of the joint airport. Each city promptly set about pouring millions into the development of its own.

Aside from continuing to engage in a certain amount of mild bickering about their respective airports ("It's Smarter to Fly Carter"—Fort Worth *Star-Telegram*. "Isn't it too bad? Fort Worth built its airport on the wrong side of town"—Dallas *News*), the former rivals now regard each other in a spirit of good fellowship as mellow and rich as old domestic wine. Instead of the perilous, two-lane, traffic-choked highway that long served as the chief, and downright forbidding, land link between the two cities, there is now a coöperatively constructed six-lane toll road that puts them only thirty minutes apart. In the spring of 1961, members of the Dallas and Fort Worth Junior Chambers of Commerce gathered to stage a ceremony in which they literally buried a hatchet. "We hope this is a symbolic example our elders will follow," a Dallas junior said. No less dispiriting to the unreconstructed elders of both cities was a recent Dallas *News* story that coolly discussed the possibility that the day may come when the two municipalities will merge into one glorious metropolis.

Pending the arrival of that golden future time, the shape of things to come in Texas—and the way they will be wrought from things of the past—can be seen to particular advantage in the Great Southwest Corporation, which, comprising five thousand and fifty acres midway between Dallas and Fort Worth, is the world's largest planned industrial community and has risen on the site of what was once the fancy horse-breeding farm and private race track of Tom Waggoner. (His father, one of the original cattle kings, amassed an empire of half a million acres, spread over six North Texas counties. When asked if he had in mind buying all the real estate in North Texas, he replied, "No, just what joins me.") In 1904, Waggoner inherited his father's cattle domain intact, along with several other useful properties, including some banks. His financial position was made more secure when, in 1911, a tremendous pool of oil— one of the historic finds in Texas—was discovered under his extensive acreage. Waggoner had nothing against oil money, but he used to lose his temper when his men, drilling for water badly needed for the cattle, found more oil. "Damn it! Cattle can't drink that stuff!" he would bellow.

Waggoner's interest in cattle was exceeded only by his love of horses, which he indulged by maintaining for many years a nationally famous thoroughbred farm in the North Texas town of Electra. That was also the name he gave to his only daughter, who by her own efforts became one of the storied figures of Texas. After attending private schools, she embarked on a round-the-world trip, returning with a brilliant butterfly tattooed on one of her legs, and soon afterward was married to a blueblood from the East, the first of three husbands she had during her lifetime. When not visiting New York, her favorite spot after Texas, she divided her time between a ranch she owned and a large residence on seven acres in Dallas, which she bought and fixed up in order to have a place in town where she could entertain. "In some rooms, as many as fifteen coats of paint were applied before she got the exact shade she desired," Frank X. Tolbert has written. "She furnished this house with about a half million dollars' worth of art objects she'd collected around the world. . . . A truckload of flowers was brought by a florist every day, [and] almost every day Neiman's would send out large stocks of dresses for Electra's selection. The dresses would have to arrive in the original packages from Paris or New York, for Electra refused to wear a dress that anyone else had tried on. She rarely ever wore a dress more than once. . . . One entire closet was filled with fur coats. Her shoe cabinet usually held three hundred and fifty pairs of shoes. And she had a new pair delivered to her daily." Electra Waggoner's life was colorful but short; she died in New York in 1925, at forty-three.

Two years later, her father, who was then seventy-six, suffered another blow when fire destroyed his thoroughbred stock farm. Instead of rebuilding on the old site, Waggoner decided to construct a new and grander establishment on twenty-five hundred acres that he bought near the town of Arlington, roughly halfway between Dallas and Fort Worth. After landscaping the entire tract, which he named Arlington Downs, and enclosing it with a solid board fence, Waggoner spent three million dollars turning it into a show place; besides an array of barns, paddocks, and similar structures, the layout included a one-and-a-quarter-mile race track, complete with a clubhouse and a six-thousand-seat grandstand, from which spectators looked out upon a meticulously manicured infield set off by a forty-six-million-gallon artificial lake. Waggoner then spent another million to stock the place with thoroughbred horses.

Since pari-mutuel betting was illegal in Texas when Arlington Downs was built, it was used only for matched racing on a "Southern-gentleman basis," in the phrase of Glen Turpin, who was Waggoner's foreman of the Downs and was later given a farmhouse and property on the premises. "A man would just bring in a good horse and match him against some other fellow's," Turpin has recalled. "It was pretty informal." In 1933, pari-mutuel racing was legalized in Texas, and the following year Arlington Downs was turned into a public track, with two racing seasons. The transformation was sanctioned by Pappy Waggoner, as the old gentleman was by then called, but the track's operation was largely directed by Waggoner's two sons—Paul, who was interested in horses, and Guy, who was interested in marriage and by then had had half a dozen wives. Though Pappy was past eighty, ailing, and nearly blind when his race track was opened to the public, he insisted up to the end on being taken to the Downs whenever the weather was good, and there he would sit, in a wheelchair in the infield, rewarded only by a blur and the pounding of hoofs as the horses thundered by.

In 1934, Tom Waggoner died, and three years later the Texas Legislature outlawed pari-mutuel racing once more. After that, Waggoner's sons lost interest in Arlington Downs. Guy drifted away and was married a couple of times more before his death, in 1950. Paul, who married only once, took up residence on the Waggoner Ranch, near Vernon, Texas, where he still lives with his wife and, in the manner of his father, takes a special interest in the breeding of quarter horses and the staging of the Santa Rosa Roundup, an annual week-long private rodeo.

Carrying on another family tradition, Paul Waggoner named his daughter (and only child) Electra, who, like her aunt, was educated in private schools and afterward spent a good deal of time in New York, where, according to an interview she gave Cholly Knickerbocker, her main interests were clothes and parties. Then, in 1937, when she was twenty-five and had been once married and divorced, she took a studio on Park Avenue and settled down to a serious career in sculpture, which she had studied in Boston and Paris. "I have given up social life and pleasures for my work," she announced, and set about executing several commissions. In 1943, she was married to a business executive named John Biggs, who is now general manager of the Waggoner Estate, the family's multimillion-dollar oil-and-cattle operation with headquarters in an imposing marble edifice in Vernon.

The Biggses live nearby on the half-million-acre Waggoner Ranch (the second largest ranch in Texas), where Mrs. Biggs —attractive, energetic, and the mother of two teen-age daughters—has continued her professional career. Her life nowadays bears small resemblance to the original Electra's. "During the Roundup, we do a good deal of entertaining, but otherwise our life here is quite simple," Mrs. Biggs remarked to a visitor a while ago. "People come for dinner. There's a good movie house in Vernon, but we seldom go. We prefer to look at TV. Then, there's a Chinese restaurant in town that isn't too bad. I go in to Vernon once a week to have my hair washed, but mostly I spend my time right here, working at my sculpture and trying to make some money."

Unlike her namesake, Mrs. Biggs shuns ostentation not only in her social life and her conversation, which is liberally sprinkled with cryptic asides hinting at impending financial doom, but also in her dress, which is fashionably conservative. "As far as jewelry is concerned," Mrs. Biggs told her visitor, "my main interest these days isn't in owning it but in making and selling it—coin-size medallions for charm bracelets, and so on. I did once have a rather nice diamond, though. It was quite a stone—thirty-five carats. I bought it on time from Harry Winston. When we moved to Vernon after the war, I decided to sell it. You can imagine what would happen if I wore it around here. I sold it back to Harry, and I made a rather nice deal, if I do say so myself. I used the money to set up two trust funds for my daughters' education. They'll need the money."

Whatever the future may hold for Tom Waggoner's great-grandchildren, it is unlikely that they will ever gratify a personal fancy on the scale of Arlington Downs, which in the years following Pappy's death deteriorated into an elegant relic and finally disappeared from the scene in the summer of 1957, when it was bought by the Great Southwest Corporation for six million dollars cash. The money, like that involved in many other Texas enterprises these days, came both from local millionaires and from Eastern men of means, including the Rockefeller brothers.

As a sentimental gesture, the president of the corporation, Angus Wynne, Jr., held the closing ceremony in the farmhouse belonging to Glen Turpin, the foreman, who had continued to look after the Downs and whose separately owned piece of property had also been purchased by the Great Southwest. This transaction was completed first. Wynne handed a check for a handsome sum to Turpin, clapped him on the shoulder, and said sympathetically, "Glen, I sure am sorry that this transfer of land has meant taking away your home." Turpin nodded, put the check in his wallet, patted it, put the wallet back in his hip pocket, and looked around the room, not uttering a word. "You could have heard a pin drop," a New York lawyer who was present has recalled. "It was one of those funny, poignant moments. For some reason, the thing that popped into my head was that Cyril Connolly line—'It's closing time in the playgrounds of the West.' When the old foreman finally spoke, he came up with what I suppose is the West Texas equivalent. 'Well,' he said, 'I guess it's time to spit on the fire and call the dogs.' And with that he walked out the door and never looked back."

It is not only the Texas landscape that is changing but also the figures on it. "Where have all the lusty Texans gone?" asked Worth Gatewood, of the Houston *Post,* upon returning home recently after eight years' residence in New York. "The limply sincere hand press and the murmured 'Howjuhdo' of the effete East have replaced the knuckle-crushing grip and hearty 'Howdy, podnuh!' of yesteryear. . . . The pear-shaped tones and tepid phrases of the East have sneaked across the Sabine to corrupt Texas talk. 'Y'all' still falls pleasantly on the ear, of course, but the lazily slurred 'somethin' has become the harsher 'something,' and not once have I heard a single 'reckon' [or] a 'yonder.' . . . The once-gaudy apparel of the Texan has all but vanished, too, in favor of the subdued garb of the East and Midwest. . . . His step is a little quicker; there is an urgency in his manner that is new to me. A little of the brusqueness of New York has crept into his attitude; he smiles not quite as readily, and spends far less time on casual conversation."

All this being true of the dramatis personae *in toto,* what about the leading characters? Where, on the changing Super-American scene, is the new crop of "Fourth-of-July kind of people," as J. Frank Dobie calls the protesters, dissenters, nonconformists—the kind of people who gave meaning to the national holiday and have since given significance to American life? Where, to get down to cases, are the new Dobies and Walter Prescott Webbs, the new Marion McNays and Ima Hoggs? Where, for that matter, is a latter-day Super-American sufficiently picturesque to be mentioned in the same breath as James Marion (Silver Dollar Jim) West, that wondrous ornament of Houston, who died only four years ago?

West acquired his nickname from his habit of carrying in his outsize trouser pockets about fifty silver dollars, which he sometimes dropped by the handful in crowded public places to create a little excitement. A rotund man, he favored vivid shirts with collar points of platinum, two-toned hand-made boots bearing his embroidered initials, a diamond-studded Texas Ranger badge, and a tooled-leather belt set off by a massive gold buckle. The outfit, completed by a pair of holstered gold-and-silver revolvers, might have been slightly less eye-catching had it adorned a figure less impressive than West's. He was a noteworthy trencherman, and at football games customarily reserved three seats—one for himself and two for his refreshments, which generally consisted of a bushel basket of hot dogs and hamburgers and a case of Coca-Cola. He was particular about his food; having a strong preference for butter churned at one of his ranches, he always carried a supply of it along to restaurants where he dined, and when-ever he made a trip out of state (generally travelling in one of his four private planes), his provisions included not only a few pails of butter but several dozen steaks from his own cat-tle. West was willing to go to a good deal of trouble to have things his own way in other respects, too. He wound up a disagreement with the Houston Lighting & Power Co. by cut-ting off its service to his residence and installing a private electric-power plant. Unable to see eye to eye with the munici-pal water-supply authorities, he dispensed with their product and drilled a couple of wells in his front yard. His younger brother, Wesley, satisfied his desire for a house with a view by building on a slight rise and having the surrounding land scooped out and landscaped. Wesley has always been known as "the conservative one."

As a rule, Silver Dollar Jim arrived at his office around five in the afternoon, put in three or four hours on business affairs, and then left to spend the rest of the night playing an adult version of cops-and-robbers. Since he was a friend of Houston's chief of police and a benefactor of practically everyone on the force, he had many willing uniformed companions as he cruised the city's streets in search of lawbreakers. The all-night patrol was made in one of West's Cadillac sedans, which was equipped with four telephones, a two-way radio (he was assigned his own call number on the police radio system), a sawed-off shotgun, a .30-30 rifle, a submachine gun, and other crime-busting paraphernalia, including tear-gas bombs. As far as is known, Silver Dollar Jim never personally apprehended a suspect, though once when he and a police lieutenant exchanged fire with a fugitive, West, according to some reports, accidentally shot the lieutenant in the foot.

Next to his police work, West's chief interest was automobiles. He maintained a fleet of eleven Cadillacs, supplemented by thirty Oldsmobiles, Plymouths, and other smaller cars, most of which he kept in a private three-story garage, in downtown Houston, that had a staff of full-time mechanics as well as a large paint shop. Silver Dollar Jim had a strong preference for a specially mixed shade of paint known around the garage as West Production Blue. He was so fond of it that once, when giving a party at his house, he instructed the parking attendants to drive the automobiles belonging to several guests who were staying overnight to his private garage; when the cars were returned the following day, all had been painted West Production Blue.

In 1957, failing health obliged West to give up his night patrol, and toward the close of the year he died, at fifty-four. A few months after his death, agents of his executors, searching the basement of his mansion, discovered a hidden cellar stashed with barrels, cans, bags, and paper sacks brimming with silver dollars. When the hoard, weighing over eight tons, was removed to a bank and counted, it turned out that Silver Dollar Jim had in reserve two hundred and ninety thousand of his favorite playthings.

In his later years, Silver Dollar Jim was regarded with mounting uneasiness by his fellow-millionaires, who cringed at the thought that the outside world would consider him typical. Their collective concern sprang from a great wave of self-consciousness that began sweeping across Super-America in the early nineteen-fifties and left in its wake a communal aversion to public notice so intense that it amounts to a persecution complex. "We have been misquoted, misjudged, and downright lied about until we are all fairly bristling with unfriendliness toward anyone who comes to write us up," Mrs. Olaf LaCour Olsen, a prominent Houston matron, explained a while ago to a visiting journalist.

However, a few Super-Americans are aware that their misshapen public image was not fashioned solely by people who came to write them up. "You have got to realize that we are the lousiest public-relations men that it is possible to be," Jake Hamon, an open-minded and widely respected independent oilman, told his colleagues a couple of years ago when serving as chairman of the American Petroleum Institute. "What you don't realize is that most people in the United States think we are a bunch of overbearing braggarts with a tax gimmick. Unless we change that unfair attitude about us, we're going to lose our depletion allowance and generally go down the drain. . . . Despite the fact that we live like peasants compared to the way wealthy people live in some other sections, we are regarded as the richest. We have got to start winning friends and influencing people, and we are starting a lot later than we should." Later by about a year, it would seem, for some twelve months earlier *Cosmopolitan* published an article about Neiman-Marcus that was accompanied by a drawing of Mrs. Hamon above a caption reading, "A typical customer, Mrs. Jake Hamon is the wife of a millionaire oil operator. Mrs. Hamon, an exquisitely groomed brunette, was interviewed in one of the store's fitting rooms while she examined a honey-colored mink stole. Her hobbies, travel and entertaining, require an enormous wardrobe, most of which is supplied by Neiman-Marcus. Last year, the Hamons were hosts to several hundred guests at a masquerade ball, and one summer they gave a 'Christmas in July' party, complete with snow."

Aside from a contretemps or two like that, the Hamons, though they are not likely to be taken for peasants, have studiously avoided looking like the richest, even in the days, not so long ago, when many other Texas millionaires were obligingly coöperative in creating the image they now deplore. In 1948, for example, *Life* published an article titled "Southwest Has a New Crop of Super Rich," which included a photograph of a pair of them getting into a Rolls-Royce, the door of which was being held by a colored chauffeur wearing a visored cap and a baggy tweed suit. "New Rolls-Royce (price $19,500) was bought by Colonel Henry Russell of Dallas as a present for his wife," the caption read. "She liked it because 'it goes with my blue hat.' The Russells claim they are just 'camping out' in their house, plan to turn it over to the servants and build a bigger one for themselves as soon as they can get around to it." The distinguished banker and philanthropist Karl Hoblitzelle did his bit by posing in an automobile showroom gingerly inspecting a Rolls-Royce, which, readers were informed, he could afford, since he "owns banks, utilities, vast tracts of real estate, a chain of 178 theatres, is worth about $30 million."

Another assist was provided by E. E. (Buddy) Fogelson, described as one of "Texas' most famous oil millionaire playboys," who sat for his camera portrait while consuming crêpes Suzette at the Cipango Club. Clarence Scharbauer, Jr., coöperating in the enterprise, was written up as an eligible young bachelor and rancher with twenty million dollars in his poke. Probably the most arresting exhibit of all was the picture of D. H. Byrd, in a top hat, cutaway coat, and false mustache and goatee, stepping down the street with his arms around two pretty girls. The caption read, "'Dry-Hole' Byrd, so nicknamed because he made 100 tries before finally hitting oil in Texas, puts on false whiskers to stroll with his two secretaries during a trip to Mexico that he took with 30 of his friends in two planes."

And so, in those days, the Super-Americans passed in review, each contributing to the composite picture of the Texas millionaire. Today, Hoblitzelle, Fogelson, Scharbauer, and their fellows have become so camera-shy that they think twice before posing for a passport photograph. To complete their reformation, many Texas millionaires (including the once ebullient Byrd) who were born with a taste for gaiety and the gift for promoting hilarity in others now employ a public-relations man, that splendid twentieth-century invention for neutralizing individuality.

"It's pathetic," a Texas newspaper editor said recently, speaking of the vanishing Super-Americans who could properly be described as "originals"—the term used by Harriet Martineau for "men and women who, in more or fewer respects, think, speak, and act, naturally and unconsciously, in a different way from the generality of men." However melancholy this aspect of the changing scene may make the few in Super-America, it satisfies the many, because it shows progress toward conformity, the touchstone of good Americanism.

Ever since de Tocqueville described our willing submission to the rule of numbers as "the tyranny of the majority," observers have found this trait central to an understanding of the American character. "Out of the mingled feelings that the multitude will prevail and that the multitude, because it will prevail, must be right," wrote Bryce, "there grows a self-distrust, a despondency, a disposition to fall into line, to acquiesce in the dominant opinion, to submit thought as well as action to the encompassing power of numbers." Santayana, though in most respects an American buff, was not favorably impressed by our penchant for obligatory togetherness. "Even what is best in American life is compulsory—the idealism, the zeal, the beautiful happy unison of its great moments," he wrote. "You must wave, you must cheer, you must push with the irresistible crowd; otherwise, you will feel like a traitor, a soulless outcast, a deserted ship high and dry on the shore." More recently, a contemporary French observer, Albert Béguin, contributed the thought that America is "a dictatorship without a dictator, exercised by everyone over everyone else."

After listening for more than a hundred and twenty-five years to similar variations on de Tocqueville's theme, Americans may understandably feel that the observations, however accurate, reflect little more than a keen grasp of the obvious. "It takes no great perspicacity to detect and to complain of the standardization in American life," Robert Benchley wrote, back in 1932. "So many foreign and domestic commentators have pointed this feature out in exactly the same terms that the comment itself has become standardized and could be turned out by the thousands on little greeting cards, all from the same type form: 'American life has become too standardized.'"

Nowadays, of course, the standardized life, like some of our other pioneering efforts, has ceased to be a local monopoly. Arnold Toynbee recently observed, "It is not only in America that people are being herded together in mammoth cities without social cohesions and are having their individuality ironed out of them by the demand for docile employees to serve mammoth organizations, private and public. The same thing is happening on both sides of the Iron Curtain." "Everywhere," said Toynbee, "organization, industrialization and urbanization are threatening between them to dehumanize us—to turn us, in fact, into subhuman caricatures of ants and bees." If we manage to keep ahead of the ants, there is nevertheless a strong possibility, Bertrand Russell has prophesied, "that under the influence of scientific discoveries and administrative possibilities and organizations, the world may get so organized that there's no fun to be had any more." The chances are better, Lord Russell has said in his more cheerful moments, that the human race will avoid that dismal end by extinguishing itself.

Meanwhile, back in Texas, the contemporary predicament is also causing concern, but the Super-Americans are not taking it as hard as Toynbee, Russell & Co. On the contrary, anybody who spends much time in Texas is apt to get the feeling that the human race has not only a future but a bright one—or, as they say in Super-America, "Everything's coming up roses." There are, to be sure, a few thorns, such as the one that prompted a recent Houston *Post* editorial titled "Biggest Things All Around But in Texas," which, after noting that a check for the biggest sum ever drawn was recently deposited in a bank in London, that the biggest skyscraper ever financed by local money was going up in Chicago, and that the biggest lake ever made by man was being constructed in Russia, concluded, "It's about time Texas came up with some 'biggests.' We haven't had a very important one since Alaska bumped Texas out of its biggest-state position."

In Texas generally, however, the old-time American optimism still reigns. The natives' conviction that tomorrow will be better than today—a belief once considered the hallmark of all Americans—is not without foundation, for the Texas progress chart, even during the depression that took the starch out of the rest of the world, has never gone anywhere but up. As a result, the Super-American atmosphere is charged with the jaunty feeling that man's destiny is success, and, consequently, that to become a millionaire is something that any Bill Jones can do. William T. (Bill) Jones, of Houston, for example, worked his way through high school as a soda clerk and dance-band leader, spent fourteen years learning the drug business, and then, in 1947, at thirty-four, opened a place of his own. Today, besides having made a million from the Jones Apothecary, a chain of nine drugstores, he has further assured his social security with highly successful operations in oil, ranching, and South American coffee plantations. It is because the Bill Jones story is repeated, with variations, endlessly in Texas, that Texans are imbued with an unshakably buoyant spirit, as if, in Camus' phrase, there lived within them an invincible summer.

Some non-Texans think the sanguine approach is overdone in Texas. Texans think it is underdone elsewhere; after all, they say, optimism was not incidental to the original idea of America. Elsewhere, it is no doubt true that, as Patrick O'Donovan remarked a while ago in the London *Observer*, "the old innocence, and at least among the intellectuals, the old absolute confidence in the righteousness and in the destiny of America have gone," but in Texas even the intellectuals are still so wide-eyed about America that they think it is abso-

378

lutely O.K. Furthermore, they have as much confidence in its destiny as the men who pushed back the frontiers—that tremendous adventure, which in Texas often seems to have taken place only yesterday. "Texas is still a last frontier," John C. B. Richmond remarked a while ago when he was British Consul-General there. "It's the part of the United States where the traditional virtues are still operating. In short, a piece of living history."

Reminders of the proximity of the frontier are everywhere: the passion for hunting and horses; the Western-style dress and the prevalence and importance of cattle ("BULL SHORTAGE LOOMS IN FALL"—San Antonio *Express*); the ubiquitous rodeos and so-called trail rides, an indigenous recreation participated in by groups of as many as two thousand men and women, who get together once a year and spend several days and nights traversing one of the old cattle trails on horseback or in covered wagons, eating out of chuck wagons, and sleeping on the ground, usually in foul weather; the horse thieves (a ring of five youthful ones rounded up last December in Fort Worth); the cattle rustling (four separate instances reported during the first six months of last year within a twenty-five-mile radius of Houston); the newspaper stories about local residents who grew up on the frontier ("OLD CAMPAIGNER, 91, RECALLS INDIAN FIGHTS"); and many other remnants of history that, in Francis Bacon's phrase, "have casually escaped the shipwreck of time."

Though the remnants, too, are disappearing, the spirit of the frontier persists, giving Texas its special tone and explaining in large part its peculiar fascination for foreigners—especially other Americans, since the frontier is the most highly cherished element in the American experience. "What the ocean was to the Elizabethans, so were the vast spaces of the West to the Americans of the last century, and the glamour and wonder of it have never faded," the London *Times Literary Supplement* has said.

In the same way that America stands as the frontier of Europe, so Texas stands in the collective American imagination as the frontier of America—the land of the second chance, the last outpost of individuality, the stage upon which the American Drama, in all its wild extremes, is being performed with eloquence and panache, as if for the first time. While the production, distinguished throughout by the Super-American genius for overacting, has drawn mixed notices, a judgment perhaps as fair as any might follow from applying to the Texan and Texas of today the words with which the brilliant English journalist George Warrington Steevens characterized the American and America at the turn of the century: "He may make his mind easy about his country. It is a credit to him, and he is a credit to it. You may differ from him, you may laugh at him; but neither of these is the predominant emotion he inspires. Even while you differ or laugh, he is essentially the man with whom you are always wanting to shake hands."

✱ ✱ ✱ ✱ ✱

Index

392